W9-DBN-019

SPORT AND SOCIETY

Series Editors
Benjamin G. Rader
Randy Roberts

A list of books in the series appears at the end of this book.

People of Prowess

People of Prowess

Sport, Leisure, and Labor in Early Anglo-America

Nancy L. Struna

University of Illinois Press

Urbana and Chicago

This book is printed on acid-free paper.

Library of Congress Cataloging-in-Publication Data
Struna, Nancy L.
People of prowess : sport, leisure, and labor in early Anglo-
America / Nancy L. Struna
p.   cm. — (Sport and society)
Includes bibliographical references and index.
ISBN 0-252-02247-5 (cloth : acid-free paper). —
ISBN 0-252-06552-2 (pbk. : acid-free paper)
1. Sports—United States—History—17th century. 2. Sports—United
States—History—18th century. 3. Sports—Social aspects—United States—
History—17th century. 4. Sports—Social aspects—United States—History—
18th century. 5. Leisure—Social aspects—United States—History—17th cen-
tury. 6. Leisure—Social aspects—United States—History—18th century. 7.
United States—History—Colonial period, ca. 1600–1775. I. Title. II. Series.
GV583.S88   1996
796'.0973'09032—dc20   95-50193
                                                                CIP

Contents

Acknowledgments

This book has been a long time in the making, and even now it remains unmade. What it may suggest, however, owes much to the many people who have offered suggestions, criticism, and other forms of support. I want to thank, first, two very dear friends, Alison Olson and Katherine Beardsley, who not only read the entire manuscript but also took time for lunches, listening, and "puzzling things out." Roberta Park, Patricia Vertinsky, and Stephen Hardy also read various chapters and offered invaluable comments. Alan Metcalfe helped, as he long has, with some thorny conceptual problems. William Baker connected me with the University of Illinois Press, and the press's readers, Benjamin Rader and Stephanie Grauman Wolf, provided many insightful suggestions for improving both my conceptualization and my writing. I shall always be in their debt. I also appreciate the discussions that I have had with colleagues in the North American Society for Sport History, the Departments of Kinesiology and History at the University of Maryland, and the Maryland Early American History Seminar. Through its General Research Board, the University of Maryland provided two grants that financed some of my research.

At the University of Illinois Press, Richard Wentworth (director), Theresa L. Sears (managing editor), and Bruce Bethell (copy editor) provided enormous support and guidance. They made the later stages of the writing and publishing process a marvelous experience, and I would work with all of them again.

My search for sources led me to a number of institutions over the years, and many librarians, archivists, and curators helped me to locate records and suggested others for me to use. I hope I leave none out: the Historical Societies of Maryland, Virginia, Massachusetts, Pennsylvania, and South Carolina; the Maryland Hall of Records, the Suffolk County (Massachusetts) Court House, the Virginia State Library, and the South Carolina Department of Archives and History; Colonial Williamsburg Foundation Research Library, the William and Mary College Library, the South Caroliniana Library, the William R. Perkins Library at Duke University, the Library of Congress, and McKeldin Library at the University of Maryland; and the Essex Institute (Salem), the Old Colony Historical Society (Taunton), the Haverhill Public Library, and the Ipswich Historical Society, all in Massachusetts.

Finally, I owe the greatest debt to my family, one special Jewett and two dozen Strunas. They have shown inordinate patience and interest over the years, and they have clarified for me who people of prowess are.

People of Prowess

Introduction

Both colonial history and sport history are rich and vibrant subfields in American history, yet their interests have rarely overlapped in recent years. Not since 1965, when Jane Carson published *Colonial Virginians at Play*, has a colonial historian written a monograph about sport in the seventeenth and eighteenth centuries. Articles and sections of chapters by Edmund S. Morgan, Rhys Isaac, and Timothy H. Breen represent the fine but few efforts to incorporate sporting practices within broader frames of colonial experiences that have appeared since the 1970s. Most recently David H. Fischer included some sports among the cultural practices that transferred with and persisted among four groups of colonists who migrated from particular regions in Britain. Sport historians, in turn, have ventured into the seventeenth and eighteenth centuries even less frequently. J. Thomas Jable examined the efforts of the early government of Pennsylvania to constrain sports. Hans-Peter Wagner described a version of the Puritan ruling hierarchy's position on sports in seventeenth-century Massachusetts in his book *Puritan Attitudes toward Recreation*. A very fine article by Elliott Gorn, who is a nineteenth-century cultural historian, and my articles and chapters extend this list.[1]

This book attempts to ground sports as social and cultural practices within the larger frame of colonial life and thus to link colonial and sport history more closely. It examines persistence and change in sporting practices within the broader contexts of and relationships between labor and leisure during the seventeenth and eighteenth centuries. *People of Prowess* begins in England on the eve of North American colonization and then focuses on the transfer of sports across the Atlantic, the subsequent loss and mutation of particular forms, and the adaptation and creation of other practices and traditions across time. It concludes with the construction of a distinctive sphere of leisure and the assignment of some sports to it by Anglo-American upper and urban middle ranks in the second half of the eighteenth century. Throughout, it considers a variety of practices, including games, contests, and matches. All these forms were primarily physical performances, and all were meaningful to people who put more stock in displays of physical prowess and in physical culture more generally than many Americans do today. Hence the title, *People of Prowess.*

The subtitle, *Sport, Leisure, and Labor in Early Anglo-America,* is also significant, in part because it indicates one of several major limits to this book. "Early America" might read better, but "Anglo-America" is more accurate, for I have concentrated on the experiences of Anglo-Americans, especially in the Chesapeake and Massachusetts. This focus was necessary; completing the research on all thirteen colonies and their various populations would have required much more time and at least another volume. It also enabled me to examine cultural transmission, since these were the areas to which English colonists first came. It did not, however, permit an in-depth look at the experiences of colonists in other regions or at those of the many non-English colonists. Another cost of my approach is that it precluded a nuanced analysis of regional variations. Even in the material about the Chesapeake and Massachusetts, I have tended to emphasize common themes and patterns at the expense of significant differences. Finally, I have examined leisure and labor patterns and relationships only through the lens of sports. This is a narrow perspective that prohibits me from suggesting even how and to what extent the colonists' sporting experiences played a role in their construction of labor and leisure as separable spheres. A comparative analysis of multiple leisure experiences—theater, reading, music, a broader range of street and tavern activities, and more—would be far more telling, not only about labor and leisure, but also about sport. But that, too, would require more time and more volumes.

My use of the word *sport* requires a more extensive discussion. I often use the term broadly, as a label for a set of experiences. In part my interests compelled this broad usage. I wanted to talk about people whose practices do not fit our own definition of sport. Ours is only one historical understanding of the term, however. Years ago my graduate adviser, Marvin Eyler, suggested that *sport* derived from the Middle English *disport,* which in turn derived from the Old French *desporter,* meaning "to carry away from." In ordinary language in the sixteenth through eighteenth centuries, people used *sport* as both a noun and a verb, as *a diversion* and *to divert, display* and *to display,* and *an amusement* and *to amuse.* The *Oxford English Dictionary* even identified "amorous dalliance and intercourse" as a meaning for the term in late Elizabethan and early Stuart England, which is where my story begins.[2] Any and all of these connotations suggest uses and understandings of *sport* for which we have only valorized and often negatively charged words.

By framing sport broadly I have parted company with many of my colleagues in American history and, in fact, with many Americans. To most people today the term *sport* usually means something quite specific. Contemporary sports are practices like baseball, football, and basketball. Some people consider nonteam games as sports, including events such as mountain climbing, auto racing, and rodeo. Few people on this side of the Atlantic, however, define chess, pool, or bridge as sports. They are games but not sports, according to popular wisdom, because they lack two of the "essential" elements of sports: physical activity, even physical prowess, arrayed in competitive formats. Categorizing hunting is a bit more difficult, at least for nonhunters. It is not a game in the classic sense, but it is a physical activity. Moreover, depending on how one views the endeavor, it may involve competition, against animals and the environment if not so visibly among humans.

Academicians have spent years classifying, justifying, and reifying sports and related phenomena. Structural sociologists and philosophers were probably the first players in what became something of a name game. The composite typology constructed by John Loy in the late 1960s remains a standard one for ordering and distinguishing terms. This continuum runs from play, to games, to sports, with the differences accounted for by varying degrees of complexity, organization, and physical skill.[3] In the late 1970s Allen Guttmann laid out an evolutionary model for the "development" of sport, as well as a characterization of "modern" sport, that has influenced many sport historians. Indeed, the abstract properties that Guttmann identified—secularism, equality in the conditions of competition and of opportunity to compete, role specialization, rationalization, bureaucratic organization, quantification, and quest for records—have become the perceived "real" features of sports.[4] If a practice does not display or is not viewed as displaying these elements, then it is not sport. The academic approach thus generally confirms what mainstream popular opinion has held as truth, that sports are structured, rule-bound contests between more or less equally matched opponents in largely physical activities that have little or no connection to "real life" endeavors.

This last sentence suggests another element that many people, both inside and outside the academy, consider to be "essential" to sports: play. Conventional wisdom maintains that sports are supposed to be forms of play, and we often hear that people are *playing* sports and that sports people are *players*. The Dutch historian Johan Huizinga secured the connection between sports and play in his book *Homo Ludens*, or "man the player," which was first published in 1938. Although Huizinga also posed the larger and potentially more controversial claim that play was the basis for culture, what has mattered most over time is his definition of play. He conceived of play as "voluntary activity" that occurs within "fixed limits of time and place according to rules freely accepted but absolutely binding." Play also has its own "aim," it should be joyful, and it is "'different' from 'ordinary life.'" As such, Huizinga maintained, play is a constitutive feature of sports, the "basic forms" of which are "constant through the ages."[5] Sports are supposed to be playful physical contests, taken seriously only in their doing.

One could use—and many people have used—Huizinga's construction of play to frame an important dichotomy: work and play. Indeed, academicians and the general public alike often conceive of work and play, or labor and leisure, as polar categories of experiences.[6] They may even be oppositional, as Thorstein Veblen contended in *The Theory of the Leisure Class,* in which he attacked what he considered to be the viperous, consumptive, and nonproductive upper class of the late nineteenth century.[7] Such a dichotomy becomes problematic when we look at contemporary sports, especially professional sports, in which what is playing to ordinary people is work to paid athletes. Huizinga, of course, condemned professionalization as a movement that subverted "true" sports, ones that drew from and existed on account of play. Few modern Americans, however, feel strongly about the discrepancy between, or the hypocrisy of our conceptualizations of, the ideal and the real. Fewer still bother to rationalize our problematic constructions. We pay to see the best players, even as we continue to believe that sport is supposed to involve play and is not "normally" work. We will even pay our best "amateurs" to play.

This book does not employ these definitions of play, sport, and the labor-leisure polarity. They are relatively recent conceptions, modern constructions that date from a particular people in a particular time and place: white, middle- and upper-class males who lived primarily in industrial and commercial cities in mid-nineteenth-century America and elsewhere in the Western world. They worked in shops, counting houses, and factories during their "work time," and then they played in their "leisure," their nonworking, discretionary time. Theirs was a neatly divided world with categories of and sites for particular endeavors, including sport, or sports, narrowly framed.[8]

The colonists who are the subjects of *People of Prowess* did not live in such a world. Many early Americans were farmers and agricultural workers. The needs of crops and animals defined their tasks; the seasons, their rhythms. Others inhabited small villages where they plied their crafts or from which they set out to harvest the resources of the seas and forests. Only a few were urban dwellers, and most were not even middle rank, let alone members of a middle class. Nor were they all white. Substantial numbers of Africans, African Americans, and Native Americans figured in the picture, and I have tried to address some of the experiences of these and other ethnic and racial groups, at least insofar as they affected the dominant Anglo-American culture.

The people discussed in *People of Prowess* produced a variety of practices that I have labeled *sports* and, on occasion, *physical recreations*. Some of their activities we would recognize. Early Americans knew games, races, dances, and animal sports organized in baits and battles. They also engaged one another, animals, or the environment in other formats, only some of which we have experienced. Matches—events that pitted one individual (or a group) against another one—were particularly common. So were other mostly individual or paired performances, some of which involved actions implied by earlier connotations of *sport*.

These practices also took place in a variety of social sites. Rituals and festivals provided one set of occasions, and some of these events had deep roots in Old World life, whereas others emerged in the colonies. Many contests and displays of prowess, especially in the seventeenth century, drew directly from work tasks and occurred in what we would call workplaces and during work time. Some early Anglo-Americans even maintained, as did their ancestors and contemporaries in Britain, that particular sports were forms of work. Horse racing, hunting, and hammer throwing may come to mind. But then, these players were not people who viewed or experienced labor as we do, nor did they conceive of labor and leisure as separable realms of experience, at least before the middle of the eighteenth century.

By necessity, then, *People of Prowess* is also about change and persistence in the relationships between labor and leisure, which both affected and were affected by what happened in sporting scenes. One change, of course, stands out. Especially in the second half of the eighteenth century, a distinct segment of the population materially and ideologically distinguished labor from leisure. They assigned each set of activities to distinct times and places, and as a part of the process, they relocated some sports from work and other endeavors in ordinary life to "leisure." Paradoxically "leisure" sports for some made work for others. Moreover, even at this time, other relationships and other forms of sports continued to exist. Consequently I have emphasized not only the plurality of labor-leisure relationships but also the conflicts and struggles that emerged among groups of people over competing notions and values of work and sports. Sports have always been political practices, and connecting them to the larger realms of labor and leisure helps us to understand how and why they were so in the seventeenth and eighteenth centuries.

People of Prowess opens in Britain, and more narrowly in England, in the late sixteenth and early seventeenth centuries. The times were complex, for the country was experiencing some of the effects of a long-running transformation, the movement from a medieval to an industrial society. Few things were unaffected—not economic or political activity, not religious or intellectual affairs, and certainly not ordinary life. Still, not everyone favored change, and for many English men and women, customary and even traditional patterns of life and living remained meaningful. Such a life was one in which most things remained connected and integrated.[9]

Nowhere was the integration that characterized traditional English society more evident than in customary sports and physical recreations. Animal contests, athletic events, games, individual displays of prowess, and more flavored popular gatherings, tavern and alehouse visits, and the rituals and festivals that had long animated and punctuated the lives of English men and women, both low and high born. Sporting practices even drew from and occurred within the course of ordinary work tasks, and therein lay a critical dilemma, at least for civil authorities and proponents of change. Ordinary people preferred games and displays of prowess to work, for many reasons. Would-be reformers, however, who included royal and local government officials, merchants and other mercantilists, and reformist Protestants, perceived the people's expressions of what one historian has called the "leisure preference" as an obstacle to economic efficiency and social discipline.[10] They wanted to get more work out of more people, and they eventually realized that to achieve this goal, they had to change not only the work practices but also the popular recreational preferences. Some critics of customary patterns even went so far as to define physical recreations as forms of labor, which enabled them to restrict the activities of laborers. Still, none of the opponents of traditional ways succeeded in containing the popular leisure preference. Resistance to their efforts mounted, especially in the 1620s and 1630s, and the tensions involving labor and leisure persisted.

These tensions transferred across the Atlantic once English trading companies sent colonists to acquire resources from the North American mainland after 1607. These early efforts are the subjects of chapter 2. The simple fact is that none of the colonization experiments ended as their planners had hoped, in part because those who were sent as colonists behaved in much the same way as they had at home. They labored intermittently, interspersing sports and work, and even the military governors who were sent to bring order out of chaos fared little better in altering traditional habits than did their contemporaries in the Old World. The architects of the colonial outposts had misread what and whom survival and prosperity in the "New World" required—but then, they also mistook North America as a "new" world. Native Americans, whose own recreations resembled British ones and actually played well for the propagandists of colonization, already lived there. Moreover, some of them assisted colonists in adjusting to the North American environment, and in so doing, they set the stage for successive and continuing cultural adaptations rather than direct transmissions of English forms.

Chapter 3 relates the experiences of the next generation of English migrants to the Chesapeake and Massachusetts Bay. Many of these immigrants were not like their predecessors. They were skilled servants and members of the island's emerging middle rank, people who managed to transform the outposts to permanent colonies. They also managed to reproduce only some aspects of customary English culture and society, including its physical recreations. Theirs was a constricted sporting life with little room for the traditional leisure preference. This pattern itself was the consequence of North American conditions, cultural attrition, and the taunt discipline maintained by authorities and superiors, but it was not evidence of a revolutionary cultural change. Even the Puritans in Massachusetts Bay did not radically reframe and relocate all sports and other physical recreations; they simply legitimized ones that drew from and benefited labor. By the 1670s, when the material conditions of life had stabilized, sporting patterns in the colonies more closely resembled English ones, even though they did not replicate them.

The next two chapters focus on the decades of the late seventeenth and early eighteenth centuries, when ordinary people engaged in a dynamic process of culture construction. Chapter 4 discusses the reinvigoration of popular culture, which a number of economic, demographic, and geographic changes made possible and which was manifested in a surge of locally made and meaningful sports and other physical recreations. These practices in turn implicated the reemergence of multiple labor-leisure patterns and the diminished power of civil and religious authorities to dictate the course and contents of ordinary life. Some sports were also products of the broader reframing of the colonial social structure and sites for negotiations among emergent ranks. Chapter 5 examines the rank-making process and the significance of sports to it in one region, the Chesapeake, where a group of large landowners came to acquire substantial economic, social, and political power. In fashioning themselves as an upper rank and negotiating with ordinary colonists to achieve the status they desired, the gentry also changed the face and the place of particular sports.

One of the subprocesses involved in rank making as it continued in the eighteenth century was the construction of distinctive sporting styles, or cohesive styles of behavior and meaning. These styles, genteel and vernacular, are the subjects of chapter 6. Both patterns drew from experiences and fashions known to people across the Atlantic, both in Europe and Africa. Nevertheless, neither the upper- nor the lower-rank sporting styles on the British North American mainland duplicated or precisely replicated transatlantic forms. Distinctive rank, race, and gender relations, as well as economic actions and the environment, ensured differences. Furthermore, neither style emerged and was elaborated independently of the other. There were multiple exchanges and interactions between upper- and lower-rank colonists, especially in the taverns. Chapter 7 discusses taverns—or ordinaries, as colonists often called them—and the recreations and sports that took place in them. For many early Americans, taverns served multiple roles: they provided food, drink, and shelter, opportunities for games and gambling, and space for the conflicts that had been emerging outside their walls. One of these was the persisting conflict about the content of labor and leisure, including what the "appropriate" content and context of physical recreations were. This conflict was not resolved in the mid-eighteenth century, but the reactions of one group of opponents to customary tavern activities did play into a broader cultural change that was already under way.

This broader change involved a relationship between labor and leisure. At the hands and in the minds of the provincial upper rank, chapter 8 maintains, the traditional integrated relationship was reframed as one in which labor and leisure were separable, although not entirely separate. For the mid- and late eighteenth-century gentry, both sides of the equation changed—their labor forms and relations, as well as their construction of leisure. So did their approach to particular sports and recreations. In fact, the lengthy process of formalizing sports—distinguishing particular performances in time, place, and mode of behavior and assigning to them distinctive expectations and values—was a means of establishing boundaries between labor and leisure. After midcentury the pace of this formalizing quickened, as both the upper rank and nongentry moved to exploit and commercialize leisure and leisure recreations. Gradually, too, the emerging urban middle class moved to emulate genteel leisure, buoyed as it was by a broader transatlantic consumer revolution. By 1800 the conception of labor and leisure—and sports in leisure—as separable spheres of life was the critical and even dominant construction within the lifestyles of early national upper- and middle-class males. It was not, however, the only construction. As the epilogue suggests, many early Americans retained other patterns and, within them, a variety of sports and recreations. The days of dominant and dominating sports lay years in the future.

⤙═◑ ◐═⤚

One final comment about this book and my intentions may be in order. In the pages that follow I try to recount some of the dimensions of popular sporting life in early America, or at least Anglo-America, and in so doing, to deepen our understanding of the colonists' lives and the experiences of living among them. *People of Prowess* locates sporting practices and attitudes broadly within the larger frame of early modern British and American social history, and by design, it is probably more in the vein of histories of popular culture than it is either classic sport history or classic colonial history. Indeed, sport historians will undoubtedly wish for more material about sports, and colonial historians will want less about early American economics, demography, and politics. But I did not write this book for them alone. Academic histories have their limits, and I would like to think that *People of Prowess* has limits of a different kind. I also hope that it will appeal to multiple audiences, including not only sport and colonial historians but also members of the broader public—people like my brothers and sisters—who are interested in both early American history and sports. After all, it is they who have made history and sports.

I

Sport in the Old World

James VI had just spent several months in his native Scotland and was about to journey southward. He might have wished that he could put off this trip, perhaps indefinitely, for there was much amiss in England this summer of 1617. Men and women who were no longer bound to people or place roamed the countryside or fled into towns and cities. The royal treasury was in dire straits, as was nearly one-half of England's population, its wage earners. A heavy load of cases entangled the dockets of royal and local courts, and parliamentary debates were heated. Food was scarce and highly priced, and the tempo of estate confiscations and enclosures had accelerated. Rural industries struggled, incidences of poaching rose, and companies of merchants scrambled to find investors and to curry royal favor.

James had to go, however, for he was also James I, king of England and its other dominions in the British Isles, including Wales and Ireland. Still, he did not hurry. Whenever the northern landscape and the local supply of deer made it possible, he stopped to indulge one of his great passions, hunting. By 11 August his entourage had traveled only as far as Lancashire in west central England, a still heavily Catholic region whose numerous lords entertained the monarch in the style to which he was accustomed. Some of them also embroiled James in a local controversy involving popular sports and other recreations that he attempted to resolve. Over the long term, however, even his solution was problematic, for through midcentury Britain's local playgrounds were also battlegrounds.[1]

On the surface the situation into which James rode appeared to be a simple one. Almost precisely a year earlier, on 8 August 1616, some local justices of the peace had issued an order mandating Sunday church attendance and prohibiting recreations, particularly "pipinge, dancinge, bowling, beare or bullbaitinge."[2] They were concerned that too few people went to church, a pattern they attributed in part to the popularity of these recreational practices among Lancashire's laborers, servants, and tradespeople. As did reformist critics across England, the Lancashire justices recognized that when sportive contests and displays of physical prowess competed with religion, the former two often won. Sunday was the "reveling day" for ordinary people, and a good piper could draw several hundred pairs of ears for every soul attracted by a preacher.[3]

This was not the first time that officials in Lancashire had attempted to limit popular recreations. Nearly forty years before, magistrates had outlawed "pipers and minstrels playing, making and frequenting bear-baiting and bull-baiting on the Sabbath."[4] Elsewhere in England, especially in large towns like Chester and York, officials had pared football matches, plays, and bull and bear baits from lists of acceptable Sunday and holy day activities. In fact, since the 1540s various groups had attacked popular sports and traditional festivals for various reasons. Most such assaults had produced acts of resistance, even overt protests among the proponents of recreations. The struggles generally ended with an accommodation of sorts, as the people resorted to alternative activities such as foot and horse races in the place of football.[5]

Ultimately the Lancashire crisis would culminate in a compromise, but not before the aggrieved players took advantage of the opportunity that the king's presence created. Encouraged by some gentlemen, the people presented a petition to James requesting that he order the justices to repeal the ban. James did intervene, but he did not fully support the petitioners' demands. After consulting with his ministers and bishops, the king accepted the people's contention that they possessed the "libertie to pipinge and honest recreation." However, he also ordered that they could exercise this liberty only after church services and that at no time did they have the right to engage in unlawful sports and games. As James recognized, there were many reasons to let the people have their recreations, but there were also problems associated with unauthorized and unbridled participation.[6]

This Lancashire settlement did not end here. Within eight months it became the core of a royal edict known as the "Declaration of Sports," which outlined national policy. As long as James was alive, his "Book of

Sports," as contemporaries called it, ensured both the sanctity of Sabbath morning church services and the acceptability of sports and other recreations later in the day. Ministers could and did preach in peace, although not necessarily to greater numbers. Ordinary people also had their dances and maypoles, and when a vicar or justice tried to prevent such activities, the players claimed that "the King did allow of it by his Book."[7] After James's death, however, the compromise evaporated as distance increased between the proponents of social change, both pragmatically inclined ones and more radical ideologues, and supporters of the status quo. In 1633 James's son and successor, Charles I, reissued the document as one act in what would become a very bloody play. Sixteen years later Charles would find the Declaration of Sports noted in his death warrant.

Why did such apparently innocuous practices produce such a spirited attack and a stubborn defense? First of all, they were never innocuous, insignificant practices in English or, more broadly, British society. For centuries the fabric of ordinary life had integrated popular recreations and sports. They had occurred at alehouses and churches, in the streets and lanes, and on fields and rivers, and they affected village and rank relations, individual economies and esteem, and levels of health and pleasure. Moreover, some Stuart practices had become customs that drew from people's fundamentally agrarian pasts, their Catholic rituals, and a hierarchical social order of "high" and "low born" that dated from the era of feudalism. Many sports had changed over the years, of course, but they had done so in subtle rather than revolutionary ways. Footballers, for example, no longer kicked about a bull's head that was dripping blood, but they still preferred to play on unenclosed fields. Maypole dancing no longer celebrated the pagan carnival, but it manifested scenes of carnival nonetheless.

Some English men and women, however, no longer approved of these scenes of carnival or ball playing on unenclosed fields. Indeed, for increasing numbers of townspeople and some independent farmers, such scenes were beyond comprehension. For them, England had changed significantly in the past two centuries. No longer a land primarily of manors, lords, and tenants, the country had begun to industrialize, to create large provincial towns, and to enjoy the prospect of agricultural and manufactured exports. It was also a Protestant kingdom whose outlook was less insular, in all the senses of that word, than it had once been.

Not everyone in England benefited from or adjusted to particular changes in precisely the same way. In 1617 the signs of things amiss that confronted James were not figments of his imagination. There were legions of poor and unfettered men and women, food shortages, and backlogs in the courts. Such conditions, as Carl Bridenbaugh concluded more than twenty years ago, left many of England's nearly four million people "vexed and troubled."[8] They were also divided. Some people clung to the past, in part because they found traditional—and in some cases even residual—practices and customs comforting or because they feared the unknown. Others accepted what must have seemed like a nearly inevitable transformation and tried in various ways to moderate its effects and to adjust to it. A third segment of the population believed that the future could not arrive too quickly and that the extent and pace of change were insufficient.

Occasionally these various collections clashed openly, as was the case in Lancashire. Here the supporters of customary ways, including recreations, came face to face with the still emerging but vociferous voices of change. Into this fray rode the conciliator, the king, who was a visible representative of the country's dominant moderating forces and who offered a salutary solution to the Lancashire incident, at least insofar as it was about the practice of popular sports and displays of physical prowess. In this hamlet of shepherds, farmers, and manufacturers, however, as elsewhere in England, the affrays on and about sporting grounds were never just about games and displays of prowess, whether on the Sabbath or any other day. Popular recreations were a part of ordinary life, and any debate about them was also about things like fences, clocks, and Calvinism. Thus, the Lancashire conflict also involved competing conceptions of time, modes of agriculture and politics, work and leisure, and social relations.[9] The situation would be much the same across the sea, in places such as Jamestown, Plymouth, and Boston.

Popular Sports and Their Traditions

Popular sports and other recreations were a part of the social landscape in nearly every corner of Stuart England. Tutbury, in Staffordshire, and Stamford, Lincolnshire, were renowned for their bull running, a no-holds-barred race against bulls that freely roamed the streets. Other animal contests, like cockfights and bull and bear baits, were popular in London among royalty and commoners alike. They were even fairly common in Lincoln, a hotbed of Puritan activity in the east. Hurling and wrestling were intensely popular in rural Cornwall, and virtually any area that had a forest, especially a royal forest, was a site for hunting and its illegal offspring, poaching.[10] At Maddington, Wiltshire, in south central England, a man who

wanted to "get him a wife" began his search by attending to "some dancing or other sports."[11] Not far away, in the Cotswolds, a hilly sheep-graz-
ing region, a spate of events ranging from dog coursing to dancing constituted a fairly highly structured athletic festival.[12]

There were many other practices as well. Village neighbors and groups
from neighboring villages competed in games like football, and individuals tested their mettle against one another in cudgeling and foot races.
Members of all ranks of English society also tested the fates in card and
dice games. Stylized performances, such as fencing and jousting, occurred
at the court and on public stages, and spur-of-the-moment challenges, such
as quoits and hammer throwing, emerged in fields during respites from
labor. Horse racing and hawking were not uncommon, and there were as
many forms of shooting as there were weapons and as many stakes as there
were expressions of confidence and valued goods or qualities. In all, there
were about as many sporting patterns and places as there were people.

Some practices were relatively simple affairs. Wrestling, for example, had
as its objective one opponent's takedown of another, either by strength or
by stealth. Although occasionally described as a producer of what even then
was a complex set of qualities embodied in the term "manlinesse," it had
few rules, and a judge had only to count to five to determine a fall and to
observe the position of a wrestler's waist to rule on illegal holds.[13] Other
practices were more complicated, as was the case with hurling in Cornwall
at the turn of the seventeenth century. Named for its major action—throwing the ball—the activity had two regional forms, "to goales" in the east
and "to the countrey" in the west. In the former, with two pairs of bushes
serving as goals at opposite ends of a field, two "ranks" with up to thirty
competitors paired off and picked their best "stoppers" as goalkeepers. The
only "indifferent" act in the contest occurred at the beginning, when someone threw up the ball for which the teams struggled. Thereafter each team
tried to control the ball and to score within the framework of particular
customs and rules, which, as described by a contemporary observer named
Richard Carew, were quite numerous and specific: "they must hurle man
to man, and not two set upon one man at once: . . . the Hurler against the
ball, must not but [butt], nor hand-fast under girdle: . . . hee who hath the
ball, must but onley in the others brest: . . . he may not throw it to any of
his mates, standing neerer the goale, then himselfe. Lastly, in dealing
[throwing] the ball, if any of the other part can catch it flying between, or
e're the other have it fast, he thereby winneth the fame to his side."[14] Anyone who breached these provisions for proper defensive maneuvers and

offsides could expect a prescribed punishment: an attack on his ears, "but with their fists onely."[15]

A few sports were quite old. Cockfights and cock shailing, for example, dated at least to the twelfth century, when, as a legend maintained, people formalized the fights as ritual punishments of the fowl whose crowing awakened the Danish masters of ninth-century Albion and enabled them to ward off a surprise attack launched by the Saxons.[16] Hunting was probably even older, a sport practiced since time "immemorial" and claimed as an aristocratic privilege by the Normans.[17] Then, too, one version of village football matches, known as the Haxey Hood contest, had its roots in a medieval ritual. Played on Plough Monday, which marked the beginning of the growing season, the match pitted one group of villagers against their neighbors for the control of a ritual hood, represented by a ball made of rope encased in a sack or bladder. The contestants tried to move the ball, either by kicking, throwing, or running with it, toward the goals situated at the bounds of the villages. In an even earlier day, however, the hood had been a freshly severed bull's head that, moved about in much the same manner, bled on the fields and ensured their fertility.[18]

Although long shorn of their original ritual intents, both cockfighting and football remained popular in early modern England. That they did so speaks volumes about their embeddedness in English social practice and their persisting appeal as traditions. In this respect they were like most English sporting practices. Hunting, wrestling, and bull running, as well as many other matches and contests, were securely wedged in the rhythms, rituals, and relations of English life. Wrestling, for example, arose out of the face-to-face exchanges between individuals for whom physical prowess was a meaningful attribute in village affairs, a village in which status was a function of lateral social stability rather than vertical mobility. Horse racing, on the other end, emerged as tests of strength and stamina, both of steed and rider, among those for whom a good horse, a winning horse, could mean the difference between life and death. Races thus were ways of measuring the qualities of the breed and of stimulating improvements.[19]

The rhythms, rituals, and relations of life were not the same for everybody in early seventeenth-century England, however. Some people lived in towns and cities and worked in shops and schools, whereas other citizens lived in villages and worked fields, fens, and mines. Still others lived in castles and great houses, attended by servants or tenants. Not all these people were, or had been, as involved in the making of recreational practices as were others. Most sports and other physical recreations had emerged within and remained meaningful to the country's two oldest groups, or ranks. One rank was the "folk," or ordinary men and women. The other included their traditional superiors: members of the court, the nobility, and even some of the island's nouveau riche, the country gentry. Both groups had distinctive styles of living and sporting practices.

Folk recreations arose out of the interests and affairs of ordinary life in England's villages and towns. The interests that moved yeomen, servants, artisans, and laborers to recreate may be self-evident. Games, races, and other practices were fun, and they could also be profitable and potent in defending customs or redressing grievances. The affairs and rhythms of these people, however, may not be so obvious. Although England was industrializing and modernizing, it was not yet a nation of managers and employees, of widely available printed sources of information, of clocks and foremen, of weekday workdays and weekends. Many ordinary men and women, both in the countryside and in towns and cities, still lived a life conditioned by face-to-face contacts, village festivals, alehouses and fairs, intermittent work, patriarchy, and church feasts. Sports and other recreations both drew from and were forms of these multiple contacts. They were face-to-face expressions of prowess, guile, agility, self-interest, and community. They were forms of discourse in what was both an oral and a visual popular culture.

Popular recreations often occurred within the context of village festivals and church feasts. Some festivals had existed for centuries, and although the numbers had dwindled under the Tudors, they still were numerous. During Henry VIII's reign the Anglican church recognized more than 217 Sundays and holidays in any given year. By the mid-sixteenth century only 78 official holidays remained, but this still meant that one out of every five days was a festive one. Combined with the local church ales and village gatherings, these feast days made for a lively calendar. New Year's, Plough Monday, Candlemas, Lent, Eastertide, Whitsun, Midsummer's Eve, Michaelmas, and Martinmas, among others, heralded days of feasting, visiting, and games. So did the innumerable markers of family and community events—birthdays, weddings, wakes, and anniversaries.[20]

The sports practiced at these celebrations were nearly as numerous and as varied as were the festivals themselves. Cockfights were customary events on Shrove Tuesday, the final festival before Ash Wednesday and the solemn Lenten season. Parish bidales featured wrestling matches, and hare coursing (rabbit chases with and without dogs), hurling, and cudgeling occurred at the spring Whitson festival. Among the local agrarian festivals, Plough Monday was perhaps the best known—and the most commonly attacked—because of its ritual associations and the roughness of its football contest. But it was not the only festive source of mayhem. May Day, a part of the broader Continental carnival tradition, drew dancers, archers, dice players, and even animal baiters, any one of whom could become disruptive and even violent in this "other-society" kind of observance. Invariably, too, the popularly elected "lord of misrule" led his accomplices in dances and games playing in which they mocked the sexual and political restraints imposed by the dominant society. Figuratively, if not literally, the young male lord of misrule was king, at least for a day.[21]

Recreations also occurred in more routine contexts of ordinary life. Visits with kin and neighbors and trips to markets produced displays of prowess, gossiping, and games of chance. Even work, which was often demanding and tedious but also frequently irregular, presented opportunities for recreation. Grain and livestock growing had various seasons, with slack times in between. Daily and weekly tasks varied in intensity and type, according to the needs of sheep and cows, fuel gathering, and in the cases of increasingly more of the rural population, some mining and local manufacturing employments.

Occasionally the tasks of work carried directly over into recreations. Among men especially, contests like pitching the bar, hammer throwing, and lifting—all of which occurred in natural breaks or as passersby appeared—expressed and reinforced the physical strength required in the tasks of building and ploughing. Women, too, had their respites, but in this society that constructed gender differences on the basis of physical characteristics and sex, there were limits to what females could do in those furloughs. Dancing, foot races, and a few gambling games fell within those bounds, but few other practices did. Moreover, as women aged, their opportunities for physically active recreations declined.[22]

Still, the fabric of recreations bore the imprint of women. Women prepared the food that attracted people to church ales and harvest festivals. They were spectators, and not infrequently wagerers, at public events, including animal baits. They were also central figures, even producers, in one of the most routine sites for popular sports and other recreations, the alehouse. Some women, especially the poorest of England's many poor, were active participants in the nearly ubiquitous sexual encounters. Still others kept alehouses, either as occasional or long-term ventures. Here they sold drink and food and opened their doors to braggarts, plotters, and passersby; in so doing they earned enough to supplement their marginal incomes or to stay in business for years.

One aspect of the business of alehouse keeping, for both men and women, was the sponsorship of popular recreations. In fact, along with churches, fairs, and markets, alehouses were substantive institutional props for folk sports and for popular culture more generally. At the local alehouse contest victors celebrated each other with toasts and made preparations for the next match or a rematch. Neighbors congregated to swap stories or display their prowess on summer evenings and long winter days, and some patrons might even find equipment and facilities unavailable elsewhere in the town or village. Ninepins alleys, bowling greens, and spaces for animal baits were popular drawing cards at local alehouses, and they became even more common and popular in Stuart England.[23]

At the alehouse as well, local village teams and individual contestants came face to face with another of their long-standing patrons, the local lord or gentleman. Occasionally these men owned the public house and treated the competitors to beer and ale, but the traditions of good lordship and good neighborhood included other forms of support for popular recreations as well. Some lords provided fields for games, funding for church ales, and harvest festival dinners. A court in south Somerset even accused Sir Edward Parham of promoting and participating in a bull bait and morris dancing at a church ale "to get the love and affection of the common people."[24] On at least one occasion in Stuart England, a "good lord" arranged for a distinctive athletic festival, the Cotswolds "Olympick" games. Organized by Robert Dover just a few years before King James appeared in Lancashire, these games took place in the wool town of Chipping Camden about the time of Whitsun in the spring. Planned as a celebration of and by many of the local inhabitants, from shepherds and laborers to shopkeepers and landowners, Dover's festival incorporated activities that the gentry and the folk had practiced for years. Two forms of dog coursing, running after rabbits and racing by greyhounds, took place, as did horse and foot races. Dancing occurred, and so did various field events, including jumping, leaping, hammer throwing, and pitching the bar. There was even a locally popular form of wrestling—shin-kicking—and a double staff version of cudgeling, or hand-to-hand combat with a club or bar. Held intermittently throughout the seventeenth century, and even beyond, Dover's games offered something for virtually everybody.[25]

Dover's personal history is uncertain, but he probably had extensive knowledge of sporting practices in the Cotswolds and took his roles as patron and defender of popular recreations seriously. He was, after all, a member of England's country gentry, an emerging but integral constituency in the country's upper ranks. The inclusion of horse racing and fencing also suggests that Dover knew something about the customary practices of members of the court, the nobility, and his genteel peers. Over several centuries this upper-rank recreational style had formalized among people steeped in the exercise of service to the state, of military might, and of thrust and parry with friend and foe alike. It was a style that revealed the powers, prerogatives, and prowess of people who displayed their sovereignty in grand and occasionally gory ways.

As befit their feudal and military past, martial combats figured prominently in the social scheme of England's upper ranks. Jousting, a contest of strength and agility in which two squires mounted and armed with lances rode pellmell toward one another, each trying to unseat his opponent, had emerged from the hand-to-hand combats of knights who followed medieval lords into battle. Tilts, on the other hand, arose out of the preparations for warfare, particularly from the maneuvers undertaken to ensure accuracy with the lance in battle. Tilting involved individual competitors riding one at a time at full speed (at "full tilt") with lance in hand toward either an object (the quintain) or a ring that they attempted to spear. Even fencing, archery, and to some extent at least, horse racing were rooted in the tasks and conditions of medieval warfare.[26]

In the sixteenth and early seventeenth centuries, the royal courts took a particular interest in these martial arts. Elizabeth I, James's immediate predecessor, revised the old medieval rules and regularized tournaments in the scheme of entertainments. The daughter of Henry VIII and a supporter of overseas exploration and England's growing power on the seas, Elizabeth rarely missed an opportunity for a martial display or combat, especially when the audience consisted of European dignitaries or when she was on progression. After her death and James's accession to the throne, at least a part of her martial legacy persisted: virtually no Stuart ceremony or anniversary celebration occurred without jousts or tilts.[27]

More than an interest in militarism and ritual martial displays underlay the commitments of the Tudors and Stuarts and their courtiers to tournaments, however. They also believed that jousts, sword contests, and tilts produced qualities required of those who sought to serve the nation. This was not, of course, a belief unique to the English; it was one of several ideas that had emerged in Italy in the fourteenth century as a component of the aristocratic cult of courtesy. Moreover, it achieved popularity and its full expression in England in precisely the same way as it had on the Continent, through courtesy manuals. The first such English manual, *The Boke Named the Governour,* appeared at the court of Elizabeth's father, Henry VIII, in 1531. Written by his secretary, Sir Thomas Elyot, *The Boke* laid out the relationship between physical exercise and able service to the state in almost lawlike terms: physical strength, mental sharpness, and moral rightness developed not by accident but by participation in fencing, racing on foot and horse, jousts, and shooting, among other things.[28]

In successive years other writers echoed Elyot's message and even more fully incorporated it within the Elizabethan and Stuart ideologies of state service. At Elizabeth's own court Roger Ascham, her tutor, and Sir Humphrey Gilbert, one of her most renowned explorers and colonizers, wrote books on the subject.[29] James also contributed to the cause with his *Basilikon Doron,* written for his son, Henry. A successful king, James advised, had to "exercise his engine" if he wished to "further abilitie and to maintaine health." All "lawful," "honest" games were essential, he continued, especially if one wished to avoid idleness and to increase his strength for travel. No king, however, should engage in rough and violent games, such as football, or exercises that excite the passions.[30]

Yet James did not always follow his own rules, about sports or anything else, for that matter. The "lawful" sport that he preferred was also one that excited his passions, hunting. One historian has estimated that James spent as much as a third of each year in the chase, and he appeared to relish the blood and gore of the kill. He also protected the sport and his access to it in a number of ways. He persuaded Parliament to reduce the number of people who could legally hunt by raising property limits, and he issued gamekeeper's licenses only to particular nobles and gentlemen. In so doing James was merely exercising his royal prerogatives, greedily and without much courtesy.[31]

He was also maintaining traditions. Although horse racing would shortly make its claim as the "sport of kings"—certainly it attracted the protection and promotion of the Stuarts—hunting was the earliest regal sport. Since the days of the Norman Conquest, English kings and queens had claimed the island's forests as royal domains and the deer as royal animals. Most of them had hunted, but perhaps none more avidly than the Tudors. As did James, Henry VIII hunted on a grand scale; he was known to have several hundred deer rounded up, all to be set on by his greyhounds.[32] During Elizabeth's reign the practice was smaller in scale but grander in style, as Robert Laneham's description of the sport during the queen's visit to Killingworth Castle in 1575 suggests. One can almost experience the "earning [baying] of the hounds in continuans of their crie, the swiftness of the Deer, the running of footmen, the galloping of horsez, the blasting of hornz, the galloping & hewing [hue and cry] of the huntsmen, with the excellent Echoz between whilez the woods and waters in valleys resounding."[33] The swift deer, the huntsmen yelling to the riders, the barking dogs—all were at the queen's beck and call.

The royal monopoly over the forests, deer, and hunting was not just a figurative one. Between 1389 and 1610 a series of edicts and laws defined hunting for many common animals and fish and the ownership of weapons as either crimes or privileges granted by the central government. Anyone who hunted illegally was a poacher, and anyone caught with illegal arms or game faced fines and prison terms. The preferments that the Tudors and Stuarts granted to certain landowners, either to be gameskeepers or for the privilege of hunting, bolstered the monopoly.[34]

Such practices were not universally accepted, however, and the hunting scene enables us to see another of the ways in which folk and high-style recreations intersected. People who had not received a license or grant from the king, whether gentlemen or ordinary citizens, ignored the provisions against hunting either on protected lands or for proscribed species. Poaching, the taking of game illegally, was one of England's most common crimes. It was also a violent form of social protest, and murders and cases of property destruction were not uncommon. Notable among the poachers were members of the lesser gentry, those with estates valued under £100 whose hunting rights had been severely restricted by a succession of statutes. They ignored the laws, armed themselves heavily, and physically assaulted the gamekeepers who were there to protect the rights of the landholders. Stiff penalties, including fines up to £200 and prison terms, did little to deter these genteel bandits. Between 1586 and 1609 they were involved in criminal cases ranging from 11 to 13 percent of the total, even though the entire rank constituted only about 5 percent of the early seventeenth-century population.[35]

An even larger percentage of indicted poachers came from other groups in English society. For each member of the gentry brought to court, six yeomen, husbandmen, servants, artisans, or laborers appeared. Their interests in breaking into enclosed or in other ways protected parks, chases, and ponds were also numerous. They needed to supplement meager diets with fresh game and to augment paltry incomes or barter stocks with furs and pelts. They might also poach in a preserve to protest enclosures or an unfair and unscrupulous liege lord, and one of the fears of England's governors, both local and royal, was that ordinary people would use hunting as an excuse to form "Assemblies, Conferences, and Conspiracies for to rise and disobey their Allegiance."[36]

The hunting and poaching scene tells us much about the contemporary English society and its scheme of recreations. To the country's monarchs and noble families, hunting was anything but "mere play." The ruling class defended its prerogative to hunt as vigorously as it defended its prerogative to rule. Moreover, the hunting-poaching distinction generally embodied the social distinctions embraced and maintained by the upper ranks. Only one who owned a preserve or chase or possessed the king's warrant to hunt in the royal forest, whether noble or favored gentlemen, was known as the "hunter." The "huntsman," in turn, was a servant to the lord. He might be tenant or bound laborer, but he was always subservient to the hunter. Finally, there were the poachers, who often owned little or no land, a condition that placed them at the bottom of the hierarchy and might even induce them to commit crimes.

Even though poaching was a crime in Tudor and Stuart England, it did not always result from simple criminal intent. For some ordinary people, poaching was a matter of survival. The deer, fish, and fowl they sought provided food and other necessary materials. Poaching was also a matter of custom, an age-old means of protesting arbitrary laws and the establishment of preserves on once common lands. In turn, the fears fed by these protests were customary and real. At least since the reign of Richard II, during the peasant's revolt of 1381, people had used hunting as a ruse for unlawful assemblies. Thereafter riots, physical assaults, and other forms of disorderly and disordering conduct persisted, both in the context of hunting and on occasions for other recreational practices.[37]

This discussion merely underscores what many people in Stuart England knew about their games and displays of prowess and their sporting traditions: they were meaningful social practices. James did not interfere in Lancashire and permit some sports and other recreations after Sabbath church services just because he had nothing better to do. He knew that baits, jousts, races, and rushbearings were as much a part of the English scene as were hamlets, markets, and castles, and he defended them as matters of common rights and vital practices. He did so in the tradition of good lordship and with the understanding that such recreations were one of the bonds between proprietors and servants and between kings and subjects. They had been so for centuries.

The Regulation of Popular Recreations

James's support of popular sports and recreations was not unique in the history of English government. For hundreds of years kings and queens and the Church had sanctioned these practices, but many English governors had also tried to regulate some recreations. Sometimes particular practices interfered with the rights and prerogatives of others, as was the case in the thirteenth century when the Church ruled against singing and games near a house in which a dead person lay, or in 1591 when the court of Elizabeth I banned stage plays at times set aside for baits because rowdy theater audiences hindered royal spectators at the latter. On other occasions the exercise of recreational rights culminated in behaviors such as fornication, theft, property destruction, and riotous assemblies. Then, too, as was the case in 1342, 1389, and 1527, civil and ecclesiastic officials responded to unbridled wakes, hunting, and a host of gambling games with decrees and laws illegalizing either the occasions or the activities.[38]

Two other situations also warranted government intervention. One involved popular sporting preferences and came to a head in 1541. Prior to that time the government of Henry VIII had become concerned about the military readiness of the people in the provinces. Officials feared that ordinary citizens would not be able to defend themselves if attacked, nor would they be fit to launch an offensive if the need arose. Their skills with the bow, the officials believed, had seriously deteriorated. Away from the center of government, archery was no longer a practical art or a popular recreation. Its place in the ordinary imagination had fallen to bowling, a contest with questionable physical merits but immense gaming possibilities. Parliament responded by enacting statutes that promoted archery and illegalized bowling, except at Christmas, among commoners whose estates or tenements were worth less than £100.[39]

The second matter involved the people's penchant for sports and other displays of prowess. Historians of early modern England have generally concluded that ordinary English people enjoyed their recreations and pursued one or another of them on almost any occasion in almost any context. That they did so suggests that such practices held a great deal of meaning for yeomen, artisans, servants, and laborers, more so perhaps than did work. Indeed, there is virtually no evidence to suggest that many ordinary English people preferred work over recreation. As long as there were few consumer goods to purchase and little incentive to save, even when labor was scarce and wages were high, most people worked just enough to earn or produce enough to ensure day-to-day existence. Real energy went into church and other community gatherings, to festivals and games, to respites and alehouse visits. In all, as Peter Mathias concluded more than a decade ago, the lives of ordinary English people manifested a decided "leisure preference."[40]

At least by the early sixteenth century, the predecessors of the Stuarts, the Tudors, began to believe that they could not tolerate this leisure preference. The popular taste for recreation could and did draw people from work, they reasoned, at precisely the time when a series of unsettling social and economic changes mandated not only greater individual output but also adjustments in work relations and rhythms. Of prime importance was a demographic explosion between 1540 and 1600 that increased the population of England and Wales from three to four million. By itself this human surge might have been sufficient to disrupt supply-and-demand patterns of food, clothing, and shelter, but it was not the only unsettling condition. The long-running agricultural and industrial revolutions, which propelled early modern England away from its medieval moorings, were also restructuring the landscape and the work force. Tenantry and wage labor had begun to replace villenage, and many individuals were set adrift. Yeomen, husbandmen, and renters were dividing and enclosing large estates, which also reduced access to the common lands on which the poorest citizens had depended. Experiments to raise grain yields, mining, and local arts and crafts turned into for-market manufactures had also emerged. For many Tudor-era people, however, particular benefits of these practices, especially secure and sufficient supplies of food and a wider array of materials and manufactures, lay some years in the future. In the meantime they had to contend with recurring food shortages and un- and underemployment on a large scale, desultory conditions attributable in part, in the eyes of the government, to the popular leisure preference.[41]

Parliament and royal officials thus cooperated in a series of measures designed to get more work out of more people. One set of efforts aimed to have people better prepared to work, as Edward VI did when he ordered that youths should be trained for the tasks of agriculture and apprenticed to craftspeople. The Statute of Artificers updated and expanded the mandate for training regimens and apprenticeships in 1563. It recognized that training workers was not the only answer to what was a complex problem. Consequently the statute also defined the hours that craft and agricultural workers (including wage laborers), servants, and apprentices should work: from daybreak to nightfall in the fall and winter and from five o'clock in the morning to seven or eight o'clock in the evening the rest of the year. The problem of work and the problems faced by workers and nonworkers persisted, however, and successive Elizabethan enactments dealt variously with the poor, supplies and prices of food, job security, and wage levels.[42]

Many of these Elizabethan prescriptions for work and workers were also proscriptions of sports and recreations. The Statute of Artificers not only stretched the limits of the workday—and in so doing cut into traditional recreational times—but it also tried to eliminate the persistent practice of intermittent work. Instead of stopping whenever they wished for whatever they wished, laborers covered by its provisions were to have only two and one-half hours per day for meals and relaxation. In 1573 another act inveighed against alehouses and the games therein as perverse stimulants to bad workers and desultory work habits. Even the various "poor laws" in 1576, 1598, and 1601 addressed popular recreations, albeit more indirectly. Such acts condemned and made provisions for those who would not work, the idlers, in whose ranks were vagrants, beggars, and gamesters. The legislation also took aim at what lawmakers saw as a pervasive condition that underlay poverty: idleness, which supposedly resulted not only from a dislike of or inability to work but also from a habitual preference for leisure.[43]

Even before James issued the Declaration of Sports, then, many English governments had attempted to limit the contexts and the content of popular recreations. Recreations were no excuse for criminal behavior, nor could they infringe on the prerogatives of the monarchy or the prescriptions for war and work. By no means, however, were all recreations "unlawful"; as James acknowledged in Lancashire in 1617 and announced to the nation in 1618, some were both lawful and necessary. Moreover, to lawful, "honest" recreations, as he also recognized, the people had their "libertie."[44]

An Emergent Order of Labor and Leisure

As the situation in Lancashire suggests, not all English people concurred with the distinction between lawful and unlawful sports. Nor did they believe that the central government effectively enforced its laws and orders regarding recreations. Especially from the 1570s onward in the provinces and provincial towns—from Chester and York in the north, to Manchester and Shrewsbury in the Midlands, to Southampton and Salisbury in the south—emerged two major blocs of people who found fault both with popular recreations, honest as well as unlawful ones, and with the royal governments' efforts to regulate labor and leisure. One group worked to control the disorder endemic in many local sporting scenes and to contain the incidences of looting, theft, drunkenness, assaults on both passersby and property, and sexual improprieties. In northern and central England this relatively moderate coalition consisted of gentlemen who had decided that they could no longer afford the expense of patronizing traditional festivals and festivities, owners and managers of agricultural and industrial enterprises who disliked the results of the leisure preference of tenants and workers, and pragmatic politicians who recognized that the suppression of local contests and matches was also an assertion of local control. As befit their often relatively narrow economic and political interests, they focused on prosecuting unlawful and disorderly recreators, on scaling down the numbers and expense of festivals, and even on challenging the royal hegemony over the forests and wild prey.[45]

To the east and in some sections of the south, on the other hand, were more ideologically bound reformers. Some even called themselves "new men," and they were willing and eager to dismiss some English customs in favor of emergent practices. A fairly diverse lot in terms of occupation, they often shared a particular brand of Protestantism, Calvinism, which had neither room for personal license nor respect for the traditional liberty to recreation. They believed that the spiraling numbers of vagrants and unbound men and women and of enclosure and food riots were not the stuff of ordinary, traditional social disorder. They also feared that the economy was on the verge of collapse and that the sins of immorality, imprudence, and idleness threatened, in the words of a Southampton jury, to unleash "the great wrath of God [which] hangeth over us."[46] Consequently, where Calvinists dominated, as in Essex and Sussex, they lashed out against simple village games "for fear of the tumult of the people," at the "superfluous numbers of idle wakes," at mixed dancing, which was the "storehouse and nursery of bastardy," and at plays that contributed "to the great hurt of the poor."[47] In Stafford magistrates even turned maypoles into fire ladders.[48] In effect such radical adversaries of recreations reduced popular practices to minor, almost aberrant behaviors. They also viewed those that remained as relics of a passing order, an order that could not pass too swiftly.

Despite their differences, these two broad sets of opponents of popular sporting practices generally agreed that many recreations often stood in the way of an emergent social regime that intended to do more than just reduce crime and bring order out of chaos. Through this emergent order they proposed to reconstruct England as an economically productive and efficient country with adequate supplies of food, textiles, and other industrial goods for home consumption and export. They sought to restructure relations among people and to base the foundations of social discipline not on inherited position and privilege but on the productive capabilities and talents of competitive individuals. They also wanted to create a godly society in which parishioners were responsible to and for one another.

Finally, members of the emergent order called for a different approach to labor. In part this was a response to England's economic malaise, a condition that even Elizabethan ministers and Parliaments had recognized. The country had to be more productive, according to policy makers, a goal that required greater output from and more efficient uses of natural and human resources. The Elizabethan and Stuart "ultimate solution," colonization of the New World, would address the problem of natural resources. Redressing the human side of the equation, however, was more complex. It required several approaches, each oriented to particular issues. First there was the matter of individuals who could not or would not work. The two-pronged solution proposed to criminalize vagrancy and jail offenders and to shore up the poor by providing "poor relief," establishing workhouses, and expanding the system of apprenticeship. The second problem was that of excess labor, which contributed significantly to the massive Stuart un- and underemployment. One remedy involved shipping the surfeit of England's human resources across the Atlantic to mine the New World's natural resources. A third issue specifically involved the structure of labor and the government of the workplace. Relying on old mechanisms, especially apprenticeships and servitude, industrial and agricultural reformers both expanded these ways of binding people and defined protobureaucracies in the factory and on the farm. Managers, foremen, and overseers emerged as late Elizabethan and Stuart-era taskmasters who were responsible to farm and factory owners and for their hired or indentured underlings.[49]

The reorganization of labor required more than just a set of old and new mechanisms imposed on laborers by employers, however. In fact, as the later history of England suggests, laborers would become significantly more efficient and productive only once they conceived of new ends for work, especially in terms of consumption. This connection lay some years in the future, but another interpretation of work was beginning to emerge, especially among Calvinists who explained and explicated the "calling doctrine." At their doctrine's core was the notion that labor was more than just necessary; it was a social duty. The message was appealing. Independent farmers, gentry, merchants, mine and factory owners, and craftspeople and artisans, among others, began to accept the proposition that labor, theirs as well as that of their servants, did produce tangible outcomes and could mean the difference between success and failure, between security and poverty. They wanted to improve their standard of living, make their small businesses successful, and achieve social and political power and influence. Moreover, they recognized another side of the argument: that thrift, frugality, and hard work were meaningless if idleness and waste persisted, if people expended profits in drink and reveling, and if a discipline in leisure did not reinforce discipline in both work and the workplace.[50]

The late sixteenth- and early seventeenth-century reformation of labor thus had to be a reformation of leisure, according to the advocates of change. This realization in turn helps to account for the sometimes vicious assault by the "industrious sort" on popular recreations. The movement to reform leisure also helps to account for the growing strength of the Sabbatarian movement, especially after 1620. For over a century proponents of a strict Sabbath had proposed legislation to ensure that Sunday would be the Lord's Day, and they had struggled (and usually failed) in areas such as Lancashire to end traditional sports and matches and to fill the churches. Never before, however, had Sabbatarians had the weight of the emergent labor order behind them. The strict Sabbath was the necessary concomitant to a rigorous and disciplined work life: it was a day of rest, the one day of rest in a week of workdays. Finally, in 1625, a law defining the Sabbath as a day devoid of labor, unnecessary travel, and "unlawful sports" did gain the assent of both houses of Parliament and the king.[51]

In practice the strict Sabbath was more austere than the law mandated. The statute did not proscribe lawful recreational practices, but some magistrates, ministers, and ordinary people in the ranks of the "industrious sort" carried the attack on recreations beyond the limits of the law. In part this was an interpretive matter of morality and social order: even lawful sports resulted in crime, drunkenness, and fornication. The attack apparently also drew on the reformers' interpretations of the relationship of sports and other recreational practices to labor. In the late sixteenth century Heinrich (Henry) Bullinger, a Swiss Protestant, had suggested that active sports were forms of bodily labor and that these practices, as well as other recreations that detracted from bodily rest and service to God, should not occur on the Sabbath. Several English Puritans, including Richard Greenham and Nicholas Bownde, came close to replicating Bullinger's position. Still others, such as William Perkins, posed a less direct relationship, arguing that some "moderate" recreations benefited labor. In subsequent years, although neither position dominated, both views did secure the dependence on labor of any values, positive or negative, associated with sports and other recreations.[52]

In the two decades after Parliament enacted the initial Stuart Sabbath statute, some men also tied the general relationships between recreation and labor and of both to the Sabbath to particular kinds of laborers. In 1635 Francis White, the Anglican bishop of Ely, declared that recreation, especially among servants, "belongs not to rest, but to labour." As such, he continued, their recreations "must be granted on days of labour" and not on the Sabbath.[53] Shortly thereafter official support for White's position emerged. In 1644 Parliament, now a fundamentally nonroyalist, radical Protestant body, illegalized two remaining Sunday recreational traditions, wakes and ales. Three years later the same body acted more directly on White's recommendation: it designated the second Tuesday in each month as a day of "recreation and relaxation."[54]

The impact of these Sabbatarian actions was both complex and, in the context of long-standing practices and views, quite radical. On the one hand White and his allies in the Parliament struck again at the customary liberty to after-service Sabbath recreations that James had upheld. Second, they proposed a new kind of day in English life, a day unencumbered by labor *and* recreation, a day for rest and service to the Lord. In effect they constructed an emergent category of social practice that had economic and theological significance.

The actions of the reformers may have had another kind of impact as well. Given that one of their goals was greater productivity and efficiency, we need to ask why other people, not all of whom were Sabbatarians, did not object, as they apparently did not, to the parliamentary order to take a day for recreation from the work week. The prohibition of work on Sundays plus the designation of the second Tuesday as a day for recreation effectively shortened one work week in a month to five days. What return on this reshaping of the calendar did other people expect?

A part of the answer may lie in White's reference to "servants." Application of the law to the work and recreation of servants probably left the practices of many others unaffected. In simple terms, nonservants could continue to toil on Tuesdays. Moreover, members of the "industrious sorts"—including merchants, mine and factory owners, lawyers, small farmers, and some gentry, who had the most to gain from the reformation of popular recreations and of society at large—often controlled the labor of those servants. Some of these people were also involved in another struggle involving recreations, an upward struggle. They had set their sights on the prerogatives of the aristocracy, especially regarding hunting, and would force significant changes in the game laws and gain broader access to the fields and forests for the sport after 1671.[55]

All this suggests that the most profound impact of this episode was on the structure and power relations of English society. Stated simply, the assaults on popular recreations, the enactment of a strict Sabbath, the linkage of sports to labor and laborers, the assignment of Tuesdays for servants' recreations, and the eventual attack on game privileges were dimensions of the remaking of society into three ranks—with the emergent middle rank wielding economic and political power. The practices under attack belonged to England's hereditary ranks, the high and low born. Many of the attackers belonged to the island's emergent and still amorphous middling rank. From this social vantage point and as the parliamentary legislation suggests, the industrious sorts succeeded in linking the recreations of servants, including both contract and wage laborers, with labor, which they could control. They also recognized that sporting privilege was a function of rank, a particular rank that all too often stood in the way of the emergent social order. Indeed, even as White spoke, England's "new men" were about to find out just how obstructionist the upper rank could be. Many of its members would assist Charles in the coming civil war.

The Resistance on Behalf of Popular Practices

Old England's high and low born did not just give way to the emerging labor order's assault on their sports and their places in the social order. Across England resistance to the reformers' recreational and labor policies emerged, and it took many forms. For dancers denied their traditional Whitsun festivities in Keevil in 1624, the Declaration of Sports proved to be an effective weapon. In other and perhaps more numerous instances, however, the protests were violent, as was the case in Stratford-on-Avon, where dancers rioted when a constable tried to take down a maypole in 1619. Property damage was also not out of the question, especially when the enclosure movement felled traditional games. This is precisely what happened in a Dorset village between 1615 and 1622 as angry bowlers found that a field that had belonged to the crown and on which they had played the game for years was no longer available to them. They reacted by destroying the hedges and other property of the current owner, a gentleman.[56]

Probably the most significant act of resistance to the reform of popular recreations occurred in 1633 and involved Charles I. It began as Chief Justice Richardson, head of the Somerset assize court, anticipated Parliament's ruling of the next decade and issued orders forbidding church ales on Sundays. After investigating the affair and determining that a number of local inhabitants favored the ales on the grounds of harmless sociability, William Laud, the archbishop of Canterbury and one of the king's most important advisers, ordered Richardson to repeal the ban. Laud and Charles also knew that Richardson's aversions to popular recreations, although the most visible at the time, were not unique; shortly thereafter they reissued the Declaration of Sports and ordered ministers all over England to read it from their pulpits.[57]

In 1633 the situation in Somerset in particular and in England more generally was more complicated than had been the case when James entered Lancashire. On the one hand, Laud, Charles, and their supporters believed that if the people were denied their liberty to "honest recreations," they would turn to the alehouses, where they would talk about "matters of church or state."[58] Beyond moving to protect episcopal and royal prerogatives, they wanted neither to lose popular support nor to drive potential supporters into the hands of their enemies. On the other hand, these enemies, largely proponents of the emergent order, were stronger and more vocal than they had been in James's day. Not only had they made some headway in the struggle to eliminate popular recreations, but they also had gained some economic and political leverage in local areas and in Parliament. Finally, Laud enforced the provision that all ministers were to read the document from their pulpits, as James never had; he also sought out dissenting preachers who refused to do so. Those who were caught were tried before the Star Chamber, and those who were not often went into hiding or fled the country, some as far away as Massachusetts Bay.[59]

As late as 1637 the campaign of Laud and Charles, which was as much a matter of harrying their enemies as defending customary sports and recreations, appeared to be succeeding. As James had discovered twenty years earlier, however, things were never quite as simple as they appeared. Success was illusory, and within a year Laud and Charles had to marshal their forces on another field, the field of battle. The Declaration of Sports would not stem this tide any more than it had stopped the larger cultural conflict between reformers and traditionalists. England was about to experience civil war, and in it the Declaration of Sports was a wholly ineffective weapon.

That it was ineffective suggests as well that the social order that the declaration had sought to protect was too weak to produce an effective resistance. "Old" England—rural, agrarian, village England with its two social ranks—was itself becoming a tradition, an invention, as are all traditions, to preserve remnants of the past. To some people it was a defensible England, and it clearly needed defending: many of their countrymen and -women had a different vision of English life, its economy and labor system, its values and religious inclinations, and in fact, its popular culture. Moreover, they had the means and the power to construct a "new" England, and gradually and eventually they would do so. Nonetheless, "old" England, including its popular recreations and their base in customary social relations and labor-leisure experiences, would not pass quietly or quickly. Some practices from this England made their way across the sea to the North American mainland, where the contemporary cultural struggle continued.

2

A Grand Scheme

The promoters of colonization did not envision the "new world" as a land of conflict. Rather, they expected that overseas plantations would resolve particular English problems and reduce the potential for conflict at home. North America, they believed, was a rich land, laden with resources ripe for the taking, resources that England needed to feed its industries and its people. In addition, by sending workers from the ranks of the poor and idle to labor in the plantations, the planners figured that they would diminish one of the social and economic burdens on contemporary England, its massive unemployment. Finally, once the overseas English population expanded, it would serve as another market for English goods. The cycle of supply and demand would thus be complete.

The plans that the Elizabethan and Stuart promoters of New World colonization constructed responded to the needs and conditions of their society. They defined the goals of the overseas outposts in terms that virtually any literate and committed nationalist could understand, and they provided a blueprint for the social structure and relations that should prevail in and order the plantations. Once some of the promoters actually saw the mainland of North America, they also provided prospective colonists with glimpses of life in the outposts, including sporting practices. Through the 1620s the promotional literature promised planters abundant opportunities for enjoyable English recreations.

None of the advocates of overseas expansion, however, ever provided a complete and accurate portrait of life on the mainland of North America. Nor did their relatively narrow conception of colonization as an economic and political movement reflect the fact that it was also a social movement, a movement of people who would reproduce the practices and patterns of English society that the planners had sought to change. So, even as they envisioned a better future for England, the promoters of this grand scheme failed to anticipate all that would happen to their contemporaries in North America. Theirs were promises made to be broken, for the transfer of traditional labor-leisure patterns resulted not in riches and relaxation but in hardships and death for many colonists.[1]

The Case for Colonization

Figuratively at least, the Elizabethans discovered the Americas for England. To be sure, their claim to the land rested on voyages made by John and Sebastian Cabot during the reign of the founding Tudor, Henry VII, in 1497 and 1498. Not until the 1570s, however, when Martin Frobisher and Sir Humphrey Gilbert sailed for North America, did this "new found land" receive the attention of more than a handful of explorers. At that point adventurous knights and expansion-minded civil servants began to envision the "westerne partes" as a source of power and glory and to plan the first transatlantic colonization ventures in English history. Still, Elizabeth herself, as well as the investors who would be needed to finance the movement, remained to be convinced of the economy of empire.[2]

An intensive lobbying campaign designed to sway the queen began shortly thereafter. At its head were men who wanted the "many large Pattents, and gratious Commissions" that Elizabeth alone had the right to grant, as well as those whose interests lay primarily in extending Britain's power and influence within the European community.[3] Among this latter group were the Hakluyts—Richard the elder, a lawyer, and Richard the younger, a minister—both of whom were well connected with military men, merchants, members of the court, and eventually, trading companies. Both of them also spent much of their lives collecting reports from explorers and framing the case for colonization. In 1584, at the urging of Sir Walter Raleigh, the younger Hakluyt presented to Elizabeth *A Discourse of Western Planting,* which distilled the arguments and expectations to date.[4]

The *Discourse* contained twenty-one chapters that explained why Elizabeth and the country should support the efforts of people like Gilbert and Raleigh. In part perhaps because he was a minister, Hakluyt listed as the first reason "thinlargemente of the gospell of Christe, whereunto the Princes of the refourmed Relligion are chefely bounde."[5] He then turned to secular goals, beginning with the country's political agenda. To elevate its standing in the European community, England required military posts and allies, and the land to the west could satisfy both needs. Its huge mass would support English people, and the native population, once converted and brought under "good" government, would undoubtedly join with England in the struggle to check the ambitions of Spain and Portugal.[6]

Hakluyt also realized that the country's political fortunes depended in part on its economic might, which at present was slight. Manufacturing in particular was an economic Achilles' heel. The country simply did not produce enough goods, and the market trade suffered. Colonization, however, could resolve at least a part of the problem, for again America had what England lacked: "commodities" to "supplye the wantes of all our decayed trades."[7] Citing those who had actually seen the New World, Hakluyt described the riches of the continents, their store of minerals, animals, fowl, fish, and vegetation. Such resources were so varied and plentiful, he declared, that in a short span of time and with a small investment, "for little or nothinge," planters could send back to England all the goods that its trades and crafts required to become prosperous again.[8]

The planner addressed one other economic dilemma that England had to resolve: its abundance of idle men and women. During the country's "longe peace and seldome sicknes," he claimed, their numbers had multiplied, and none of the statutes enacted on behalf of industry and industriousness had "deliver[ed] our common wealthe from multitudes of loyterers and idle vagabondes."[9] Anticipating by several decades the directions of the emergent labor order, Hakluyt also recognized that the problem of not enough people doing not enough work would require solutions beyond those mandated by statute. Some of England's idle persons would find work once raw materials from the West were available to fuel English industries. Moreover, the planting of overseas colonies would create a new "vent" for English goods, a new market that would further stimulate employment at home.[10] By themselves, however, these changes would not resolve the problem of unemployment. There were so many poor and idle people in England, the *Discourse* maintained, that "they can hardly lyve one by another, nay rather they are readie to eate upp one another."[11] Left to their own devices, they could also threaten the peace and stability of the nation.

The younger Hakluyt thus proposed to send these idlers, particularly those who were "pety theves," to overseas plantations. There they could fell timber and make masts for ships, or plant sugar cane and raise silk worms, or mine the earth for minerals and the seas for food. There were appropriate tasks, as well, for the young, the old, and the lame. Indeed, there would be enough work in the West for five times the number of idle men and women that England actually had.[12] And as long as they worked, regardless of their ability or occupation—and Hakluyt identified more than seventy occupations needed in a colony—the laborers could expect a common benefit: they would be "kepte from idleness, and be made able by their owne honest and easie labour to finde themselves."[13]

The *Discourse* projected the planting of the West as a grand development scheme, at the core of which would lie outposts that would replicate English social relations and responsibilities. For her part, Elizabeth would provide grants of land to the adventurers who planned and invested in the colonies and who came from the ranks of nobles, gentlemen, and merchants. The adventurers, to whom Hakluyt promised significant material gains, would then recruit their sons, as well as other gentlemen and respectable tenants, to go abroad as planters. These colonists in turn would be responsible for achieving the "noble endes" of colonization: finding resources, taking English civilization and Christianity to the native peoples, and enhancing the prestige and fortunes of the queen and the nation.[14] With workers provided from the ranks of the unemployed, the hierarchy was complete. The poor and idle would perform the manual labor tasks required in the plantations, and they would support an English style of life for the planters, some of whom, as Hakluyt eventually recognized, could "take delight in hunting" a variety of animals and "hauks [hawks] of sundry kindes."[15]

In the short term the *Discourse* proved to be prophetic, at least about the matter of resources on the North American mainland. In 1585 Sir Walter Raleigh sent a band of colonists to establish a plantation on the Virginia land for which he had received a patent from Elizabeth. Within a few years the entire company on Roanoke Island had mysteriously disappeared, but not before two of its members had reported their observations. In September 1585 Ralph Lane, who was in charge of the landing party, wrote to the elder Richard Hakluyt that the land had a "greate abundance" of commodities, some of which existed nowhere else in the world.[16] Thomas Harriot, a mathematician and naval expert, also saluted the region and its resources. The climate was good and the "soile so fertile, and yeelding such commodities," he maintained, that nobody could find any "cause whereby the action [establishing other plantations] should be misliked."[17]

During the next twenty years instability at home and war abroad stalled English development on the North American mainland. Thereafter, however, conditions stabilized, and trading companies prepared to restart the colonization process, beginning with a plantation along the central coast of Virginia sponsored by the London Company in 1607. As the Hakluyts had suggested, the company instructed its men to explore the land, to trade with and Christianize the native inhabitants, and to seek minerals and other commodities. Two years later, when the London adventurers sought investments to finance additional colonists, they issued a pamphlet, "Nova Brittania," that expressed the "noble endes" of the plantation almost exactly as had the *Discourse of Western Planting*. The company was in Virginia to "advance the kingdome of God," enhance the "honour of our King," and promote the good of the country by "furnishing our owne wants of sundrie kindes." Further, the bulk of the relief party was to come from precisely the population whom the Hakluyts had proposed to send as workers, the "swarmes of idle persons, which having no meanes of labour to releeve their misery, doe likewise swarme in lewd and naughtie practises."[18]

The Appeal to Planters

As "Nova Brittania" suggests, the Hakluyts' vision of the "westerne partes" became a standard part of the lore and lure of the Stuart colonizers. Through the 1620s, and beyond in some cases, individuals and trading companies alike invoked the honor of God, king, and country.[19] They particularly stressed the commodities that the New World offered the Old, to the extent that these became "abundant" commodities, or more simply, just "abundance." In 1610, for instance, Sir Thomas Gates, who wrote to reassure his superiors in the London Company that its plantation at Jamestown, Virginia, would eventually return a profit, confirmed that "all things before reported were true; . . . the country yeeldeth abundance."[20] Two years later William Strachey, who had been the company's secretary in Virginia, filled his *Historie of Travell in Virginia* with anecdotal evidence of the land's abundance. He had seen fowl that were more numerous and larger than most English varieties. In fact, there were so many partridges that hunters could kill them "with their smale shott sometyme from of a tree, 5 or 6 at a shoot."[21] Two decades later, while exploring the more northerly Delaware River country, Thomas Yong raised the possible kill ratio to forty-eight partridges "at one time."[22]

Strachey's *Historie* was the first of many lengthy reports written as much for prospective colonists as for investors. As such, they differed slightly, especially in terms of content, from the literature produced by men like the Hakluyts, who never set foot in North America. Their treatment of the native inhabitants of the "Indies," or the "Indians," is a case in point. For centuries North America had supported a large population that was as ethnically and culturally diverse as was that of Europe, but of these people the English knew little. The Hakluyts had extracted some information about the Native Americans from the reports of explorers, but they had used that information primarily to argue that English culture and religion would benefit the natives and that they would assist the English in any struggle against the Spanish and Portuguese.[23] In contrast, Strachey and his contemporaries, most notably John Smith, provided prospective planters with some descriptions of the conditions and affairs of ordinary life among the indigenous people, usually in terms that Englishmen of some means could appreciate.

The Stuart colonization propagandists described several North American practices that had parallels in English society. One involved work, for which Native Americans had a gender-dependent work scheme not unlike their own. Among the Virginians, Strachey recorded, the men "fish, hunt, fowle, goe to the warrs, . . . and such like manly exercises," whereas the women "as the weaker sort be put to the easier workes, to sow their Corne . . . dresse the meat brought home, . . . beare all kyndes of burthens, and such like."[24] Twenty years later Edward Winslow, a member of the Plymouth plantation in Massachusetts, observed a similar gender-based division of labor among the local tribes. The men "employ themselves wholly in hunting, . . . except at some times they take some pains in fishing." The women, in contrast, "live a most slavish life"; they "carry all their burdens," plant and harvest the corn, and "have all household care lying upon them."[25]

Given the contemporary English connections between labor and leisure, it is probably not surprising that the white observers also commented on Native American recreations, which they recognized and occasionally approved. "In their hunting and fishing," declared John Smith after he had traveled among them for more than a decade, the Indians "take extreame paines," and "they esteeme it a pleasure and [are] very proud to be expert therein."[26] Their pride was not, however, a matter of simple male vanity. Rather, "by their excelling therein," Strachey concluded, "they obteyne the favour of the women."[27] Native males were also inveterate gamblers. "They use gaming as much as any where," asserted Edward Winslow, and while trading among themselves, they "will play away all, even their skin from the backs; yea, and for their wives' skins also."[28]

The Indians had one final set of practices for which there was a corollary in England: festivals. Whether as preparatory or as celebratory events, festivals were a regular feature in the lives of Native Americans, as they were in traditional English life. They concluded the growing season and preceded battles, and they enabled the tribes to invoke the gods and invest their children with the rights and responsibilities of adulthood. Usually large-scale affairs, such festivals also involved "dauncing and singing, . . . Musique," and "sprorts [sports] much like ours heare in England." One of these sports, according to Captain Henry Spelman, who lived in Virginia for a decade and a half, was "football play, which women and young boyes doe much play at" and "make ther Gooles [goals] as ours only they never fight nor pull one another doune."[29] Strachey also recognized among the festival recreations of the native Virginians a ball game akin to the "auncyent game" of English bandy, a wooden ball and curved bat contest that, in the next century, bore on the not-so ancient game of cricket.[30]

Precisely why men such as Smith, Strachey, and Winslow recounted in such a positive manner the work and recreational practices of Native Americans, particularly when much else they wrote was distinguishing and even discriminatory, remains something of a mystery. Strachey's efforts are particularly vexing, because he rarely wrote anything positive about the native Virginians. His overriding judgment was that they had a "disposicion fearefull."[31] As an agent of the London Company, however, he may have wanted to assure his employers that these people were not entirely unlike the English. Smith and Winslow, on the other hand, spent extended periods of time in North America, and both men recognized that Indian foods and farming practices were important to English survival. Consequently it seems reasonable to suggest that each of these observers was intent on finding some features in native culture that could serve as the basis for communication and trade between them and their English neighbors.[32]

Smith may have had another interest in describing native affairs. Born into a small farming family from Lincolnshire, he was a professional military officer who spent more than two decades governing, exploring, and writing about the mainland after 1607. Like the Hakluyts, Smith believed in the riches of the New World and the significance of overseas colonies for England, and he offered extensive evidence and arguments on both points in works such as *A Description of New-England* (1616) and *The General Historie of Virginia, New-England and the Summer Isles* (1624). He was also more sanguine about the role of able and committed planters in the overseas development schemes than the Hakluyts had been, and he clearly wanted to spark their interest in migration. Consequently he spoke directly to prospective planters about the demands of life in the colonies and about the pleasures they would enjoy.

Smith specifically addressed the matter of work, and in so doing he portrayed life in the North American outposts a bit more realistically than had the Hakluyts. All planters should realize, he advised, that the business of "planting and discovering" required time and effort on the part of all colonists.[33] After all, minerals did not rest on the surface, animals would not miraculously shed their furs, and the soil would not just sprout food. Nevertheless, the toil that the planters would have to perform would not "be insupportable," a conclusion that his descriptions of the Native Americans underscored. Given that Hakluyt-like workers would do most of the ordinary labor in the plantations, a planter would probably have to spend no more than three days each week "to get more than hee can spend" and, by implication, to live comfortably.[34]

Smith then tried to reassure potential colonists that their lives would not be too hard. As he wrote in *A Description of New-England,* the "nature and liberty" of the region would produce far more "sweet content," including recreations, than one could realize at home.[35] Planters would find great "delight" in hunting, for, Smith implied, the New World was really a large and unfettered version of the Old World manor parks, and its teeming forests and skies offered planters a marvelous variety of animals and fowl. Colonists and their families did not have to limit their recreations to the land, however. "What pleasure can be more," Smith asked, than that to be had "where man woman and childe, with a small hooke and line, by angling, may take diverse sorts of excellent fish, at their pleasures?" Planters could also "recreate themselves before their owne doores, in their owne boates upon the Sea," after they had grown "tired with any occasion a-shore, in planting Vines, Fruits, or Hearbs."[36]

Smith may have been the most effusive of the Stuart promoters of colonization about the prospects for recreations in the New World, but he was not the only one to make the point. Strachey had linked recreations with his descriptions of the natural riches of the mainland. Other men followed suit. In 1630, for example, Francis Higginson, whom the Massachusetts Bay Company had sent to minister at its post in Salem, maintained that the New World fowl were not only more numerous than their counterparts in the mother country but also larger. In the vein of Strachey, Higginson recounted one occasion on which he had been walking through the woods and surprised "a partridge [pheasant] so big that through the heaviness of his body could fly but a little way." He immediately added, "they that have killed them say they are as big as our hens."[37] Even as late as 1656, when promotion by tracts and relations had virtually ceased, John Hammond offered one more complimentary assessment of Virginia. "The Country is not only plentifull but pleasant and profitable," he concluded. There was an "abundance of game" and "recreation for the gentry."[38]

Recreations thus became a common theme in the colonization literature published by the Stuart promoters, probably for several simple reasons. First, they served as appropriate enticements for the men of means whom people like Smith, Strachey, and Higginson hoped to draw to the mainland of North America. Recreations were experiences, even customs, shared by the writers and their readers. Second, they were concrete exemplars of the benefits of New World abundance, which had been and remained one of the pivotal messages of the propagandists. Finally, they enabled the promoters to demystify the New World and to make the point that even in an unfamiliar land familiar patterns of life could root. English patterns of work and leisure were appropriate to life on the mainland of North America, as even some aspects of the native inhabitants' culture illustrated. In fact, the promoters suggested, whatever planters had done at home, they could do better or more easily on the land across the sea.

Still, the experiential orientation of men like Strachey and Smith did not substantially alter the broad vision of the "western partes" that their Elizabethan predecessors had created. Their underlying message remained the Hakluyt message: the mainland of North America was a rich and appealing land. Indeed, and in contrast to what Perry Miller argued for so many years, neither the Hakluyts nor their Stuart successors offered any hint of the uninviting wilderness in which Miller's Puritans lived and of which William Bradford spoke.[39] Rather, as David Cressy has concluded, the colonization propagandists consistently portrayed the North American mainland as a "garden or a park, a generous land."[40] Such a land was appropriate either for military garrisons and company supply stations or, eventually, for permanent plantations peopled with families. It would support English government and English industry, and in time the society that emerged would look very much like that in England. Of all this John Smith was so certain that he even called a portion of the mainland "New-England."

The Reality of Life in the Outposts

In the early seventeenth century trading companies led the way in implementing the development schemes on the mainland of North America. Each was a joint stock company composed of men who pooled their resources, lured other investors with promises of profits from trade in the commodities of the region, and acquired charters and patents from the king. In 1606 the first of these firms, the London Company, completed its plans for the plantation that it called Jamestown in honor of King James. Toward the end of the next decade, the same company, in concert with a group of West Country merchants headed by Thomas Weston and some Yorkshire gentlemen who were looking for another home for their nonconformist brethren, proposed a commercial fishing and fur-trading plantation in New England. This outpost became the colony of Plymouth on the shores of Cape Cod Bay. After 1623 a third group, the Dorchester Company of Adventurers, which soon reorganized as the New England Company and eventually as the Massachusetts Bay Company, also sent colonists to develop the forests and the bays around Cape Ann and, finally, Salem, Massachusetts.[41]

For these companies, however, as well as for their colonists, the promotional literature's promises about the garden and park of the New World mainland proved to be a pipe dream. None of the plantations produced a profit for its investors. Virginia did not even produce an exportable commodity until 1613, and that was an unanticipated one, tobacco. In New England inconsistent supplies of and unstable markets for fish and furs thwarted the commercial goals of the plantations' developers. Moreover, in neither region did many planters ever realize their expectations for English-style lives filled with diverse recreational opportunities. Instead the planters and the workers whom they were to govern experienced deprivation and, not infrequently, death. Nearly 90 percent of the colonists in Virginia died over the course of the first decade, and the Plymouth plantation lost half its members in the first year alone.[42]

The problems that confronted planters and workers alike began the minute they stepped off English soil onto the ships that would take them some 3,000 miles across the Atlantic. The journey was a long and tiring one; for six weeks or more the passengers occupied leaky vessels that rocked with the waves and lurched through storms. Packed like fish, they endured unsanitary quarters, little exercise, and even less fresh food, especially fruits and vegetables that would have prevented scurvy and dysentery. In time the sight of land might raise the colonists' spirits, but the landing itself could recast the pale.[43] When the Pilgrims arrived in Plymouth in 1620, recalled William Bradford, they had "no friends to welcome them, nor inns to entertain and refresh them, no houses, much less towns, to repair unto to seek for succour."[44] Moreover, having landed in December, the Plymouth colonists suffered through winter in New England; by mid-March, as Bradford lamented, the "living [were] scarce able to bury the dead."[45]

The colonists' distress continued once they began the painstaking process of building shelters, planting crops, and exploring their environs. Their strength diminished by the ocean journey, many of them became ill, a condition exacerbated by the climate and inadequate food supplies. In Virginia the colonists also confronted the native inhabitants, about whom they knew only what the Hakluyts had written. The information was inadequate even for the simplest of exchanges, and as the Jamestown colonists bullied their way among the Indians, what they received was not the expected offer of alliance but overt resistance. Over time, only John Smith and John Rolfe worked to develop relations beneficial to both peoples, and their efforts were not enough to save the lives of hundreds of English colonists and Native Americans through 1622.[46]

In New England the English immigrants, who did have access to the works of Smith and Strachey, treated the Native Americans differently than had the colonists in Virginia. New Englanders avoided the antagonize-and-attack cycle that contributed to the persistent weakness of the Virginia plantations, at least for a time, and some planters did cultivate the native population. In Plymouth and at the private plantation of Mount Wollaston especially, the planters and servants traded with the Indians and learned how best to plant crops. Some men also came to realize that they shared interests in feasting and recreations with the native inhabitants. At Mount Wollaston Thomas Morton achieved an unparalleled degree of notoriety among his English contemporaries for the "revels" to which he invited his native allies.[47] The governors of Plymouth also invited "many of the Indians . . . whom for three days we entertained and feasted" to marriages and harvest festivals.[48] Then, too, when planters went to native villages to trade, they could expect celebratory feasts and an occasional contest, although not always on grounds dictated by the white visitors. In 1623, for example, Edward Winslow and his companions challenged the tribesmen of King Massasoit "to shoot for skins." The Indians refused, proposing instead that "one of us shoot at a mark." The event ended, Winslow concluded, with the Native Americans left in a state of wonderment "to see the mark so full of holes."[49]

The New England colonists did share one fitful and nearly fateful set of experiences with their brethren in the South, however: few of them worked enough to ensure their survival, let alone to secure products and profits for the companies. The pattern of insufficient labor, which also entailed a strong preference for leisure, had deep roots among the rich and poor alike in England. Moreover, it had been precisely this pattern that the planners and promoters of colonization had intended to alter, if not eliminate, by sending individuals from the ranks of the idle poor to labor in the colonies. By putting the plans into effect, however, all the trading companies did was to ensure that the pattern transferred across the Atlantic, first to Virginia and then to New England.

As the Hakluyts had prescribed, the London Company sent two primary groups of colonists, men of means and laborers, to Jamestown in 1607. The gentlemen, who had come to achieve "noble endes," were a fractious lot who were more disposed to yelling at one another than to felling trees. On the other hand, the workers, whom the company had sent to labor, either lacked manual skills or had little inclination to use what skills they had. Employed as company servants with no incentives to work for themselves, they quickly rejected weeding corn and making clapboards in favor of hunting gold, bowling in the streets, or escaping to live idly among the native peoples.[50] In short, as Edmund Morgan has argued, the Virginia Company had sent "the idle to teach the idle."[51]

Efforts to re-form the labor-leisure patterns of the inhabitants of Jamestown were intermittent and only partially effective. An early attempt occurred in the fall of 1608, when John Smith assumed command of the plantation. With winter on the horizon, Smith found that food was in short supply, despite his efforts to trade with the Indians, and the cabins and palisades needed repairs. He thus divided all the men, gentlemen included, into teams that spent "4 hours each day" in work. The rest of the time, as Smith himself admitted, they devoted to "pastimes and merry exercise."[52] He could get no more from them, he later explained, because the laborers "were for the most part footmen," and the "adventurers brought to attend them . . . never did know what a dayes worke was."[53]

Another plan emerged after May 1610, when the first of three military men, Sir Thomas Gates, arrived with new orders from the company. The London stockholders had given Gates, Lord De La Warr, and Sir Thomas Dale, both of whom arrived shortly thereafter, the "full and absolute power and aucthority [*sic*] to correct, punishe . . . and rule" in accord with common law.[54] The disciplinary code that they imposed, however, actually resembled military law. Their "Lawes Divine, Morall, and Martiall, etc." regulated most behaviors; major transgressions, such as blasphemy, treachery, and unlawful trading with the Indians, warranted strict punishments, including death.[55]

Discipline and retribution for breaches of it also applied to ordinary endeavors, particularly work and recreations. Each person had to "daily attend his worke upon his said trade or occupation," and no one was to lose or break a tool. Those who did not comply faced a range of punishments, from having one's "entertainment checkt" for a month to confinement in a galley for up to three years.[56] Furthermore, no one was to "play at Cards or dice," "play away his Armes," or waste gunpowder by "shooting it idly away, or at birds, beasts, or fowle."[57] Nor did the code permit anyone "to use any unlawfull and prohibited games . . . or give themselves to excesse of drinking" under any circumstances. Being placed in irons, whippings, galley service, and even death awaited offenders.[58]

The precision and severity of these laws, especially compared to the provisions of common law, suggest that the governors of Virginia viewed the lack of work and the preference for leisure as significant impediments to safety and stability in the colony. The order to work daily was more straightforward than was any provision in the Statute of Artificers, while the prohibition against unlawful games was one of the few rules that resembled its counterpart in the legal code of England. As was the case at home, however, enforcing the code and altering the discipline and productivity of the colonists proved to be the real challenges for Gates, De La Warr, and Dale. There is little evidence to suggest that they succeeded in meeting this challenge. In fact, in 1611, when Dale went to see whether conditions had improved in Jamestown, he found that "most of the companie were at their daily and usuall works, bowling in the streets."[59] Four years later, when Captain Samuel Argall visited the plantation, he, too, saw how ineffective the laws had been. Of the nearly 400 inhabitants, only about half were "fit for husbandry and tillage." Many others continued "to wait and play than worke."[60]

In the 1620s the practices and preferences of English laborers also concerned the New England planters. At Plymouth Governor William Bradford concluded that the company's servants would require close supervision, and he had assigned all "single men that had no wives to join with some family."[61] But he apparently had not anticipated either that the laborers who "were most able and fit for labour" would be so unwilling to "work for other men's wives and children" or that they would devise ingenious excuses to avoid work.[62] In 1621 he confronted one of these excuses when some of the company's servants claimed that it was "against their conscience" to work on Christmas day. Bradford did permit them to stay behind as he led the other colonists, who were reformist Protestants and did not recognize Christmas, to work. When the governor returned, however, he found the laborers "in the street at play openly; some pitching the bar, and some at stool-ball and such like sports." Bradford immediately ended their recreations and turned their argument on its head: it was "against his conscience that they should play and others work."[63]

Traditional holy day recreations were not the only behaviors that disturbed the planters at Plymouth or the governors of other plantations in New England. On the first anniversary of the landing at Plymouth, minister Robert Cushman reported that the colony still had too many "idle drones."[64] It also had troublemakers, including two servants who engaged in a duel with swords and daggers and other "ill-conditioned people" who sought refuge from Separatist restraints in some nearby private plantations, which provided customary revels and alehouses.[65] The lack of a sufficient number of "industrious men" also complicated life in the nearby commercial fishing plantation at Cape Ann.[66] In 1625, after its ledgers showed an income of £480 and expenses totaling £1,200, the New England Company concluded that the depressed market for fish and the rising shipping costs did not entirely account for the deficit. Another part of the problem lay with "our Land-Men, who being ill chosen and ill commanded, fell into many disorders and did the Company little service."[67]

In 1628 the New England Company established one final plantation in Massachusetts, at Naumkeag, or Salem. Here, too, colony officials struggled against the tide of customary labor-leisure preferences and practices. A year later, when the company had reorganized as the Massachusetts Bay Company, its council went so far as to dismiss "divers servants" whose "ill life might be prejudicial to the Plantation."[68] Still, the planter-governors in residence at Salem had to contend with "idle drone[s]" and other men who tended to "that inordinate kind of drinking as to become drunk."[69] They also had to deal with men from neighboring plantations, particularly Thomas Morton, whose recreational practices set an example that the Salem leaders did not wish their own men to follow.

Morton was a minor partner in a small private fur-trading venture at Mount Wollaston, and by his own account he enjoyed the New World park.

It offered him five kinds of hawks, which he "reclaimed, trained, and made flying in [a] fortnight."[70] Trading with Native Americans for furs proved to be less fruitful, however, and many of Morton's companions left the plantation with their commander, Captain Wollaston, for Virginia. Soon after their departure Morton and the men who remained planned a festival for the upcoming May Day "after the old English custome." They brewed a "barrell of excellent beare" and erected an eighty-foot-high maypole "with the help of Salvages." With "buckshorns nayled . . . unto the top," the pole stood not only as a "faire sea marke for directions" but also as a focal point for traditional festive practices. Around it Morton, his men, and their native allies danced, drank, and according to the company's critics, engaged in "great licentiousness."[71] They continued to do so long past May Day—until the Salem planters cut down the pole. Eventually the authorities at Boston arrested Morton, accused him of crimes that had no basis in English law, and shipped him back across the Atlantic.[72]

⊷⟹◖⟸⊷

In retrospect we can probably concur with Morton that his treatment was unfair, particularly given that he was simply living the kind of life that the promoters of colonization had promised planters. This was an idyllic life, an ideal life, a traditional life—a life of limited work and unlimited recreations. It was a life that sounded fine on paper, which was what propagandists for English overseas expansion had intended since the 1580s. The Hakluyts, John Smith, William Strachey, and others all had noted and promoted sports and recreations as if they were the preferred activities of Englishmen and -women—which they had been and remained for some people. The story the colonization propagandists told to prospective adventurers and planters, in short, was one of continuity. Indeed, it was about continuity.

It was not, however, a story that had a happy ending for thousands of mostly English men. Multiple sports and recreations may have been desirable practices, even the ends of desires, in the North American "garden" and "park"—had the players recognized the boundaries of their existence. The lack of food, climates to which they were not accustomed, indigenous people whom they did not understand, and diseases, among other things, were challenges for which the prior experiences and present knowledge left laborers and governors alike ill-equipped to meet. Such conditions required changes in traditional practices and rhythms, changes that only gradually emerged after 1620.

Ironically perhaps, Thomas Morton was the product of one such change. Even though he may have thought that he had no superiors and no fetters in the game park of Massachusetts because he paid no homage and fealty to traditional lords and rulers, he actually had many "masters." Morton had gone to the New World as an agent in the market-driven enterprise that English colonization of North America was becoming, and his bosses were the shippers who transported his furs, the hatters and clothiers who turned them into finished goods, and the consumers who purchased them. Moreover, the Salem and Boston authorities who captured Morton came from this emerging reformist Protestant, capitalist community. They saw themselves as his superiors, and his disputes with them stemmed from the irreconcilability of his preference for leisure and their emergent work discipline. From their perspective, Thomas Morton was a man of an older England, and in neither Europe nor North America were such men and their practices as much in favor in the late 1620s as they had been earlier.

Had he been a more astute reader of colonial policies, Morton might have anticipated an important alteration in the grand development scheme of colonization some ten years before the Salemites captured him. In 1618 the London Company introduced a policy that changed the process of and prospects for colonization and, ultimately, labor-leisure patterns. This was the headright system, which provided fifty acres of land to planters and adventurers for each colonist they recruited and financed. In the next decade the New England–Massachusetts Bay Company also offered land to people who would either invest in the company or bear the risks and the costs of transporting their households and servants overseas. For both regions the demographic consequences of this policy change were particularly significant. In Virginia the population nearly tripled between 1619 and 1628, and by 1634, 2,000 colonists were arriving annually in New England.[73]

The new recruiting policy, however, changed more than just the dimensions of the population. Insofar as it established a new interest for migration, it also drew a different blend and, in some cases, even a new breed of colonists. In the past the trading companies had recruited the sons of nobles, a few gentlemen, and laborers and unemployed Englishmen, few of whom had any direct stake in the success of the colonies beyond their own survival and most of whom had neither incentive nor inclination to behave in other than traditional ways. With the promise of land, on the other hand, the companies provided a direct interest for colonists, the one that John Smith had forecast would be needed to secure the colonies. "I am not so simple, to thinke," he had written, "that ever any motive then wealth, will ever erect there a Commonweale."[74] He was right. The new policy drew individual proprietors, families, skilled servants who expected to become free men and women, and even some of England's "new men." Their migration disrupted the freewheeling ways of Thomas Morton and altered the course of work and recreational practices among the English colonists.

3

Change and Persistence in Colonial Sporting Life, 1620s–1670s

The thirty or so years after 1618 constituted a watershed in the histories of sports and other recreations in England and its colonies on the mainland of North America. In the Old World King James's "Book of Sports," which had confirmed the people's right to lawful recreations after Sabbath morning services, also committed the Stuart royal house to support some recreations at a time when economically and religiously motivated reformers were becoming more concerned with the undesirable consequences of those practices. During the next three decades, as royalist and reformist forces struggled for power in England, the persisting practice of traditional recreations remained a matter of political import. By 1649 the weight of the royalist order had diminished, and the process of containing expressions of the leisure preference and suppressing popular recreations proceeded. With Oliver Cromwell at its head, the emergent labor order had won the day.

Simultaneously the new recruiting policies of the trading companies set in motion the re-formation, if not the transformation, of recreational life in the North American mainland colonies. Gradually in Virginia after 1618, and more quickly in neighboring Maryland and Massachusetts Bay to the north, expressions of the leisure preference became less prevalent. Work regularized. A relatively strict Sabbath prevailed. Games, contests, and matches were not only irregular but also lacked the relatively complex structures and multiple locations of English forms.

A number of factors, beginning with a change in the dimensions and composition of the population, account for this picture. Through the mid-1640s thousands of men and women migrated across the Atlantic Ocean. Some of them were members of England's middling ranks—small land-holders, craftspeople, ministers, professionals, shopkeepers, and mer-chants—who came to take up land for themselves. In the process they also abandoned sports like baits and jousts as artifacts that they either could not or would not transfer with the rest of their cultural baggage. Other immi-grants, especially those who came as servants, were coerced into giving up some recreations once they arrived on the shores of North America. They had been brought to labor, to complete the many tasks necessitated by survival and society building, and not to play or be idle.[1] For most colo-nists as well, a marginal material culture and institutional infrastructure, a narrow range of social relations, and the physical environment of North America either abetted their decisions or encouraged their compliance with the dictates of authorities to forgo many recreations, at least until midcen-tury. At that point the colonists were able to reinvent some traditional practices, but through the 1670s they neither replicated particular forms exactly nor reproduced the full range of English sports. They had moved, historically as well as geographically, away from the customary patterns of their homeland.

The Chesapeake

The earliest scenes in the process of changing the course of English recre-ations took place along the shores of the Chesapeake Bay. *Chesapeake* is an Algonquian word for "country on a big river," and the big river is actually an arm of the Atlantic Ocean that veers inland about 200 miles in a north-westerly direction. In the process it separates Virginia from Maryland and divided both colonies into eastern and western "shores." The shoreline of the bay is about 3,000 miles long, broken by innumerable rivers and creeks of various widths and lengths. Surrounding the bay is a broad plain known as the tidewater. North and west of the plain the land rolls gently to the fall lines of major rivers where cities such as Baltimore and Richmond eventually emerged, and even farther west is the piedmont, or the foothills of the Appalachian Mountains.

It was on the coastal flatlands, and especially along the rivers that flowed through them, that English colonists initially concentrated in the seven-teenth century. Jamestown was there, as were the numerous private plantations that appeared westward along the James River after 1618. North of another river, the Potomac, in what became Maryland, manors and small farms emerged after 1634. Where the plain had relatively fertile soil and good drainage, it supported the commodity that John Rolfe had learned about from Native Americans, tobacco. Gradually, this "sotweed" came to dictate the rhythms and dominate the lives of Virginians and Marylanders. By midcentury it also supported a still largely immigrant population of nearly 20,000 men, women, and children, many of whom lived and worked on individually owned farms and plantations.[2]

Among these colonists sports and recreations were less evident than they had been among their predecessors who had worked irregularly for the Virginia Company. This is not to suggest that no colonists in the Chesapeake played games or displayed prowess in other ways. Some of them hunted, played cards and gambled, and engaged in wrestling, cudgeling, fencing, and ninepins. A few members of the governor's council in Virginia even raced horses. None of these events, however, was as formalized or as stylized as was its corollary in the Old World. Nor did these practices achieve the same fit or regularity in the course of ordinary life as popular recreations had in England. From Virginia there is little evidence to suggest that either servants or their owners took much time from work to play games, to visit with passersby, or to go to a tavern or alehouse for midday or evening meals and a game or two. To the north in Maryland, as well, the records are virtually silent about sportive contests and displays of prowess interfering with work and about owner-servant conflicts over labor-leisure practices.[3]

This movement away from customary Old World patterns and the construction of a relatively stable tobacco culture did not occur overnight. In the 1620s in Virginia especially, some patterns evident in the company outposts persisted. The death rate was not far below that in Jamestown a decade and a half earlier. Nearly 75 percent of the immigrants died within a few years of their arrival, the victims of illness, ignorance, and their inability to get along with the Native Americans. Basic commodities that an efficient labor force might have produced, such as food and clothing, remained in short supply. Women were few, and Africans had not yet arrived in substantial numbers to take the place of white indentured servants. In fact, the London Company still recruited servants and apprentices from the ranks of Britain's un- and underemployed and from the ample stock of destitute boys in London. Individual proprietors like the Lords Berkeley, whose ancestral home lay in the Vale of Berkeley in Gloucestershire, had also begun to send shiploads of servants and tenants to work newly acquired lands. Their private plantation, known as Berkeley Hundred, consisted of nearly 100 people from the Vale, many of whom had lived at or below the poverty line as farm and woolen workers.[4] Their presence did not eliminate criticisms of laborers, however. There were still many "lasie servants, who had rather stand all day idle, than worke, though but an houre . . . ," the Reverend Jonas Stockam concluded in 1621.[5]

The structure of society remained as it had been as well. Virginia retained two ranks, planters and workers, or governors and governed. In turn two forms of discipline prevailed, both predicated on the customary hegemony of masters over servants and, more generally, of superiors over inferiors. One form was the local, personal oversight that planters and their overseers exercised. They assigned tasks to servants or went with them to the fields, and they held laborers accountable for their work.[6] Isolated as they were, planters were able to treat their workers as they wished, and as the London Company heard in 1623, "divers" masters "do much neglect and abuse their servants there with intolerable oppression and hard usage."[7]

The establishment of a resident legislature, the Virginia Assembly, and the presence of company and eventually royal officials provided a second means of securing discipline. They produced formal acts and laws that were less capricious than personal governance but still harsh. Some rulings aimed directly at the "Idler or renagate," whether free person or servant, who was to be put to work "till he shew apparant signes of amendment."[8] They also focused on the activities that planters apparently believed led servants and free colonists alike from work. In the case of "gaming at dice or cards," the victor stood to "lose all his or their winninges," and all players faced fines of ten shillings.[9] Another form of legislation tried to ensure that workers were sufficiently rested at the beginning of each work week. Six years before Parliament adopted a similar measure, the proprietor at the private plantation of Berkeley Hundred ordered his servants and tenants to refrain from labor and recreation and to keep the Sabbath "in holy and religious order."[10] The assembly applied this prescription to the colony as a whole in a series of acts through 1629.[11]

The court records are too incomplete to permit an accurate assessment of whether the legal statutes were enforced, let alone any judgment about their effectiveness. Nevertheless, there are indications that some change, if not a radical alteration in the conditions of society and the practices of colonists, had begun to emerge in Virginia by the late 1620s. First, tobacco exports reached one-half million pounds in 1628, or more than ten times what the colony had shipped a decade earlier. Second, the rate of production also rose, from approximately 50 pounds per worker in 1618 to between 600 and 700 pounds in the late 1620s and 1630s. Finally, the criticisms of laborers moderated in terms of both frequency and tenor in the 1630s.[12]

The tobacco production gains may be particularly telling about changes in the conduct and context of ordinary life. Some of this increase may be attributable to the fact that there were more people. In 1618 only 1,000 colonists, mostly men, lived in Virginia, whereas there were some 2,600 people ten years later. As historians of the Chesapeake have maintained, however, a more efficient labor force probably accounts for a larger portion of the increase. The rise in per laborer production, which was particularly steep in the decade after 1618 and more steady through midcentury, supports this argument.[13]

By the early 1630s, then, colonists in Virginia were apparently laboring longer and more regularly—at the cost of sports and other recreations—for several reasons. Prospective landowners faced many tasks once they arrived in the Chesapeake, whether they came primarily to profit from tobacco or not. Unlike their contemporaries in New England, few immigrants to the region in the 1630s and 1640s found living quarters or adequate food supplies readily available, either with neighbors or on their own farmsteads. Consequently they quickly had to construct shelters for themselves and their animals, clear and seed fields, and prepare and store food. Given the dispersed pattern of settlement, planters had to do much of this work themselves; neighbors and kin lived too far away to provide immediate or regular assistance. Some planters did have help from bondsmen and -women who had exchanged their freedom for passage to the Chesapeake. If these servants survived the "seasoning," if they adjusted to the climate and did not succumb to disease, they could reclaim their free status and acquire land. In the meantime, however, they too faced years of labor.[14] Sometimes the labor was unremitting, as is clear from the words of one indentured servant recounted in a ballad, appropriately subtitled "The Distressed Damsel." Since she arrived in Virginia from England, the piece begins, "the axe and the hoe have wrought my overthrow." For five years she knew only "sorrow, grief and woe." Each dawn brought a common routine—"so soon as it is day, to work I must away"—and what play she had was only "at Plow and Cart." Her story closes with hopelessness: "in misery I spend my time that hath no end."[15]

More than just the harsh demands of tasks regularly performed limited opportunities for recreations, however. Many workers, whether free or bound, worked in relative isolation, in climatic extremes, and in a physical environment that was different from that in England. The work environment, in short, was not conducive to many contests and games. Nor did the colonists' material culture, which was bare by English standards, support a range of familiar and enjoyable practices. Except for their carbines, muskets, and an occasional sword, personal estates rarely held equipment that Chesapeake colonists might have used in British games, contests, and festivals. Even tavernkeepers do not appear to have owned the goods that they had available in the Old World, and the few taverns that existed were sites for drinking but not for many sports and games. Horses were also not numerous, a fact that restricted racing to a few owners. Hunting, for which equipment did exist, lacked the grandeur and the gore of the sport in Britain, and at least in Maryland, plans for game preserves did not materialize before midcentury.[16]

There was one other barrier to the reproduction of recreations: the governing structures and strictures in what remained hierarchically organized societies. On the manors in Maryland the presence of overseers and manor courts combined to secure labor and to deter expressions of the leisure preference. In both colonies as well, the organs of official culture, especially the assemblies and county courts, continued to define expected behaviors and to penalize publicly visible breaches of work discipline and social order more generally. Both legislatures prohibited traveling, unnecessary labor, and recreations on the Sabbath, and they proscribed acts of violence and waste of gunpowder, as well as drunkenness, fornication, and adultery. The resultant legal codes thus resembled, and in fact drew from, those enacted by contemporary British Parliaments in which Puritans and other reformers dominated.[17]

As did their peers within the emergent labor order in England, legislators in the Chesapeake did more than prescribe penalties for lawbreakers. They also held the masters and mistresses, be they planters or tavern owners, responsible for the actions of their servants, family members, and customers. Planters and proprietors paid for the infractions of their charges, sometimes dearly, as a court case from the eastern shore of Virginia suggests. In 1636 the Accomack County court cited William Ward, a herdsman, for deserting the cows he was tending to play ninepins at a nearby house. This was not the first time that Ward had left his duties, the court determined, but it left his punishment to Ward's owner. The court did specify Lady Dale's penalty, however. It fined her 385 pounds of tobacco, which was slightly more than half of what an able servant produced in a year.[18]

By Chesapeake standards a servant's annual tobacco production was a significant sum to lose, and the threat of such penalties probably encouraged other planters to maintain vigilance over their servants. No other case of what was apparently an expression of the traditional leisure preference surfaced in the court proceedings before midcentury, and this pattern is probably not simply a function of incomplete records. Popular English recreations were, at most, irregular practices in the Chesapeake from the late 1620s onward, and neither planters nor servants had a vested interest in making them otherwise. Their interests lay in land, tobacco exports, and especially for servants, freedom. Not until midcentury did a critical mass of colonists realize these interests, however. Only then, as the Chesapeake entered what Russell Menard has called the "age of the small planter," did the prospects for sports and other recreations improve.[19]

Massachusetts Bay

In the fall of 1636 Robert Ryece wrote to his friend John Winthrop, who had moved from the family estate in Suffolk to Massachusetts Bay six years earlier. Ryece had remained in the East Anglian province, where conditions, which had not been good for some time, had actually worsened as an economic depression settled in the textile trade. Almost daily the signs became more ominous. A drought had parched the soil and the crops, and then a rain so heavy that the ground could not absorb it flattened what remained of the grain. Finally, a plague had struck London, which lay not far to the southwest. All these calamities, Ryece maintained, were the results of God's judgment that too many of his contemporaries were devilish and disorderly, especially on the Sabbath. The Lord had good reason to be so distressed, he concluded. Some months earlier the bishop of Norwich had ordered "all weekely lectures putte down" and "many mynisters sylenced, suspended, & putt from there places for not . . . readinge the Kings boocke for liberty & recreation on the Lords daye." Now, Ryece continued, employers "cannot contayne there servantes from excursions into all prophane sportes & pastimes on the Lords daye." Oh, such wickedness, he ended, implying as well that Winthrop was fortunate to be gone.[20]

Ryece's interpretation of local events was not unusual for "new men" such as he. They were Puritans who believed that God controlled the fates of individuals and that he punished individuals who failed to live righteous lives and to labor on his behalf. Climatic extremes, such as drought followed by a deluge, did not just occur; God inflicted them on humankind as retribution for acts of disobedience. Before 1636 there had been many such acts of disobedience, people like Ryece believed, including the persisting practice of recreations on the Sabbath and a more general inattention to individuals' callings. There were more such acts yet to come, they also suspected, especially since the Catholic-leaning son of James, Charles I, now occupied the throne and appeared to be doing the work of the devil through his reissue of the Declaration of Sports and his bishops' harassment of nonconforming ministers. If England persisted on its ungodly and uneconomic course, they wondered, how would God react? Did retributions worse than drought and depression lay in store?[21]

Men like Ryece faced two choices in these turbulent years of the 1620s and 1630s. They could stay in England, as Ryece did, struggle to maintain their way of life, and possibly face more of God's wrath, or they could leave, as Winthrop had. For Winthrop, the decision to leave England had not been an easy one. He had a country estate at Groton, a law practice in London, and a large family. After several years of thinking about his options at home, however, he had concluded that "this land growes wearye of her Inhabitants." Economic conditions in particular were so bad because people acted in such "deceiptfull and unrighteous" ways that "it is allmost impossible for a good and upright man to maintaine his charge and live comfortably in any of them." Insofar as succeeding and, ultimately, profiting in one's calling were necessary both for earthly comfort and as a possible sign that a person was one of God's elect, that he or she was predestined to achieve heavenly salvation, Winthrop had to go where it was possible for a man and his family to "live comfortably."[22]

Winthrop consequently migrated to Massachusetts Bay, where he became a landowner and the first resident governor. The opportunity had arisen after the Massachusetts Bay Company had formed and made plans to transform its sparsely settled outposts into a network of towns and villages in 1628. Two years later the "great migration" began, with Winthrop in the first wave of a movement that would bring more than 20,000 men, women, and children to the shores of Cape Cod Bay through the early 1640s. As was Winthrop, many of the immigrants were of the "industrious sorts." Numerous servants accompanied these middling-rank men and women, but only a minority were of the "poorer sort."[23]

For many migrants, the company's offer of land was an opportunity to leave behind the unsettled conditions of their homeland and to achieve what Daniel Vickers has described as a level of "comfortable independence," or economic "competency."[24] The precise meaning of this term varied among individuals. Some immigrants wanted to acquire sufficient land and material goods so that they and their families could live without fear of failure. Others intended to maintain, and perhaps improve, their status. Most colonists expected to achieve their "competency" in an English manner, with farming, commercial fishing, crafts, and trading as the economic mainstays. Moreover, they established English institutions such as taverns and courts, assigned English names to their towns and villages, and replicated English gender and rank relations.[25]

The immigrants did not reproduce all English ways, however. Winthrop and his peers did not have to deal directly with the Declaration of Sports or with large numbers of servants who sported on the Sabbath. The declaration seems to have figured in the early history of Massachusetts Bay only insofar as a few ministers who had refused Bishop Laud's order to read it from their pulpits in Britain migrated to the region. Here the strict Sabbath prevailed, and the courts indicted only two Sabbath sporters through 1640. Traditional festivals and rituals also produced no recreations; they did not transfer from Britain. Unlike the situation in the Chesapeake, however, neither laws nor brutal masters can account for the infrequency and irregularity of recreations in Massachusetts. Through 1645 the colonial assembly, the General Court, directed only one piece of legislation against recreational practices, an order for all householders to get rid of cards and other gaming devices in 1631, and owners and employers apparently did not forcibly coerce servants and wage laborers into unrelenting work.[26]

Also inadequate in accounting for this change in the recreation pattern is the explanation offered by earlier historians, that Puritan civil and religious leaders such as Winthrop opposed and suppressed most recreations in New England.[27] In fact, some members of the ruling hierarchy viewed some recreations as necessary to life. A case in point was recreational practice that resulted, as Governor Winthrop himself concluded, in "strength to the body, and vigour to the mynde."[28] Long hours of reading, writing, and government service had left him "melancholick and uncomfortable," his mind clouded by "a great dullnesse and discontent." As was his habit, he looked for the cause of his troubles in his own behavior and determined that his distress was of his own making. He had stayed at his duties too long, all the while abstaining "from suche worldly delights as my heart most desired." He thus turned to "outward recreation" and thereafter found himself "much refreshed."[29]

This was not the first time that Winthrop associated mental and physical stimulation with physical recreations. He had come to a similar conclusion some years earlier, as he suffered through what for many immigrants was one of the most grueling experiences of the colonization process, the Atlantic crossing. In 1630 strong waves rocked the *Arbella,* which carried the governor and some 200 men, women, and children across the ocean; most of the passengers had become ill and had taken refuge in their cabins. Only after they had returned to the deck and "stirred themselves," Winthrop recalled, did their conditions improve. The captain also observed this effect, and he subsequently "set our children and young men to some harmless exercises." In the end, Winthrop concluded, such "play did our people much good."[30] Five years later a similar situation occurred on board the *James,* the ship that transported Richard Mather, the minister and progenitor of the famous Mather family, to the Bay Colony. This time, however, the ship's crew provided the relief. They caught and then carved up on deck a "great porpoise." For the weary travelers, Mather concluded, the experience was a "marvellous merry sport" that provided "spiritual refreshing to our souls" and "delightful recreation to our bodies."[31]

The Puritans also expressed an interest in "delightful recreation" on land. This was particularly true of hunting, fishing, and fowling, which they had known in Britain and whose prospects both the earlier colonization literature and the colonists themselves promoted. In 1633, for example, William Hammon wrote to his former master in England, Sir Simonds D'Ewes, about the bounty that surrounded him in the village of Watertown. Codfish and bass were so plentiful, he maintained, that three men or boys could catch 300 to 400 of them in about twenty-four hours. Around him as well was a "good store of deer," and "had we but a kennel of great hounds we should hunt them from our plantation."[32] About the same time William Wood described for his English readers a natural wildfowl preserve at Rumney Marsh. An eight-square-mile plot of land at the mouth of the Saugus River between Boston and Salem, the marsh contained numerous creeks, an abundance of fowl, and "convenient ponds for the planting of duckoys."[33] Four years later Winthrop's brother-in-law, Emmanuell Downing, proposed to hunt "wild foule by way of duck coy" on common land near Salem, a plan that the General Court approved in part because it promised to promote the "publike good."[34]

The approval and interest that Puritans manifested in some recreations complicate the question of why traditional sports and other displays of prowess were relatively uncommon in Massachusetts Bay in the 1630s and early 1640s. Some of the same evidence, however, does provide clues about one part of the answer. To hunt in an English manner required dogs, as

Hammon implied, and neither he nor other individuals apparently acquired them before midcentury. Nor did the colonists bring with them, or craft and raise once they arrived, other equipment and animals that English recreational practices incorporated. Except for holding a few fishing lines and carbines, estate inventories contained almost no goods employed in Old World recreations. Moreover, the horses and other domestic animals that the colonists might have used in racing or baits were too few and too valuable to be used in sports.[35] In short, like their contemporaries in the Chesapeake, migrants to the Bay Colony lacked the material culture to support a variety of recreations.

There is also no evidence to suggest that Downing's proposal for a wild-fowl preserve ever moved beyond the petition stage, perhaps for several reasons. For one thing, the abundance of wildlife and land in the New World may have rendered such a preserve unnecessary, if not impractical and uneconomic. In addition Downing did not migrate until 1638, and then he did not stay long, a pattern typical of English lords and gentry and one that may have limited recreational practices. In the old country nobles and landed gentlemen had been the patrons of recreations. In the new one, however, only a handful of either group came, even fewer stayed as full-time residents, and apparently none assumed the role of patron.[36]

The migrants to Massachusetts Bay thus lacked two of the props that underlay recreational practices in their homeland, a critical mass of material goods and upper-rank patrons. Had either of these elements been present, however, the colonists still might not have reproduced the full range of English recreational practices, for two reasons. First, many colonists, although by no means all, were committed to the ideological primacy of labor and to the broader reformist Protestant tradition linking labor and leisure. Second, the demands and rewards of work itself were greater in the New World. Both factors worked against the reproduction of Old World labor-leisure rhythms and for the subordination of sports to work.

The Puritan ideology that raised the specter of and the stakes for labor drew from both theology and their economic interests. The central theological root was the calling doctrine, which maintained that people whom God had called, or chosen, to share in the afterlife had a responsibility to labor on his behalf. In practical terms this meant that such people had to do good works and to labor assiduously at their occupations. To do so would not ensure that an individual was one of the elect, but even this uncertainty was preferable to the certainty of damnation that Puritans accorded to those who did not work. Labor thus was a part of the ordinary order in community life and a means of ordering its members.[37] It was critical for individuals as well. As Winthrop implied, only by laboring could one "maintaine his charge and live comfortably."

This set of beliefs clearly informed Winthrop's and Mather's comments about sports and other physical recreations. In fact they apparently borrowed from William Perkins, one of England's leading Puritan theorists, the notion that sporting practices benefited and complemented labor. Both men believed that contests and displays of prowess replenished the vitality depleted by either the rigors of shipboard life or the demands of work on land. They viewed sports as antidotes to the physical, mental, and spiritual labors that engaged and fatigued human beings.

Another experience that Winthrop had before he left England suggests that he may have flirted with the more radical view on the relationship between labor and leisure to which Francis White subscribed. The matter involved hunting, about which Winthrop recorded a long personal debate. As a young man the future governor had enjoyed the sport, but then he had married and acquired responsibilities to family and clients. Under these conditions, Winthrop wondered, could he justify pursuing the pleasures of the field? No, he could not, he concluded, for a number of reasons. First, the sport was unlawful for one such as he, a gentleman who was supposed to have either permission or a license to hunt. Second, hunting consumed a good deal of time and physical effort, and consequently, "it toyles a mans bodye overmuch." In addition, the sport was dangerous, both physically and to one's economy, and if Winthrop were caught hunting, he would have to pay a monetary fine. In all, he maintained, the risks were great, and for what? Only on occasion had he succeeded in killing the prey. "Most commonly" he returned home with "nothinge at all towards my cost and laboure."[38]

Whether Winthrop viewed hunting as a form of labor or simply believed that hunting required labor remains unclear from this conversation. In fact none of his writings, or those of his peers in the ruling hierarchy of Massachusetts Bay, clarifies as precisely the relationship between labor and leisure as did the literature of their English cousins. They did produce a social policy about sports and idleness, however, both of which they judged against their standard for labor, productivity. They constructed the policy in the typical English fashion, with categories of behavior ordered hierarchically. At the pinnacle were "lawful sports and recreations." Although the terminology was English, the Massachusetts Bay category was narrower in scope than was its corollary in common law, which probably reflected the Puritan bias toward "productive" sports. Lawful practices included athletic contests, archery, hunting, fishing, and fowling, all of which benefited the health and fitness of the individual or abetted the public good in various ways.[39] Unlawful recreations, in turn, were practices like gaming, which was unproductive at best and even costly at times, as well as baits, which destroyed animals and brutalized humans. Finally, there was the most damnable practice, idleness. In the Puritan scheme of things, idleness was the antithesis of labor. It was a sin.[40]

It was idleness, rather than unlawful recreations, that alarmed the leaders of Massachusetts from the beginning. In fact, not until 1646, when the General Court illegalized "play or game for any mony or mony worth," did it enact any legislation against any unlawful sports outside the context of Sabbath prohibitions against all recreations.[41] The first injunctions against idleness, in contrast, emerged before the great migration began, when the Massachusetts Bay Company ordered John Endecott to ensure that "all be kept to labor as the only means to reduce them to civil, yea a godly life" in 1629.[42] Over time the concerns of the authorities persisted, even as the perceived stimulants changed. In 1633, for example, Winthrop argued that high wages were the cause of idleness, because workers could earn enough in one day to "keep them a week."[43] After wages declined slightly in the middle of the decade, drinking and smoking acquired the blame. Colony leaders also associated idleness with persons who either ignored or attacked authority, with those who led "dissolute" lives, and with "unsettled persons."[44]

Ideology rather than experience apparently drove these criticisms. Compared to the numbers of indictments on other offenses in this litigious society, idleness was probably not a common practice. In his analysis of crimes among women in New England, Lyle Koehler uncovered only eight indictments for idleness in the Court of Assistants and county court records over the course of the seventeenth century; these documents record 706 charges of fornication and 180 instances of theft over the same time period. There is no comparable analysis for men, but a cursory look at the court records suggests a similar pattern.[45] The matter may be a function of incomplete records, which prevent historians from testing the proposition directly, but there is another body of evidence that indicates that the leaders' harangues are inadequate indicators of widespread and persisting idleness. This is the evidence about the colonists themselves as workers and about the reality of work, and on this matter the histories of Massachusetts Bay and the Chesapeake converge. As did their contemporaries to the south, many migrants worked long and hard.

Few English immigrants who landed on the shores of Cape Cod Bay in the 1630s and early 1640s could have missed the fact that the transfer of English culture and society required work. The efforts of the small number of people whom the Bay Company had sent to build houses and grow crops in 1628 and 1629 notwithstanding, the men and women who composed the great migration had to construct virtually everything from scratch. Whether they owned land or worked it as tenants, they had houses and barns to build, fields to clear and plant, and animals, gardens, and orchards to tend. Craftspeople built shops and filled orders for local use, while fishermen and loggers produced commodities for the international market. Finally, although many migrants to Massachusetts Bay apparently brought with them a larger supply of household goods and other equipment than did their contemporaries in the Chesapeake, they also had to resupply their stocks with handmade items and to attend to the hundreds of tasks that emergent village life and trade demanded.[46]

Several indicators suggest that much of this work was done. First, the colonists built not just one English-style village but eight by 1633, and within two years the population had spread thirty miles beyond its center at Boston. Second, Massachusetts exported fur, timber, and dried fish; of the latter, some 300,000 were sent to market in 1641. Third, and perhaps most telling, the mortality rate was low, at least in part because food was plentiful, a fact that more than one colonist reported to friends in England.[47] In 1632 Thomas Weld, a minister who had migrated from Essex to Roxbury, told his former parishioners that "here is plenty of corn [so] that the poorest have enough."[48] Another minister, Edmund Browne, who had moved from Sussex to Sudbury, offered a similar assessment in 1638. "I saw much good corn of all sorts this year," he wrote, and fruits, fish, game meat, and domestic animals were also plentiful. In fact, he noted, "in many towns there be two hundred head of cattle," a not insignificant number in either Britain or the colonies.[49]

Thus many colonists apparently adhered to the advice that the Reverend William Wood offered to prospective migrants in 1634, that "all New England must be workers in some kind."[50] What is less clear is why they worked as they did; no single explanation suffices. Some colonists undoubtedly shared the views of their leaders about the ideal social order and the efficacy of work. They too were Puritans who deplored the disorder at home and who had left England in search of a better life. These men and women in turn may have enlisted as servants people who, if not as ideologically committed, at least were willing and able to work. Certainly Winthrop did.

He selected "boys and young maids of good towardness," which meant that they would take orders, behave themselves, and work.[51] In addition the moral suasion of superiors, the Puritan practice of placing single men and women within families and family discipline, and the threat of expulsion may have encouraged recalcitrant laborers to adhere to the dictates and rhythms of a work-driven society.[52]

Yet there appears to be one other possible explanation. Despite the existence of servants and the fact that tenant and free farmers and their families hired themselves out to neighbors for day work, there were never enough workers. As a result wages were high. Carpenters earned three shillings per day, double the rate they had known in Britain, and even unskilled laborers apparently received more money than they would have had they not migrated. The pattern may have affected other people as well, for the General Court unsuccessfully tried to limit the wages of many workers and the prices that goods sold for on the local market.[53] People who performed needed tasks had options in Massachusetts that they had not had in England, as John Eliot, the Puritan minister at Roxbury, recognized in 1633. This was especially true of "fair conditioned" workers, those who were "workful" and who tended to "desire freedom."[54] If employers would not pay the going rate, laborers could move elsewhere. Alternatively, if they saved enough money, they could acquire land or open a shop.

Labor thus had significant material consequences in Massachusetts Bay, and coupled with Puritan ideology, this fact elevated the importance and the value of work. Both factors also raised the value of workers, who in turn had a vested interest in working. Consequently the demands and rewards of labor and the economy of Massachusetts probably operated to undermine or at least to delay the gratification of whatever interests workers may have had in recreations. Unlike England, where wages were low, terms of servitude long, and workers had little hope of substantive gain, the economy and ideology of the Puritans in the New World enabled servants, wage laborers, and artisans to earn substantial wages, a stake, and freedom.

Assessment and Aftermath

Part of what remains to be seen in this chapter is how we should interpret the experiences of this generation of colonists. What sense should we make of them in the context of both the early Anglo-American and the English scenes?

On the colonial front several things seem clear. One is that the migrants to the Chesapeake and Massachusetts Bay in the 1620s and 1630s failed or refused to reproduce many English practices, as well as the extensive web of festivals and institutions that embraced sports and other recreations at home. Simultaneously they also worked more regularly than their predecessors and assigned a different value to labor. This is not to suggest, of course, that they worked just because they had work to do or that they played less because they worked. Such a dichotomy had no base in either the experiences or the conceptual schemes of people in the seventeenth century.[55] It seems likely, however, that the Winthropian generation had moved some distance from traditional English practices.

That they did so is not particularly surprising. Colonization itself was a movement, a physical movement with significant cultural implications. The migrants to the Chesapeake and Massachusetts Bay had uprooted and removed themselves from England, carrying only the goods and practices that they considered moveable and important and for which they had room. Three thousand miles later, they found themselves an ocean apart from their traditional cultural sources, the locales of the Old World; this spatial gulf made the replication of traditional ways difficult, at best.[56] They also found themselves on a different continent facing multiple challenges, some naturally occurring, some not. It would take time, certainly more time than a single generation had, to adjust and adapt to North America and to determine once and for all which Old World ways were and were not worth keeping.

Their physical voyage also accelerated another kind of voyage on which the migrants had embarked even before they left Britain. This was a historical journey, the transformation of traditional culture, which was underway before 1618.[57] Forces beyond their control had moved some colonists away from some customary cultural practices. They had seen owners enclose common lands, Parliament enact restrictive legal statutes, and the crown eliminate long-standing holidays. People such as Winthrop, Lord Berkeley, and some of the small farmers who made their way to the colonies also had sympathized with the goals of the emergent labor order. Its members had opposed particular recreations and the leisure preference, they had supported efforts to regularize labor, and they had followed a strict Sabbath. Some of them had even left the Old World, at least in part, to escape what they considered to be the unsavory residue of traditional English culture: limited access to freeholds, social disorder, immorality and impiety, and expressions of the leisure preference.

Still, the English migrants who made their way to North America in the 1620s and 1630s did not complete this historical journey. Ordinary colonists did not reject all cultural forms, including some sports, that they had known at home. Nor did their leaders move beyond the English reformists' construction of the relationship between labor and leisure, let alone define an alternative to it. Certainly the Puritan authorities in Massachusetts Bay did not. They maintained the connections between labor and leisure that men such as Francis White and William Perkins had proposed rather than conceive of different ones. The attitudes of their counterparts in the Chesapeake are less clear, but the laws they enacted against idleness and unlawful sports indicate both a similar hierarchy and a similar reformist Protestant position on lawful recreations. Such practices were either to be laborlike, to be productive, or at least to be beneficial to workers. No one constructed labor and leisure as separable categories of experience.

What happened once the colonists were more nearly able to sustain themselves economically and demographically, as they were by midcentury, both confirms and clarifies the limits of this historical journey. Two points are pertinent. First, some colonists were able to construct some sports, games, and labor-leisure rhythms that were similar to those they had known in England. At no point before 1680, however, did they reproduce the full range of English practices, past or present. Thus the cultural loss instigated by earlier migrants persisted, and at most the colonists' sporting life in the third quarter of the seventeenth century became more English-like.

We can see one English-like pattern among colonists for whom agriculture persisted as a critical economic activity and for whom the tradition of recreations occurring either as respites from or as forms of labor remained powerful. As early as the 1640s in Massachusetts Bay and elsewhere in New England, for example, small farmers incorporated field sports—fishing, fowling, and hunting—within their daily regimens. So did field hands in the Chesapeake. Here, as the number of small and middling-size plantations mounted in the middle decades of the century, the supply of laborers remained too small to meet the demand. Consequently labor retained its value, and male servants at least were able to negotiate for respites and recreations within their work.[58]

During the 1650s and 1660s other English-like sports and displays of prowess also reemerged in the context of popular gatherings, both impromptu and prearranged, that were at least festive even if they did not constitute festivals in the Old World style. These gatherings were the products of emergent kin and neighbor networks and of the celebrations and performances of social tasks that came with the farm, village, and society building in which more colonists engaged by midcentury. The recreations in turn drew from long-standing British practices. Youths met on village greens, where they played ball games. Neighbors challenged one another to a game of ninepins or a horse race as they passed on the streets and lanes or congregated at the local tavern to conduct business or attend court.[59] Funerals at plantations begot wakes with extensive drinking before the burial and, afterward, "intertainment part of too days" more.[60] In port towns weekly markets, seasonal militia trainings, and arriving ships drew crowds to the streets and harbors, precipitating "many drinkings . . . singings & musick" and even "unreverent carriage and behavior."[61]

Even animal baits, although rare, appeared in forms that were reminiscent of affairs in the Old World, as a description provided by John Josselyn, an English visitor to Massachusetts Bay in 1664, suggests. During one of his frequent stops in the colony, Josselyn accompanied some men of the "better sort" on a wolf-hunting expedition. They found a wolf "asleep in a small dry swamp," but they did not shoot the animal, as Josselyn had expected. Instead they set their largest dog on him. The dog cornered the wolf until the hunters could get a rope around its neck. The men then tied it to a stake and began, in the English manner, to let their smaller dogs attack the creature. The baiting continued, and the men "had excellent sport" until the dogs "knockt out his brains."[62]

This wolf bait was an adapted version—or better, a reinvention—of a popular Elizabethan sport, and it illustrates the persistence of traditional English practices in North American settings in the third quarter of the seventeenth century. The match between Old and New World forms was not exact, of course. The colonial baiters had used a wolf, a common predatory animal, instead of an expensive bull or an uncommon bear. Still, as did Josselyn, most contemporaries would have recognized and understood the practice.

A kind of negative evidence also speaks to the reemergence of some Old World sporting patterns, as well as to the social tensions they provoked, in the third quarter of the seventeenth century. In keeping with their reformist Protestant social visions, civil officials enacted a series of acts and laws through which they apparently intended to maintain order and discipline among recreators and in recreational contexts. The substance of these regulations was similar across the colonies. First, the legislatures passed— or better, restated and added haranguing preambles to—Sabbath laws that ordered colonists not to do unnecessary work, to travel, or to sport on the

Sabbath, which began at sunset on Saturday and ended at the same time on Sunday.[63] Second, provincial and local governing bodies alike moved to protect lives and property, albeit in regionally specific ways. In 1655, for example, the Virginia Assembly prohibited colonists from shooting while they were drinking. The practice, it seems, wasted powder, resulted in injuries to passersby, and produced false alarms at a time when a gun shot was a warning of danger. In Salem, Massachusetts, on the other hand, civil authorities did not permit inhabitants to race horses on the streets because they, too, injured pedestrians, and the selectmen in Boston ruled against football games by boys for the same reason.[64]

A third set of regulations governed what, to the modern mind at least, were personal actions that occurred primarily although not only in recreational contexts, such as drunkenness, smoking, and fighting. Among people for whom the modern distinction between public and private had little meaning, however, all behaviors required scrutiny. Moreover, insofar as drunkenness, fighting, and "common coasting" (walking) could detract from social order, productivity, and moral expectations, such behaviors created problems for which colonial authorities and citizens alike were ill-prepared to deal. These practices especially troubled authorities in Massachusetts Bay and elsewhere in New England, all of whom were more proscriptive of personal behaviors, or misbehaviors, than were their counterparts in the Chesapeake, perhaps because of the arrangement of people in towns and their Puritan ideology. Through the early 1660s colonywide statutes and local acts identified many recreational practices and contexts as "unprofitable," hindrances to the "due preparation for the Saboath" and the public peace, and conducive to idleness and "the dishonour of God."[65]

Civil authorities in Massachusetts and the Chesapeake did agree on another matter that affected recreational life and the course of ordinary life more generally. This was the tavern, or the "ordinary," as such institutions came to be known, in part because they filled ordinary needs for food, drink, and shelter. In fact they were so important that British law required communities to have them. Beyond the licensing of the owners, however, Old World statutes provided few guidelines about their operation. The colonial legislatures thus moved to regulate the number of taverns, which was increasing, the rates tavernkeepers charged for food and drink, and what behaviors occurred therein. No tavernkeeper was to permit "evil rule," which generally meant drunkenness, idleness, and "debauchery," but the term embraced other behaviors.[66] In Maryland "evil rule" included gambling among servants and apprentices, who the Assembly feared would leave their work and wager their owners' money or goods. Tavernkeepers in Massachusetts, on the other hand, were not to permit shuffleboard, bowling, and dancing, which the authorities believed led to gambling, illicit sexual intercourse, or idleness.[67]

It is difficult to assess the effect of these acts and laws. The fragmentary court records do not enable one to determine whether the proscribed behaviors occurred with any frequency or even whether local magistrates regularly enforced the laws. From the records that do exist, however, one gets the impression that none of these things happened. There were some prosecutions of Sabbath offenders, but these were not common. Nor were the offenses especially threatening to the public peace or church discipline. Moreover, the courts heard cases of tavernkeepers and patrons violating the laws two or three times a decade, a relatively small number compared to other legal violations and crimes. In other cases a few incidents at most appear to have precipitated the legislation.[68]

Still, the laws do provide information. They help us to gauge the limits of the colonists' movement away from traditional English culture. The civil authorities in the colonies at midcentury acted as English governors had for decades. They employed the only means they knew other than personal influence to maintain social discipline: the law. Whether social discipline was diminishing or merely changing course, this was probably a reasonable decision. Other than local churches, there were few institutions in the colonies that could serve as brakes on what provincial leaders viewed as misbehaviors, and the popular gatherings and informal networks in which recreations occurred did not always dissuade their members from particular activities. As events would soon demonstrate, civil authorities had reasons to fear what could happen if individuals and crowds were left to their own devices. By the mid-1670s Nathaniel Bacon was ready to lead a crowd against the ruling party in Virginia, and John Coode and Jacob Leisler unsettled their peers in Maryland and New York shortly thereafter.

The lawmakers also had come from a place where authorities had long viewed some popular recreational practices as problematic, and for the most part, officials in the Chesapeake and Massachusetts Bay still knew only traditional sports and games and other displays of prowess. Indeed, only two patterns indicated substantive departures from traditional practices. One pattern—a temporal one—emerged among a small group of colonists, men of means who lived in the largest towns in Massachusetts Bay and who stayed abreast of current English fashions. They had developed a broader set of economic activities and work relations, which helps to account for their emergent and distinctive patterns of labor and leisure. In Boston, for example, merchants and ministers made time in their schedules to travel, occasionally for several weeks and invariably in the summer, to towns with nearby "hot" springs. These were founts of medicine and entertainment that had become popular with gentlemen in England. In the 1650s at Harvard College as well, officials tried to contain the traditional practices of students with a nontraditional means. They imposed on the students' drinking, games, and gambling a set of rules that at once regularized and confined recreations to three periods daily: a half-hour at breakfast, an hour and a half at dinner, and a less defined span between evening prayers and nine o'clock. In effect the clock and the "season," rather than work tasks, had begun to dictate times for recreations.[69]

The other pattern involved ordinary colonists and incorporated practices that civil authorities supported and that had changed, although they had not yet been transformed, in the New World setting. These were field sports—hunting, fishing, and fowling—which became relatively more widespread in the colonies than in England for reasons that seem clear. First, as people whose livelihoods depended largely on agriculture or fishing, many colonists had a vested interest in field sports. Wild game and fish were important foodstuffs for ordinary people at midcentury, constituting about one-half of their dietary intake and contributing to their diminishing mortality and rising birth rates. Second, some colonists were able to act on this interest, since by midcentury they either owned or had access to muskets and carbines, as well as poles and string. The fact that militias had either decimated or forced out the Native Americans whom hunters had once feared was probably also significant. It certainly helps to account for the mobility of hunting parties, some of which roamed far and wide for game.

Not coincidentally provincial and local governments encouraged field sports in two ways. First, acting on English precedent, the colonial legislators recognized and institutionalized the claims of property holders that hunting and fishing on one's own land were inviolable rights. Given that a larger proportion of the colonial population either owned land or had access to untitled, if not unclaimed, lands, this practice not only underlay the spread of hunting and fishing but also made proscriptions of poachers and game preserves unnecessary. Then too, legislatures and some town officials offered bounties for the hides and heads of vermin, destructive or dangerous animals such as wolves, squirrels, and deer.[70] In time the bounty system would encourage commercial hunting.

The role of civil authorities in field sports warrants a final comment. Although there is no way to gauge the impact of the policies of official culture on the expansion and regularizing of hunting and fishing, it seems clear that the actions of provincial and local officials did not limit popular practices, as was the case in England. In fact the bounty system probably stimulated hunting insofar as it promised some economic, as well as ecological, benefits to people who worked the land and who needed to augment their incomes. By sanctioning field sports, however, local and provincial authorities did more than recognize or support local interests. By encouraging or enticing ordinary colonists to engage in field sports, the authorities also urged them to engage in lawful recreations, sports that were either laborlike or beneficial to laborers. Hence, especially to the extent that colonists applied for patents and bounties, they also submitted to the interests and, indeed, the control of civil officials.

⊷⊜⊶

Acknowledging the control that provincial authorities exerted on field sports, and on the colonists through field sports, brings us full circle in this episode about recreations in the English colonies on the mainland of North America. The actions of one group of authorities, the leaders of the trading companies, set the stage for what turned out to be a substantive change in the course of popular sports and other recreations—and of ordinary life more generally—once they started recruiting a different set of migrants. These men and women, either pursuing their own ends or bowing to coercion by landholding superiors and civil officials, chose to work more regularly in exchange for freedom and their own land. Many sporting practices suffered as a result, and although the loss was never total, it persisted. Through the 1670s the provincial recreational scene, even as it became more English-like, remained constricted.

More than the course of sports and other recreations changed after the 1620s, however; so did the content of colonial sporting life. Many English practices never made their way across the Atlantic. Cockfights, rush bearings, dog coursing, jousts, hurling, and other sports were among the costs of the physical and historical journey that was English colonization of the North American mainland. Other practices did reemerge, but only in English-like forms, for although traditional practices had not yet become residual ones, remnants of earlier forms and formations, some of them were reinvented, reshaped, to fit North American contexts.[71] Sports and other recreations occurred once more in the course of work but not in religious festivals.[72] Wolves replaced bulls in baits, and horse races became bursts of speed on streets and roads rather than endurance matches on formal courses. Field sports were possible for many at a variety of times and places as the availability of land and water and abundant wildlife altered colonial hunting and fishing practices and relations in ways that the most resolute English assaulters of aristocratic privilege never did.

In effect colonial sports were becoming elastic, civil practices that resembled but did not replicate traditional English forms precisely. This construction subsequently achieved fuller articulation and underlay a broader menu of sports and meanings attributed to physical performances than any English colonists had so far imagined. Such a time came after 1680 when, in the context of the ongoing transformation of traditional culture, colonial locales achieved a vitality they had not had, and ordinary men and women went about remaking provincial popular culture.

4

⤙⟹◯⟸⤚

Sports and Colonial Popular Culture,
1680s–1730s

In 1686 John Dutton, an English bookseller, had been in the colonies for
some time, traveling about and seeing the provinces firsthand. Now he was
staying with the Stewart family in Ipswich, Massachusetts, so he had an
opportunity to write to his wife about some of the things he had seen.
Recently, Dutton noted, Mr. Stewart and he had traveled to Rowley, which
lay six miles to the northeast. They had gone to see "a greate Game of
Football" between the townspeople, many of whom were clothiers, and
some neighboring villagers. Dutton had seen such games before; they were
"common in England." This game was different from Old World affairs
in two respects, however. First, the participants played in their bare feet,
which Dutton considered to be "very odd" until he realized that they did
so "upon a broad Sandy Shoar free from Stones." Second, the players were
not "so apt to trip up one anothers heels, and quarrel as I have seen 'em in
England."[1]

The game that Dutton saw was probably an unusual event in the mainland British colonies of North America in the late seventeenth century.
Outside of southern New England, there is no evidence that colonists
played football, and even there, apparently only boys and craftsmen had
an interest in it. Moreover, neither football nor other ball games had sus-
tained roots in the colonies. Consequently the origin of this practice is
something of a puzzle. Native Americans and English villagers had played
football for centuries, especially in the course of spring festivals. It is pos-

sible that earlier villagers adopted, or adapted, the game from Native Americans at some point before racial hostilities resulted in King Philip's War in 1675. It seems more likely, however, that the Rowleyites either drew on their memories of such games in the old country or learned about it from visitors.

Less problematic is what the game involved. Dutton is clear about the fact that the players were villagers who were competing, in groups if not teams, against one another. They were also likely economic competitors— both collections of players appear to have been textile craft workers—and that relationship may have encouraged the rivalry on the beach. His description also suggests what the action of the game itself was probably like. Since the players did not trip one another, which was the conventional English means of interfering with opponents, they probably relied on foot speed and accurate passing to move the ball, which may have been made of cloth or an animal bladder. The contest, then, was probably a form of keep-away, rather than a high-scoring game, in which individual displays of prowess mattered. Certainly something drew onlookers such as Stewart and Dutton, who traveled a considerable distance to the site. They also went expressly to see the game, which apparently was not associated with any other community gathering.

This football game on the beach at Rowley draws us into the recreational experiences of late seventeenth- and early eighteenth-century colonists, who now inhabited much of the eastern coast of North America. Compared to their predecessors in the early English colonies, residents of the Carolinas, the Chesapeake, the middle colonies, and New England enjoyed a broader variety of sports and other displays of cunning and prowess. Moreover, many of these practices were like football in particular ways. First, they resembled but did not replicate Old World recreations. Second, sports like football, as well as some emergent practices, achieved a fit in the course of ordinary life, sometimes as nearly autonomous events but also in the context of work and community gatherings as useful competitive recreations. Finally, many forms were locally devised practices, testaments both to the surge in cultural production in many locales evident by the 1670s and 1680s and to the centrifugal force of given locales at a time when the colonies had no cultural core. Indeed, what the Rowley clothiers did for football— defining the site and the time, the manner of playing, and the object or stake of play—other colonists did for hunts, races, and tavern games.

The game that John Dutton observed thus illustrates two themes evident in colonial life in the late seventeenth and early eighteenth centuries.

One theme is that the movement away from traditional culture practices and relations continued. The other is that ordinary colonists, rather than institutions of official culture, were the primary agents in this movement. In effect popular culture revitalized—from the bottom up—and it did so at a propitious time. Across the colonies a number of dynamic events unsettled the agencies of official culture. Rather than dissolve into chaos, however, provincial society remained orderly and ordered as ordinary people constructed and reconstructed a range of social practices, such as football on the beach. To these recreations they assigned particular meanings—social, economic, political—and through them they mediated important social relationships.

Local Forms and Sites

In the latter decades of the seventeenth and the early years of the eighteenth century, many popular recreations were locally, or at most regionally, defined endeavors, either adapted from older forms or constructed anew to fit the conditions and interests of the people. Skating and sleigh races, for example, were relatively common practices in the middle colonies—New York, Delaware, and Pennsylvania—where substantial numbers of colonists of Dutch and Swedish ancestries lived. Both practices were suited to the long winters when snow covered hills and roads, waterways froze, and travel became difficult without a pair of skates, a sled, or a sleigh. Animal baits were confined primarily to New England farmers and New York laborers, both of whose roots lay in British village life, whereas some of the emergent large landowners in Virginia, in the fashion of Old World gentlemen, organized cricket games and occasional foot races. Horse racing was more widespread, but even it lacked a single form. In New York the British upper-rank mode of distance racing on a course emerged with the royal governor after 1664, whereas colonists in the Chesapeake favored quarter-mile sprints. Contemporary New Englanders arranged races on roads, village commons, and beaches with horses bred to travel at steady speeds and occasionally with wagons and carts in tow.[2]

Like horse racing, hunting was also less a single type than a collection of local practices. The diaries of New England farmers are full of references to hunting for deer, wolves, and pigeons, usually with firearms and almost always in pairs or small groups of neighbors and family members.[3] Different practices prevailed in the Carolinas, which eight proprietors had secured from and named for Charles II in the 1660s. Here, as Samuel Wilson recounted, "all the considerable Planters," some of whom had migrated from Barbados and viewed themselves as British gentlemen, hired Indian "huntsmen" to procure game and to lead them in hunts.[4] Here, too, enslaved Africans, who formed the backbone of the colony's emergent labor force, apparently drew on their experiences in their homelands or in the Caribbean Islands, from which many were sent. While touring the rice plantations established on the coastal islands and inland along the rivers, another English visitor, John Lawson, observed "Negro's and others" who "swim and dive well . . . go naked into the Water, with a knife in their hand, and fight the Shark, and very commonly kill him."[5] Even Marylanders who lived by the Chesapeake Bay and hauled in large fish did not pursue them this way.[6]

Other forms of hunting emerged in Virginia. As William Beverley, a large landowner and chronicler of contemporary life, maintained, the colonists "entertain themselves in a hundred ways" in the pursuit of game. They hunted by horseback and on foot and for nearly every species of fowl and animal. They relied on devices such as decoys to lure ducks and traps for turkeys. There was also the "diverting" practice of "vermine hunting" in which planters set out on moonlit nights to stalk raccoons, opossums, and foxes, all of which damaged cornfields. The chase began when the hunters sighted and treed the "vermin." A "nimble Fellow" then climbed the tree, "scuffle[d] with the Beast," and threw it on the ground, where dogs lay in wait. Then "the Sport increases," claimed Beverley, as the "Vermine encounter those little Currs." Such a hunt did not always end here, however. If the prey was a rabbit, it was sometimes intentionally freed so that the chase could continue.[7]

Throughout the Chesapeake colonists also practiced forms of hunting that they had learned from Native Americans. One of these endeavors was wild horse stalking, the object of which was to capture horses bred from domestic stock but foaled in the woods. Young people especially pursued this valuable prey, either by lying in wait behind rocks or trees in the uplands or while mounted on another horse. The chase was often hard and fast, and not infrequently the horse on which the hunter rode was injured. The wild steed, if captured, thus became a replacement rather than the desired addition to one's stock. Then there was fire hunting. This began as the colonists herded deer, which trampled or ate crops and transmitted disease to domestic stock, into a thicket or a patch of woods. Thereafter the hunters surrounded the herd and set fire to the woods. Finally, as the frightened deer tried to flee from the flames and smoke, they were easy marks for the waiting hunters.[8]

Fire hunting was not exclusive to the Chesapeake, but it was apparently more common there than in other regions. It fit neatly within the life schemes of small landowners and their descendants, some of whom eventually carried the practice west as they migrated to the Ohio and Tennessee valleys. Fire hunting was a cooperative endeavor among people who valued neighborliness, and if not a form of labor, it was certainly born of the necessary task of destroying troublesome animals when their instincts and the rhythms of agriculture made it possible. The hunts were primarily fall affairs. They took place once the tobacco leaves had been harvested and hung to dry and before the corn was entirely picked, a time when emboldened deer took to the fields and the rains had stopped. They ended with hordes of deer dead and the economies of the planters and the ecology of the neighborhood preserved.

Its particular significance to the common planters of the Chesapeake notwithstanding, fire hunting also illustrates a broader provincial pattern: work was a common site for sports and recreations among late seventeenth- and early eighteenth-century colonists. Many of the hunting practices described earlier took place within the course of ordinary labors, either as forms of or as respites from work. So did tests of strength and skill. New England–based fishing and whaling crews employed a weight used in their work to secure canvas and other materials in a particular distance-throwing contest. Known as pitching the bar, the event occurred in the almost natural breaks in the crews' tasks, either between the casting and hauling in of nets on board ship or between the mending of nets and doing chores for their families onshore. A similar practice, and a similar pattern of intermittent labor and leisure, emerged among field hands in other locales. Instead of pitching bars, however, they threw hammers and stones. Especially in the middle colonies as well, wrestling bouts resulted from the challenges and boasts of laborers and wagoneers. Even in New York City cart drivers eventually began to meet and issue challenges, literally on the spot, for a horse race or for a match between sleighs or sleds in winter.[9]

In some locales colonists linked work and recreation in ways that approximated Old World festivals. In New England, for example, colonists transformed particular tasks, such as house and barn construction, into productive and festive gatherings. "Raisings," as these events were called, drew neighbors and family members from miles around, not only to help with timbers and planks but also to compete in contests and races and to partake of refreshments. Fairs and harvest festivals emerged where the population was more dispersed and the economy primarily agricultural, as was the case in the Chesapeake and in some parts of the middle colonies. Fairs served as regional markets for livestock and produce, and harvest festivals marked the climax of the grain or tobacco growing seasons. As sites for business and social exchanges, both events featured recreations and sports that an individual of wealth and influence occasionally arranged for those who attended, be they free or slave, men or women.[10]

There were other popular gatherings in which sports and recreations figured. Some affairs, such as funerals and weddings, were nearly universal ceremonies marking particular events in an individual's life. Other celebrations recognized locally important achievements. College graduations and ministers' ordinations in New England, for instance, involved drinking and feasting by the celebrants, sometimes for several days and usually in mixed company, which may in part explain why card and dice games but not more physical recreations also took place. Unlike some of their contemporaries, New Englanders did not arrange physically demanding competitions between men and women. In addition there were celebrations of royal events, especially military victories and the birthdays and accessions of James II, his successors, William and Mary, and their daughter Anne, all of which played well in the largest towns. Festivals celebrating the colonies' ties to the British empire, these were affairs of particular significance to individuals of wealth and influence who gathered in Boston, New York, and Charleston to drink healths and then were joined by their wives for dinner and balls. Finally, traditional English festivals such as April Fool's Day, Shrove Tuesday, and St. George's Day emerged among distinct groups of men or boys in a given locale. Laborers in Boston celebrated Shrove Tuesday, the day before Ash Wednesday and Lent, with cock shailing in the streets. April Fool's Day (1 April) apparently appealed to young boys and was a time for tricks. St. George's Day (23 April) was a festive day in the South, where men competed in shooting and sword contests, races, and wrestling.[11]

These martial contests also emerged in the context of the musters, or militia trainings, that regularized in some colonies. Four to six times a year local commanders drilled what were volunteer defense units on village commons, fields, or specially designated training grounds. The precise nature of the training, however, did vary from colony to colony. Entire troops in New England towns took part in sham battles and shooting contests, whereas their peers in the Chesapeake favored matches between individuals in foot races, wrestling, and cudgeling (a form of hand-to-hand combat with sticks held by both hands). Occasionally a Chesapeake commander provided prizes—swords, pistols, or guns—to the strongest, swift-est, or best shot.[12] At the end of the day, however, the regional differences vanished. The local guard marched "away in Triumph" to "great applause, as winners of the Olympiack Games"—and into a local tavern, where the revelries continued.[13]

Especially for men, taverns became important social centers in the late seventeenth and early eighteenth centuries. Many villages and even cross-roads hamlets had at least one, and larger towns such as Philadelphia, Boston, and New York had many. Provincial and local efforts to regulate the ordinaries by requiring licenses of owners and defining lawful activi-ties notwithstanding, tavern owners were businesspeople, both men and women, who at least had to break even if they were to remain in business. The food, drink, and rooms that the law required tavernkeepers to provide drew some patrons, and recreational practices enticed others. Card and dice games were especially common and easily undertaken as patrons sat with friends to eat or drink. By the end of the seventeenth century tavernkeep-ers and owners of English coffeehouses in some locales had begun to ca-ter to the recreational interests of various constituents.[14] In 1687 in Bos-ton, for example, a tavernkeeper turned over one of his rooms to a man "to shew tricks in" to a paying audience, until the magistrates intervened, as they had earlier against a dancing teacher.[15] Even here, however, tavern-keepers and coffeehouse owners allowed patrons to play on ninepins alleys without much interference. So did their contemporaries in New York, Philadelphia, and Williamsburg.

The Provincial Context

Practices like football and fire hunting rooted in a number of profound events that altered the social environments and experiences in many colo-nial locales in the decades after the 1670s. Some of these were latent events, things that people were either not fully aware of or not aware of at all.[16] First and perhaps foremost were the demographic changes. By the fourth quarter of the seventeenth century, not only were people living longer, but there were more people, primarily from natural increase. The British and Anglo-American population alone expanded from approximately 35,000 in 1640 to a quarter of a million in 1690, and there were substantial numbers of other ethnic and racial groups as well. Coupled with broader transat-lantic economic forces, this population growth stimulated faster and more numerous divisions, or acquisitions, of land and other holdings. Property realignments in turn influenced living standards, internal mobility, and the political unrest that occurred throughout the North American mainland in the final decades of the seventeenth century. In addition migrations of indentured servants slowed, and in some areas halted, as the labor surplus in Britain diminished. Consequently African slaves and the least self-sufficient farmers, fishermen, and sailors became a lasting labor force and, at the extreme, an underclass whose presence was evident in a vibrant and public street culture. Finally, the British government moved to imperialize the colonies as never before, and royal charters, the Toleration Act of 1690, navigation acts, and metropolitan celebrations figured prominently.[17]

The dimensions and effects of these changes varied from colony to colony and even within a colony, but their general impact is evident in, for example, New York City. Until 1664 New York City had been New Amsterdam, the primary port of entry and a major trading post for Dutch colonists in North America. It was little more than a hamlet, and the course and content of its social and economic life were not unlike those in towns and villages inhabited by migrants from Britain. Few colonists, especially those who were tenants or servants, had substantial opportunities for physical and social mobility. Civil authorities and the owners of large estates required work and imposed a relatively strict social discipline. Sabbatarianism was an abiding force, even though it was not universally practiced. Equipment for popular Dutch recreations was minimal, as were feasts and festivals. Sports and other displays of prowess were constrained, if not entirely contained.[18]

By the end of the century the situation in New York was quite different. For one thing, the Dutch town had become a British city of nearly 4,700 people, or slightly more than had lived in Virginia in 1640 and about double the population of its social and economic competitor, Philadelphia.[19] It also had a varied economy; numerous trade, communication, and political links with Europe; and a distinctive mix of people. Besides Anglo-American and British citizens, there were residents of Dutch, French, and African ancestries. Even Native Americans came to trade, and a visitor could see recreations drawn from the homelands of many of these people or created here. Skating was Dutch, as were the "merry makings," a local harvest festival that focused as much on the "merry" as on the collective work of gathering crops.[20] British civil servants had laid out a course for horse racing on Long Island, which they named after the Newmarket course of James I. They also frequented English coffeehouses, where they conducted business and wagered on their luck at cards. Just beyond the limits of the town, one could watch a bait made possible by an English farmer who supplied the bull. Along the way a traveler might pass a "low pot-house," or tavern, that a woman might run and that catered to carters, dock workers, and other laborers.[21] These laborers included free and enslaved Africans who gathered at taverns, on the streets, and in the still numerous orchards to plan escapes, organize hunts, or gamble, occasionally with bones instead of wooden dice.[22]

With its varied recreational scenes, New York City was not typical of most colonial settings at the turn of the century. Its population was larger and more diverse than were those of smaller towns in the North or even the triracial South. Yet neither was it entirely dissimilar. Most locales experienced substantial population growth, which meant that there were simply more people to act as producers and consumers of recreations. Moreover, many places acquired a different mix of people, who transferred customs and practices from their homelands and entered into exchanges with other groups. Both practices enlarged the local recreational repertoire.

Certainly this was the case with hunting practices in the South. In the Carolinas, for example, two forms of hunting not evident elsewhere, shark hunting and deer hunting with "huntsmen," apparently emerged only after Africans and English planters migrated from the Caribbean and then tried to reproduce the labor-leisure patterns and the style of life they had known in the islands. Also striking were the hunting practices in the Chesapeake, some of which the colonists themselves attributed to Native Americans. Despite the large-scale destruction of native tribes and cultures that whites had managed by the 1680s, some Indians did survive among colonists in Virginia and Maryland, especially in the back countries. This contact enabled colonists of European and African descent to adopt Native American modes of hunting. In time some of these practices, like fire hunting, proved to be so effective that colonial hunters provided a relatively stable supply of hides and furs for markets in Europe.[23]

The recreational scene in New York City hints at another demographic alteration that affected the forms and sites of some practices in some places: the presence of increasing numbers of women. It is not a coincidence that events like harvest festivals appeared on plantations in the Chesapeake only near the end of the century, when the gender ratio neared equality. In their traditional roles as providers of food and drink, women, for whom these affairs provided opportunities for contacts with neighbors and relatives, made these festivals possible.[24] In small towns such as Annapolis and Williamsburg, as well as in larger ones such as Charleston, New York, and

Boston, women triggered changes in the content of public celebrations for military victories and royal anniversaries. The men who organized these affairs no longer gathered just to drink a "health," or a toast. They now arranged balls so "that the Ladies might also partake of the Rejoicings on this extraordinary Occasion."[25] Particularly in New England, where families and villages remained significant structures, some women owned the equipment with which they and their husbands and neighbors played games, especially card games. As did their contemporaries in the Chesapeake, they also contributed to raisings, and they joined with men to fish, sail, or "drink cydor & recreate our Selves."[26] Some women became virtual partners in the expanding realm of village and small town social life.

Women also played a role in the expanding tavern trade, particularly in the largest towns. Indeed, the increasing numbers of women, along with the population growth more generally, may help to account for the proliferation of taverns. Certainly tavernkeeping was an occupation into which women had moved only recently. As Lyle Koehler has indicated, no women had licenses in Boston at midcentury, and there is little evidence to suggest that the pattern was different in other places. By 1690, however, 45 percent of the licensed tavernkeepers in Boston were women; although the precise proportions in other towns are unknown, they, too, probably rose.[27] The expansion of occupations for men and the economic needs of some women may account for this movement. As the seventeenth and eighteenth centuries met, tavernkeeping was one of the few public, commercial positions in the colonies to which women had access. The income, although not always stable, probably helped to maintain widows, who constituted a substantial portion of licensed tavernkeepers and who would otherwise have depended on a small bequest from the deceased husband or the goodwill and support of the eldest son, who inherited the major portion of an estate. The stakes may have been even higher for single women, who also obtained licenses. In addition tavernkeeping probably enabled both groups of women to achieve a degree of social status that might otherwise have remained out of reach. Tavernkeepers were invariably tolerated by neighbors, unless they ignored local standards of behavior, and occasionally they were respected members of the community.[28]

The involvement of women in taverns and the proliferation of taverns more generally was not, of course, a result simply of demographic growth. Critical to both trends were significant economic changes that both fed and were fueled by the population expansion. One catalyst for these changes lay in European markets, which initially depressed the prices of colonial goods and interrupted the supply of laborers. Eventually the markets and prices rebounded, and demand diversified and expanded, but not before the colonial economic system and structure had altered substantially.[29]

One of the economic processes affecting recreational life in some locales was the expansion of commercial activity, which was itself in part a response to the economic dislocations of the era. Taverns were at once ends and means of commercial exchange. They produced some income for the proprietors, some of whom either were or had been farmers, merchants, or widows, and their rising numbers may have been tied to changing market and occupational conditions. Some keepers also catered to particular segments of the population, and to the extent that they offered particular recreational events or facilities—baits in the back lot or bowling greens—they probably also contributed to the occupational and rank specialization of recreations.

The commercialization of recreations extended beyond the walls of the taverns, however. Merchants who not only were aware of what was happening in Britain but also wanted to expand their inventories and their customer base imported goods for recreations. This was not an entirely new movement, of course. Ships had carried cards and even hunting dogs to sell in the colonies since the 1650s. What was different was the range of goods, many of which made possible the reproduction of particular European, and especially English, recreations such as cricket, lawn bowling, and billiards. Moreover, the rising colonial demand for sporting goods, which was evident primarily among the British civil servants and the emergent provincial gentry, also encouraged—and perhaps was stimulated by—the work of colonial artisans and craftspeople. Colonial printers made and sold cards in towns and cities, and carpenters made tables and some leather goods.[30]

Especially in the largest towns and cities, local government officials and entrepreneurs responded to the demands of their citizens and patrons for commercial entertainment options. In New York City, for example, the matter was simply one of constructing a public dock from which people could fish; on the neck of Boston authorities guaranteed hunters a piece of marshland where they could shoot ducks. Both actions had a commercial base; they were supported by public money and established on public lands. Provincial and town governments also organized lotteries, which were forms of gambling whose proceeds funded buildings and other civic endeavors. Even entrepreneurs commercialized recreations in some urban areas. Announcements for horse races, pig runs for boys who tried to catch and hold the animal by its tail, and animal baits appeared on the walls of taverns and in newspapers once they became available in the larger towns.[31] By 1724 one could see "slack rope and tight rope dancing by men and women" in Philadelphia.[32]

The commercialization of recreations was not strictly an urban process. Some of the craftspeople who made sporting goods were rural artisans who sold their wares to supplement incomes. Their customers were tavernkeepers, merchants, and especially in the South, an emergent upper rank of tobacco and rice planters who had both the means and the interest in owning equipment for English-style recreations. The commercialization of sports and other recreations also was evident from New York southward in the local fairs that planters and planter-merchants organized in part to stimulate local economic exchange. Then too, in some areas, European market demands transformed hunting and fishing into full or part-time occupations that paid handsome dividends. This process had begun some years earlier among New England fishing crews, but by the 1680s it also involved small farmers in the backcountries of many colonies, including recently established Pennsylvania. With a twist on the old colonization theme of New World abundance, propagandists for the proprietor, William Penn, encouraged residents and prospective migrants alike to pursue the game available in "Penn's Woods" not for traditional bounties but for markets. Turkeys that weighed as much as fifty pounds and had valuable feathers, the literature maintained, were a source of both "Food and Profit," whereas mink, muskrats, beavers, and whales were good "for Profit only."[33] That turkeys were readily available for sale locally and that furs and blubber boiled down into oil were shipped overseas suggest that some colonists heeded the recommendations.

The ongoing commercialization of hunting hints at another process that affected sports. In particular locales colonists experienced substantial alterations in the tasks and relations of work, and these in turn affected recreations. The experiences of a hunter in the middle colonies suggest the connections and complexity of this process. Before someone hunted for the market, he (the colonial hunter usually was a male) had irregularly searched for and shot animals or birds or fished. When he went depended on the migratory patterns of animals, the weather, and the needs of crops or cattle. A hunting trip was rarely far or long, a week at most, a day or two more commonly, and neighbors or relatives generally went along. Then the market intruded, and things were never the same, for the hunter or anyone else. Hunting for quantity, let alone specific species, demanded regular trips, of considerable distances and time if need be, and by oneself. Other relationships changed as well. Markets and merchants were the hunter's emergent bosses; they may even have become more important than the local large landowner if the hunter was a tenant. Moreover, to the hunter's wife fell the responsibilities for tending the homestead, crops and cattle, and children. She in turn looked to relatives and neighbors for assistance to bring in the crops, build a barn, or sell a cow. Perhaps she did not miss the irony in this turn of affairs. As her husband labored at what had once been a supplemental activity, she found some relief from the isolation and tedium of farm and family work in the emergent recreations of harvest festivals, raisings, and fairs.[34]

In particular colonies, especially the older and more heavily populated ones, the dynamic economic and demographic events of the era combined to produce multiple labor-leisure patterns, and we can locate particular recreational forms and sites within the labor-leisure patterns of distinct groups of people. Massachusetts is a case in point. For example, we have already seen the locus of pitching the bar. Members of the North Atlantic fishing crews, whose work was sporadic and physically demanding and who shared the traditions and relations of British laborers, favored it. A second set of practices emerged among the British civil servants in the colony and the provincial merchants, ministers, and professional men who were their allies and beneficiaries. Their recreations were not the physical contests and displays of laborers, nor did they occur primarily in irregular respites from work. Rather, they were practices popular among upper-rank Britons: balls, lengthy and elegant dinners and formal gatherings, and formalized and stylized races. Most of these practices also were prearranged events that consumed blocks of time in the evenings or on days designated as special occasions to the state or royal house and that occurred not in the primary workplace but at coffeehouses, estates, and even specialized sporting facilities. In short, although work and recreations did not yet constitute separate realms of experience for these colonists, neither were they linked in a traditional manner.[35]

Then there were the practices common to the small farmers, farmerministers, and farmer-lawyers who inhabited the small coastal towns and inland farms and villages—an occasional hunting foray with neighbors and kin, a raising or muster, and an irregular game of cards or ninepins. Many of their ancestors had moved to the Bay Colony during the "great migration," and they retained the Winthropian generation's commitment to regular labor, Sabbatarianism, and other reformist Protestant practices and values. In fact, among these people the Winthropian approach to recreation had become a custom. Recreations were not normative practices during the day except between seasons when work was not possible or when, as with hunting, they were incorporated within work as an ordinary endeavor. Rather, they occurred primarily in the late afternoons or evenings, with family members and neighbors who worked on the farms present.[36]

The Rowley football experience hints at another pattern that had not appeared earlier and that may have been specific to coastal Massachusetts. At issue in Dutton's description is when the game occurred. It probably did not take place on a Sunday. This was, after all, Massachusetts. Nor is it likely that the match occurred on a Saturday. Given the six-mile distance between the beach and Ipswich, Dutton and Stewart would probably have had to make the return trip after sunset, when the Sabbath formally began. That practice also was unlawful, and violators were punished if caught. Dutton indicated no such penalties or fear of penalties.[37]

Consequently it seems likely that this football game occurred on a Tuesday, the day set aside in the parliamentary legislation of 1647 for the recreation of servants. The Rowley clothiers were not, of course, servants in the traditional sense; they were skilled workers and possibly even property owners. Nevertheless, they may not have controlled their own labor entirely. Whether or not they worked under a supervisor, they probably worked at the behest of merchants and traders and perhaps for wages. The football players thus were an emergent breed of servants, skilled laborers. Moreover, they lived in a village that contained other people whose values and customs were not entirely distinct from those held by inland farmers. They were middling English people by tradition, and they probably had relatives in that radical Parliament of 1647, even if the clothiers did not.

Another event lends support to the possibility that the football game occurred on a Tuesday, in good reformist Protestant tradition. This was a bull bait that in both time and place was not far removed from Rowley. The town was Marblehead, another coastal town; the year, 1702, only sixteen years after the football game. As described by the Reverend Josiah Cotton, the bait had been planned, apparently by a local farmer in conjunction with the fishermen and laborers who made up the bulk of the town's male population, for a Tuesday. It was to occur on the public grounds of the schoolhouse, where "an abundance of People" had gathered to see dogs attack the bull, "as they do in England." For some unspecified reason the bait did not occur. Instead the bull's owner rescheduled it for another day, one that had come to be associated with recreations and with English workers: 5 November, or Guy Fawkes Day, the anniversary of the Gunpowder Plot against James I in 1605. Moreover, in the tradition of the good patron, the owner of the bull promised to "give him to the poor" once he was dead. Cotton's reaction to this development was simply that "our great men" should be so generous.[38]

Popular Culture

Beyond reinforcing the possibility that Tuesdays had become customary days for sports and other physical recreations in coastal Massachusetts, this bull bait is intriguing on another count that bears on our understanding of late seventeenth- and early eighteenth-century recreations. In an earlier day—such as at midcentury, during the life of Josiah's forebear, the renowned and influential Puritan divine Reverend John Cotton—even the planning of a bait would have been unlikely, if not impossible, for two reasons. First, bulls were few and expensive, and almost certainly no owner would have put up one to be killed in a bait, regardless of who would have eaten well afterward. Second, baits were unlawful, and had even the planning of a bait become public knowledge, the local authorities almost surely would have moved to stop it.[39]

In 1702 at least one of these conditions persisted: baits remained illegal. This fact apparently mattered little, however, if at all. Nobody—not Cotton or the local magistrates—seems to have interfered with the event, and the farmer who owned the bull, as well as his prospective audience, was apparently unconcerned about either the legal status of the bait or the penalties that awaited convicted baiters and gamblers. The question thus is why this was the case. Why could the planning of an illegal sport proceed so openly? Did the religious and civil leaders, other than Cotton, not know about the plans? Or did they not care about the bait and the fact that it remained illegal?

Unfortunately the Marblehead records do not help to answer these questions. They are all too silent. The records of other places, however, suggest that what we may be seeing in the bait—an illegal practice openly planned and even justified—was not only possible but also probable. Most colonies, as well as some towns and counties, maintained laws or acts that either restricted or prohibited particular recreations. As was the case in Marblehead, however, many of these practices still occurred, and they did so on more than an incidental basis. Gambling, for example, was illegal everywhere. Nonetheless, not only was it widespread, evident in many contests and matches and among many ranks and races, but individuals and government agencies were also moving to institutionalize gambling as they organized lotteries to raise money for one cause or another. Moreover, gamblers were rarely indicted, let alone convicted. In addition, along with unnecessary work and travel, recreations on the Sabbath were not to take place, but they did. So did other behaviors that the authorities had illegalized: lengthy tavern visits, hunting by nonlandowners, and even the destruction of town fishing weirs.[40]

Precisely why this discrepancy between the legal status and the real life scenes of particular recreational practices emerged is unclear. A part of the answer probably lies in the interests of the participants in illegal sports and other recreations. Such practices were enjoyable, they might contribute to one's material position or social standing, and their illegal status may have added to their allure and challenge, their "sport." Another part of the answer involves the efforts and interests, or lack thereof, of civil authorities. Given the spread and the mobility of the people, as well as the popularity of some behaviors, they may simply have found it impossible to enforce some laws. Especially in the case of a practice like gambling, this seems to be a reasonable suggestion. Reluctance or apathy on the part of officials may have figured in other cases. The nature of some laws suggests this possibility. They replicated the language adopted a generation or two earlier, when both the conditions and the population in an area were different. The Sabbath laws fit this case, and outside New England these statutes seem to have had little support from either magistrates or ordinary people. Even in New England, however, other continuously enacted laws, such as those that prohibited tavern sports, emerged without the extensive and haranguing preambles that lawmakers at midcentury had written. Such a change was small but probably not insignificant. It suggests a moderating of ideological zeal, if not of commitment.[41]

Regardless of the precise reasons, the pursuit of illegal recreations and the failure or inability to pursue illegal recreators may signal a broader inattention to, perhaps even the attenuation of, the authority of law and official culture in general. Other historians have described this phenomenon more fully. In many places, they have argued, the power and authority of the organs of official culture diminished in the wake of the demographic, economic, and political events of the era. Churches faced theological and political struggles. Assemblies and courts endured disputes about sovereignty. Philosophical and geographical movements diminished the authority and efficiency of military forces. Unrest arose in councils, congregations, and counties in virtually every corner of the colonies, as was evident in Bacon's Rebellion in

Virginia, the revolts of John Coode and Jacob Leisler in Maryland and New York, and even the witchcraft trials in Salem, Massachusetts.[42]

Importantly, however, colonial society did not collapse. Remarkably, and perhaps paradoxically, neither pervasive chaos nor even significant bloodshed accompanied the rebellion and upheaval affecting the institutions of official culture, which were also the traditional agents of social cohesion. The social exchanges that prevented destructive conflict continued. Many of them just took place outside official culture.

This alternative location for social exchange was what the British social historian Peter Burke has called the "unofficial" culture, or popular culture.[43] A popular culture had always existed in Anglo-America, but its vigor and authority had been reduced, first by the movement to the New World and then by the rigors of early colonial life. Indeed, the pre-1680s colonial culture was a constricted one partly because its unofficial system of behaviors and values had been cut off from its source in Britain. As a result the institutions of official culture—especially legislatures, local governing bodies, and even churches—had acquired extraordinary authority and significance in Anglo-American life compared with other spheres of the British world. In the decades immediately before and after 1700, however, colonial popular culture revitalized, and the balance between official and unofficial cultures shifted.[44]

Late seventeenth- and early eighteenth-century popular culture was socially flexible, rooted in the central places of ordinary and local life—fields, streets, shops, and taverns. Here ordinary colonists, as well as some "extraordinary" ones in their unofficial capacities as planters, merchants, and neighbors, displayed and assigned meanings to behaviors and values. Here, too, they engaged in the social exchanges that secured social stability, and they did so in a manner that Darrett Rutman has described as one of "jostling" and "accommodation."[45] Stated more simply, people both competed and cooperated, especially when their interests coincided. Occasionally they jostled or accommodated formally, as when individuals and groups went to a court to recoup a debt or when they signed contracts and covenants that defined rights and responsibilities. At other times they did so less formally, by working a crowd at an election, by participating in a race, or by organizing raisings and militia trainings to fulfill the needs of neighbors and the community. Either means enabled ordinary colonists to accomplish what the agents of official culture had previously done. They either bound people together or distinguished one from another, and they regulated behaviors.

Some of this jostling and accommodation occurred within a particular realm of popular culture, physical culture, which was significant to early Americans in ways that their modern descendants rarely acknowledge. Many colonists labored physically, often long and hard, at farming, home building and tending, and manufacturing, in an early sense of the word. Even doctors, ministers, and lawyers, whose ordinary tasks were primarily mental ones, valued physical prowess and health. As had Winthrop earlier, they linked mind and body in a simple way: the body was the housing for the soul and the mind.[46] For most colonists, as well, physical characteristics such as strength and speed, skin color, hair, and sexual attributes were markers of identity and status. Skin color in particular was an important basis for the subordination of Native Americans and Africans, and a range of biological and physical differences figured in the construction of gender differences. Finally, some colonists communicated physically, via gestures, and more than a few let their fists do their talking. In short all manner of things physical—appearance, dress, work, and prowess—were matters of ordinary life and discourse.

It is in this context of an invigorating popular culture in which physical behaviors and characteristics were important that the expanding and locally based array of recreational practices becomes more meaningful. Sports and recreations were physical performances, albeit ones that involved a little luck and mental acuity, and they were one of the means by which colonists jostled and accommodated. When members of fishing crews pitched a bar or passing wagon drivers challenged one another to a race, they were engaging in a contest that the members of each occupation understood. They had, after all, constructed the event, including the goal and the conventions that defined allowable behaviors. Within each group, however, the men were also competitors, not only in the physical contest but also for prestige, place, and power in the local community. A similar combination of jostling and accommodation probably occurred in the football game on the beach near Rowley. The Rowleyites had to agree on the action of the contest, not only among themselves, but also with their opponents. The event may have involved two layers of contesting, as well. The visible action involved running, kicking, and controlling the ball, for football was, if nothing else, a physical rivalry. Another kind of rivalry, however, may have encouraged the physical one. Both sets of townspeople were clothiers, and in the broader scheme of things, the world beyond the beach, they were economic competitors vying for place in an emergent industry.

This is not to suggest that games playing merely drew from, or was generated by, external competition. Nor was the significance of physical contests and matches simply metaphorical, although some colonists did recognize this possibility. As Samuel Sewall, a justice of the Massachusetts Supreme Court, concluded after another man refused to end a disagreement, "we are at Foot-ball now."[47] Physical skills such as throwing, running, shooting, or riding and the attributes generally collected in the term *prowess*—physical strength, speed, or agility—were real skills and characteristics. They were observable. They could be developed, refined, or even diminished, as they often were. One could improve such skills by practicing them or performing frequently in shooting contests or hunting, and age usually diminished one's physical performances. Particular skills were also more meaningful and valuable among some groups and in some places than they were for others. Thus, more than being a means for jostling and accommodation, the sports and recreations that collected and displayed these skills were also their products.

As the products of particular groups, some sports and recreations were also significant in expressing oppositional interests, or even in repudiating traditional relationships. The Reverend Cotton's snide comment about the "great men" in Marblehead suggests that possibility. So does a situation involving cock shailing in the streets of Boston. The practice itself was an old English sport; it occurred in the mid-1680s much as it had for centuries, except that the symbolism of the cock had apparently been abandoned over time. On Shrove Tuesday, the last festival day before Lent, one man led a cock with a bell around its neck down a street. Having paid for the right, his comrades threw sticks or stones at the bird, which they intended to kill, after which they would march off in triumph to celebrate at the nearest tavern. What happened in the interim, however, was that the sticks and stones landed not only on the cock but also on passersby and building fronts and windows. Personal injuries and property damage were thus common results.[48]

The timing and social location of cock shailing provide us with some clues about its particular significance. The sport had not appeared in the colonies before the 1680s, and at that point it emerged in the one region, New England, where authorities had long repressed residual festivals. Its appearance thus may suggest either ignorance of or resistance to Puritan hegemony. There certainly were other contemporary forms of opposition to the Puritan minority that was trying to retain power and influence.[49]

Another dynamic may have figured in this situation as well. These men were laborers, for whom conditions in Boston in the 1680s were anything but ideal. Apprenticeships remained common, bound servitude was not unknown, and wages were relatively low. Moreover, and regardless of their precise status before the law, many laborers were finding John Smith's vision of land and profit increasingly difficult to realize.[50] Thus, more than an act of resistance to ministers and other churchgoers, cock shailing may have been a form of defiance meted out by laborers against wealth and property holders. It may even have been an instance of what the dominant culture considered to be the residual leisure preference. As such, it was also an effort on the part of laborers to reestablish control of their leisure practices and, in the process, reclaim an advantage for themselves as workers.

The actions of the Boston laborers may have been extreme. Contemporary records contain few similar overt acts of resistance. The interests, conditions, and the manner in which these men lived, however, were not unique. Indeed, the laborers of Boston resembled the small planters of the Chesapeake, the Rowley clothiers, and the North Atlantic fishing crews in important ways. As were Boston's cock shailers, some of these people were poor; a few were even bound, either to persons or to places. They were small landowners and tenant farmers, laborers, servants, and slaves. Their recreations—locally specific displays of strength and prowess, hunting and fishing, blood sports, and gambling games—drew directly from the course and condition of their lives. They lived and worked in the open, in the streets and fields, and their holdings were meager. Muskets, knives, lines of cord, and wooden die and bowls were instruments for both work and play, which often occurred in tandem. By genteel standards, as well, they were ill-educated, relatively poor, and consigned to the margins of the expanding web of colonial social relations.

Far above them were the colonists who came to constitute, for the first time in Anglo-America, a native-born upper rank. The primary basis for their position lay in a variety of economic enterprises, shipping and merchandising in New England, landholding and money lending in the South, and numerous ventures in the middle colonies. Their wealth made possible experiences and conditions not available to ordinary colonists: education, direct contacts with Europe, political influence and power, and a relatively extensive material culture. These contacts and their wealth in turn underlay a host of sports and other recreations, some of which were adapted from forms popular among their aspirational peers, gentlemen and -women of the Old World. Some of these we have seen: billiards in English coffeehouses, horse racing on the Newmarket course outside of New York City, and hunting with "huntsmen" in the Carolinas. There were also balls and celebrations of royal anniversaries, lawn bowling and fencing, and a variety of card games, some of which took place out of public view and employed specialized equipment. Many of these practices occurred as well in places and at times that bore little connection to work, at least the work of the players. The early colonial upper rank were not a "leisured" elite in any Weberian sense, but they did speed the material and ideological separation of labor and leisure.

In the context of these two groups of colonists, one final pattern involving the many locally based forms of recreations in the late seventeenth and early eighteenth centuries emerges. Instead of being isolated acts in a provincial recreational scene that was inexorably and inevitably expanding, recreations like football on the beach and cock shailing on the one hand and English-like horse racing and hunting on the other were really components of cohesive patterns of behavior and meaning—recreational "styles" or "traditions"—that distinctive groups of colonists had begun to construct. One pattern belonged to ordinary men and women and was a colonial variant of Old World "folk" cultures. The second was a provincial version of the British "high style," the pattern of gentlemen and gentlewomen, or at least would-be gentry.

This notion of emergent sporting styles helps us to make sense of the dramatic developments in colonial sporting life in the late seventeenth and early eighteenth centuries. Especially compared to the preceding period, these decades witnessed extraordinary changes: population growth and diversification, geographic expansion, a near explosion of commerce and communication networks, and extensive social exchanges. All these factors help to account for what appears to have been the unprecedented, at least in the British North American provinces, sporting interest and activity. This is not to suggest, of course, that an increasingly dynamic sporting life was the inevitable consequence of these events. Rather, the surge in sporting production resulted as a critical mass of people, confronted with dynamic circumstances that were often rooted in events beyond their locales, competed and cooperated with one another on a social and cultural terrain with which they were familiar and in which they had facility: the arena of public physical performances. Making games, contesting physically one on one, displaying prowess—all were meaningful acts of communication, of presentations of self, of representations of values in what remained primarily visual and oral cultures. Also important is that few of the colonists' physical performances were entirely novel—in time of occurrence, in social location, or in form or format. Many sports and recreations drew from their pasts—as Europeans or Africans, as agriculturalists or seagoers, as men or women, as laborers or quasi professionals—even though they had been adapted to North American settings. Consequently the emergent styles blended past and present behaviors, rhythms, and meanings in practices readable by contemporaries. Sporting styles in effect made clear from where people had come, in both historical and geographical senses, and who they were or wanted to be. They were the results of the everyday boundary making that shaped and ordered ordinary life.

One particular set of boundaries constructed by colonists in the late seventeenth and early eighteenth centuries to which the emergent sporting styles were related remains to be discussed: the boundaries associated with the formation of ranks, which were essential structures in the social hierarchy after 1680. Through sports on the streets and in the fields, colonists expressed the manners and norms of a particular rank, as common planters did in fire hunting and clothiers did in football. Such performances also defined and signified differences between the ranks. Cock shailing in the streets of Boston surely set the laborers apart from, if not against, their employers and church and civil officials. Horse racing, balls, and billiards among gentlemen had a similar effect. In fact, some members of the colonial upper rank consciously performed in particular ways to distinguish themselves from ordinary colonists. Such was the case with the native-born large landowners, the emergent gentry, in the Chesapeake. Among them we can see more clearly how sports and labor-leisure rhythms and relations figured in the making of social ranks.

5

⊰✦⊱⊜ ⊜⊰✦⊱

Sport and Rank Making in the Chesapeake

About the time that the clothiers of Rowley, Massachusetts, were adapting the centuries-old game of football, a second group of colonists who lived farther south had begun to reinvent another physical recreation, horse racing. Known as the "sport of kings," horse racing had a long tradition in British history, especially among the upper rank. It had occurred only sporadically in the Chesapeake, however, until the final quarter of the seventeenth century, when some men of means began to approach it seriously. In fact they went to court to settle disputes about races, and from a few surviving records, we can piece together how the practice changed.

One site of this drama was Henrico County, Virginia, which straddled the James River some fifty to seventy miles west of the Chesapeake Bay. The curtain opened in 1689 when three men, all planters who raised tobacco on the rich bottomlands along the river, appeared at the county court. William Randolph was the first witness. He had started the race, of an unspecified distance, between William Eppes and Stephen Cocke at Malvern Hills. Before the event the principals had agreed on a ten shilling wager and on a few matters of conduct. The race was to begin with a "fair start," neither man was to touch the other rider or his horse, and each horse was "to keep his path." Eppes and Cocke had also agreed that if the latter went ahead by "two or three Jumps" [lengths], he could move into Eppes's lane. Therein lay the dispute. Once the race began, Randolph testified, Cocke "endeavored to gett the other rider's path as afores'd according to ye agreem't." He failed to do so, however, and the contestants "Josselled upon Mr. Epes [Eppes] horse's path" for most of the race. Afterward Eppes sued Cocke for breach of covenant.[1]

About a decade later the Henrico court heard another dispute about a race, this time between Richard Ward and John Steward Jr. Again the basis for the suit was a covenant, but it was one that left little to either chance or a rider's imagination. The race was to be a precise length, a quarter mile, at the "race-place commonly called ye Ware" on 1 July. Each rider was to weigh "about one hundred & thirty weight," and both men agreed to "fair Rideing." Moreover, because Ward was riding a mare, he was to have a five-length (ten yards) head start, and he could win if he finished within five lengths of Steward's horse. In the end the mare did win, but Steward refused to make good on the wager. Ward sued, and the jury, which recognized the covenant as a legally binding one, decided in his favor.[2]

These two cases enable us to see a complex sport in the making. In the first case Cocke and Eppes had agreed to just enough conditions to ensure that theirs was no ordinary ride. They had defined the wager and the manner of riding beforehand, but little else. A decade later Ward and Steward specified virtually everything. Their match involved a set distance, a standard and measurable distance, a replicable distance. They consented to weight limits on themselves and to a handicap that mitigated the size and presumably the speed advantage of the male horse. Both constraints probably made the race more competitive, the outcome less predictable. Ward and Steward backed their skills with a wager that was worth 200 times the sum staked by Cocke and Eppes. They also made it possible for others to watch the race, having designated the place and the time in advance. The site was a "race-place" that planters used frequently and probably only for racing, even if it was not a formal course in contemporary British terms.[3] Why they picked 1 July, on the other hand, is not as clear. Neither a holiday nor the date of a court meeting, it was probably a slow day in the cycle of tasks demanded by tobacco culture. It was a good day for racing.

Both cases also suggest what the reshaping of racing in the Chesapeake among men like Ward and Steward likely involved. Over a period of several decades they had transferred some procedures and conventions from Britain, where racing had undergone a renaissance of sorts among post-Restoration gentlemen, who were the aspirational peers of provincials such as Ward and Steward. Certainly standard jockey weights and handicaps came from abroad. Nevertheless, Chesapeake racing was not an exact replica of British racing. One major difference was the length: a quarter mile in the Chesapeake but several miles in Britain. The adaptation was necessary. The planters' horses were small, capable of short bursts of speed rather than performance over great distances, and they ran on ill-cleared fields and roads rather than tracks.

The race covenants agreed to in both instances also speak to the construction of distinctive behavioral, geographic, and temporal boundaries around racing. By the 1690s planters like Ward and Steward were setting their matches apart not only from the speed contests of other colonists but also from other affairs of ordinary life. Their version of racing—quartermile racing—thus was an extraordinary practice. It was a customized, formalized sport, and it quickly became a custom in the Chesapeake. By the early eighteenth century quarter-mile racing was as well known, and perhaps better known, to many colonists in the tobacco counties of Virginia and Maryland than either football was to the inhabitants of Rowley, Massachusetts, or cock shailing was among Bostonians.

Who were the planters who transformed horse racing? For the most part they inhabited the lands along the major rivers that flowed into the Chesapeake Bay—the Patuxent in Maryland, the Rappahannock and James in Virginia, and the Potomac, which divided the two colonies. Some of them were descended from minor English gentry who had migrated after midcentury and acquired some political offices and several thousand acres of land. A few came from merchant families and had gained prestige and property through family businesses or independent trade. Still others, having made the most of their abilities at a particularly dynamic juncture in the history of the region, had emerged from the ranks of common planters and indentured servants. All together these "great planters" never constituted more than about 5 percent of the population, but they became a powerful minority. From their base in land they traded, bullied, and negotiated their way into local and provincial leadership. As the seventeenth and eighteenth centuries met, they were an emergent elite.[4]

They were not, however, a hereditary elite. The large landowners and merchant planters of the Chesapeake had to negotiate their hegemony, and it was within the process of doing so that sports like quarter-mile racing and other physical recreations figured prominently, as Timothy Breen first suggested in the late 1970s. As the rank emerged, Breen contended, sporting contests, particularly those involving gambling, translated values—pride, materialism, contentiousness, display—that were immensely important to these men. Their most visible public contests, the quarter-mile horse races, "strengthened the gentry's cultural dominance."[5]

The races and gambling were also aspects of a distinctive and distinguishing gentry sporting style. This chapter describes that style and what led to its construction. The beginning of the story predated the gentry, emerging in the decades after midcentury as the economy stagnated and the agencies of official culture responded with measures that contributed to the stratification of Chesapeake sporting life. By the 1680s and 1690s the scene shifted to the great planters. Having acquired substantial acreage, contacts with Britain, and political responsibilities in the colonies, the large landowners had both the interests in and the means of redefining recreations such as horse racing. They also had access to an increasingly prominent labor force, enslaved Africans, whose presence in part underlay the distinctive view of labor and leisure that the great planters held and that quarter-mile racing manifested. Slaves also help to account for another un-British pattern. Even as the would-be provincial elite organized events only for themselves, they also encouraged racing, as well as other useful physical recreations, among common planters. By the 1720s and 1730s quarter-mile racing was *the* sport in the Chesapeake.

The Stratification of Sporting Life

There were few signs of a distinctive gentry sporting style in the Chesapeake in the middle of the seventeenth century. Some men of wealth and influence had migrated to the region, but they had not produced distinctive or distinguishing recreations. Moreover, as chapter 3 discusses, sporting life in the Chesapeake remained constricted in the middle decades of the seventeenth century. The high value placed on work, the scarcity of workers, and the bare material culture ensured that few recreations were possible, especially on a regular basis. Horses, for instance, were few and neither particularly strong nor fast. Consequently racing was sporadic at most. The same was true of game playing. Few planters owned equipment for contests like ninepins, bowls, and cards, nor did they possess goods that might have sufficed for balls, jacks, or weighted bowls. To engage in such contests planters and servants alike had to visit the taverns, whose owners sometimes permitted gambling games and even provided the equipment and credit for them.[6]

Hunting, on the other hand, was more widespread, in part because land and wildlife were abundant and unfenced. Moreover, the demands of plantation agriculture, although rigorous, were also intermittent. The seasons of crops and cattle, as well as other tasks necessary to the ongoing process of farm building, ensured blocks of time in which planters could pursue the game that supplemented their diets. Given the scarcity of labor, servants were also able to negotiate with their employers for breaks in which they might hunt; as George Alsop, who had been an indentured servant in Maryland, maintained, "every servant has a Gun, Powder and Shot allowed him." Especially on holidays and in the winter, when the primary task associated with tobacco was planting seed for the year's crop, servants with "Ingenuity" could "hunt the Deer, or Bear, or recreate themselves in Fowling."[7]

In effect one's wealth and local social standing had little bearing on recreational practices in Virginia and Maryland at midcentury. What recreations were possible were possible for many, which is not surprising given that the Chesapeake had entered what Russell Menard has called the "age of the small planter."[8] Not until the middle of the seventeenth century had all the appropriate conditions—migrations of families and servants who could expect to complete their terms, political stability, and economic development—combined to produce the first period of real security in the Chesapeake. Land was available to those who escaped early death, and the proportion of middle-size holdings (500–700 acres) to either the very small or the large ones increased, as did per capita wealth. Housing was fairly uniform, and one-room dwellings were the norm. Household goods were simple and neither numerous nor fashionable. A feather bed was a luxury; a china tea set, virtually unknown. Clothing did not yet distinguish small planters from either their servants or the few well-to-do landowners and merchant-planters who lived and traded among them.[9]

This relative prosperity did not last long, however. In the late 1660s the economy began to contract. Tobacco prices fell, and increased productivity and declines in the cost of production no longer offset lower prices. Fewer families migrated from England, and the number of servants decreased. Instead of skilled workers, criminals, debtors, and other British poor once again constituted much of the servant population. Thus, by the mid-1680s the social structure of the Chesapeake was more stratified than it had been since the 1620s.[10]

The gradual differentiation of Chesapeake sporting life rooted in these altered economic and demographic circumstances. As the economy began to falter in the 1660s, the legislatures—the agencies traditionally responsible for ordering society—attacked anew one ubiquitous and fundamentally economic endeavor in British sporting experience. This was gambling, or gaming—betting with money or goods—which had long been unlawful.[11]

Not since the 1620s in Virginia and never before in Maryland, however, had the legal statutes been so specific and even discriminatory. In 1663 the Maryland Assembly cited the "many & great greivances that have happened unto many Mastrs . . . by the infidellity of their Servts" as the reason for suppressing gambling among these nonpropertied colonists.[12] By 1668 the Virginia burgesses identified the tavern as the major haunt of persons who neglected "their callings" and "mispend their times." This body limited the number of taverns and eventually prohibited ordinary keepers from extending credit to laborers and bound workers.[13] In the 1670s Maryland also limited the number of taverns.[14]

The assemblies apparently intended to restrain the actions of only some colonists, however. The laws identified one segment of the population, men without property, who were vulnerable to legislative control on several counts. First, regardless of whether they were free men or servants, they did not have a voice in the law-making process. Second, and probably more critical, British and colonial authorities alike had long associated laborers, servants, and other unpropertied colonists with unprofitable and unproductive expressions of the residual leisure preference, an association that, at the very least, contemporary gambling did not undercut. Obviously the propertyless lacked collateral—material wealth—to back up their wagers. They were also people whose perceived failure to work regularly and whose indebtedness diminished not only their own chances of success, and possibly their survival, but also those of their employers and the tavernkeepers. In all, the daily actions and debts of the propertyless could affect the fragile economy of the region. Consequently, as had their predecessors in late sixteenth- and early seventeenth-century Britain and as did their contemporaries in Massachusetts Bay, the agents of official culture in the Chesapeake apparently believed that their society, which was still in the making, had to be protected from the damaging residual practices of the propertyless.[15]

The assemblies' acts, however, did not speak specifically to gambling among men of property. Landowning colonists continued to gamble and to contract debts in a variety of contexts, including recreations, as court cases in the 1670s confirm. In Maryland the plaintiffs in these suits were winners of uncollected wagers rather than constables or other officers of the law. The victorious bettors could indeed sue, but they did not always reclaim the debts owed. In 1671 Edward Steevenson initiated a claim against John Drywood for "1200 pounds tobacco & Caske." Drywood's lawyer asked for a delay in the trial so that he could locate "a statute of England that Play debts aboue the value of 40s (shillings) is not pleadable" for his client's defense. The judge granted the delay and never did render a decision on the plea.[16] In another suit the next year, a defendant maintained that a debt (200 pounds of tobacco) was "a wagger at a Horse Rasse and therefore Not Acconable [actionable]." The plaintiff failed to prove to the satisfaction of the court the contrary, and the judge ordered the suit abandoned.[17] In both cases the defendants were men of property who apparently understood English conventions differentiating play debts from other forms, a distinction accepted by provincial courts. They were also direct participants in the action, a factor absent in another court case in which a justice ordered a defendant, who did not invoke the play debt argument, to pay a debt incurred at a horse race.[18]

That the courts treated play debts differently from other debts in the early 1670s is clear. Precisely why this difference emerged, as well as what the immediate and specific effects were, however, is less clear. The concept of play debts derived from British law and gambling practice, but in the colonies it was applied to a society that lacked a mature, British-like social hierarchy, with its relatively clear distinctions between ranks and the informal brakes on recreational behavior that rank relations in the Old World made possible. Consequently, by invoking the play debt distinction, provincial justices and the men who initiated and defended the suits—all of whom were men of property—may simply have attempted to translate gaming debts into social distinctions.

Nonetheless, it seems reasonable to suggest that the play debt distinction was first and foremost an economic measure. The Chesapeake economy was tenuous, in part because it was tied to an unstable international economy. Property-owning colonists thus could do little directly to stabilize their positions. Court officials who were responsible for imposing discipline, however, could eliminate one source of economic flow by restricting recovery of debts incurred at play. As the colonial economy entered a no-growth and, quickly thereafter, a depression phase in the late 1670s and 1680s, the courts excluded play debts from those that could be recovered by the litigious men of property. Again, the maneuver apparently worked. The few court records that exist suggest that cases involving gambling debts during these years were rare, although probably not because colonists suddenly and simply ceased to wager. In fact gambling cases do exist in the records from the 1690s. Consequently one may suspect that only men who could afford to lose the irrecoverable play debts may have chosen to wager significant sums. Others, if they wagered, limited their bets. Conceived of in this context, the play debt distinction was a response to economic conditions, one that had social implications. It accomplished what the laws of the 1660s and 1670s had not done. It mediated relations among men of property in the Chesapeake. The play debt distinction separated small and marginal player-gamblers from their wealthier neighbors.

Court suits of the 1690s support this explanation. They also signal another phase in the stratification of the Chesapeake gambling scene. No longer did either plaintiffs or magistrates invoke the play debt distinction. Moreover, the sums debated before juries were greater than they had been: 4,000 pounds of tobacco and forty shillings in one case, 1,500 pounds of tobacco in another, 1,000 pounds of tobacco and twenty shillings in a third, and five and six pounds sterling in a fourth case. At a time when the average yearly tobacco harvest ranged between 1,500 and 3,000 pounds, these wagers represented significant investments. Furthermore, the men involved had substantial property and prominent names: Randolph, Cocke, Eppes, Kenner, Gardner, Baker, Humphrey, and Steward.[19] These cases thus suggest boundaries around gambling actions that were not evident earlier. The boundaries were predicated on the existence of at least three groups of colonists: the propertyless, planters with small or marginal holdings, and landowners whose incomes more than covered their wagers. In the case of gambling at least, the age of the small planter had come to a close.

Whether the process of stratification affected other recreational practices remains uncertain. Field sports, although they remained relatively common, probably did bear some effects of rank differentiation. Estate inventories suggest that wealthy decedents owned a broader variety of firearms and fishing equipment, which presumably underlay different modes of hunting and fishing. The bounty system, even though it was not as extensive as it was in New England, may also have encouraged rank differences. Men of means do not appear to have sought bounties with any regularity, and it is possible that their poorer neighbors and dependents who did cared primarily about killing efficiency. Finally, archaeologists' readings of soil samples and bone deposits indicate that wild game remained important in the diets of poor and marginal planters and servants but less so for families of substantial wealth.[20]

Economically driven social distinctions may also have affected horse racing. In at least one locale a county court redefined who could legally race. In 1674 the York County, Virginia, court heard arguments about the legality of a match initiated by James Bullocke, a tailor who had run his mare against a horse owned by "Mr." Mathew Slader. The court ruled against Bullocke on the grounds that it was "contrary to [British] Law for a Labourer to make a race, being a sport only for Gentlemen." The justices also criticized Slader, however, although not because he had raced against the tailor. Having run his horse "out of the way that Bullock's mare might win," Slader had committed "an apparent cheate," and the court censured him for this behavioral breach.[21] Thus, besides acting to curtail the freedom of action of a propertyless man, the court had ruled once again against the lack of restraint evidenced by a man of means.

This court case may have involved a unique public display of legal rank discrimination in a Chesapeake sporting event prior to the 1680s, when the covenants among men of means with which this chapter begins became relatively common. No similar incident has surfaced, and given the vastness of the colonies in which the still irregularly run races occurred, one must doubt whether officials could have effectively enforced the "only for Gentlemen" law. Another factor, too, may have prevented repetitions of the Bullocke case: few colonists owned horses at this time. Estate inventories registered in Maryland during 1674–75, the same time as the York County case, suggest that the probability of laborers and small planters racing against large landowners was small. Of a total of 217 horses registered in 105 estates, slightly more than half were owned by the wealthiest 20 percent of the decedents (estates of more than £415). The poorest 20 percent, in contrast, registered only 8 of the 217 horses, and nearly 80 percent of the colonists at the lower end of the economic scale owned no horses at all. Middling estates, a full 60 percent of all the estates (and valued within a broad range from £21 to £415), held the remainder.[22] Furthermore, the assemblies in both Maryland and Virginia had begun to curtail the stock that was most available to poorer people, the inbred and undesirably small horses that roamed the land and created "detriments."[23]

As had been the case with gambling, the economy and the invocation of British legal precedents by agents of official culture apparently combined to define who could and who could not race, at least in public. In fact, the economy, contracting as it was, seems to have been the primary factor in the tiering of Chesapeake society and sporting life after 1660. Men without property were the first to find their options diminished; gradually and later, some men with property experienced similar constraints. Particularly for marginal planters (estates valued at £100 or less), few horses and the irrecoverability of play debts had probably diminished their abilities to compete against their wealthier neighbors by the 1680s.

The Gentry's Sporting Style

By the late 1680s and the early 1690s the differentiation by rank in sporting contests had become stark. What the York County court case and the play debt distinction anticipated became clear: separate events, sporting contests arranged by and for a minority of Chesapeake inhabitants. By 1691 Sir Francis Nicholson, the governor of Virginia, arranged contests at the annual St. George's Day celebration for the "better sort of Virginians onely who are Batchelors," and he offered prizes "to be shot for, wrastled, played at backswords, & Run by Horse and foott."[24] Probably more common than major public events like these were recreations at individual plantations. Particularly after the turn of the century, wealthy landowners swam, held running and walking races, skated on frozen rivers, fished, fenced, and protected stumps in a cricketlike game.[25] At his Westover estate on the James River, William Byrd II even made his wife "out of humor by cheating her" at piquet.[26] Men like Byrd also spent hours and even nights, as Breen has already detailed, wagering among themselves on their skills in various games.[27] Throughout this array of forms the interests of the participants varied—from entertaining guests, to providing an outlet for friendly rivalries, to improving or maintaining one's health—but the performances usually were closed affairs. Separate events were the base, the given of the emergent gentry's sporting life by the 1690s.

What they did within the frame of separate events, however, also set the large landowners apart from other colonists in the Chesapeake—and from some of their peers in other colonies. As their approach to horse racing suggests, they had begun to fashion a distinctive sporting style, a cohesive pattern of behaviors and meanings that drew on both contemporary British practices and their own experiences and expectations. As did other men at home and broad, the gentry competed in a variety of physical recreations: athletic events and field sports, household and tavern games, and horse races. At a time when recreations were proliferating in the Chesapeake, just as they were in other regions where popular culture was reinvigorating from the bottom up, however, not all sports engaged the aspiring elites, and what they did not do serves as a starting point for describing their style. They did not, for example, participate in either fistfighting or cudgeling, which was a duel between men who attacked each other with stout sticks. Holding the sticks in both hands, the contestants pushed, shoved, and occasionally struck the opposing cudgeler until one of them could no longer continue the fray.[28] Nor, as William Byrd suggested, did men like himself take part, at least publicly, in the "unmerciful sport" of fire hunting, a form in which both the hunted and the hunters suffered.[29]

Such a practice, the owner of Westover maintained, was more appropriate for the "barbarous" than for one such as he. What made it so were the manner of the performance and its outcome. As chapter 4 indicates, fire hunting began as hunters torched the brush and trees that harbored a herd of deer. In what was an "unfair way" of sporting, Byrd continued, the fire burned inward, ringing the "poor deer" and causing them "extreme distress." With such a destructive advantage, the common planter hunters slaughtered the deer en masse. For their cruelty, however, the marksmen were occasionally rewarded with more than just large quantities of game. They were "hurt by one another when they shoot across at the deer which are in the middle." In all, Byrd concluded, "'tis really a pitiful sight."[30]

To men of Byrd's stature the actions that constituted the event and the outcome mattered. Fire hunting was unfair and cruel, and cudgeling and fistfighting were, if not explicitly contrived and unfair, at least brutal and less ordered than were other forms of recreative combat. Sixteenth- and seventeenth-century courtesy manuals classified such sports as plebeian, and none of the activities engaged the large landowners. Furthermore, in sports in which they did compete, the gentry attempted to prevent, or at least contain, what they considered to be acts of brutality, opportunities for cheating, and the possibility of winning obvious physical mismatches. Race covenants checked precisely such behaviors. The "fair start" mitigated the cheat—the bolt in the beginning—while handicaps redressed size and speed advantages, and either winner or loser could prosecute an opponent who breached the provisions of a covenant. Moreover, the gentry's concerns about proper behavior did not stop at the physical boundaries of the race path. They expected "Decency and Sobriety" from race spectators.[31] A landed hunter "regretted when his party "butchered" a quantity of prey greater than it was "able to transport," for "this was carrying out sport to wantonness."[32] Even in gambling, when a locally influential man like Major Ben Robinson of Caroline Country, Virginia, found himself in debt because of "his gaming and idleness," he committed himself to clearing "his old scores" and to refraining from such excess in the future.[33]

"Fair riding," "decency and sobriety," and moderate hunting and gambling speak to an emergent set of "right" actions, a set of behavioral boundaries by which genteel sportsmen framed their physical performances after 1680. Given the fluidity of recreational practices, some of these actions operated as conventions defining what behaviors were and were not a part of the performance, what behaviors were and were not a part of a sport. Fair riding, for instance, mandated behaviors that no rule book or custom ensured. The term specified no whipping, no forcing an opponent off the path, and no false starts at a time when there were only a few unstandardized rules and conventions that ordered and differentiated competitive recreations, both from one another and from other forms of action incorporating the same movements. Race covenants, therefore, literally convened the contests and bound participants to an accepted manner of riding. They also differentiated races from other equestrian activities, just as the limits on game distinguished recreational hunting from wanton slaughter.

These "right" actions constituted a code of conduct that translated particular qualities valued by the great planters. As the race covenants and the phrase "decency and sobriety" suggest, one of these qualities was orderliness, which the gentlemen deemed important not just for a recreational performance but also for the construction of a stable, governable society. The Chesapeake upper rank thus prescribed regular, controlled actions—right behaviors—in and about the entire sporting scene. They did so by agreeing about the manner of racing, by objecting to "all Immorality" among spectators, and by competing in relatively well ordered practices.[34] Rather than pursue activities with ill-defined numbers of participants or ones that climaxed in disorder, such as fisticuffs and cudgeling, the gentry fenced in pairs, played established card and dice games, and raced over predetermined distances according to conventions that spurned disordering behaviors.

A second quality embedded in the right actions was moderation. Moderation is a relative term derived from comparisons with contemporary common planters and servants, as well as with the gentry's peers and superiors in Britain, comparisons that some gentlemen occasionally did make. It suggests the recognition and imposition of limits, limits beyond which wantonness, contrived competition, or debilitating debts occurred. A moderate sportsman was, in Robert Beverley's words, "but a small Sports-man." In the context of hunting, the small sportsman was one who killed only what he could carry—and always less than his common planter neighbors.[35] Compared to contemporaries in the mother country, even as gamblers gentlemen like Beverley were small sportsmen. Certainly they were avid gamblers, perhaps in part, as Breen has inferred, because gambling was a social glue.[36] But the evidence does not suggest that their fondness for gambling led many of them to replicate Major Robinson's actions. Through the 1730s few of the Chesapeake squires wagered the large sums that were relatively common among their peers in Britain, and they did not face the debts and bankruptcies that threatened some of their sons and grandsons. Instead they staked several hundred to several thousands pounds of tobacco, which in terms of eighteenth-century specie equaled from one to ten pounds sterling. They also wagered from a few shillings to five or six pounds in cash, but not the hundreds and thousands of pounds sterling put up by the aristocracy at the courts of the later Stuarts, amounts that reached the ranks of the gentry at Newmarket during the reign of William III.[37] At no time did a provincial commentator decry, as the Englishman John Evelyn had in the days of Charles II, the "deep and prodigious gaming . . . vast heaps of gold squandered away in a vain and profuse manner."[38] Nor did antigambling laws in the Chesapeake cite the large landowners directly, although parliamentary actions during the reigns of both Charles II and Anne did attempt to limit the gambling actions of the landed elite in the mother country.[39]

Precisely why the Chesapeake upper rank did not wager the large amounts found among Britons remains a question. Several factors apparently figured in what may have been a conscious decision not to bet inordinate amounts. First, these men operated on tobacco sales, with which they balanced accounts, and debt was a fearful condition to men who desired to "live in a kind of Independence on every one but providence."[40] Not until the late 1720s and 1730s did the economy stabilize; until then, sotweed revenues primarily financed necessities, especially land and slaves. Crop receipts did not cover luxuries, including large wagers, things that made one "too much of this world."[41] Second, these working squires who avoided conspicuous consumption, who wanted to be "not too gaudy or rich, yet genteel," had a moral sense that blended Enlightenment and Calvinist strains.[42] Men who desired ordered and moderate sporting competition expected themselves and their children, if not all their common planter neighbors, to be "well moral'd," to show "good morals and . . . agreeable obligeing behaviour."[43] Excessive wagers, in contrast, were evidence of neither. Finally, there was the reality of their situation, both as an emerging upper rank and as inhabitants of a transatlantic province. Unlike their cousins in the Old World, the great planters of the Chesapeake possessed no birthright to rank or status, and they existed in a colony where life itself remained something of a gamble. Gambling for relatively small wagers, then, may have been a means of dealing with the competitiveness of life as Breen has argued, but it was also one that did not threaten either the fragile relations among the gentlemen or their economic conditions and moral notions.[44]

A third expectation embraced by the gentry's code of conduct involved a belief in the importance of useful, productive action and the desire to avoid unproductive endeavors. Chesapeake gentlemen disliked idleness, which, as did other reformist Protestants, they considered to be the most unproductive condition; some of their recreational practices even occurred, according to Byrd, to "avoid the imputation of idleness."[45] To Byrd and others the primacy of productive activity was unquestioned, a dictum that applied both to the environment in which sport occurred and to men's actions. A deer park, wrote Governor William Gooch of Virginia in 1727, could be and was "turn'd to a better use I think than Deer, which is feeding of all sorts of Cattle."[46] Robert Carter applied the same line of reasoning to his workmen and his sons. On one occasion when two of Carter's Cornish laborers claimed the right to certain holidays and free time on Saturday afternoon, Carter responded, "You pretend to holidayes and what not; but I forbid it you and order him [the overseer] to make you work dayly as the rest of my servants that are there do day by day."[47] At another time Carter reprimanded his eldest son, John, when the youth was studying in England because he seemed to prefer the "pleasures of the town" and was "so taken up with your diversions."[48]

Carter's criticism of his laborers and his son is telling about more than just the significance he attributed to proper conduct. It also reveals a change in the mental world of the great planters from that of their predecessors concerning the substance of proper conduct, including their expectations for productive work and leisure practices. At the very least Carter did not tolerate expressions of the residual leisure preference, as some planters had in the middle decades of the seventeenth century. No claims by his field hands for their rights to holidays and breaks from work moved him. Nor did he countenance his son's "diversions," which were not unlike laborers' breaks from work. Carter had sent his son to London to acquire an education, and he expected the lad to labor assiduously at his books. Work, even mental tasks, was one's first responsibility.

It seems clear that men like Carter had adopted at least some elements of the approach to labor and idleness that reformist Protestants, including the Puritans, had clarified more than a half-century earlier. The hierarchical and oppositional relationship between labor and idleness remained meaningful to the large landowners of the Chesapeake. They could and did mandate productive work, which they valued. Idleness, in contrast, was the antithesis of work. Although not quite a sin, as the Puritans had termed it, idleness was a waste of time and energy. It was unproductive activity. It was a behavior of ordinary planters and field hands, who also engaged in recreations such as fistfighting and cudgeling.

Their own practices, however, were another matter. These suggest that the great planters had moved some distance beyond the earlier reformist Protestant view of the relationship between labor and leisure. As chapter 8 will clarify, this generation of provincial gentlemen had begun to construct a specific notion of leisure as a distinctive time and set of experiences, which meant not free, discretionary time but time, as well as tasks, that were different from the physical labor required by tobacco culture. In short they had begun to conceive of labor and leisure as discrete endeavors, as separable—but not yet separate and certainly not opposite or oppositional—spheres of life. Moreover, experience rather than abstract thinking underlay this conclusion. They knew what they saw, and what they saw was that what they did differed from what others did. Gentlemen raced horses in an orderly fashion, and they gambled at virtually everything, albeit moderately so. They did not, they believed, waste time or energy; they were not idlers. Nor did they engage in recreational practices that looked more like melees and slaughters than fair, competitive matches and hunts.

It is this conception of leisure that the great planters expressed as they formalized quarter-mile racing. Quarter-mile racing took place in times and places and with a goal and conventions that set it apart from ordinary riding, necessary transport. The same boundaries also distinguished it from impromptu contests, be they for diversion or when people had nothing better to do. Importantly, as well, genteel race men also appropriated from Britain a formal rationale for the sport. Organized racing helped to improve the quality of the breed, men like Carter and Byrd believed. A fairly run match separated winners from losers. It set the swift, hardy horses and mares that should be used to breed or bear the next generation of steeds apart from animals that should, literally as well as figuratively, be put out to pasture. For anyone who might miss the connection, provincial laws—which the great planters helped to write and, as justices of the peace, enforced—made it clear. As was the case in Britain, statutes in the Chesapeake protected and promoted racing.[49]

The great planters who formalized racing thus apparently conceived of it as a useful, productive recreation. It was distinct from labor and other endeavors in life, although it continued to advantage work in the agricultural society that the Chesapeake remained. But then, these men could afford the subtle transformation in the relationship between labor and leisure that they had experienced. Their leisure, their time to engage in activities that benefited but were clearly not the physically demanding tasks of tobacco culture, depended in part on a change in the composition and relations of labor in the plantation society.

The critical matter was the expansion of chattel slavery. Dutch traders had brought the first enslaved Africans to Virginia in 1619; thereafter small numbers of Africans, as well as Native Americans, worked side by side with indentured servants. By the 1680s, however, British servants were no longer as available as they had been, and provincial planters began to purchase more African slaves. Their numbers, and their percentage of the total tobacco work force, increased only gradually, but they did expand. In 1700 African slaves constituted about one-third of tobacco laborers, up from just a few hundred in 1670. A half-century later they made up nearly two-thirds of the work force.[50]

Sheer numbers do not tell the whole story, however. Also important is the fact that only a few planters owned more than one or two slaves, even though the practice of slaveholding was fairly widespread. The great planters controlled the bulk of the slave population, which lessened their labor costs even as it enabled them to maintain or enlarge output. Coupled with declining competition from small planters, the large landowners thus enjoyed significant advantages even though the tobacco market remained unstable. Moreover, they continued to acquire land, establish new "quarters," and hire overseers to manage the slave laborers and conduct the daily campaign of tobacco culture. They were also able to forgo the harsh physical labor that both their predecessors and their small planter contemporaries had to perform. They thus had time and energy to devote to other tasks, including politics, land speculation, rearing families, and racing horses.[51]

It is probably not coincidental, then, that this generation of native-born large landowners elevated the significance of labor and degraded idleness. Freed from the drudgery of ordinary work by slaves, the great planters could value it. They could also attach enormous significance to physical endeavors that were productive but not onerous. Their code of conduct, which proscribed some behaviors and prescribed others, suggests as much, as do their comments about the activities of ordinary colonists. On a surveying trip through the Roanoke River region in south central Virginia in 1728, William Byrd met Epaphroditus Bainton, a frontier planter whom he admired. Bainton's accomplishments, recorded Byrd, included walking twenty-five miles "in a day" and killing more than 100 deer yearly.[52] In another case Colonel Phillip Ludwell, the auditor of royal revenues in Virginia in

1710, expressed his amazement at the feats of a woman who lived and worked with her husband, Francis Jones, on their small farm near the Virginia-Carolina border. Mrs. Jones "is very civil and shews nothin of ruggedness," Ludwell wrote, "yet she will carry a gunn in the woods and kill deer, turkeys, &c., . . . and perform the most manful Exercises as well as most men in those parts."[53] A third, and caustic, reaction appeared in the commentary of an Anglican minister, the Reverend Hugh Jones, who was posted in eastern Virginia near the bay. Speaking about common planters, Jones judged that they led "easy lives" and "don't much admire Labour or any manly Exercise, except Horse-Racing."[54]

What the genteel observers had focused on in the activities of contemporaries was a single element, an element whose presence merited approval and whose absence warranted criticism. Ludwell and Jones admired "manful" or "manly" exercise, euphemisms for a task requiring physical prowess. Combining strength, skill, bravery, and even gallantry, prowess encapsulated the gentry's physical performance expectations and was significant in practical and symbolic ways. On the one hand, a man without physical strength, stamina, and courage lacked qualities that were important for survival, let alone for the achievement of wealth and power, in the late seventeenth- and early eighteenth-century Chesapeake. Furthermore, for men who suffered from gout and other physical ills in an age when the mortality rate remained high and medical treatment was occasionally traumatic, the development of prowess was, in a Lockean sense, a practical necessity.[55] Byrd, who suffered from gout, thus walked to "make a man of tolerable vigor an able footman" and swam to "restore our vigor."[56] The surveying party led by Governor Alexander Spotswood exercised itself by hunting bear in 1716,[57] and in 1729 Colonel William Woodford accepted his son's daily riding and fishing in the hopes that both activities would help the son to "escape a Seasoning."[58]

Prowess was also an observable quality. It differentiated men from women, as well as men from one another. The latter especially was an important goal of the large landowners who were emerging as a native-born upper rank. Since the cult of courtesy had pervaded the British court in the sixteenth century, courtiers and civil servants had magnified the importance of prowess as a sign of ability, potential, and achievement. Those who trained their bodies and cultivated prowess, announced the literature, served the state and gloried in its greatness. Those who lacked prowess were destined to anonymity, to the mass of humanity. The sentiment was not lost in the Chesapeake. Both real life and the courtier manuals in their libraries transmitted a similar message to the gentry and to would-be gentlemen.[59]

Located both in experience and in rhetoric, then, prowess was a historical concept that remained significant to the large landowners of the Chesapeake. It helps to explain why Byrd scoffed at the fire hunters whom he considered brutal; why Mathew Slader's cheating earned the court's retribution; and even why gentlemen engaged in particular recreations, such as racing and hunting, but not in physical combats that they considered to be plebeian. It also provided what the other components of the great planters' sporting style, the code of conduct and separate events, did not establish: a rationalization and justification for participating in competitive recreations, the importance of which extended far beyond the boundaries of the region. Although members of the British upper rank, whom the Chesapeake gentry took as their model, might not appreciate the precise forms of the sport common among Chesapeake gentlemen, they could at least appreciate the prowess displayed by their provincial cousins. Prowess thus linked the great planters to a broader and longer-running sporting style of British gentlemen.

Mediating Relationships

What accounts for the construction of the emergent gentry's sporting style at this time? Part of the answer lies in what they had. These men had the material means to acquire goods and horses, to entertain themselves, and to wager, frequently if not excessively. They also had contacts with British gentlemen, from whom they appropriated some recreational fashions. Yet what they did not have also mattered: status. The large landowners of the Chesapeake were a nonhereditary elite who had to negotiate their status, both among themselves and with others. In so doing they also produced a distinctive sporting style, for physical recreations were both the context for and the outcome of these negotiations.[60]

The construction of the gentry's distinctive sporting style involved three particular social relationships. As the earlier discussion of gambling suggests, one such relationship included the men themselves, who were clearly contentious individuals. They competed for land and offices and in the councils and assemblies—sometimes among themselves and occasionally with others. They also had to accommodate one another, however, to cooperate among themselves to consolidate their individual and collective positions and prerogatives. As the seventeenth and eighteenth centuries

met, these individuals had become quite adept at jostling and accommodation, or competing and cooperating, and they had begun to develop their
sporting style, including its small-wager gambles.[61] Unlike the economic
and political contests that were shaped by market conditions and institutions, however, the sporting practices that enticed the great planters had
few conventions—and even in Britain no governing bodies—to constrain
and regularize competitors. Thus the "right" actions that emerged as the
gentlemen competed among themselves and observed other colonists convened and ended the competition and deterred "cheats." In other words,
as did the small wagers, right actions kept sporting contests competitive.
The code also kept events ordered, moderate, and productive, so that sporting performances could translate genteel ideals and values and thus proceed as shared activities for health, for enjoyment and entertainment, for
displays of prowess, and for the ubiquitous gambling.

A second set of relations involved the provincial gentlemen and those
who provided the elite model: large landowners and merchants in the Old
World. Numerous newly regular connections between the provincial squires
and their metropolitan brethren emerged in the late seventeenth and early
eighteenth centuries. Affluent men of the Chesapeake sent their sons to
school in England, imported household and agricultural goods, became land
agents for British lords, and engaged in physical recreations that at least
resembled Old World forms. Moreover, besides testing and contesting with
one another in the fashion of the British upper rank—in separate events—
the provincial gentry also began to purchase Old World books and equipment. Along with prowess, these accouterments simultaneously enabled the
large landowners to identify with genteel sportsmen in the Old World and
provided them with the means of formalizing recreational practices in the
new one. That specific forms of sport, such as horse racing and hunting,
differed from their corollaries abroad apparently mattered little, if at all.[62]
The perception of Britishness was important. By 1724 Reverend Hugh Jones
believed that the emulation had succeeded. Provincial gentlemen, he concluded, "behave themselves exactly as do the Gentry in London."[63]

The great planters of the Chesapeake adopted one other practice from
the British upper rank just as a third relationship, between themselves and
their smaller landowning neighbors and servants, was also changing. This
was patronage, the practice of a gentleman supporting, arranging, and even
paying for the recreational opportunities of others. The particular ways in
which the large landowners supported and cultivated common planters and
servants varied. In the case of horse racing, for example, gentlemen attended

races among neighboring small planters, they permitted common planters to race on their fields, and they even helped to arrange contests. Some men of means also patronized members of the local community, either of the immediate plantation or of the broader neighborhood, when life warranted celebrations in which physical recreations figured prominently. The recently emerging harvest festivals, along with the shooting and athletic contests that took place within them, for instance, required the commitment of time and provisions by the large landowners, as did the musters and other martial displays that had begun to enliven the course of ordinary life. As commanders the majors, colonels, and provincial governors arranged target, wrestling, cudgeling, and running contests. They also provided the prizes—rifles, swords, saddles, boots, and money.[64]

These forms of patronage undoubtedly affected the gentry's relations with other colonists. Consider the sequence of events within the broader society. In the decade and a half before 1690, some degree of social unrest surfaced in the Chesapeake. The disturbances and discontent took many forms and involved many people until or shortly after the turn of the century. By that time a more stable economy and the expansion of slaveholding, an increase in the number of women and families, out-migration, and the cooperation of royal governors and major planters had combined to reduce internal tensions.[65] The patronage of common planters and servants by their wealthier neighbors and employers also served this end. Particularly after 1700 the provincial squires helped to organize or at least attended sporting events that occasionally had been sites for extended drinking and fisticuffs among common planters, and they discouraged "all immorality" at the gatherings.[66] Furthermore, as their own horse races regularized and neighbors gathered at what became local public events, the gentry had an arena in which they could display their own right conduct and reinforce their actions with calls for decency and sobriety.

Genteel patronage also coincided with another development in the Chesapeake that this chapter alluded to earlier and that the patronage of the great planters neither disrupted nor discouraged. Throughout the region ordinary colonists were participating in a variety of sports and other physical recreations, frequently if not regularly as matters of pleasure and entertainment. As Robert Beverley noted, poor planters entertained others gladly, as did their wealthier neighbors; if a "Churl" did not "comply with this generous Custom, he has a mark of Infamy set upon him."[67] Common practices were shooting contests, races, hunts, and combats, and even if ordinary colonists lacked specialized equipment, which most did, they made do with the goods they had and with animals and environmental conditions as they were. The western areas of Maryland and Virginia, especially in the foothills and the Appalachian Mountains, were home to large game that had all but disappeared in the east, and surveying parties still encountered Native Americans, whose hunting and fishing practices often amazed but eventually aided the surveyors. Throughout the region, on the other hand, tavern visits and gambling games therein remained relatively common, despite legal proscriptions, and horse races proliferated as the number of horses increased. Race paths and fields dotted the landscape in many counties, and Saturday became a major race day.[68] By 1702 the Maryland Assembly believed that the "frequent" racing on Saturday contributed "very much To the Prophanacon of the Lords Day following," and it condemned the practice.[69] Ill-enforced and even offset by genteel support for the sport, such legislative actions did not discourage the events, however. Facilitated as they occasionally were by gentry arrangement and approbation, horse races in particular—and other recreations more generally—had emerged in the Chesapeake as a medium of social exchange, a part of common parlance, a customary endeavor in which various ranks of provincials engaged.

The case of horse racing suggests that the gentry chose to encourage the commonness of the sport. The large landowners did patronize racing, and they did not enforce the laws concerning horses and gambling. From their positions as justices of the peace and given the long-standing British legal position that racing was a sport only for gentlemen, the great planters could have attempted to exclude others. They did not do so, however, apparently for several reasons. On the one hand, exclusivity provided few if any advantages among men who were eminently practical.[70] Maintaining racing only among themselves at the very least would have been an unrealistic goal, given that colonials were spread out over many miles. Then, too, such a practice might have been counterproductive. The great planters believed—and made clear in statutory form—that racing advanced the goal of quality horseflesh. They also apparently had some understanding of what modern physiologists recognize as a conditioning effect. Because the matches tested, and perhaps stretched, the prowess of the jockey and the steed, they improved the abilities of rider and horse alike to endure the physical demands of plantation life and provincial travel.

A final explanation for the gentry's actions lies in their social status, or more to the point, their aspirations to status. Although land and gradually chattel slavery were the preeminent factors in the creation of a native-born upper rank in the Chesapeake, they did not by themselves guarantee the rank's power and authority in a society that lacked a long-standing landed aristocracy. In part at least, power and authority depended on the deference and the respect earned from inferiors and on the reputations recognized by royal governors who could grant political offices and preferments. Deference and respect, in turn, derived from appropriate performances in appropriate circumstances—superior performances and the performances of superiors in activities meaningful to many. Sports in general and horse racing in particular became activities in which gentlemen could secure deference and reputations because, as were land, tobacco, and voting, they were relatively common and appreciated by many members of provincial society. Throughout the Chesapeake colonists appreciated the prowess of the rider and his horse. Genteel riders, already set apart by extensive land ownership, augmented that distinctiveness by reaping indirect benefits of the contests—personal prestige, renown, and enhanced reputations. Separate gentry events, rather than the construction of a sport exclusively for gentlemen, however, were the key. As Breen implied, quarter-mile racing was and remained the central event not only in the gentry's recreational scheme but in the universe of popular recreations in the Chesapeake.[71]

Quarter-mile racing held this position because it was common, and commonness may have been an important base for eliteness, at least in the colonies, where a native aristocracy had not existed. Indeed, it may have been because many colonists had access to a shared material culture—and more broadly, to a shared popular culture—that a social system modeled on the closed, birth-defined hierarchy in Britain did not emerge in the Chesapeake. In any event, in the late seventeenth and early eighteenth centuries, when conditions and relations were relatively dynamic in the Chesapeake, those things that either were or became relatively common—especially land and slavery—figured prominently in the construction of a stable Anglo-American society by defining relations among the ranks of the dominant population. Gradually many whites achieved both, with property holding existing as the critical feature of the hierarchical plantation society and, as Edmund Morgan has argued, slave ownership serving as the basis for the white alliance that secured internal peace and perhaps even freedom.[72]

By no means did sports and other physical recreations affect Chesapeake society in the same way or to the extent that land and slavery did. Nonetheless, as sports became more widespread over time, particular ones—especially quarter-mile racing—not only translated gentry values but also mediated social relations, especially the one that was critical to the recognition of the large landowners as an upper rank, that between the gentlemen and common planters. A distinctive gentry sporting style, derived and formalized out of common experiences and uncommon expectations about proper conduct, then, reproduced the paradox that characterized Chesapeake society in the eighteenth century. Like land and slavery, sports simultaneously linked and separated Chesapeake colonists.

⋯⇌◯⇋⋯

In subsequent years the sporting style that had begun to emerge among the native-born gentlemen of the Chesapeake in the decades surrounding 1700 became more elaborate. In making it so, great planters on the James and Potomac were joined by other upper-rank colonists. By midcentury sports and physical recreations became a common language, a shared tradition among men and women of wealth and power across the colonies. But the process of culture making was not the domain solely of the provincial elite. A more full-bodied sporting style also emerged among ordinary colonists after 1730s. It is to these two styles, genteel and vernacular, that I now turn.

6

⌁⟹⟸⌁

Mid-Eighteenth-Century Sporting Styles

Traditions, Eric Hobsbawm tells us, are sets of practices constructed by people to make sense of themselves and their world. They are "normally governed by overtly or tacitly accepted rules," and they may have important symbolic functions. They express particular "values and norms of behaviour" that draw from experience, and they frequently emerge during periods of substantial change. Thus traditions, whether invented or less consciously produced by a group, link past and present. They establish continuity over time, as well as stability and cohesiveness in time, and they enable the makers to present and represent themselves in understandable ways.[1]

In the middle decades of the eighteenth century, colonists on the mainland of North America probably needed traditions. These were dynamic decades. Excluding Native Americans, the provincial population ballooned to nearly two and a half million by 1775. Many of these people were creoles, or native-born Anglo-Americans and African Americans, but there were also thousands of new migrants from the British Isles, western Europe, and Africa. Altogether they constituted a population both relatively youthful and mobile. Some colonists moved west, as far as 150 miles beyond the Atlantic, to start or restart the processes of farm and home building, while others remained along the coast, either in the burgeoning towns and cities or on farms. Those who stayed put sometimes found the soil less fertile than it had been, a fact that encouraged agricultural diversification.

For others, crafts specialization, manufacturing, wholesaling, and retailing brought in needed income. There was, however, little predictability in economic matters. The boom-and-bust phases of the economy, for which events abroad were partially responsible, enabled some colonists to profit, but others saw their standards of living decline. More than a few colonists also came to experience the vicissitudes of wars, the peaks and valleys of religious revivals, and the intellectual and practical consequences of the Enlightenment. Indeed, had Charles Dickens lived in the colonies in the middle of the eighteenth century, he might have offered the same judgment that he did of life in England and France in 1775. Living in the British North American provinces could amount to "the best of times" or "the worst of times"—or anything in between.[2]

It is in this context that the sporting styles that upper-rank and ordinary colonists alike had begun to construct in the decades surrounding 1700 matured. These cohesive patterns of behavior and meaning came to constitute traditions in Hobsbawm's sense of the word. They expressed particular values, connected past and present, and had "rules." Although rarely written, the rules were widely understood guidelines about ways of behaving and expectations. They were also boundaries that deterred some practices and differentiated genteel from vernacular. But then, boundary making was a critical process in the mid-eighteenth-century colonies, not only between and among people, but also between past and present. The construction of autonomous or nearly autonomous sporting events suggests as much. Moreover, these emergent forms of recreation also indicate that colonists in both ranks had begun to shape nontraditional cultural forms and to frame labor and leisure as separable experiences.

The Genteel Style

John Adams shared some views about sports and exercise with John Winthrop. In 1756, just as he turned twenty-one, Adams declared his disdain for "rakes and fools," some of whom "waste the bloom of Life, at the Card or biliard [sic] Table." He was not inured to the "pleasure of ranging the Woods," however, especially if, as had Winthrop more than a century earlier, he anticipated "some Boon in Return." The boon might be health, for Adams realized that "exercise invigorates, and enlivens all the Faculties of Body and Mind." It "spreads a gladness . . . over our minds and qualifies us for every Sort of Buisiness [sic]."[3] The words were different, but the connection was similar. To the future American president, some physical recreations and exercises benefited labor, much as they had for the first governor of Massachusetts Bay.

On other matters regarding recreations and sports, however, Adams was not at all like Winthrop. Four years after his protestations and rationalizations, the now twenty-five-year-old farmer-lawyer spent an entire day fishing from a boat. Adams had needed no excuse; he had gone expecting a "Day of Pleasure." At day's end, however, he had caught no fish and had "none of the Pleasure of Angling" and "very little of the Pleasure of Sailing," so it mattered little that the activity was "wholesome." He experienced only the "fatigue of Rowing, and some of the Vexation of Disappointment."[4]

John Adams obviously did not mind pleasurable recreations, especially ones that he could enjoy with company. Just prior to his marriage to Abigail Smith, he half-jokingly scolded her that she had "been extreamly negligent in attending so little to Cards." Card games were a "noble and elegant Diversion," but Abigail played them "with a very uncourtly, and indifferent, Air." John hoped that she would shortly make "a better Figure in the elegant and necessary Accomplishment."[5] Abigail, however, apparently did not share John's views entirely. Some years later he again lectured her about recreations, this time among their children. John insisted that they should learn the "pretty" amusements: dancing, skating, and fencing.[6]

The Adamses may have lacked the great wealth of some members of the colonial upper rank but not their interest in sports and other recreations or their understanding that some forms were requisite practices. Men and women of the Adamses' social position expected to play and display their prowess in such endeavors in the middle decades of the eighteenth century. Many practices were pleasurable, and pleasure was not unimportant to upper-rank colonists. Moreover, people who would be gentlemen and gentlewomen required some facility in physical recreations. Sports, games, and dancing had long been popular among the British upper rank, whose fashions influenced provincials.[7] A British gentleman was not only literate, witty, and relatively well mannered, at least in public, but he was also a man of grace, power, and agility. A gentlewoman, although physically different from and considered inferior to men, was to be healthy, gracefully mobile, and conversant in the rules and conventions of the arts of physical improvement and refinement: the sports of men and the sports of "society." To be cultivated she, as well as he, needed to acquire skill in and knowledge about recreations such as fishing, sailing, dancing, cards, and races.[8]

The sports of the Anglo-American gentry were quite varied in terms of both form and forum by the middle of the eighteenth century. Some practices were regionally popular, as had been the case since before the century began. Sledding and skating, for example, were most common from Pennsylvania northward, whereas cockfights occurred from New York southward. The same was true of water sports. In the Chesapeake men and women paddled canoes and, on occasion, ventured onto a river or the bay in a slave-powered galley. Their peers in New England sailed small boats and sloops, and New Yorkers raced on the Dutch-designed packet, the yacht.[9]

Other recreations were more widespread. Up and down the seaboard youths especially swam in the warm summer months, and field sports appealed to their parents, although not equally to both women and men and not always in the same manner across the colonies. Fishing drew women as hunting did not, a consequence of the persisting and constraining perception of women's lesser physical strength, their lack of access to firearms, and their own interests and relations. Fox hunting on preserves engaged gentlemen in New York, Pennsylvania, and the Chesapeake, while their Carolina contemporaries hunted the wily animal wherever they could, and New Englanders did not bother with it at all. They preferred other forms of hunting. Card games and dancing were ubiquitous, as were many kinds of races: foot, boat, and horse. In fact, as it was in Britain, horse racing was emblematic of gentry life and a focus of transcolonial competitions.[10]

The provincial elite pursued these recreations with a scheduled regularity that had no precedent in colonial experience. Winter was the time for balls and assemblies, virtually every fortnight in towns, as well as for indoor card games, outdoor skating, and club dinners. Early spring, when rains swelled the rivers, marked the beginning of the fishing season, which lasted until early fall. Cockfights, ball games, and horse races began about the same time and peaked between April and June. By the 1770s one could attend a race virtually every week in a different town in Virginia and Maryland, and a calendar of sorts ensured that races did not occur in two areas at the same time. July and August were for cricket games in the South, swimming everywhere, and the beginning of the hunting seasons that, with different animals and fowl in turn, lasted through early winter. By September the fall races began; when they ended in November, they overlapped with hunts and the beginning of the dancing season. In short, there was a sport or two for every season, and recreations were always in season.[11]

Beyond its extensiveness, this seasonal program of sports and other physical recreations represents a departure from several previous patterns. First, genteel recreations were no longer as dependent on other gatherings, such as royal anniversaries and community rituals, as they had once been. These affairs persisted, but contests and displays occurred in other social settings as well.[12] A few sports, especially horse races and cockfights, emerged as autonomous events. Especially among men, they generated intense interest, keen competition, and the almost inevitable gambling. The prospect of such pleasures enticed spectators and participants alike; as had Adams, they needed no other justifications to attend.

The range of settings and the autonomy of some events suggest that the most popular and visible recreations had ceased to be bound up in the same way with the rhythms of work, or perhaps that the rhythms of labor and leisure had changed. Most colonial historians agree that many upper-rank men and women were a working gentry, and there is little evidence to suggest that, except for some gentlemen in coastal Carolina, they constituted a Weberian leisure class. Nor did they conceive of labor and leisure as entirely separable spheres of life and social activity or behave as if they were. Nonetheless, many gentlemen and gentlewomen did face tasks and work relations different from those that their predecessors had faced. Managing a plantation or fleet or large house, running a farm or law practice, and operating a mill or store required particular skills, mental astuteness rather than raw physical strength, and the ability to dictate work and dispatch laborers.[13] With some planning one could make or take time for recreations. One could fit recreations into a day's or a week's regimen.

From at least the 1740s there is considerable evidence that some upper-rank men and women did precisely this. A case in point was Eliza Pinckney, the daughter and wife of rice planters in South Carolina. From the time she was a teenager, Pinckney thought it important to construct and follow "a plan for our conduct in life," a blueprint for how and when to behave.[14] As a young woman she apparently did just that. After 5:00 A.M., when she rose, Pinckney assigned one- and two-hour blocks to different tasks: reading, walking, breakfast, music and French lessons, practicing shorthand, teaching her house slaves, dining, seeing visitors, "going abroad" on some afternoons, and so on. As an adult with the responsibility for managing the plantation in her husband's absence, Pinckney's regimen changed little in form, although much in content. She moved from task to task, in the house and around the plantation, each in its turn. But her diary and letters hint at her efforts not only to fulfill her responsibilities but also to make time for recreations. Pinckney worked long and hard, and in times of crises, such as the smallpox epidemic that devastated Charleston in 1760, she would put off recreations—her walks, balls, music, watching the races, and riding horses. Eventually, however, she would reincorporate them in her schedule.[15]

Pinckney's account suggests one important component of the upper rank's scheme of life that bore directly on their ability to make time for recreations. Many of these people had hired or bound employees—wage laborers, house servants, or slaves—to whom they assigned many tasks, especially the manual work that some masters and mistresses, in the South and middle colonies at least, not only disliked but came to disavow. This attitude in itself affected particular recreations, as will be seen. More to the point, however, the labor of these workers became one of the material and human props for the gentry's sports and displays, just as they had earlier for the great planters in the Chesapeake. Having given the day's instructions to his overseer about what his slaves were to do, George Washington, for example, was able to focus on his own tasks: he could spend hours readying the grounds for fox hunts.[16] The presence of slaves and overseers, along with a father and brothers, also helps to account for the extensive recreational pursuits of Robert Wormeley Carter, a grandson of Robert "King" Carter. In the 1770s in the northern neck of Virginia, the young Carter exceeded even the expectations for sport among his contemporaries, many of whom prided themselves on their sporting prowess. Time after time he abandoned his work for a horse race or a cockfight. On one occasion he left home as his wife was giving birth. Children and crops had little hold on Robert Wormeley—at least not until his own son replicated his behaviors. Only then did recreations cease to drive Carter's time.[17]

Robert Wormeley Carter's behavior was not typical of the actions of many other young men, even in the race-loving Chesapeake, as well as farther north. Still, it illustrates the interest that some members of the upper rank manifested in some sports, as well as a broader process affecting ordinary life among the gentry. This was a specialization, or an emergent segmentation, of work tasks and relations, of endeavors in time, and of sports and recreations in relation to daily and weekly work and time. This process of specialization appears also in the seasonality of recreations, the sequencing of sports and contests in time.

There were many dimensions to this specialization and the other processes related to it, the formalizing of recreations and their emergent separation from ordinary life and work. One dimension involved the transformation of local networks of gentlemen into voluntary organizations and even formal clubs. One of the earliest was the Schuylkill Fishing Company, which formed outside Philadelphia by 1732. Shortly thereafter jockey clubs in Maryland and South Carolina organized, quickly languished, and then reorganized in these colonies and elsewhere at midcentury. In the 1740s merchants and lawyers established a "Physical Club" in Boston, and merchants and rice planters around Charleston organized two hunting clubs, which merged by 1761.[18]

Beyond providing a link to British upper-rank clubs, these organizations served as forums for the closed, corporate participation in recreations that gentlemen came to value and for discussions that affected the shape of particular practices. Members of the Schuylkill Fishing Company, for example, drew up "rules and regulations" for their sport, as eventually would other clubs. The Philadelphians also clarified the social location and significance of fishing. It was a "handmaiden" to other endeavors, a necessary and useful practice.[19] The precise meaning of that phrase probably emerged in deliberations among the members, although these have been lost. In addition to defining rules governing performance, club members shared and debated ideas, as they did in other contemporary voluntary associations—local political clubs, literary societies, and subscription theaters. Jockey clubs discussed breeding and bloodlines of horses, as well as weights and techniques of riding. The Boston Physical Club focused on all "sundry physical matters"—health, diet, exercise, and ways of playing—that were meaningful to men who sought to "strengthen and render active their Bodies."[20]

Concurrent with and probably a force in the rule and ideology making of the clubs was the proliferation of sport-specific equipment, although this movement was not confined to the gentry. Tavernkeepers had long owned sporting goods, and especially after midcentury middling-rank colonists had access to some equipment. Still, gentlemen and gentlewomen became consumers as never before. From Europe they imported a range of goods, including battledores for an indoor version of badminton, stopwatches to time races, ivory billiard balls, and quail and dog calls. Provincial craftspeople supplied other equipment, especially card and billiard tables, swords and foils, sleds and carriages, and an assortment of leather goods. Animals for sport also came on order: French hunting hounds, cocks for fighting, and horses.[21]

This equipment and stock in turn found its way into specialized facilities. Especially in urbanizing areas after midcentury, coffeehouse owners found competition for the gentry's recreational time and their dollars increasing. Entrepreneurs were building not only theaters but also assembly rooms, race courses, and tracks. They also had to contend with the increasing number and variety of private facilities, some of which were built by planters and urban merchants who had enough income or credit to own a second home in a town or the countryside. Stables on the grounds of plantations and estates housed the thoroughbred racehorses that improved stock, earned stud fees, and transported the owner quickly and gracefully from place to place. Bowling greens, which were sites for entertainment and parts of the symmetrical pattern of the outdoors, spread across expanses of grass between estate entrances and great houses. Game preserves stocked with deer encompassed hundreds of acres of meadows and woods and served as experiments in land conservation and arenas for the chase.[22]

These facilities were not architectural appendages. Rather, they merged commerce and fashion, practicality and symbolism, as befit the material and ideological interests and conditions of people who were aspiring to be like their British peers. The performances that occurred on the grounds and in the buildings served this same function. Many contests and matches were anything but haphazard practices; both rules that laid out behavioral expectations and limits in writing and conventions, or orally transmitted procedures, governed them. Some guidelines came directly from Britain, via visits or books, as was the case with cricket and many card games. Others drew on British ways of playing but incorporated colonial experiences and expectations as well. Such was the case in thoroughbred racing.

Thoroughbred racing was one of several forms of horse racing known to gentlemen and gentlewomen. By the middle of the eighteenth century quarter-mile racing still drew some great planters, at least as patrons, and in New England trotting and pacing events were probably more common than were thoroughbred affairs. Nonetheless, the crowning colonial affair was the last form. In its British format, a distance contest on a straightaway, the event probably emerged first among civil servants, military officers, and large landowners in New York. It flourished in the Chesapeake, however, once large landowners began to import full-blooded stock from England to improve their small native stock after 1730. From there race men reached north and south for competition, sales of horses, and renown. By the 1760s thoroughbred races were vibrant public affairs from New York to Georgia. Occasionally the races matched an owner-breeder from one colony against his peers from another.[23] Even New Englanders knew enough about the sport to attend contests in towns in other regions and to praise or criticize a victorious rider who "assumed the airs of a hero or German potentate."[24]

Few behaviors were left to chance in thoroughbred racing. Some planters kept meticulous breeding and foaling records, as well as accounts of stud fees, club dues, prizes won, and wagers won and lost. An annual assessment of income and debts helped to identify and cull losing horses, as well as wayward, wagering children. By the mid-1760s newspapers announced not only race meetings but also the formula by which pairings for match events (between two horses) and the entries for subscriptions (races to which all entrants contributed) and sweepstakes (winner-take-all contests) were determined. The two variables in this formula were the "bloodedness" of the horse and the weight of the jockey. Full-blooded horses had to carry the heaviest weights, whereas one-eighth-blooded horses carried less. The basis for modern handicapping, these predetermined equivalences were important to setting up "fair" races.[25]

The codification of race-track behavior was not just a process involving the equine performers, however. There were also the humans who bred, rode, and watched them; although few human behavioral guidelines were committed to paper, they existed nonetheless. Indeed, prescriptions for proper conduct were transmitted in ways far more visible and important than literary form. Riders followed the generations-old "fair riding" code, which itself had become a tradition. Competitors were not to use their whips against one another, to bump an opponent's horse, or to bolt before the formal start. The structure of the races transmitted another aspect of the code. Thoroughbred contests were for gentlemen only; there was no interrank competition. A third component defined gender relations, which the built environment expressed and institutionalized by the 1770s. Specific stands accommodated, or segregated, women, who were not to mingle with the crowd or endure the inevitable jostling at the rail, even though they might wager. Genteel women were to act and to be treated as gentlewomen. Finally, gentlemen were not to act as ordinary men, at least in the open. They were to limit their drinking, their wagers, and their demeanor. They might behave as Robert Wormeley Carter did in private, or even in the semiprivate spaces of taverns, but at the major public events, such as thoroughbred races, they were to behave as gentlemen.[26]

It is not surprising that what became the premier event in a province-wide sporting style clarified and expressed what John Adams had tried to relate to Abigail. Highly visible genteel sports displayed not just prowess but the cultivation and refinement that bound the colonial upper rank to the contemporary British gentry. Genteel men and women were to be "noble and elegant," not "uncourtly and indifferent." Even Benjamin Franklin, who lampooned himself and his contemporaries with the beaver cap, was never entirely comfortable with the persisting image of the provincial boor. He told and retold of his ability to swim and of his feats in the water, for he understood the special and specialized significance of physical prowess and sport to the British upper rank.[27] The effect was not lost on their peers from abroad. By the mid-1760s William Eddis, a British civil servant stationed in Maryland, put the matter succinctly. "We have varied amusements and numerous parties," he wrote back home, such that "very little difference is, in reality observable in the manners of the wealthy colonists and the wealthy Briton."[28]

The Vernacular Style

A second style also became more resonant in the middle decades of the eighteenth century. This was the vernacular style, the recreational pattern not of *a* people but of *the* people, ordinary colonists—artisans and small farmers, slaves and sailors, housekeepers and shopkeepers, and more. Some of them lived in towns or cities, whereas others spent their entire lives on family farms, small plantations, or isolated cabins in the backcountry. None was rich, by anyone's standards, and more than a few were poor, surviving on the economic margins. For most of them, place still mattered, and the rhythms and relations of life shared by the group or the community were the critical boundaries of experience. Thus, to speak of the vernacular style as a singular pattern is misleading. It consisted of many locally, or at most regionally, constructed practices, some of which were as different from one another as many were from contemporary genteel forms.

The sports of ordinary colonists were not simply a disparate collection of nongenteel practices, however. Many vernacular forms had much in common with one another, as well as with the "folk" recreations constructed by the lower ranks across the Atlantic. First, conventions governed many activities, which is not surprising given that many ordinary colonists continued to express themselves orally and physically rather than in written form. Second, they constructed many of their practices with what lay at hand and within the context of ordinary affairs. Specialized equipment was rare, and even the horses and boats used for racing doubled for travel and transport. Workplaces—fields, forests, lanes, docks, houses—remained common sites for physical recreations, and the tasks and relations of agriculture, aquaculture, trapping, trading, and domestic chores continued to shape when, with whom, and how one engaged in a contest or display. Finally, many sports remained structured as they had been for decades. Matches, or events that pitted one person against another, were common, as were small group and communal events; with the notable exception of card play, few of these activities could be classified as formalized games. Instead, they were practices like baits, field sports, displays of prowess, and even "outings" that incorporated physical skills that remained important in ordinary life. In short, as had football on the beach near Rowley a half-century earlier, many vernacular recreations in the middle decades of the eighteenth century resembled older forms.

On this point field sports are perhaps most telling. The most nearly universal of all vernacular recreations, hunting and fishing especially had deep roots in ordinary life. Many colonists spent much of their time out-doors, and whether they lived in rural areas or towns, few of them were far from forests and streams. Many people, as well, owned carbines or muskets or had lines of cord or nets. Thus, except for legislatively defined seasons, there were few official or popular limits on hunting and fishing. These were the practices one undertook for relaxation, when sustenance or variety in the diet was the object, or when one had "nothing to doe," when whaling crews could not put out to sea or when southern planters had slack spells during the winter.[29]

The various regional patterns of field sports also evoked ones known to prior generations. New England farmers and ministers, some of whom were part-time farmers, for instance, proceeded much as their predecessors had. Each autumn when the weather and work permitted, individuals and small bands of neighbors stalked and shot "vermin," troublesome animals such as squirrels, wolves, and bears. In the middle colonies and the Chesapeake the repertory of hunting practices was more extensive, and rambling and frolicking were not out of the question. Fire hunting, with its camaraderie and danger, persisted in the latter region, but common planters and field hands also spent hours and even days pursuing ducks and geese, laying traps for fur-bearing animals, and chasing deer and turkeys on horseback. Far south in the Carolinas and Georgia varied species of wildlife remained abundant, exchanges between whites and Native Americans were still rel-atively common, and hunting practices remained varied. As they had for decades, Anglo- and African-American colonists ambled after deer on fall afternoons with muskets, as well as with bows and arrows. Planters even spent upward of ten days at the chase, which became more challenging when they pursued any wary prey through a natural obstacle course such as dense woods and underbrush. In the Carolinas, at least, men also hunt-ed alligators, either by shooting the amphibians from a boat or by diving into a river and then wrestling and stabbing one.[30]

Resemblances to past patterns are evident as well in the placement of recreations within the web of family and community affairs—weddings, fairs, frolics, holiday celebrations, and evening gatherings. These events had been, and remained, important venues for social and economic exchanges, for enjoyment and "merry making," and for expressions of belonging to both Old and New World communities; most achieved a distinctive place in the annual, local calendar. Frolics, for example, were forms of harvest festivals in the North in the late summer and autumn, as well as youthful celebrations on days such as May Day. Fairs were semiannual events, especially in the middle colonies and the Chesapeake. More broadly, holidays recognized both Christian and civil events: Christmas, Easter, royal anniversaries, and days of note in a colony's past. The holiday calendar was particularly rich in the South, but northern villagers were not without joyful gatherings. Their physical proximity made possible frequent meetings on greens, roads, and ponds, especially in the naturally shorter workdays of winter and spring.[31]

Physical performances figured prominently in all these events, as they long had. Dances were traditional practices at weddings, although the precise forms varied from group to group. Africans favored jigs and individual rhythmic performances to the accompaniment of fiddles, whereas New Englanders of British stock practiced country dances, which were variants of reels. Fairs in Pennsylvania and Maryland featured races, both on foot by white and black runners and on horseback. Frolics begot relatively simple games, drinking and eating, and sexual license—the practices of carnival.[32]

The similarities between Old and New World practices, in terms of both the gatherings and the precise forms of physical recreations, require some comment. As many historians have recognized, ordinary colonists in the eighteenth century remained linked to Old World traditions—of political activity, of social relations, and of recreations, among other things—despite their physical distance from both Europe and Africa and despite important economic, demographic, and environmental differences between North America and the lands across the Atlantic. Shared histories, economic exchanges, and not entirely disparate styles and standards of living help to account for the similarities, as does the fact that migration from abroad persisted, and newly arriving immigrants brought with them the customs of the homeland. The continual infusion of Old World people and practices maintained the cultural linkages even as they added to the internal variability of colonial cultural forms.[33]

We can see this cultural transfer in physical recreations tied to the wedding celebrations of two groups of people. One involved German colonists, who arrived in substantial numbers after 1714 and made their way from coastal ports especially to the piedmont and western valley regions of Pennsylvania, Maryland, and Virginia. In their New World settlements they maintained a particular throwing contest as a part of the nuptial festivities. Known as "throwing the stocking," the event began once the newly married couple went to bed, surrounded by the celebrants. The women balled a stocking and threw it at the bride; the men did the same at the groom. A hit on the target signified that the thrower was the next person, of both genders, to be married.[34] Some Scots-Irish migrants, on the other hand, transferred from the British Isles a match that highlighted both the athletic prowess and the drinking interests of young men. Either on horseback or on foot, two contestants ran a race for a bottle of liquor; the rougher the terrain, the better. The key, of course, was the physical display of raw speed and agility in the face of rocks and downed trees. The winner then not only drank lustily but also improved his standing among the young unmarried women.[35]

The transfer of particular practices from the Old World also helps to account for the appearance of some ball games in the context of community festivities in Georgia, the final British-claimed colony on the mainland of North America. Established in 1732, its population initially consisted of a few English people of means; religious dissenters from Salzburg, Austria; and tenants and laborers from north of London. This latter segment in particular brought with them games they had known in England— cricket, football, and quoits—for which opportunities in North America were regular if not frequent. In keeping with customs at home, both the trustees who remained in Britain and the migrating planters permitted, and perhaps encouraged, an extensive calendar of holidays. Included in these holidays were a number of days between Christmas and New Year's and then, in the spring, the Monday and Tuesday after Easter. The multiple royal anniversaries—George I's birthday, his coronation, and his accession to the throne—were also joyous occasions. Finally, St. George's Day, 23 April, and 5 November, the anniversary of the attempted assassination of James I by suspected Catholic plotters more than a century earlier, were annual events. For ordinary workers, cricket and football were the games of the day, and virtually no holiday passed without them.[36]

Nevertheless, the particular history of ball games such as cricket and football also suggests that we should not overemphasize the similarities between Old and New World practices. In Britain at least, ball games not only remained popular among ordinary people but also formalized and became rule-governed rather than strictly convention-bound in the eighteenth century. Such did not happen in the colonies. By the 1760s and 1770s in Georgia and elsewhere, cricket play was rare, limited to British soldiers, officers, and merchants, and primarily boys engaged in football.[37] British ball games apparently had no staying power among colonial adults. They were residual practices that did not become traditions.

A part of the reason for this failure lies in the gender relations of ordinary colonists. In the eighteenth century few family and community events were about the construction of simple, vertical dominant-subordinate relationships between men and women. Instead, they were opportunities for shared experiences, for community making. They relieved the tedium of ordinary work and the physical isolation of many people, including women, who as co-producers of the events had considerably more social power than they did in daily affairs. Thus ball games, which drew from and magnified male physical prowess, were less meaningful in the context of such gatherings than were other practices. These other events joined men and women in recreations in which the physical differences that were important in the construction of gender—and the gendering of recreations—either mattered little or were critical to the practices. Such recreations were numerous: dancing, throwing balled stockings, fishing, sledding, card play, canoe and sleigh races, and of course, sexual intercourse. In east central Pennsylvania, where the Quaker commitment to equitable social relations manifested itself in ordinary life, men and women even raced horses against one another, with wagers on the outcome.[38]

A second reason for the constriction of ball games over time, especially in the context of popular gatherings, lies in the fact that holidays, especially those associated with holy days, were not nearly as extensive, either numerically or geographically, in the colonies as they remained in Britain. New Englanders celebrated only a few occasions, and mostly secular ones; their contemporaries in the middle colonies, a few more. In both regions the social power of particular reformist Protestant sects contributed to the diminution of holy days. On both political and theological grounds, some latter-day Puritans, French Huguenots, and Dutch Calvinists explicitly rejected holy days become holidays and the extensive cycle of British royal anniversaries. Only in the South did a British-like pattern prevail. From the Mason-Dixon line southward large landowners, common planters, and slaves relished holidays, and at least until the Revolution, many British holidays had some currency among men and women there.

Even in the South, however, ball games did not become customary endeavors for a third reason. The skills and the structure involved in ball games simply had no fit in the experiences of southern males. The physical skills of throwing, catching, and batting were not the actions one took to obtain food, to settle a dispute, or to gain renown. Racing horses, fighting with fists or cudgels, and shooting were. Then too, ball games had historically involved men participating in groups, if not teams, of from ten to twenty on a side. Although such collections were not unknown, they were also not the norm, except in the deep South among enslaved Africans who worked the fields in gangs. More commonly, ordinary male southerners lived and worked in small groups—a father and son and a slave or servant or two, for example—or they worked alone. The significance of individual action, although not necessarily individualism, in the eighteenth century thus cannot be downplayed.[39]

The failed staying power of ball games also suggests a limit to the significance of persistence in vernacular recreational practices. As was the case among their genteel peers, physical recreations among ordinary colonists were traditions in the making, not static practices, and there was more dynamism in the forms, the locus, and the meanings of popular recreations than the preceding discussion suggests.[40] Other residual sports suffered the fate of ball games. Cock shailing, for example, ceased to matter among laborers in the streets of Boston, or any other urban area. They turned instead to the expanding realm of commercial recreations, especially in the taverns, where equipment for cards and ninepins was available, where liquor and women made for lively entertainment, and where few authorities dared to interfere. They also turned to the streets and greens for shooting and cudgeling contests, and they began to construct large group, ritual affairs such as Pope's Day.

Popular recognition of Pope's Day, or Guy Fawkes Day, probably emerged in coastal Massachusetts towns in the late seventeenth century. Laborers seized the occasion of the anniversary of the failed Catholic plot to blow up Parliament on 5 November 1605 to hold bull baits. Not until the mid-1730s, however, did they formally and visibly celebrate the day as a holiday with its own distinctive meanings, anti-Catholicism and, eventually, antiauthoritarianism. About the same time laborers in New York City followed suit; in fact the celebrations were similar in both regions. Groups of workingmen, including white servants and African Americans, marched through the streets in the evening, parading effigies of the pope, the Scottish Stuart "pretender" to the British throne, and the devil. The festivities culminated with a bonfire, fireworks, drinking, and property destruction. In both places as well, wealthy citizens often stood off to the side, both literally and figuratively, drinking toasts and watching the marchers—at least until the mid-1750s, when the actions of the crowds became more pointed. By then the "mob," as contemporary critics called the marchers, had begun to turn against local civil authority and the colonial upper rank that presumed to wield it.[41]

Paul Gilje, who has studied the Pope's Day festivities in eighteenth-century New York City, suggests two points that bear on this discussion of changes in vernacular recreations. One is that the celebration was an early patriotic, secular holiday, even though it had religious overtones, and it moved from being an evening event to a daytime, day-long affair. In part this was a matter of official action. Civil authorities perceived the destructive, even violent crowd actions as more troublesome and uncontrollable in the dark of the evening than in the light of the day. Thus they banned parades at night. Second, and related to the extending of the affairs, the Pope's Day ceremonies became ritualized. Year after year, the procedures—not only in Boston and New York but also in Marblehead, Salem, Newbury, and Plymouth—acquired the weight of custom, of convention.[42] The parade proceeded with the effigies in place and the messages contained in the images unmistakable. The organizers at least knew where the parade would end; the marchers, the goals. They enjoyed themselves, drinking, carousing, occasionally falling "upon one another wch ye utmost rage & fury" in fisticuffs and wrestling, and especially in the affairs in Boston, joining laborers from different sides of town in a "Union."[43] In short, what civil authorities saw as mob action the marchers saw as an enjoyable experience in community making and resistance to authority.

Historians might view the Pope's Day marches as transitional recreational practices. On the surface they bore little resemblance to the specialized sporting affairs, such as horse, pedestrian, and boat races, that became relatively common in nineteenth-century urban areas. Instead they looked more like the village community affairs, the harvest festivals and wakes, of seventeenth-century Britain, especially in the sense that matches and displays of physical skills were embedded in the broader frame of merrymaking. Yet Pope's Day marches were not residual affairs. They were at once both ends and means of an emergent community of laborers, whose skills in street brawling and active political resistance the organizers of the opposition to Britain would draw on during the 1760s and 1770s.[44] They were also annual rituals and, before the Revolution, nearly autonomous, secular holidays. They were, in effect, not unlike the assemblies and thoroughbred races of the gentry.

The semiautonomy of Pope's Day marches was evident in the sports of other groups of ordinary colonists as well. By midcentury, for example, small planters in Maryland, Virginia, and North Carolina needed no excuse to arrange quarter-mile races, although they continued to do so when the rhythms of tobacco and, gradually, wheat culture permitted. In fact in the latter two colonies the races generated such interest that common planters, tenants, and servants crossed their respective borders either to compete or to gamble on the contests of others.[45] Shooting contests also regularized and occurred independent of gatherings like musters and fairs after the 1730s, when the needs to conserve powder and to avoid popular confusion about whether the shots were alarms of impending danger had diminished. In population centers such as New York and Boston colonists set up targets at distances of a hundred yards or more, and after paying an entry fee, the marksmen took turns shooting. In rural areas, and especially in the backcountry, tavernkeepers or locally renowned individuals organized similar events. Towns like Hagerstown, Maryland, became known for their shooting contests, some of which were distance events whose limits were not absolute measures but a range permitted by the musket barrel. Other contests occurred indoors, where restricted space and the imaginations of the marksmen combined to produce short-range accuracy events such as shooting at candle flames.[46]

In the southern backcountry another recreation that emerged as a nearly autonomous social practice was fistfighting, which Elliott Gorn has examined in detail. Although it had been and remained a means of resolving conflicts among colonists, both ordinary and genteel ones, fistfighting regularized and acquired distinct conventions primarily among farmers, laborers, and itinerant trappers and traders who lived in and near the Appalachian Mountains during the second half of the century. These people lived on the margins (in many senses of the word) of the tidewater civilization from which some of them had migrated in search of cheaper, more fertile land. They were relatively self-sufficient individuals, although never simply subsistence farmers and hunters. Theirs was a predominantly male culture, an oral culture, and a culture in which status was personal and fragile. Among them fistfighting—or as contemporaries called it, "rough and tumbling"—drew from and reinforced their physical, personal styles. The conventions of these contests, which were affairs of honor among intensely competitive individuals, were simple. The contestants used any and all of their skills—kicking, slugging, wrestling, and gouging—until an opponent could no longer continue. Not all the rough-and-tumbling battles were of a kind, however. There were distinctive "abelarding" matches reserved for the most skilled fighters and the most serious challenges. The primary action was gouging, in which the fighters used their fingernails, which they had grown long and then hardened in wax. Using these knifelike nails, the contestants had only one object: to cut off the opponent's sex organ.[47]

Part of the key to understanding why ordinary colonists would set all these affairs apart from ordinary life lies in the fact that they incorporated physical skills that remained useful. In this sense horse races, shooting matches, and fistfights were unlike ball games. This was probably most evident in less settled regions, but even in urban areas the skills remained viable and meaningful. Many colonists, at least the men, continued to settle disputes personally and physically, with fisticuffs. They also owned and traveled by horses, and they needed to augment their diets with game. Thus few ordinary people could afford not to become skilled riders and shots. In addition some colonists enlisted in the militias, where all these skills came into play. Moreover, in both rural and urbanizing areas, ordinary men often derived some measure of their identity from their riding or fighting prowess and their skills with guns.

Not all the recreations that regularized and became nearly autonomous practices, however, incorporated physical skills that retained their utility. Consequently, we should not overemphasize this point or understand it as a condition for the emergent separation of recreations in time and place. Some practices were grounded in the memories and past experiences of groups of colonists. Then too, in coastal towns and cities the transition to capitalism—and with it, the occupational and gender specialization of labor, the redefinition of necessary skills, and the separation of work and play spaces—was underway by midcentury. In Philadelphia, for example, one of the central recreations of laborers, both free and bound, was bullbaiting. Either near taverns or just outside the city limits, butchers commonly provided the bulls and staged the baits in the evenings when dockworkers, servants, and apprentices could steal some time for themselves.[48] Not entirely different were the spinning contests of New England townswomen. Spinning was a traditional female skill, but among these women it was also a residual skill. For several decades they had been purchasing yarns and even ready-made cloth rather than spinning the threads and making their own textiles. In the 1760s, however, when colonists refused to import cloth and clothing from Britain, they resurrected the task as a political act and transformed it into a competitive recreation. Dividing themselves either by neighborhood or by skill level, they raced to see which group could produce more yarn. They also raced for a prize other than skeins of yarn, which were used locally.[49]

Even more than do Pope's Day marches, practices like quarter-mile races and spinning contests—whether they incorporated still viable physical skills or drew on traditional practices that remained meaningful—suggest a subtle but important change in the social locus of some vernacular recreations. These were no longer as thoroughly embedded in the rhythms and relations of ordinary life as preceding practices had been. They were no longer "folk games," to borrow Benjamin Rader's description.[50] Shooting matches, baits, and spinning contests occurred at distinct and occasionally prearranged times and, in the case of some horse races, at specialized tracks. They had conventions governing the performances that producers and consumers alike understood, and as did fistfighting, some of them permitted preparation, if not formal physical training, before the match. They were, in short, emergent forms of recreation, distinct and distinguishable in time and performance from ordinary life.

As such they attest to a broader movement that historians generally have not attributed to ordinary people in the eighteenth century: an emergent separation of labor and leisure. Certainly not all ordinary colonists participated in this movement, nor did it visibly affect sports other than quarter-mile races, shooting and spinning contests, abelarding, and bull baits. One should also not assume that the construction of nearly autonomous matches and other displays of prowess constituted a conscious redrafting of the matches as "modern" leisure practices. Task cycles still largely defined the windows in time for recreations, and one still played with the people with whom one worked. Nor is there much evidence to suggest that ordinary Americans conceived of leisure as a distinctive sphere of life and activity. In fact, reactions to work tasks and conditions, rather than actions taken to expand or predicated on an understanding of leisure as nonwork time, probably propelled the separation. This is particularly clear in the South, where the emergent separation of labor and leisure was pronounced and where an ideological shift had occurred. As early as the 1720s white common planters and servants alike had begun to suspect, if not to suspend, physical labor as something that Africans did. Thereafter few common planters or backcountry farmers bothered to argue that horse races and fistfights were laborlike or even beneficial to labor.[51] They just moved to organize the events.

Events such as horse races and spinning contests were particularly significant to ordinary colonists. Had this not been the case, probably no group would have set a recreation apart from ordinary life. These were exciting and entertaining matches in which individuals earned renown and perhaps material gain and through which groups signaled and cemented their collective interests and identities. In so doing they also set themselves apart from others, both spatially and behaviorally. Moreover, as the experiences of the Pope's Day marchers suggest, they exercised a measure of cultural autonomy and control that some of them rarely achieved otherwise, especially in their work. Indeed, the construction of nearly autonomous recreations by laborers, common planters, and townswomen was no small feat at a time when the upper rank held substantial political, economic, and cultural leverage. Beyond indicating the persisting significance of physical recreations, then, baits, races, and spinning contests testify to the persisting agency of ordinary people in the making of popular culture.

Exchanges between the Ranks

The discussion so far has ignored an important point: there was a good deal of interaction between the ranks. Neither style developed in isolation, as even the boundaries themselves suggest. Gentlemen and gentlewomen were conscious of the practices of ordinary people, just as laborers, common planters, and artisans were of those of their "superiors." They lived too close to one another not to know what the other was doing and saying through physical recreations. They shared public spaces: roads, docks, and fields. They traded for or purchased goods and animals from each other. They observed each other's races and fights, and they appreciated a sterling physical display of strength and speed when they saw one. To the extent that sporting matches and displays of prowess drew from common interests and served as a common language, as they had in William Byrd's day, they deterred the nonporous rank boundaries evident in Britain.[52]

Exchanges between elite and ordinary colonists took many forms. There was, for instance, the matter of borrowing recreational forms, by which each rank extended its repertory. In New England assembly participants in towns such as Boston, Salem, and Newport incorporated within their programs country dances drawn from their less wealthy neighbors. Boat racing in New York apparently originated with the upper rank, especially Dutch descendants; after the turn of the century, however, workingmen who transported goods along the Hudson River or worked the docks in New York

City adopted and adapted the practice. In other places as well, the assimilation of recreations was relatively common and beneficial to the borrowers.[53] The process extended the range of practices known to either rank and expanded the cultural core.

Other exchanges affirmed physical recreations as core cultural practices. This was perhaps most evident in the numerous commercial exchanges between the ranks. At midcentury most provincial legislatures maintained the bounty system, which gave official support to hunting and provided colonists who existed on the economic margins with some income. Colonial craftspeople sanctioned the sporting tastes of the upper rank as they made goods, ranging from billiard tables to leather riding crops, for sale to and use by gentlemen and gentlewomen. In time and in turn, however, these goods would also be in demand by an emerging urban middle rank for whom genteel refinement had become meaningful.[54] The shared interest in commerce thus mitigated the self-interest manifested in distinctive and distinguishing sporting styles.

On rare occasions as well, exchanges between genteel and ordinary colonists produced something that affected an entire community. A case in point was thoroughbred racing in the Chesapeake, which became the paramount secular ritual in the tidewater region of Maryland and Virginia after midcentury. As suggested earlier, the sport was particularly significant to the upper rank. They flocked to the races to see and be seen. Pictures of stallions and mares hung on the walls of great houses. Racing stables figured in the design of the plantation grounds. Terms from breeding and racing seeped into daily conversation.[55]

Still, thoroughbred racing was not simply a construction of the upper rank, nor was it a mirror image of British racing. Chesapeake gentlemen did race only against one another, and they did run their horses in heats, as British race men did, with two or three heats over distances of two, three, and four miles constituting a match. They did not, however, race on the flat, be that road or field. Instead they built oval or round tracks that were often a mile in circumference. And they did so, it seems, to accommodate the "others." Thousands of spectators swelled the populations of small towns such as Williamsburg, Annapolis, and Richmond, but only a few were gentlemen waiting for their turn to race. Among the rest who watched the horses go round and round were ordinary colonists, including common planters who were prospective buyers of stock and semen. Others were slaves, who sometimes attended a horse and his master but who also came to watch, gamble, and visit friends and relatives. For them, as for most people, the races were extraordinary occasions, no matter how often they occurred.[56]

In effect thoroughbred racing in the Chesapeake was a negotiated practice. The gentry owned and ran the horses, but they did not "own" the sport. Horses and racing were too important to many people in the region to be controlled by the few. Moreover, these few never had the cultural power that their peers in Britain had. They were not a hereditary elite, nor could they, on practical economic and political grounds, operate as independently of common planters and servants and slaves as did the British upper rank. They also existed within a larger imperial context in which the great planters were a less than powerful minority. They were actually on the margins. By British standards, they were relatively poor, a fact reinforced by their debts to British merchants, and relatively powerless, as their inability to create a colonial alliance or to gain representation in Parliament suggested.[57] Only the War for Independence would alter this relationship. Even in that event, however, the provincial upper rank would depend on the alliances developed with ordinary colonists in practices such as thoroughbred racing.

Perhaps because the status of the provincial upper rank was fragile and subject to ongoing negotiations, the holders of status felt compelled to protect their prerogatives, to secure the boundaries that separated genteel and vernacular, in particular circumstances. The boundaries between the ranks were real, and relations between ordinary and genteel colonists were not always so cordial and absorptive as they were in thoroughbred racing. Gentlemen did use their sporting prowess, their equipment, and even their thoroughbreds to dominate, to remind ordinary farmers and servants of their place, especially in contexts in which genteel self-interest weighed more heavily than community solidarity. Moreover, the laws enacted and enforced by upper-rank colonists who sat in provincial legislatures and town councils and as selectmen and justices of the peace point to a dislike for, and even a rejection of, particular vernacular experiences. Gambling by people of marginal means, sporting on the Sabbath, riots and property destruction associated with popular gatherings like Pope's Day marches—all were subject to proscription in statutes and acts. Critics believed that such endeavors threatened the peace and economic stability of a locale, as well as the order of society. In what remained a hierarchical society, men of means continued to see themselves, if not as authoritarian governors, certainly as champions of the public interest—especially when that interest coincided with their interests.

Ordinary colonists in turn occasionally reacted to genteel efforts to dominate and control, as well as to what some people viewed as residual privileges. Expressions of fear were not unknown, as was the case with Devereux Jarratt, the son of a small farmer in New Kent County, Virginia, who "would run off, as for my life," when a gentleman approached on a road.[58] Probably more common, however, were instances of opposition and resistance, especially on the part of white colonists. Rhode Island farmers, for instance, demanded and then defended in public what they viewed as their rights to fish in local rivers.[59] Throughout the colonies laborers, craftspeople, and small landowners alike either ignored or actively protested, depending on one's interpretation, some of the laws passed to constrain particular behaviors. Some people engaged in "Sporting, Laughing . . . and drinking rum" on Sunday afternoons, whereas others turned to "cudgeling and breaking of heads" after a disputed election.[60] The worst-case scenario, however, at least for the gentleman, was the physical attack. In 1779 a doctor in Virginia lost an eye when a small planter with whom he had been playing billiards turned on the doctor and beat him with the cue stick.[61]

These acts of domination and resistance on the part of genteel and ordinary colonists speak to the limits of traditions in a multirank, multiracial, multigender society such as the British colonies on the mainland of North America were in the middle of the eighteenth century. Traditions bind people to particular ways of behaving and thinking, but they are meaningful only in particular contexts, and they are binding primarily on the makers. They are not a panacea for all the troubles and tensions faced by a group of people, and they do not resolve differences between groups. Indeed, traditions express and even intensify differences between groups, which is precisely what the sporting patterns of genteel and ordinary colonists did. As fairly elaborate cultural statements, both styles-become-traditions clarified differences between the ranks—their means, their gatherings, their relations, their values. No manner of borrowing and assimilation could entirely overcome the differences captured in practices such as thoroughbred and quarter-mile racing, or yacht and canoe races, or hunting on preserves and diving after alligators.

Nor for that matter could the frequent exchanges between genteel and ordinary colonists at the taverns, which remained common sites for sports and other physical recreations, overcome the differences between them.

Here there was significant sharing, to be sure, even to the point of gentlemen and ordinary men competing against one another. Tavern experiences thus might result in the suspension of style preferences and differences, but not their abandonment. Moreover, common tavern recreational practices helped to clarify, especially for members of the upper rank, another critical boundary—that between labor and leisure.

7

Taverns and Sports

Today, about twelve miles east of Winchester, Virginia, near the intersection of state routes 340 and 7, is the small burg of Berryville. The town acquired its name from Benjamin Berry, who operated a tavern there in the middle of the eighteenth century. As was true generally of the Appalachian foothills before the War for Independence, the area surrounding Berryville had a small and scattered population. Some people who had left the tidewater in search of cheaper, more fertile land lived and worked on plantations and farms. Itinerants were also present; immigrants from Europe and from the eastern parts of the mid-Atlantic colonies, they were making their way south or west, beyond the Blue Ridge Mountains. Other passersby were hunters and traders who harvested the produce of the forests or exchanged goods with the Native American tribes to the west. Finally, there were teamsters, the wagon drivers who transported goods and people throughout the region now bisected by Interstate 81. Benjamin Berry served them all.

In Berry's day the village had not acquired its current name. Locals called it "Battletown"—because of what occurred at the tavern. Apparently Berry was an astute businessman. Not only had he wisely placed his tavern where people were or would be, but he also offered what prospective clients needed and wanted. He provided services that colonial laws mandated of tavernkeepers: beds, food, and stabling for horses. He sold alcoholic beverages, some of which he probably brewed, both by the glass and by the bottle, and as his customers sat and drank, they could join in a card or dice game or venture outside to play at ninepins or watch a cockfight. He also encouraged other sporting "battles": bear baits, fistfights, and wrestling matches. Outside the tavern Berry constructed a pit for the animal contests, and he retained some local strongmen to fight the wagon drivers when they stopped for refreshment and entertainment. After the teamsters had finished, they returned to drinking his liquor.[1]

Benjamin Berry was not necessarily a typical mid-eighteenth-century tavernkeeper. As a promoter of sporting events, he had few peers. Nonetheless, no keeper could entirely ignore what Berry saw clearly. Patrons of all ranks, races, and genders came to the taverns not just to conduct business or to refresh themselves but also to play and display their prowess. As were food and drink, sports and other physical recreations were a part of the ordinary fare of the taverns, or as contemporaries often called them, the "ordinaries."

Taverns were the most visible sporting houses of the eighteenth century. In fact, except for the impromptu matches that erupted on the streets or in the fields, taverns offered the "only game in town" in some communities. Many taverns played to the irregular rhythms that still characterized the lives and lifestyles of many colonists, especially ordinary colonists. They also occasionally catered to particular groups of colonists, and to stay in what became an increasingly competitive business, keepers had to provide their customers with what they wanted—liquor, food, and sports popular among their clients—even if that meant running afoul of laws and critics. By the 1770s some tavernkeepers found it difficult not to become embroiled in controversy. Taverns and tavern sports and other displays of prowess lay at the center of a sometimes virulent conflict about the course and content of popular behaviors.

Taverns and Tavernkeepers

Taverns were ubiquitous in colonial life. In the seventeenth century they appeared wherever people congregated, occasionally before the local church did. Rural taverns emerged at ferries, along major thoroughfares, and at crossroads where enough people met to warrant the construction of courthouses, and as one eighteenth-century observer snidely remarked, thus began the linkage of taverns and the "advancement of justice."[2] Some of these "public houses" were independent structures, but others were rooms within or attachments to people's houses in the style of poor English alehouses. Town taverns were not much different. They were simply more numerous, in part because there were more customers.[3]

Over time taverns became more widespread. In rural areas the expanding web of farms and plantations made taverns more rather than less necessary in the latter half of the seventeenth and throughout the eighteenth century. They were places to which locals came to conduct business and drink with friends and in which travelers rested before they took to the road again.[4] Urban taverns also proliferated as the population increased and economic and social activity expanded. The trend was particularly evident in the largest towns, for which numerical estimates are possible. In 1685 William Penn, the proprietor of Pennsylvania, authorized seven ordinaries in Philadelphia "for the Intertainment of Strangers and Workmen, that are not Housekeepers."[5] In the next decade a dozen taverns existed in the burgeoning town, prompting Penn and the assembly to agree that "there are too many" such establishments.[6] Their opinion apparently mattered little, for in subsequent years the numbers increased. By 1731 there were nearly 100 legal taverns in Philadelphia, a figure that rose to 120 in the mid-1750s, when the population neared 18,000. Similarly, New York City had approximately 100 taverns at midcentury, for a population that was only slightly smaller than its southern competitor's.[7] In effect both colonial cities offered one licensed tavern—and untold numbers of unlicensed houses—for every 150 citizens, a ratio eclipsed only by older and larger cities such as Paris and Amsterdam. Estimates for the former metropolis suggest the existence of one legal drinking establishment for every 100 citizens in the middle of the eighteenth century.[8]

Why were taverns so common? Contemporary expectations and demands provide a part of the answer. Throughout the colonies the assemblies assigned particular functions to ordinaries, especially the provision of overnight lodging, food, and drink for travelers, and laws specified the price and quality of these services.[9] But taverns were sites for other activities as well. Indeed, colonists also knew them as "common houses of entertainment." Local residents came to the ordinary to catch up on the news and to discuss and debate politics; merchants, ship captains, and visitors, to receive their mail. Farmers, merchants, and artisans conducted business at the tavern, either in public view or, if the tavern was large enough, in a back room, and they attended court meetings in taverns. Passengers on the stage lines boarded their vehicles outside the building, while political allies and, eventually, factions and parties met inside. And after, or even as, colonists completed the tasks at hand, they could quench their thirst from the keeper's store of alcoholic beverages and play at or watch a contest in progress. Eighteenth-century taverns were quintessential "public houses."[10]

Taverns also underlay individuals' economies. Tavernkeeping was a common occupation, although it could also be a short-lived one. In Baltimore County, Maryland, for instance, only 180 of 325 keepers between 1755 and 1780 had licenses for two or more years, and only 26 operated for a decade or more.[11] The fact that many proprietors did other work, authorities' support of widows' applications for licenses, and inventories of deceased keepers' estates all suggest that some colonists entered the business to sustain themselves at a level approaching the Puritans' "competency." With so many licensed keepers, especially in towns and cities, the trade was competitive, but the prospect of earning enough money to supplement one's income no doubt led some people to invest in or acquire on credit the stock and building needed to set up shop. Certainly tavernkeeping rarely led to substantial wealth. Honest keepers did earn respect and even some leverage among their neighbors and customers. Few of them, however, were ever as well off as Samuel Fraunces was in New York City in 1762. Of African descent and a migrant from the West Indies, Fraunces purchased the three-and-a-half-story mansion of Stephen Delancey for the relatively large sum of £2,000 and then transformed it into the Queen's Head tavern, at which he served the city's elite. Even Fraunces, however, was not able to maintain his wealth. He moved from tavern to tavern and even from city to city as his personal fortunes waxed and waned.[12]

Who were the tavernkeepers? In the eighteenth century most tavernkeepers were white, and until after the War for Independence, perhaps two-thirds were men.[13] They also represented a range of occupational and wealth groups. Rural male taverners were farmers or planters and, on occasion, ferry operators or small storekeepers. Tavernkeepers in towns were tradespeople and artisans—scriveners, hatters, watchmakers, even blacksmiths—whereas others had been mariners or ship captains or were shopkeepers and constables. A few were substantial merchants and manufacturers or, on occasion, professional tavernkeepers like Fraunces. Women, in contrast, were primarily housekeepers who had little access to other occupations and for whom tavernkeeping was an important source of income. Many female tavernkeepers were widows and single women, and some of them inherited a tavern from a husband or father or had a male relative post a bond so that they could establish a tavern. On occasion as well, a husband and wife both held licenses and jointly ran an establishment, or the woman managed it while her spouse worked at another trade.[14]

Running a tavern was never a simple or certain enterprise. Probably the easiest task was to obtain a license, for which one posted a bond with the county or mayor's courts and paid a fee, usually under £10 pounds. Securing a building was more difficult, especially when a prospective tavernkeeper was poor. In urban areas few tavernkeepers apparently owned their taverns; they rented or managed someone else's tavern. Some rural keepers did own their taverns, or the room in the house that served as the tavern, but ownership did not guarantee success. Finding a good location, a potentially profitable site, was always a challenge. Then there were the outlays for stocking the tavern with furniture, food and drink, and provisions for horses. Keepers also had to pay taxes, even on billiard tables, and to face authorities. Additionally, compared to other enterprises in the colonies, taverns faced many regulations. Besides defining minimum services and furnishings, provincial laws and local acts established retail prices, how much and to whom a keeper could extend credit, what behaviors they could permit, and in some places, how late they could stay open. To struggling tavernkeepers the fact that few local authorities regularly enforced the laws or that the patronage of a genteel patron might encourage stalwart constables to look the other way probably provided little relief.[15]

Finally, there was the important matter of attracting customers. From the beginning taverns were service enterprises dependent on demand. Even having the only tavern in an area did not guarantee success. If local planters or laborers did not like the type and quality of a keeper's services, they found alternative sources of refreshment and entertainment. In the eighteenth century tavern customers had other options, even in rural areas. Planters welcomed travelers to their homes for overnight or longer stays; urban boarding houses opened; liquor and other beverages were available from many sources, including private stills; and sports and games occurred in numerous venues. Then too, as ranks formalized and society stratified, tavernkeepers found themselves catering only to some people in a block or a county. Urban taverns in particular specialized as the eighteenth century proceeded. In cities such as New York, "low pot houses" and English coffeehouses were no longer the only distinctive forms. Taverns for merchants and planters, for seamen, for artisans, and so on emerged. The trend toward customer specialization was not as evident in rural areas, but even there tavernkeepers had either to offer multiple services to attract patrons from many ranks or to be content with a narrow range of clients and at best marginal profits.[16]

It was in the context of the quest for customers and their dollars that sports and other displays of prowess figured in the operation of taverns. Colonial statutes had long emphasized the lodging and eating functions of taverns, and many ordinaries did offer these services. Tavern patrons, however, also enjoyed and demand other options, especially for liquor, games, matches, and socializing—all of which amounted to "entertainment" in a different sense than lawmakers intended. Tavernkeepers, in turn, obliged their customers, even to the point of risking fines and imprisonment for permitting proscribed activities.

Sporting Life in the Taverns

Taverns were hubs of activity from daybreak, and sometimes before, to late evening and sometimes beyond. Laborers, seamen, and artisans occasionally began their days there with a dram and a meal, as did stage drivers, post riders, and travelers, although they started later; tavernkeepers often provided the formal breakfast at nine o'clock. Thereafter other locals stopped by for a drink, to get the news, or to rent a room, if there was one, for a meeting later in the day. Shortly after noon on an ordinary day, the first card or ninepins games began, along with the inevitable wagering. Tavernkeepers then served dinner about two o'clock and drinks throughout the afternoon. Customers continued to appear erratically, unless a court meeting, a political debate, a cock main, or a fistfight were on the docket. In the evening the pace quickened: supper at seven o'clock, more drinks, a shooting contest and card play, a rendezvous in a back room, a round of dancing, a fight between inebriated adversaries, a political or philosophical discussion. All and more were framed within the collage of tavern life.

Sports and other physical recreations were core activities in eighteenth-century taverns. Some practices were particularly suited to—indeed, were partly defined by—the internal environment of the ordinary, and they were nearly as common as were taverns themselves. Card and dice games required only tables and chairs and were easily played, or perhaps better played, as people sat, conversed, and drank. Shooting contests in which the targets were things normally found indoors, such as candle flames that a marksman tried to "snuff," also occurred, as did dancing and more than a few fistfights.[17]

Outside the tavern were space and, occasionally, equipment and facilities for other practices. Many keepers provided places for ninepins, if not formal alleys. Urban proprietors permitted this traditional bowling game in the lot or lane behind or next to the tavern, whereas rural taverns usually had enough land in front. The physical requirements were minimal and unstandardized; a narrow strip of ground, minimally twenty or thirty feet long, was sufficient to allow contestants to take turns at trying to knock down the pins, arrayed in three rows of three, with a wooden or stone "ball." Quoits was similar, in terms of both space and format. Originally a game played by agricultural laborers who took breaks in their work to toss stones at a target in a field, mid-eighteenth-century quoits required only a straight-away, a meg or stake, and a doughnut-shaped stone or piece of iron with a hole in the center. The object of the thrower was to "ring" the meg with the quoit, or at least to toss the object closer to the stake than the opponents did. Eventually horseshoes would serve the same purpose.[18]

Tavern grounds were also the sites for more physical matches between humans or animals. Cricket games between teams of gentlemen took place at taverns, as did the bull and bear baits that appealed to laborers. Horse races occasionally started or were arranged at the ordinary, and especially in the backcountry, tavernkeepers like Benjamin Berry permitted and even promoted fistfights and wrestling bouts. Perhaps the most common sport on the grounds of the taverns, however, was cockfighting, which, outside New England at least, drew people of all ranks and races. Tavernkeepers were well aware of the popular interest in the event. Some of them built formal pits, which ranged from simple holes in the ground covered by boards when not in use to elaborate stagelike facilities. Others provided open spaces for matches, or single contests between fighting birds, as well as "mains," which were a series of fights.[19]

Cockfighting flourished in the eighteenth century, especially from New York southward. Precisely when, where, and in what form battles between fighting chickens first occurred in the colonies remains unknown; the second half of the seventeenth century, when Shrove Tuesday celebrations re-emerged, seems likely. By the turn of the century cockfights were relatively common in the environs of New York City, owing in part to the region's trade in goods and people with the West Indies and especially Barbados. In 1724 Hugh Jones, an Anglican minister posted in Virginia, noted that the sport was already popular there among common planters. Tavernkeepers in the Carolinas were building pits by 1732, and before midcentury the sport had spread to the towns surrounding Boston. By the 1740s it was a staple of tavern life, although the fights certainly occurred in other venues, and it was popular among servants and slaves, as well as free colonists.[20]

Cockfighting was like other eighteenth-century sporting practices in that it was both simple and complex. The battle itself was the simple part.

Owners loosed their fighting fowl in a ring, preferably an enclosed "pit" that provided protection for spectators. Spectators standing around the pit watched the birds strike one another with beaks, claws, and metal spurs, or gaffs, attached to each leg. The fight, which could be over in seconds or a few minutes, ended once one of the birds was either dead or too maimed to continue.

More complex were the preparations, which were not only extensive but also pursued with a seriousness usually reserved for life-and-death struggles—or for horse races. Planters and tavernkeepers, as well as farmers and merchants, either raised or imported fowl that were specifically bred for limb speed and ferocity. They also clipped the birds' wings and feathers, fed them special diets, and trained them via mock fights to enhance their aggressiveness. Finally, some owners either assigned a servant or slave or hired a neighbor to care for the birds and oversee their training.[21]

Why would colonists go to such lengths when there was little certainty that one's bird would survive to fight another day? The inferences drawn by scholars who have examined the sport and the patterns of its adherents are suggestive. Clifford Geertz, who observed the sport on the Indonesian island of Bali, provided the classic psychological explanation. The fighting cocks, Geertz wrote, were surrogates for their owners' personalities. Their battle required and displayed immense physical prowess, and it was often a fight for status, which was crucial to life itself and to individuals' conceptions of themselves in the hierarchical society on Bali. Owners thus saw the stakes as enormous, perhaps higher than they could ever realize or rationalize, and the practice of gambling and the multiple layers of wagers reinforced the stakes.[22] Cockfights were, in short, instances of what Jeremy Bentham meant by the phrase "deep play."[23] Everything and anything of significance was on the line in this contest, which was by no means playful in any abstract, modern sense. Moreover, the owner of a winning fighting cock was not likely to recoup all that he—the owners were men— had invested, psychically or materially.

More recently Rhys Isaac applied Geertz's and Bentham's reasoning to cockfighting in mid-eighteenth-century Virginia. Isaac noted the commonness of cockfights and the seriousness with which producers and consumers approached them, and he suggested that what Geertz had observed in Bali also occurred in the British colony. Virginians manifested a not entirely rational affinity for deep play, Isaac argued.[24] That they did so was likely of matter of persisting traditions, at least in part. In Virginia and elsewhere in the South, some Anglo-American men disavowed hard, physical work and valued particular physical recreations, as had their ancestors in Britain. Cockfighting thus linked them to prior generations for whom play, rather than work, was meaningful. It was, in short, a contemporary manifestation of the traditional leisure preference.

The contemporary social power of cockfighting rested on more than the ways of a still meaningful past, however. As it did in twentieth-century Bali, the sport had a particular appeal in light of the stratified social structure and prevailing rank, gender, and—in Virginia—race relations. According to Isaac, cockfights and other public sporting events enabled the human participants to suspend ordinary social conventions and boundaries.[25] Indeed, cockfights were the produce of social rules suspended; they were practices negotiated by a variety of people in an extraordinary setting where what was ordinary did not hold sway. Owners of the cocks incorporated any training maneuver or match strategy deemed advantageous, regardless of the social position of its developer—a position that usually mattered in other contexts. Then, too, free men, women, and slaves attended the mains, not as passive spectators, but as wagerers, people whose gender and race differences did not deter the gambling contests among themselves. On occasion as well, members of both ranks, who otherwise would have competed in separate events, actually cooperated in constructing the central battle. They pitted their fighting chickens against one another's, literally on the same plain. For both, the fight—on which they might also wager substantial sums—was no laughing matter, and for the moment the divisions between them eroded. One who won, won big: some thing, perhaps money or tobacco of material value, and almost certainly respect or acclaim.[26]

The social leveling effect of tavern sports such as cockfighting thus was real, but it was also fleeting, at least in the South. After a match a human victor was not likely to find much changed. The sums won did not equal the investment of time and money, nor were they sufficient to propel the common planter into the upper rank, the great planter downward, or women and slaves anywhere. Moreover, except for cockfights, opportunities for interrank and interracial contests were infrequent. Separate contests for gentlemen, for common planters and small farmers, for laborers, and for slaves were more common, although gentry often supported the events of the others.[27] Indeed, the practice of genteel patronage, which had itself become a custom, reinforced socially constructed and persisting rank and racial lines. As was the case with horse racing, gentlemen who permitted or actively supported cockfighting among their neighbors and laborers probably gained much, at least in terms of local goodwill and work force harmony, at relatively little cost. Beyond the shadow of the cock pit, the gentleman's extensive material holdings held sway.

Neither taverns nor tavern games and matches were inherently capable of overcoming persistent social constructions of difference, particularly but probably not only in the South. Some historians have claimed that taverns, regardless of location, were great democratic melting pots and that customers tended to put aside their differences and either to "belly up to the bar" or to congregate at the gaming tables and cock pits as if they were one people.[28] This broad effect seems unlikely, especially given persisting rank, gender, and race divisions throughout the colonies. Occasionally, of course, in the context of popular public rituals such as horse races and cockfights, the physical environment of taverns, the fanatic interest in the sports, and the effect of liquor did encourage colonists to cross social boundaries. Still, the passage was short-lived. Once a race or match had ended and the bottle was empty, social differences and divisions reemerged.

Particular differences actually deepened within the taverns and in the course of tavern sports as the eighteenth century advanced. One obvious pattern, as noted earlier, was the specialization of taverns by rank, occupation, and race. Taverners in turn provided for physical recreations of interest to their customers. Urban keepers whose clients were large landowners and merchants, for example, had billiard and card tables, and they were likely to have multiple rooms, one of which could be turned over to dancing for men and women, at least until assembly rooms appeared after midcentury. Taverns whose customers were hunters and trappers, small planters, laborers, seamen, and African Americans, both slaves and freed people, tended to sponsor or permit practices popular among their clients. In such places bull baits, shooting matches, ninepins, and country dances, among other practices, were common. Some taverns even became locally renowned as centers for particular vernacular sports.[29]

For ordinary people, taverns appear to have been especially important recreational centers in the eighteenth century. This is not particularly surprising given the marginal infrastructure of facilities and institutions supporting popular sports. Moreover, taverns had long been social centers for ordinary people, and eighteenth-century colonists continued to see them as such. They went to the ordinaries for many reasons, not the least of which was to enjoy themselves. Tavernkeepers like Benjamin Berry, in turn, actively catered to ordinary people; they came from their ranks and were neighbors, relatives, or friends. They thus permitted practices such as drinking and gambling that civil authorities had legislated against but that remained popular. They also kept their doors open for hours to accommodate the often irregular rhythms of ordinary peoples' lives, and they were not immune to the commercial possibilities of particular physical skills and performances. In the taverns many sporting entrepreneurs—exhibitors of equine skills, tumblers, acrobats, fighters, and eventually, people who claimed card playing and other gambling games as their means of making a living—found homes and audiences.[30]

Taverns also had historically been places for respites, even refuges from the outside world, and their appeal as such persisted among ordinary people in the eighteenth century. In the taverns ordinary colonists could do what was either more difficult or impossible to do elsewhere. They could engage in shooting matches that stretched for hours and concluded only after an inebriated human assumed the role of target and ended up dead. They could go to a tavern after a disputed election, drink heartily, and then resume the unresolved contest with cudgeling. They could momentarily escape the shackles of servitude or slavery by dancing away the night, women and men intimately coupled in a physical and social relationship that was rarely achieved on the plantation or the ship. They could even vent their rage at the "cheat" or the privileged upper rank. A fistfight with a gentleman or beating him senseless with a billiard cue was no small matter of besting one's superior in a society where opportunities for more permanent gains were limited.[31]

Running through many of the accounts and records of tavern life is a behavioral theme that appears to be, if not a normative dimension of affairs there, certainly not an abnormal one: violence. Colonists rarely used the word; they spoke of assaults, beatings, and even battery instead. And there was probably a fine line between, and much ideological mediation of, actions understood or intended as violent ones on the one hand and the displays of strength, stamina, power, speed, and agility observed in physical recreations on the other. Moreover, the two sets of actions were not entirely separable, for instances of excessive force and other forms of abuse occurred in the course of some sports. Sometimes men were involved as both aggressors and victims. Occasionally fistfights and shooting matches between ordinary colonists culminated in violent ends, sometimes including the death of one of the contestants. Then too, retribution against a gentleman was not unknown.[32]

Women also committed and suffered from violent actions. Like their male contemporaries, female patrons resorted to physical violence, especially in urban taverns and at least against other women. Such was the case with Isabella Arena, who had been drinking heavily in an ordinary run by Elizabeth Kelly in Annapolis, Maryland, in 1747. After Kelly asked Arena to leave, the inebriated customer snarled and then swung at the owner; Kelly apparently returned the favor.[33] More commonly, however, women were the objects of attacks, abuse, and other aggressive acts. Some of them were barmaids whom male customers verbally upbraided for not delivering the drink or the meal quickly enough. Female patrons and keepers also endured physical assaults, and not always from other women. Finally, a few of the abused women were prostitutes, who were present in the taverns as producers of physical recreations. Their labor entertained male tavern customers, and had the women not toiled at sexual tasks, some of them might have been out on the streets begging.[34]

These encounters point us toward a larger picture of what was happening in the taverns in the middle decades of the eighteenth century. Taverns were sites for social contests, of which sports and other displays of prowess were one form. Horse races, cockfights, and games like ninepins pitted the strength, speed, and cunning of one participant against another. Even mixed dancing could involve contesting. William Black, a traveling Pennsylvanian, thought he observed precisely that at a ball in an Annapolis tavern in 1744, where the women rather than the men generated the action. They were testing the "strength and vigor" of their partners, as well as trying to convince the men of their own "Activity and Sprightliness," Black concluded.[35] He clearly was amazed, although he need not have been. In a society that continued to value physical prowess and expressiveness, taverngoers often constructed scenes in which physical discourse had center stage.

There were other contests in the taverns as well. Embedded in court meetings were struggles for social justice, as judges and juries heard and then rendered decisions about the claims of accusers and accused. Taverns also housed political debates and election disputes, as well as contests that were less formally arraigned and arranged but still highly charged. Tavernkeepers who allowed African slaves to gather in their establishments, for example, implicitly if not explicitly challenged local or provincial authorities. A gentleman who refused to "stand a round" confronted the customary expectations of common planters and small farmers, and the latter two groups were free to withhold their votes or their deference.

Taverns were more than simply sites of contests for social power, however. They were also contested domains, their content subject to ongoing negotiations. Patrons, keepers, and surrounding communities all played a role, and probably multiple roles, in the bargaining, mediation, and overt challenges that involved services, prices, permitted behaviors, activity-governing conventions, and the positions and prerogatives of people of various ranks, genders, and races. Also playing a role in these negotiations were agents of official culture, especially members of the provincial legislatures and local governments, who attempted to regulate taverns and tavern activities. Absent regular and effective enforcement of most laws and acts, and given the interests of taverngoers, however, many of the behaviors deemed undesirable and illegal by official culture were common. So, in the middle decades of the eighteenth century, critics of tavern life went on the offensive, and the contest for what went on in the ordinaries became more heated.

Criticisms of Taverns and Tavern Activities

The decade of the 1730s was pivotal in the history of tavern criticism. Prior to that time most concerns appeared in preambles to laws and in ministerial sermons. Thereafter membership in the chorus of criticism expanded, and the tone and content of the litany grew more harsh and pointed. Individuals and groups of colonists voiced their concerns through petitions, instructions to prospective tavernkeepers, letters in newspapers, and orally. Their messages originated in diverse movements—the Great Awakening, the Enlightenment, changes in the political cultures in some colonies, and the nascent economic diversification and restructuring—but they converged on a common theme. Taverns were no longer simply necessary establishments, or even necessary evils, the critics maintained. Especially but not only in urbanizing areas, they had become dens of iniquity that threatened the peace, stability, and moral rightness of colonial society, a society in which many of the critics had a stake. Whether as governors, officers in the churches, or private citizens, many of the objectors to contemporary tavern affairs were men who belonged to the upper and emergent middling ranks.

The attack on taverns was two-pronged. On the one hand, some critics maintained that tavernkeepers bore some responsibility for what the Braintree, Massachusetts, selectmen termed in 1761 the "present prevailing Depravity of Manners."[36] They tolerated many behaviors, including "Quarreling and fighting," sexual license and other "lewd lascivious behavior," illegal sports and recreations, gambling, rioting, and excessive drinking.[37] But the source of the "problem" extended beyond keepers who maintained lax discipline.

Ordinaries had become the "haunts" of "loose, idle, and disorderly" persons, other detractors charged.[38] Here "many People," especially of the "poorer Sort," came to "loiter and waste their Time."[39] Here sailors and servants "spent all their wages" or expended their owners' or employers' credit in tippling and gaming. They also used tavern visits as excuses to "run away."[40] Here "youths" were "greatly corrupted [and] in their Morals render'd disobedient, unruly, and Insolent."[41] Here, as the ruling council in Georgia in 1742 succinctly put the rank bias shared by would-be censors throughout the colonies, the "common people" came to "debauch themselves."[42]

At the core of this "debauchery" lay a trio of particularly problematic behaviors, according to unsympathetic observers of taverns. One was "tippling," or habitual drinking, which was quite different from the ordinary, necessary, and nearly universal consumption of alcoholic beverages. In fact, many colonists probably agreed with John DeBrahm, a surveyor in the South at midcentury, who maintained that a "person otherwise of healthy Disposition may preserve his Health by . . . mixing always the best Spirits with his drinks."[43] Tippling, however, exceeded ordinary consumption, in terms of both frequency and amount, and it could lead to drunkenness. Drunkenness not only injured one's health, the critics charged, but also led to fighting, property destruction, riot, runaways, indebtedness, and poverty.[44]

Tavern critics also maintained that tippling and drunkenness went hand in hand with idleness, another of the problematic behaviors. Drunkards, they believed, tended to be idlers, a combination that worsened the situation not only for the drinkers but also for the tavernkeepers and for society at large. Drunken idlers, or idle drunkards and tipplers, could never pay for what they consumed, so somebody else bore the expense.[45]

Implicit in this argument was the tavern opponents' belief that idleness was "uneconomic." It was unproductive, even wasteful, and it was surely not work—nor, as will be seen in the next chapter, was it "leisure." Methodist and Baptist ministers in the South, where evangelical Protestantism was particularly vibrant, also argued that idleness was immoral, but even they tended to view immorality as a consequence, or at least a derivative, of the uneconomy of idleness.[46] Whether tavern visits and rhythms encouraged or accommodated idleness, however, was an open question. Some critics associated idleness with "sloathfulness" and, by extension, with "lazy" people, many of whom were of the "poorer sort," even vagabonds and beggars, servants, and slaves. Again, the rank bias was at work. Other objectors depersonalized idleness. For them, idleness was the unproductive use of time, which taverns and the unproductive activities popular there abetted.[47]

Just as tavern critics linked drunkenness and idleness, so they also coupled idleness and the final "problem" behavior: gambling and, in an extreme form, gaming. Gambling was the practice of staking something of value, usually material value, on one's or one's animal's prowess. It involved risk taking in a contest or a display, recreative or not, and for many colonists, gambling appears to have been the sine qua non of sporting matches and contests—horse races, bull baits, cards, and more. The greater the risk, as when the skills of the players were relatively equal or when multiple factors beyond the control of the participants might influence the outcome, the higher the stakes and the more numerous the wagers or bets.

Contests with significant and multiple risks were the stuff of dreams for "gamesters," people who wagered habitually, often excessively, and on occasion, deceitfully. Indeed, as George Webb, a justice of the peace in New Kent County, Virginia, concluded in 1736 after he had spent considerable time trying to interpret an English law involving gambling in games and other contests, deceit lay at the heart of an important distinction: "Playing at Cards, Dice, and the like, are not prohibited at Common Law, but only that Deceit shall not be used in such Play; neither are they evil in themselves, abstracedly [*sic*] considered: And therefore, the Statute [33 Henry 8. cap. 9] which prohibits them to certain Persons, and Places, yet exempts others, and tolerates them to All, at certain Times, and on certain Conditions: The Intent and Policy of the Statute appears to be, to prevent unlawful, crafty, and deceitful Gaming, and the inordinate haunting Alehouses, and Tipling Places."[48] Over time Webb's phrase "deceitful gaming" became something of a redundancy, and legislatures in many colonies, including Virginia, prohibited just "Gaming for Money or other Gain" or the amorphous "excessive" gaming.[49] The latter phrase especially was sufficient to distinguish gaming from gambling for small stakes—without extinguishing the suspicion that gamesters also cheated.

This distinction between gambling and gaming was not unlike that between drinking and drunkenness, and it drew from a similar rationale. Gaming and drunkenness were out-of-the-ordinary, immoderate forms of gambling and drinking, respectively. Gambling, of course, was like drinking in that it was a common practice. In fact, it was probably so common, even in New England, where some people still considered it sinful, that no official could or would have eliminated it from ordinary life.[50] Certainly gambling knew no human boundaries. Africans wagered on their skills and, if they were slaves, those of their owners. Native Americans were also fond of gambling, and European-American travelers regularly remarked on

American Indians' wagering in sporting events. Women of all ranks and races bet, and even older age was not a deterrent. Just prior to the War for Independence, Philip Fithian, who had returned to New Jersey from his position as tutor for the children of Councillor Robert Carter, went to visit his "old aunt" and found her playing at cards and betting on her skill and luck. Ever the naive soul, Fithian was clearly surprised at his aunt's actions, but he probably should not have been. Colonists who saw the practice about them and who may have gambled even as children probably thought gambling was an ordinary endeavor to be enjoyed throughout one's life.[51]

Several historians have tried to account for the prevalence of—indeed, the passion for—gambling, especially in the South. Timothy H. Breen, Rhys Isaac, and Bertram Wyatt-Brown have focused on how gambling incorporated and derived from the patterns of living, the social relations, and the values of particular social groups. In the late seventeenth- and early eighteenth-century Chesapeake, Breen suggested, gambling enabled native-born gentlemen to express important cultural values and to do so in contests that united rather than divided them.[52] Among later Virginia colonists, Isaac contended, gambling "was inseparable from the ubiquitous competition in politics and high living."[53] Even in the nineteenth-century South, according to Wyatt-Brown, gambling persisted as an important mechanism by which individuals "brought the code of honor into very serious play."[54] Markedly integral to and integrated in life, gambling was neither irrelevant nor compensatory. It was not a means of providing for something—a challenge, a thrill, or whatever—that was absent from life, as some modern Americans have claimed. Rather, formalized and conventional, gambling was an expression of life itself in the eighteenth century.

For their part, contemporary critics, who rarely attended to the legal distinction between the practices or distinguished between urban and rural patterns, had few illusions about the consequences of gambling and gaming. Some of them recognized that gambling produced no money or anything else of material worth for the society. Gamblers merely exchanged goods or money, although the exchanges were never even: one won and another lost. Thus gambling, like idleness, was "uneconomic." Worse, opponents claimed, the practice might leave the loser destitute. Critics cited the personal and societal consequences of gambling among poor and dependent colonists who risked insolvency with even a small loss. Moreover, when the poor lost, the refrain against gambling continued, other people stood to lose as well: owners and employers whose money or goods the gamblers sometimes wagered, tavernkeepers who extended credit and then could not recoup it, and families and dependents who lost the money for food and shelter. The suffering thus was widespread, the denunciators of gambling apparently believed. A society without adequate social safety nets, even for the nongambling poor, would be hard pressed to deal with or care for the gambling poor.[55]

Some critics of gambling thus framed the "problem" of gambling and gaming in rank terms, as they had that of idleness. Legislators went so far as to disallow recovery through the courts of money lost at or lent for gambling on many sports and almost always for any tavern gambling. They also ordered fines and loss of licenses for tavernkeepers found guilty of permitting gambling.[56] Through 1760 the Massachusetts General Court revised and reissued several times a law apparently aimed directly at artisans, laborers, and craftspeople. "Games and Exercises although lawful," the court granted, "should not be otherwise used than as innocent and moderate Recreations." Under no circumstance, it continued, should such practices, or gambling on them, be engaged in "as Trades or Callings, to gain a Living."[57] Even more clearly in 1764, the North Carolina Assembly laid out the prevailing assumption that gaming among lower-rank colonists was both "natural" and intolerable. The province was suffering immeasurably, the lawmakers judged, from the "many idle disorderly, and evil disposed persons . . . who are frequently found Loitering, gaming, and misbehaving themselves." One had only to look about, they continued, to see "the Discouragement of Industry, corruption of Youth, and Destruction of Families." What the legislators never said, however, was that one also had only to look about to see that they enacted this law at precisely the time when the Regulator movement had begun to coalesce. Not coincidentally its members were small planters in the backcountry who organized to oppose the authority and privileges of the large landowners in the East.[58]

Throughout the century nothing undermined the assumption that gambling and gaming were particularly problematic and "pernicious" to and among ordinary people. The corollary assumptions—that colonists of means could afford to gamble and that society could tolerate their habits—did, however, lose its certitude in the face of real experiences and the downturn that affected the provincial economy during and after the 1750s. In 1752 the *Pennsylvania Gazette* posed, albeit tentatively, a question that had not been asked publicly: "If G-m-g [Gaming] be destructive of the publick Peace and Welfare . . . , may it not be supposed to be generally as pernicious to People in high as in low Stations, some Allowance being made for the Difference of Fortune and Education?"[59] Apparently concerned about offending some readers, the author developed the answer slowly. Midway through the discussion he even suggested that "all Wagers and Betts at Horse Races, Cock Matches, Boxing Matches, &c." might be excluded. In the end, however, the writer displayed his Whig sentiments and ceased to equivocate: "If Riches and Dignities be no absolute Security against being led into Evil, can any good Reason be assigned why . . . the Prohibition ought not to be general, and the Penalties so continued as may best deter all Ranks and conditions from offending?"[60]

Contemporaries in Massachusetts and Virginia were more direct in their criticism of upper-rank gambling. In 1752 William Stith, the president of William and Mary College, implored the members of the Virginia Assembly to limit their gambling before they lost "all their weight and influence with the generality of the People."[61] In the next decade a young lawyer, John Adams, identified gamblers and gamesters as "rakes and fools," people whose gambling led to other crimes, even to "debaucheries of young girls."[62] His Virginia contemporary, the planter William Nelson, actually saw the "Dissipation & Expence" to which "all kinds of Gambling" by a "young wild raw lad" could lead. Deeply in debt, Nelson's neighbor, Jeffrey Grisley, went to jail.[63] It was Landon Carter, however, another of Virginia's wealthy landowners and a son of Robert "King" Carter, who registered some of the most vituperative criticism found in the records of both the opponents and victims of gambling. Having seen his son and his grandsons spend substantial money and time gambling—with nothing to show for their actions—Carter stated the matter in terms no planter could have misunderstood. "No affrican," he cried, "is so great a Slave, as such are to their Passion for gaming."[64]

The racialization of habitual and costly gambling and gaming suggests just how seriously men of means such as Carter viewed the practice. After all, they were European Americans who harbored no doubts that they were superior to Africans and African Americans, and for white planters to be likened to—let alone considered beneath—a slave was a harsh attack indeed. It was also an attack by men on other men. When women entered the fray in the 1780s, empowered as they had been by Republican ideology as caretakers of "virtue," they framed the matter differently. Elizabeth Foote Washington, distantly related to George by marriage, stated the gendered criticism of gambling clearly. She condemned the "itching for gaming" that men she knew displayed. The lure was "so great," she believed, that "they would spend a whole day, or days, in playing with the most indifferent creatures." And for what? she asked, in a tone reminiscent of Carter's: "What excuses, what contrivances will they not make to blind a wife to get to a dice table—or card table. How much do I pity . . . a fine woman . . . left at home to lament the loss of her husband's company, who is really not worthy of her."[65] The message to genteel gamesters thus was complete. They were no better than the slaves whom they presumed to own, and they certainly did not merit their wives' respect, or perhaps even their wives.

Why were upper-rank men and women so caustic in their condemnations of heavy gamblers in their midst? As did Nelson, some of them saw the negative material consequences of the practice. Men like Carter's son, Robert Wormeley, and William Byrd II's son, William III, who lost sums ranging from £1,000 to £10,000 at single sittings, did ruin their economies. The younger Byrd, in fact, went bankrupt. And at a time when the colonial economy had begun to stagnate and some members of the gentry believed that their indebtedness to British factors and merchants was rising, large gaming losses and bankruptcies were serious matters. They both presented and represented real threats to personal and provincial economic independence.[66]

Perhaps the larger challenge that genteel gamesters and drunkards posed to their relatives and neighbors, however, was to the rank's conception of itself. As had their predecessors earlier in the century, gentlemen and gentlewomen expected their peers to act with restraint, to behave responsibly. They were also to serve as behavioral models for others, to lead by example and, in so doing, to maintain social order. Genteel gamblers who wasted "their Time & constitutions to very little Purpose" could do none of these things.[67] They were "idlers" who threatened the security of their families, as well as their own reputations. Indeed, insofar as genteel critics conceived of persistent, rampant gambling—and the heavy drinking and other "evils" associated with it—as anything but Adams's "noble and elegant" and productive sporting practice, they saw it as a threat to the style they had consciously cultivated. Gaming, in effect, countered gentility and refinement.

→═◯═←

Try as they might, then, the critics of taverns and tavern activities could not reduce drunkenness, idleness, and gaming to simple matters of rank, especially the traditional ranks. The gaming habits of some young gentlemen were too obvious to ignore. Moreover, some of the critics were not members of the upper rank. Rather, they belonged to the economically better off segment of ordinary people which was beginning to emerge as a distinguishable middle rank and whose members had vested interests in the practices of taverngoers. Some of these people were small farmers and planters to whom the gamblers' debts were threatening, not because the debts were to them, but because indebted persons were less likely to make good on a wage or a payment of some kind. Others were neighbors who lived near the taverns and employers of tavern visitors, and the practices and rhythms therein inconvenienced them all. Even some tavernkeepers, whose businesses were precarious under the best of circumstances, had to be concerned about customers whose behaviors exceeded the norms of either local authorities or the community at large. By extending credit to gamblers they exacerbated their own financial troubles, and in harboring drunkards and idlers they risked public censure and loss of respect.

It seems likely, then, that one dimension of the conflict over tavern activities was about the relative positions, prerogatives, and power of various segments of the colonial population. The risks to the gentry were real. By their own hand people such as William Byrd III, Jeffrey Grisley, and Robert Wormeley Carter stood to lose not only their material possessions and, consequently, the base for their political and social power but also their claims on deference and respect from those below. Deemed unfit to lead, they were readily replaceable by small farmers, shopkeepers, and the rising tide of professional people—doctors, lawyers, and newspaper editors—whose personal economies and value systems were already setting them apart from other ordinary colonists. In effect the tavern scene and their reaction to it advantaged the emergent middle rank and sped the reframing of colonial social relations.

What made this social movement possible, however, was the larger contest played out in the taverns: the contest for the content of life in the ordinaries, or even the content of ordinary life. To some extent mid-eighteenth-century taverngoers were doing only what generations of patrons had done. Taverns had long supported drinking, talking, and sitting around, as well as physical recreations, usually with gambling, and they would continue to do so. They would not, however, go unchallenged, for the conditions and interests of the opponents of customary tavern practices had changed. The critics no longer tolerated what they saw as threats to the public peace, wastes of time and money, and disruptions—or interruptions—of that which they had regularized and valorized: work.

Thus, more than resurrecting old questions, tavern activities in general and the perceived prevalence of gaming, idleness, and drunkenness specifically brought into stark relief an emergent set of concerns about public conduct—in particular, tavern conduct. Would taverns persist as refuges from necessary endeavors, from productive, economic activity? Would they continue to support or encourage lifestyles that were incompatible with the messages of the Great Awakening, the Enlightenment, and emergent Republican ideology, which emphasized "improvement" and personal responsibility and restraint, messages made more urgent by the economic downturn and altered imperial policies after 1750? Would they, in short, persist as residual institutions in a society dominated by a vociferous coalition of upper- and middle-rank people who had rejected much from the past and were constructing an alternative culture that stressed commerce, trade, and capitalist communities?[68]

Underlying these changed questions was an emergent set of socially constructed dichotomies that prior generations of colonial authorities had not framed as clearly. The tavern critics had chosen their words carefully. Gaming, drunkenness, idleness—all were "uneconomic." Idleness, in fact, became the antithesis to "economic" activity, to work, and idle drunkards and idle gamesters were to be treated as criminals.[69] Sports associated with idlers or leading to idleness were also "uneconomic." They were unproductive and wasteful "evils." They were practices like baits and fistfights and day-long shooting matches that drew people—workers—from their shops, ships, homes, and fields. They were also primarily the sports of the lower rank, a few wayward gentry notwithstanding, and along with gaming and drunkenness, idle sporting pursuits warranted banishment from the face of the earth.

So the conflict centering on taverns was clearly framed. It was not, however, clearly or simply resolved at any point in the eighteenth century. On the one hand, opponents continued their assault on "uneconomic" tavern activities through the 1770s. In fact, just before the War for Independence began, the Continental Congress and local committees of safety broadened the attack. As a part of the effort to "encourage frugality, economy, and industry," the order of Congress intoned, "We . . . will discountenance and discourage every species of extravagance and dissipation, especially all horse-racing, and all kinds of gaming, cock-fighting, exhibitions of shews, plays, and other expensive diversions and entertainments."[70] On the other hand, and as was evident even in the face of the congressional mandate, tavern visits, drinking, and sporting practices continued. Some gentlemen and gentlewomen did halt their balls and horse races, but others did not. Ordinary colonists, as well, did not stop patronizing taverns or participating in proscribed activities. Among them customary practices persisted, and taverns remained critical gathering places for many colonists, especially those on the economic margins who lacked access to other forms and facilities for meeting, eating, and playing.

Despite their emphasis on economy and productivity, then, the opponents of tavern activities, including games and displays of prowess, did not succeed in eradicating long-standing patterns. Still, this episode was not inconsequential. Even as opponents were criticizing what was happening in the taverns, they were busy constructing nontavern alternatives for themselves, sporting practices in keeping with the broader emergent culture they were defining. At the center of this emergent culture lay a reconceptualization of the stuff of life itself. For some middle- and upper-rank colonists, it was a life divided, defensibly on economic grounds, between work and leisure, with some sports designated for "leisure."

8

⋅✧⇾⇒◉⇐⇽✧⋅

Upper- and Middle-Rank Leisure and Sports

In 1775 the printers of the *Virginia Gazette,* John Dixon and William Hunter, offered for sale "Sketchley's New invented Conversational Cards." Ornamented with forty-eight copperplate cuts, the cards must have been wonders to behold. "The more they are played with the more they will improve and instruct," claimed the advertisement. They "will exercise the Imagination, enlarge the Understanding, and everyone that plays with them are sure to be Gainers," it concluded. The appeal to "economic" minded colonists could not have been more obvious.[1]

Sketchley's cards were not for everyone. The announcement did not specify the cost, which may have been Dixon's and Hunter's way of saying that anyone who had to ask about the price probably could not afford them. Stylistically as well, with their copperplate designs, Sketchley's cards were not "common cards," nor did the printers apparently intend them to function as such. In what was a veiled reference to gambling, Dixon and Hunter expressed hopes that players would avoid "the bad Effects" of most card games, their "pernicious Consequences." These cards, the printers claimed, were "calculated to amuse and improve the Mind," and the sellers apparently anticipated that participants would pass the cards around, perhaps exchanging or even collecting as many of them as possible rather than playing a game of whist.[2]

Sketchley's cards were one of many products sold for sports and other recreations on the American consumer market in the late eighteenth and early nineteenth centuries. Consumers could have purchased some pieces of equipment earlier, but they had not had access to the quantity or the range of goods specifically for sporting contests and displays as now appeared. Neither had earlier goods been as ideologically charged, as laden with expressive language, as were Dixon and Hunter's appeal to "gainers," their use of the phrase "calculated to . . . improve," and their disdain for the "pernicious consequences" of other games. But then, producers and advertisers in the colonies had not sold many of their sporting goods for use in a distinctive and ideologically charged sphere of life, "leisure."

The construction of a historically specific notion of leisure and the assignment of some sporting practices to it occurred gradually in the colonies in the eighteenth century. The initial agents were members of the upper rank, who were themselves following the lead of Britons. Even before midcentury gentlemen had consciously fashioned leisure as a category of social experience, separable from both labor and idleness but suitable for some sports and physical recreations. Thereafter the genteel demand for leisure practices mounted, especially in urban areas. Entrepreneurs responded, and extensive commercial activity resulted. In the latter decades of the century as well, the burgeoning world of consumer goods enabled some middle-rank citizens to emulate genteel practices, and leisure and leisure sports ceased to be the domain of the upper rank. For gender and rank relations, the consequences of leisure sports and commercial leisure were profound—as was their impact on labor and laborers, for leisure sports made work.

Constructing Genteel Leisure

If one conceives of leisure as time away from work, it seems clear that engaging in recreations during leisure was anything but a novel experience in the eighteenth century.[3] The novelty lay only in the conscious association of some sports and other physical recreations with a historically specific notion of leisure by some colonists. Before 1700 ordinary Britons and Anglo-Americans had long participated in sports, games, and festivals when they were not laboring in the fields, the house, or the shop, as well as when they were. Indeed, the leisure preference that Peter Mathias noted in earlier periods was real, and work was problematic, as the struggle in Stuart England to regularize and valorize labor suggests.

The dichotomy that this conceptualization of labor and leisure sets up, as work and nonwork time, respectively, is both misleading and inadequate as a way of understanding how people framed time and activity. It not only suggests boundaries around experiences that few early Americans or Britons constructed, but it also ignores other conceptions of time and activity. Early in the seventeenth century, for example, Puritans were framing the Sabbath as a distinctive time for prayer and reflection, which were to proceed with no interference from work, sports, or anything else. Moreover, many Stuart critics of customary sports conceived of yet another kind of time: idleness, which was time put to no "good" use in any endeavor. To constrict idle time, as well as to prevent servants from taking time from their tasks for pleasures, Stuart reformers set aside a day of labor for recreations. They did not, however, conceive of this day, Tuesday, as one of leisure. Such a time was still in the making.

The construction of a historically specific notion of leisure in Britain was a two-part process. One part involved objectifying, measuring, and dividing time; the other, deciding what one did within particular frames of time. For the former, changes in views of time and the technology for keeping it were important. Some Britons, especially urban dwellers, had conceived of and calculated time by clocks rather than seasons or even tasks for several centuries. Still, the measurement of time in this way had remained fairly gross, until the transfer of the pendulum to clocks enhanced the precision and the accuracy of time recording by the late 1650s. Subsequent improvements in technology and production methods made clocks more readily available and cheaper. In the second half of the seventeenth century many Britons used clocks not only to reckon and measure time but also to gauge tasks against time and to standardize working days in terms of hours, regardless of weather or seasons.[4]

The long-running transition to capitalism stimulated the interest in time and clocks. Employers, especially mercantile and industrial capitalists but also some landowners and farmers, avidly segmented and kept track of time and encouraged artisans to improve clocks. As E. P. Thompson has noted, merchants, farmers with hired hands, mine owners, and others had begun to conceive of time as "currency," which was "not passed but spent."[5] They began to count minutes and hours as they did specie, and clocks became their most accurate means of keeping track of time. They enabled ambitious, efficiency-minded owners to ensure that everyone spent time well.

The middle and upper ranks did not conceive of leisure merely in terms of time, however. They also assigned to it specific activities, which the division of labor and the development of bureaucracies in emergent capitalist businesses in part made possible. The former resulted in the assignment to employees of many physical tasks, both skilled and gross, in mining, manufacturing, and agriculture. The latter left managers and overseers in charge of ensuring that laborers stayed at their tasks and that schedules for products and produce were kept. Freed from both laboring physically and watching laborers, owners and employers could thus turn their attention to—they could spend their time on—other tasks. Some of these endeavors, such as corresponding with investors or customers, were necessary to the success of these enterprises, and they constituted emerging forms of work. In part, however, because many people still constructed work as physical labor, they also designated these other tasks as "leisure" activities.[6]

After the Restoration leisure as a category of social practice expanded to include endeavors that enlightened and entertained; middle- and upper-rank Britons rationalized many activities as beneficial in their lives and to their work on both counts. Newspapers and newspaper reading spread. Theaters were rebuilt and constructed anew for a broader audience. The keeping of pets, gardening, and listening to or making music became nearly commonplace, as did rambling in the fields and on the moors, visiting with families, and partaking of the entertainments provided in emerging resort towns such as Bath and Tunbridge Wells.[7] Not coincidentally as well, in the final decades of the century English breeders got themselves out of what one historian has termed the "genetic mess" that earlier generations had made of the horse stock, improving the breed by importing purebred horses from the Middle East, especially Arabia.[8] Their offspring were the mares and stallions that underlay the resurgence of horse racing in the eighteenth century.

Elaborate sports and other recreations became fashionable as leisure practices acquired a large following among Britain's entrepreneurial and professional citizens largely in the eighteenth century. Such a development, however, rested on the material and ideological changes engineered earlier by the "industrious sorts." Informed both by reformist Protestant beliefs and by capitalist interests and work relations, they had constructed leisure as a distinctive time for necessary and productive activities, and they had broadened their view of it to include the sports and recreations that they could justify as beneficial endeavors. In effect, by the late seventeenth century in Britain, middle- and upper-rank agents of capitalism had constructed leisure not as the opposite of work but as time both for less physical forms of work and for recreational activities that they believed benefited their capacities to work.

On the other side of the Atlantic, as the centuries met, a few merchants and planters, as well as recently arrived British émigrés, conceived of and used leisure in the post-Restoration British sense, as a portion of time to be devoted to necessary but not necessarily physical labor. In 1711, for example, Dr. Francis LeJau wrote to the secretary of the Society for the Propagation of the Gospel in London requesting directions from the society about how he should proceed to resolve a problem in the Carolinas. LeJau asked that the secretary respond "when your leisure do's permit."[9] Thirty years later LeJau's conception of the term persisted. In Georgia in the early 1740s William Stephens, the secretary to the trustees of the colony, recorded that since "nothing of any Moment [was] happening to call me abroad, I had the more Leisure to get forward such papers as were requisite to lay before the Trust." On another occasion he found himself with "no Business of much Significance relating to the Public," and consequently, "I found leisure to employ my thoughts about what was doing at Bewlie" (Beaulieu, his estate).[10]

Between LeJau's and Stephens's times in the colonies, use of the term *leisure* to designate time for other endeavors became more widespread among upper-rank men. Importantly, they had bound or hired laborers to do the physical labor required by agriculture and shipping, as well as managers to keep workers at their tasks. This pattern was especially evident in the South, where wealthy planters had been acquiring substantial numbers of African slaves since the 1680s. Even in the North, however, some merchants and fleet owners were reproducing British capitalist work relations and structures. Consequently, men like Stephens in Georgia—or Robert Carter and William Byrd in Virginia, James DeLancey and Robert Livingston in New York, and Peter and Andrew Faneuil in Massachusetts—were able to undertake other tasks—useful, necessary tasks—in their "leisure." Significantly as well, only the wealthiest planters and merchants, and only the men among them, had such leisure.[11]

Upper-rank colonists probably followed the lead of their cousins in Britain and expanded their repertory of leisure practices early in the eighteenth century. Direct evidence dates from the 1730s, when the genteel sporting style was emerging as a fairly elaborate pattern in the context of altered work relations and rhythms, but the process likely occurred earlier. Some gentlemen had formalized particular sports as early as the 1680s, and they had extended and regularized opportunities for exchanges with contemporaries abroad about reading, music, and travel at about the same time. In the Chesapeake at least, the emerging gentry's code of conduct and their association of physical prowess and health with particular sports, especially races and field sports, also suggest that some men had begun to conceive of these practices as leisure activities early in the eighteenth century. Indicative of this conception as well are the governing conventions they imposed on racing and hunting and, subsequently, the specialized facilities they built. Indeed, all these practices indicate that provincial gentlemen, especially but not only in the Chesapeake, no longer viewed their sports as either ordinary forms of labor or practices for ordinary laborers.

By midcentury particular tavern behaviors probably encouraged upper-rank men to clarify their conception of leisure and appropriate leisure practices. Certainly the timing suggests as much. As the antitavern rhetoric heated up, discussions and prescriptions for leisure also became more common and focused, especially on a theme that ran counter to that expressed in many tavern criticisms: economy. The *Virginia* and *Pennsylvania Gazettes* spoke to and for many colonists on precisely this point in a series of articles printed in 1751 and 1752. There was no mistaking what leisure was, according to these upper-rank organs. It was neither idle time nor work time but the "hours which . . . Employment leaves Unengaged." There was also no doubt about how one should spend leisure: it was time for "new Advantages, new Schemes of Utility," and for "Relaxation and Diversion" that the "Imbecility of Nature obliges."[12] Leisure was, in short, time for fishing, which the Schuylkill Company had already defined as the "handmaiden" to other endeavors. It was time for thoroughbred races that secured "diversion," profit, and status. It was time for assemblies and the "relaxation" engendered by dancing. Little wonder, then, that genteel sports were occurring with an unprecedented regularity by the 1760s. Leisure and leisure sports were driving time.

Exploiting and Commercializing Leisure

Leisure and leisure sports also came to drive a good deal of commercial activity. Patrons, promoters, and other producers of recreations had invested time, money, and goods of value in recreational scenes for many years, of course, and they had occasionally reaped some material gain from their expenditures. Little of this activity, however, occurred on the scale of the operations and transactions evident in the second half of the eighteenth century, when both the gentry and various entrepreneurs exploited genteel leisure.

Before the Revolution the gentry were visible capitalizers and providers of sports and other physical recreations as leisure practices. As mentioned in chapter 6, they organized horse and boat races, balls, barbecues and fishing parties, card and dice games, and cricket and bowling matches, among other things, and they usually did so in places that they had either built or subsidized. Arranging such practices was an expensive proposition, however, and the costs rose as time passed. Gentlemen invested substantial sums of money, either directly or indirectly via their commitments of laborers' time, to build elaborate facilities: bowling greens, racing stables, and even grandstands erected at race courses to accommodate women and other spectators of note. As will be seen, equipment and animals were also more available, varied, and costly. By the end of the century the average price of a card table was slightly higher than that of a fine mahogany dining table, and many gentry homes had at least a pair of them, valued as high as $40. Pleasure boats, ranging from dories and dinghies to sloops or yachts, required even larger outlays of cash, as did race horses. Before the Revolution a good horse cost the equivalent of several cows and calves. Two or three decades later one might spend from $75 to $125 to purchase a potential racer, and for the same money a planter or merchant could buy a young female slave or two. Then there were the smaller but frequent expenditures on clothing for balls and races, club dues, and of course, gambling. The well-established subscription process also took money. To join the weekly or fortnightly winter assembly circuit just after the Revolution, a gentleman could spend about £3, which was only slightly less than he would pay to support and have access to the resources of the local lending library for a whole year. Race subscriptions, entry fees, and the costs associated with visiting hot springs resort towns added to the expenses associated with gentry-run recreations.[13]

Probably few gentry earned substantial sums from their investments and other disbursements. There were, of course, monetary prizes for winners of horse and boat races, as well as stud fees. Neither source of income, however, appears to have offset the costs of purchasing and maintaining stables. Moreover, except for gambling, there was little possibility of income from other practices.[14] Consequently the genteel sports accounting register rarely balanced, which helps to account for the emergence of some entrepreneurs on the sporting scene in the second half of the century and especially in urbanizing areas. These people were rarely members of the upper rank, but they were willing to invest in or fully assume the financial risks of owning and maintaining facilities. Race course operators were among the first to appear. They either bought existing courses or purchased land and laid out new ones, and local jockey clubs then paid to use them.

Owners of coffeehouses and assembly rooms also became more prominent capitalizers of genteel recreational options, and in the decades surrounding the War for Independence, many cities and even smaller towns had such facilities. They housed dancing, card games, billiards, and bowling—all for a fee—and gradually supplanted subscription affairs.[15]

More than economic interests underlay the presence of entrepreneurs in the second half of the eighteenth century. Fashion, or what was in vogue among their transatlantic peers and superiors, also intrigued the colonial gentry. Despite the distance, the late colonial and early national upper rank sooner or later had access to fashionable European leisure options. Indeed, even before midcentury a North Atlantic market in genteel leisure provided for by entrepreneurs existed, and some of these people made their way across the ocean once the North American upper-rank interest in leisure had become sufficiently clear and well formed to be read as demand.[16] In 1752, for example, traveling theater troops from London put on plays in cities along the Atlantic coast from Charleston, South Carolina, to Boston. Music "masters" offered concerts, and the genteel interest in music apparently encouraged periodic waves of dancing school organization.[17] By the 1760s electricity lectures and displays were in vogue, encouraged by astute pitchmen. Everyone should be aware of this "Branch of Natural Philosophy," asserted the generator of a demonstration in Baltimore, because "our bodies contain enough of it . . . to set a House on Fire."[18] Some enterprising souls even arranged puppet shows for young and old alike, while others displayed exotic animals, especially leopards, tigers, and camels, obtained in Europe and Africa. Eventually journeys to the Great Plains of North America produced buffaloes for these exhibitions, as well as for hunts constructed like fox hunts.[19]

Within this emerging tradition of North Atlantic commercial leisure, two groups of entrepreneurs were particularly visible and responsive to the provincial upper rank's interests in fashionable physical culture experiences. One group consisted of resort and pleasure garden developers. Some resorts—at Bath, Virginia, and Bristol, Pennsylvania, for example—had existed for some time as sites of hot springs, or medicinal springs, to which gentlemen and gentlewomen came seeking cures. Especially after the Revolution, however, their owners built more extensive and elaborate facilities for housing, races, dances, and other indoor recreations, which beckoned genteel guests to stay for a week or more at a time.[20]

Pleasure gardens in urban centers competed with hot springs resorts for genteel clients and probably outdrew the springs because of their location.

Provincial gardens also drew on sites long popular in Britain, even to the point of taking the names of Old World esi ıblishments, and they offered a comprehensive, European-style program of entertainment. The elaborate and carefully designed outside environment of trees, shrubs, and flowers through which paths meandered appealed to gentlemen and women who wanted to stroll or walk, for healthful exercise or perhaps other reasons. The grounds were also appropriate for concerts and fireworks, while the indoors had space for balls and cards.[21] Creating "pleasure" was the goal of garden operators, and they occasionally let prospective customers know that they had spared no expense in preparing "a genteel and entertaining place of resort." They also informed the larger public that not everyone would be admitted. The gardens were open only to people whom the proprietors judged to be "genteel in character."[22]

The owners did not, however, treat all the upper rank alike, and within the world of the pleasure gardens we can see one of the critical dynamics of genteel leisure. This was a gendered world in which the differing physical characteristics, assigned moral attributes, and rhythms and tasks of men's and women's lives mattered. Genteel leisure as unengaged time for schemes of utility was itself a male construction, and few upper-rank women, let alone women in other ranks, had the means of, or perhaps the interests in, constructing and experiencing leisure as men did. Women rarely claimed leisure, and few of them probably ever found themselves with unengaged time. Some leisure practices, of course, were not likely to occur without them—dancing, for instance—and many upper-rank women did attend races, assemblies, resorts, exhibitions, and the pleasure gardens. In these venues, however, women rarely participated in the same ways as men did, or even in the same ways as earlier women had. The construction and exploitation of leisure limited women's experiences in sports and physical recreations. It took them off the track and placed them in the stands, especially in public. It allowed them to walk the paths of the gardens but not to run. It allowed them to fish or go boating, but not to do so seriously. Leisure in effect marginalized upper-rank women as performers in contests and matches. They were cheerleaders in the making.[23]

Especially after the Revolution, women were also the moral arbiters of male leisure, a role assigned to them by the makers of the dominant ideology. Republican ideology held that virtue was a feminine attribute and that only women could ensure that virtue would prevail in the young nation.[24] They thus became the guardians of desirable morality, a role that some pleasure garden operators recognized. In 1801, for example, Joseph Delacroix, a French émigré who had just completed a "grand Amphitheatre" for the Fourth of July celebration at his Vauxhall Garden in New York City, ended his announcement of the proposed entertainments with this warning: "No gentleman will be admitted without [being] accompanied by a lady." Delacroix had planned nothing special for them, but he wanted them present to ensure that their male adjuncts would not resort to unruly behavior. He wanted them to do what they did in their homes.[25]

As social engineers the proprietors of pleasure gardens probably had few peers in the final quarter of the eighteenth century. They did have rivals in the genteel leisure business, however: the physical culture performers who were themselves adding to the variety and the specialization of leisure practices by taking skills and movements out of their traditional contexts in games and sports and displaying them in exhibitions. Some of these people had crossed the Atlantic and made their way to port cities shortly after the initial wave of stage actors, puppeteers, and musicians. One of the earliest performances in the colonies occurred in New York City in 1752, with a "famous Posture-maker" who "transforms his Body . . . with many Curious Dancings and Tumblings."[26] A year later the "celebrated" Anthony Joseph Dugee, a mixed-race man who had earlier entertained the royal family, performed "on a Slack Wire scarcely perceptible, with and without a Balance." His wife then completed the act with "wonderful Feats of Strength and Activity." She, too, was well known abroad and in male terms as the "Female Sampson."[27]

The Dugees gave several performances in New York City in 1753, which testifies to their popularity. Their subsequent history, however, remains a mystery. What is clear is that tumbling, acrobatic, and weightlifting exhibitions remained a part of the urban, genteel leisure scene well past the turn of the century. In the 1760s Henry Hymes, "Balance-Master," displayed his skills in Boston and elsewhere, and after the war other skilled performers performed their "art."[28] Some of these individuals also came from England, probably for the revenue to be had in the now independent nation. Tickets remained expensive, usually a dollar or more, and the men and women who owned the building and rooms that housed the exhibitions advertised the performers widely.[29] Promoters even made prospective audiences aware of the achievements and pedigrees of the entertainers. Certainly this was the case with "Dr." Joseph Doctor, who demonstrated "Ground and Lofty Tumbling, With many Postures and Equilibriums," in Alexandria, Virginia, in 1795, as well as with "The Incomparable African" who performed "incomparable Feats on the Slack wire" at Louis Roussell's ballroom in Baltimore in 1787.[30]

Although its precise effect remains unknown, the redundancy within Roussell's promotion was probably necessary. Competition for the acrobats' audiences was coming not just from musicians, actors, and pleasure garden owners but from other physical culture exhibitionists as well. Prior to the Revolution professional pedestrians, or long-distance walkers, arrived from England to entertain "astonished . . . natives" with their feats of agility.[31] Professional equestrians also demonstrated skills with which many people were familiar and that they respected, the skills of "horsemanship." In the 1770s Joseph Falks (or Faulks, as his name was also spelled) was probably the best-known equestrian. An Englishman, Falks thrilled crowds from Williamsburg to Boston with his "wonders," which included riding three horses at a time, and earned something approximating a national reputation.[32] After the war Falks's mantle passed to Thomas Pool, who was as skilled as his predecessor but, importantly, was also "the first American" to ride in public.[33] His nationality, as well as his military service, undoubtedly helped to draw crowds, as did the fact that he controlled his own publicity, which included direct appeals to "Ladies and Gentlemen," and used facilities that included boxes for the upper rank and pits for others. Between acts Pool had orchestras play. He provided, in effect, a more extensive program than had Falks and one that aimed directly at the upper rank.[34]

Pool's successor was John Ricketts (sometimes Jacob), who exploited the commercial possibilities of "horsemanship" more fully than had Pool. Originally from Scotland, Ricketts had spent several years touring Europe, adding to and refining his performance before the crowds and crown heads whose pride in their equine prowess showed in the value they assigned to Ricketts. In the new nation in the 1790s, he found that similar interests prevailed; in fact, planters and merchants were still trying to rebuild the horse stock devastated during the war.[35] Ricketts offered them a wide-ranging display of riding skills and maneuvers, and at least one newspaper concluded that "nothing like his performance was ever seen before" in New York City.[36] The fact that he turned over the proceeds of one performance in New York for purchasing fuel "for poor families" and those of another in Baltimore for "repairing the Streets " undoubtedly aided his reputation.[37]

Ricketts's contributions suggest that he was well aware of what had become traditions on the American leisure scene by the end of the century. As the provincial and then early national upper rank had maintained, leisure was time for "schemes of utility," and Ricketts's equestrian performances were undoubtedly schemes. No one normally rode several horses at a time, nor did a person usually ride even one horse in an inverted position, as Ricketts did. But his acts also paid off, for both civic governments and himself. Precisely what Ricketts earned is unknown, but apparently the income was sufficient to enable him to build his own facilities, each one larger and more elaborate than the last and at least one in each of the country's three largest cities: New York, Philadelphia, and Baltimore.[38] Moreover, Ricketts styled himself as an artist, which was in keeping with the traditions of genteel leisure, or at least those of the entrepreneurs who provided the gentry with leisure activities. He also appealed directly to the upper rank for their support. The amphitheater that he opened on Broadway in New York City in 1794, for example, was "erected at great expense to render it commodious," capable of seating a "Brilliant Company of Ladies and Gentlemen, upwards of 1000." His handbills even designated the seating arrangements. Gentlemen and gentlewomen were to sit in boxes for which they paid a dollar, whereas others paid half that sum to watch the show from the "pit."[39]

Ricketts's longevity and success undoubtedly owed much to his ability to operate within the context of genteel leisure. Even that was changing, however, as Ricketts apparently also realized. The inclusion of a pit in his amphitheaters suggests as much. Originally the site of animal contests, the pit had become the place where the lower ranks sat to watch various public performances in late Elizabethan and Stuart Britain, and it had remained a feature of British entertainment facilities. In the colonies, however, pits did not become widely available until the 1780s, although a few theaters had contained them before the Revolution.[40] The spread of the pit suggests that the popular interest in genteel leisure practices had broadened considerably.

Ricketts's organization of a circus is another indicator of this movement. Not long after his arrival in the United States, Ricketts combined his displays and those of other performers within what was a multiact affair. Ricketts himself gave the centerpiece performance, his equestrian displays. The program also included pantomimes, musical solos and duets, and a clown who had performed with the "Royal Circus" in London.[41] With a repertory broader than that of other contemporary leisure enterprises, except perhaps the pleasure gardens, Ricketts's circus apparently offered something for anybody who was willing and able to pay the admission, minimally a half-dollar. The sum was steep enough to exclude urban laborers, who generally earned a dollar or less a day, but not too high to deter those who aspired to what had been the domain of the upper rank.[42]

Beyond what it suggests about the widening interest in genteel leisure practices and the ongoing expansion of what constituted acceptable public leisure practices, the circus is telling about another consequence of the exploitation of leisure. Hidden within the efforts of entrepreneurs to capitalize on upper- and middle-rank interests and to commodify leisure is the fact that these people were also workers. They were laborers who filled the demands of the provincial and early national upper rank for "relaxation and diversion" and "schemes of utility." That contemporaries rarely recognized them as such, however, suggests that many early Americans continued to view labor as manual work. In subsequent years this construction persisted, and it was one of the factors that prevented leisure workers—including actors, jockeys, and eventually ball players and others—from gaining the legal and economic options and rights earned by other laborers.[43]

Still, people such as Pool and Ricketts, as well as the owners of pleasure gardens, billiard rooms, and tavernkeepers, hired "leisure workers." In 1790, for example, Louis Roussell sought a "person who understands keeping a BILLIARD-TABLE, and can be recommended for his Honesty, and Sobriety."[44] On the wall of a Fells Point tavern in Baltimore appeared an advertisement for what was essentially a magician's assistant. Desired was a "sober young man, of an affable and obliging temper, whose Pride will not Conquer his Reason."[45] Such genteel personal qualities, however, were not requisites for other positions that the expansion and specialization of leisure practices encouraged, especially those people who labored at the leisure practices that primarily men consumed and that the general public often did not see. Unlike magicians' assistants and billiard-table keepers, members of boat crews, faro dealers, prostitutes, and even prize fighters did not have to be genteel. Likely to have come from the ranks of laborers in the first place, the men and women who filled these jobs had only to bring their physical skills to the tasks.[46] Thus, even as it heightened cultural differences between the late colonial and early national upper and lower ranks, the exploitation of genteel leisure also produced divisions among the ranks of leisure workers, divisions that would persist through the twentieth century.

The larger point in all this, however, is that leisure made work, which was a significant development on several levels. First, and despite the persistence of gambling, it actually added a dimension to the construction of leisure as economic, productive activity. Leisure was an emergent industry that provided occupations and at least some income for laborers. As such, it also provided owners, organizers, and consumers of leisure enterprises with another means of controlling laborers. Second, it broadened conceptions of what were appropriate activities for relaxation and diversion. Gentlemen could, if they wished, create their own leisure practices. They could hunt, race, sail, or dance—but they did not have to be as physically active as that. With an emergent breed of workers to provide for their needs, they could sit back and watch.

The making of work in leisure suggests how far upper- and even some middle-rank Americans had proceeded in transforming the traditional British labor-leisure relationship and, in fact, traditional culture. Theirs was no longer a culture in which leisure practices, especially sports and other physical recreations, drew from and occurred within traditional work contexts, community gatherings, or agricultural and religious festivals. Leisure practices were separable, although not entirely separate from, common labor forms, places, and times. Indeed, the exploitation of genteel leisure in general sharpened the frames of time understood and experienced by the upper and, eventually, the middle ranks. They had work time, and they had leisure time; for the latter, evenings and, importantly, Saturdays—except in New England—became the standards. In the mid-Atlantic region yacht races and fox hunts regularized on Saturdays, and even in a small town like Richmond, Virginia, by the 1780s the genteel quoits club met on that day, as did the jockey club in Annapolis, Maryland. Scheduling shifts in traditional events like races, from the Wednesday-Thursday-Friday sequence of rural and small town events to a Thursday-Friday-Saturday pattern, also occurred in places such as Baltimore and New York City. Even Sundays, to the consternation of local officials, were no longer devoted to churchgoing and prayer. They were fine times for swimming and cards, especially in the privacy of the home. The weekend had begun to take shape, with sports and other recreations consuming blocks of time within it.[47]

Emulating Leisure and the World of Sporting Goods

Like Sketchley's cards, which had been produced for use in it, genteel leisure was a wonder to behold. It was a marvelous invention that was part and parcel of the dramatic changes in the way the upper rank experienced and viewed life in early America. Leisure as distinctive time and activity—indeed, a separable sphere of life—enabled them to shape practices that prior generations either had not forged or had experienced in the contexts of work, community building, and churchgoing as necessary and enjoyable in their own right: music, dance, reading, sport. It encouraged changes in language and emotions, such as love, enjoyment, and excitement, and it supported emerging social relations. Nuclear families, friendships, and ranks becoming classes were among the products of people for whom leisure was meaningful. Leisure also accommodated endeavors that became important to the gentry's social power: learning, correspondence, health-seeking, politics, and distinctively fashionable forms of and forums for play.[48]

The ideological and experiential distancing of genteel practices from what for the elite were residual patterns and practices and, importantly, from the affairs of ordinary colonists was thus complete—but not for long. Leisure as unengaged hours, as time for "new Advantages, new Schemes of Utility," including particular sports, was immensely appealing. It was something that other people envied, and especially after the War for Independence, nongenteel colonists endorsed, embraced, emulated, and exploited leisure and pursued matches, games, and other displays of prowess as leisure practices. In part this was a matter of interest. Some ordinary people understood and relished the options and opportunities for leisure and leisure sports that the gentry possessed. They had observed changes in British fashions and practices, as well as the cultural impact of the Enlightenment. They had also learned well the messages expressed in the genteel style about power, prerogatives, and the cultural and material advantages associated with gentility and refinement.

Some of these people were able to make and use leisure as well. As had the upper rank, they had experienced substantial changes in the conditions and rhythms of life over the course of the eighteenth century. Their standards of living had improved; they had contributed to and benefited from the expansion and diversification of markets and manufactures; and they had improved their production methods and enhanced the efficiency of their labor. They had even hired laborers and assumed some of the same necessary but not necessarily physical labor tasks of the gentry. They had moved, in short, materially and ideologically closer to the gentry and constituted an emerging middle rank.[49]

They also benefited from and encouraged what historians have come to call the "consumer revolution." Extending as it did over several decades, this movement was probably less a revolution in a classic sense than a gradual transformation in the production and consumption of material goods and, ultimately, in the course, relations, and meanings of ordinary life. At its core were furnishings and other goods that had once been available only to the rich and high born but that had become accessible to many people. Popular consumption, in turn, became a concrete form of emulation, and emulation via consumption included the instruments—books, self-help manuals, china dishes, eight-day clocks, and card tables—of genteel leisure.

The consumer revolution of the early modern Anglo-American world began in Britain as middle-rank people demanded goods that they had once considered amenities and luxuries. From the late seventeenth century onward producers developed manufacturing and distribution systems to supply the goods required, things ranging from furniture and clothing to personal care items and pets. Farmers responded to demands for groceries, while freight and shipping houses and merchants moved to transport and sell larger quantities and a more diverse range of goods and food. Before mid-century Britain's production and sales network for consumer goods was relatively extensive, efficient, and able to accommodate more purchasers.[50]

Across the Atlantic the provincial gentry were the initial consumers of British-made goods. Between the 1740s and 1760s, however, demands for similar kinds of goods arose from the emerging middle rank. Economically better off than either their ancestors had been or some contemporaries remained, they purchased immediately usable items first: bedsteads, tables and chairs, linens, and cooking and eating utensils. Orders for mirrors, greater varieties of specialized furniture and cookware, and chamber pots followed. Then came the "message" items, the emblems of respectability and refinement, if not quite gentility: wigs, silver teapots, and clocks.[51]

Specialized sporting equipment and animals constituted another segment of the consumer market, and they were one of the means by which the middle rank literally bought into genteel leisure practices. As previous chapters have suggested, some trade in goods for games and other contests had proceeded since the 1680s and 1690s. In the final third of the eighteenth century, however, that trade expanded significantly, in terms of both amount and variety, despite the interruption of imports from Britain during the Revolution and even though mass production and consumption lay some years in the future. Local leather crafters produced fine saddles, including sidesaddles for women. Farmers and planters bred and trained their own horses to produce hunters, pacers, and trotters. In Williamsburg, Virginia, one could obtain a copy of *Hoyle's Games* at the post office, and down the coast in Norfolk a colonist could purchase "billiard balls, all sizes at 10 sh. a pair," from Hardress Waller, who shaped them from the ivory he had on hand.[52] By 1790 a Baltimore harness maker offered for sale an item that illustrated, perhaps more clearly than anything else, the extent of specialization and fashion among patrons of racing in the young nation: the jockey cap.[53]

Estate inventories from Maryland and Massachusetts provide us with a fuller picture of the types and distribution of sporting goods. Inventories recorded what people owned on their deaths. This ownership indicates only possession, but in that day and age people were not likely to have goods that had no meanings for them. Consequently, ownership also suggests some knowledge or awareness of the "expressive roles" constructed for specialized sporting goods and perhaps their use, if not in matches and contests, at least in signifying fashion and refinement.[54]

The inventory data encourage several other general comments. First, and in the context of the larger picture of colonial and early national popular consumption, people acquired goods sold for sports and other physical recreations relatively late in the process. Such equipment remained amenities longer than did household furnishings, clothing, and even vehicles for travel. Second, acquisitions of sporting goods expanded as the eighteenth century drew to a close. Even then, however, the kinds of equipment registered suggest that either the demand or the supply, or probably both, was for goods usable in visible and widely understood sports and games, especially ones popular among the gentry. The interests of producers and consumers alike lay in goods for field sports, races of various kinds, and table games played in parlors as well as taverns. Not until the turn of the nineteenth century did novel items emerge.

Table 1 summarizes the content of inventories registered in six counties representing different regions in Maryland after the point when assessors started noting identifiable, specialized sporting goods among decedents' personal property. In 1770 only 6 percent of the estates contained sporting goods, most of which were furniture for gambling and equipment for riding or racing, hunting, and fishing. The numbers were small; one billiard and one backgammon table, three fowling pieces, seven sets of fishing hooks and lines, two hunting saddles, and a hunting horn. Twenty years later 18 percent of the inventories registered equipment, and both the quantities and varieties had increased. Through 1810 the upward trend continued. Early in the nineteenth century one out of every four deceased citizens of these counties owned equipment for sports and other displays of cunning and prowess, much of it usable only in such practices.

Table 2 provides a similar description of the contents of one county in Massachusetts, Suffolk, over the same period. The types of equipment are similar; they were for field sports, races, and table games, which had traditionally involved gambling. Suffolk County citizens, it seems, shared the interests of Marylanders in these practices. The northern inventories, how-

Table 1. Sporting Goods in Maryland Estate Inventories, 1770–1810

Equipment	1770	1790	1810
Backgammon tables	1	6	5
Billiard tables	1	0	3
Card tables	0	9	45
Dice and dice box	0	0	1
Fishing hooks and lines	7	4	9
Fowling pieces	3	6	15
Hunting saddles	2	2	2
Packs of cards	0	5	2
Pleasure boat	0	0	1
Shuffleboard/checkers	0	0	4
Sleighs	1	5	7
Sulkeys	0	0	4
Totals	15	37	98
Total estates	239	206	361
Estates with sporting goods (%)	6	18	27

Sources: 1770 Inventories, Prerogative Court Records, vols. 104–5; 1790–1810 Inventories, Probate Records of Baltimore (Inventories, 1789–95, 1809–11), Anne Arundel (Inventories, 1787–90, 1808–13), Frederick (Inventories, 1786–97, 1808–10), Prince George's (Inventories, 1787–91, 1798–1815), Talbot (Inventories, 1788–92, 1809–1811), and Worcester (Inventories, 1783–90, 1804–10) counties, Maryland State Archives, Annapolis. 1790 and 1810 inventories also included "Walker's Amusements," racing gear, and a sword and wire mask.

ever, do suggest a more substantial expansion of ownership by 1810, when 68 percent of decedents registered sports-related goods. There was, as will be seen, a particular dynamic at work in Suffolk County consumption.

Both sets of inventories also enable us to see who held these goods. In terms of race the picture is clear. All the equipment appeared in the inventories of European Americans, which was partially a result of the racial skewing of inventory registrations.[55] County courts rarely ordered the enumeration of estates of deceased African Americans, the majority of whom were slaves without estates. The results by gender are similar. Across time and in both regions, decedents whose estates registered recreational

Table 2. Sporting Goods in Suffolk County Estate
Inventories, 1769–1810[a]

Equipment	1769	1790	1810
Backgammon tables	2	3	7
Card tables	1	7	33
Fishing goods	0	4	5
Fowling pieces	0	0	3
Packs of cards	0	0	9
Sleighs	1	4	6
Pigeon nets	1	2	0
"Hoyle's Games"	1	1	0
Totals	6	21	63
Total estates	108	145	93
Estates with sporting goods (%)	6	14	68

Sources: Suffolk County Probate Records, Suffolk County Court House, Boston.

a. The inventories for 1770 were missing, so I had to use the ones from 1769.

equipment were predominantly and even overwhelmingly male. In two counties, Suffolk in Massachusetts and Baltimore in Maryland, men's estates contained all the goods in 1769–70 and 88 and 96 percent, respectively, in 1810. A few women did own equipment, but they may have inherited the goods from husbands instead of having purchased them. In Suffolk County, where one is able to distinguish between single and married or widowed women, 80 percent of the recreational goods existed in estates of the latter, making inheritance a real possibility.[56] The prospect of inheritance, in turn, further diminishes the probability that women, like African Americans, were active agents in the sporting goods market.

The inventories also speak to the matter of rank. Table 3 depicts the percentages of selected sporting goods (backgammon, billiard, and card tables; fishing goods; fowling pieces; sleighs; packs of cards; and sulkies) in Baltimore and Suffolk counties by rank, as defined by estate value. One pattern is striking. Across time in both counties the poorest colonists owned relatively little equipment, at no point even a quarter of the goods inventoried. This pattern does not, of course, suggest that lower-rank colonists

Table 3. Percentage of Total Selected Sporting Goods in
Baltimore and Suffolk County Inventories, by Rank[a]

County	1769–70	1790	1810
Lower rank			
Baltimore	0	8	6
Suffolk	20	22	18
Middle rank			
Baltimore	0	46	66
Suffolk	50	30	60
Upper rank			
Baltimore	100	46	28
Suffolk	30	48	23

Sources: Prerogative Court and Probate Records of Baltimore County, Maryland
State Archives, Annapolis; Suffolk County Probate Records, Suffolk County
Court House, Boston.

a. Across the period from 1770 to 1810, I maintained a constant percentage of
estates within each rank: 30 percent, lower rank; 60 percent, middle rank; and 10
percent, upper rank. Although most analyses of colonial inventories present estate data in constant pounds, the resulting rank demarcations (£49–50, £225–226,
and £490–491) appeared to be inappropriate for the post-Revolutionary decades,
when estate values rose and currency values fluctuated. These studies, however,
do suggest that inventory percentages derived from constant pounds fall between
25 and 30 percent for the lowest rank and about 10 percent for the upper rank.
The precise estate value ranges per rank varied over time; poorest 30 percent:
1770, £1–59; 1790, £1–83; 1810, £1–133; wealthiest 10 percent: 1770, £600+; 1790,
£1,000+; 1810, £1,500+; middle 60 percent: 1770, £60–599; 1790, £84–999; 1810,
£134–1,499. When dollars had to be converted into pounds (1810), I used the
conversion factor of seven and one-half shillings per dollar.

did not engage in sports and other physical recreations. Indeed, many games
and matches required no specialized equipment, and not all the goods,
equipment, or animals used in sporting contests and displays were used only
in those affairs. Nonetheless, the data do indicate that colonists on the
economic margins lacked specialized, fashionable goods, equipment considered necessary for some practices by wealthier contemporaries. The
absence of many goods from the inventories of poor people may also indicate their lack of interest in or their material inability to emulate genteel
practices.

Beyond confirming that middle- and upper-rank estates (the wealthiest 70 percent) owned the majority of sporting goods across time, table 3 also indicates that the relative proportions of goods located in middle- and upper-rank estates differed regionally and changed over time. In 1770 the upper rank in Baltimore County, as elsewhere in Maryland, had a virtual monopoly on specialized sporting goods, whereas the Suffolk upper rank owned only about a third of all the goods. Regional types and rates of economic development and diversification account for these differences. In Baltimore County the shifts in crop production, as well as the expansion of industry and the transport and merchandising sectors, were relatively recent and had not yet affected the balance of economic power between the middle and upper ranks. The social and economic structure of Baltimore County, in short, resembled that of many other southern tidewater counties where large landowners remained dominant. Suffolk County, on the other hand, already had a viable middle rank and a more diverse economy.[57]

These initial differences between the two counties diminished over time. By 1790 not only were the proportions of goods held by each rank in both counties more similar, but the gaps between upper and lower ranks had narrowed as well. In fact, in Baltimore County each rank held 46 percent of the goods. Twenty years later, however, the gap had widened yet again in both countries, but this time the middle rank held the majority of specialized equipment. Given few major changes in gentry practices—they certainly had not withdrawn from sports and other recreations that they had favored for three generations—this shift in ownership does not mean that the gentry had moved out of the market. Rather, it suggests that the middle rank had moved in, in greater numbers than ever before, and that they had adopted the goods and practices that gentlemen had once maintained almost exclusively.

By no means, however, was the middle rank moving into the sporting goods market in all places at the same rate. The inventories enable us to see where the owners lived and to examine another pattern suggested by tables 1 and 2. These simple lists and counts of specialized equipment for games and other contests indicate that a higher percentage of Suffolk County inventories registered goods than did those in the Maryland counties. A key to this pattern probably lies in the demography of Suffolk County. Even before the Revolution Suffolk was an urbanizing county, and although some people lived on farms in outlying areas, many others inhabited what was then the third-largest colonial city, Boston. By 1810 this demographic trend was even more pronounced: Suffolk County had essentially become greater Boston. Most of the inventories registered that year were those of urban dwellers, and most of the sporting goods—98 percent of the total county sporting goods—appeared in Boston inventories.

The Maryland inventories enable one to test for this possible rural-urban ownership difference. Table 4 presents the percentages of selected sporting goods in four Maryland counties. The oldest of these administrative units was Anne Arundel, which had existed since 1650 and contained the provincial and then state capital, Annapolis. The county itself was predominantly agricultural, and Annapolis was by no means a large city. Throughout the eighteenth century its population of 2,000–3,000 was fairly small and stable. In contrast, both Worcester, which was carved out of Somerset County on the eastern shore in 1742, and Frederick, located in central Maryland and organized in 1748, were rural, agricultural counties. The former area was a tobacco-growing area, whereas farmers in the latter raised livestock and grains. Finally, Baltimore County, which was located on the northwest shore of the Chesapeake Bay, received a patent in 1660 but had a small population until the 1770s. Its population then rose significantly, in large part because the hamlet of Baltimore "Town" emerged as a city. By 1810 it had become a booming port with a population of 46,600, enough to surpass Boston and become the third-largest metropolis in the United States.[58] At that point Baltimore County decedents held half of the sporting goods registered in these counties, and the inventories of people who lived in the city of Baltimore contained 51 percent of that half. In effect, one-quarter of all the sporting goods registered in the inventories of decedents in these four counties in Maryland in 1810 belonged to urbanites. When it came to owning sporting equipment, Baltimoreans resembled Bostonians.

The overall picture suggested by the inventories thus reinforces and clarifies the conclusions about leisure and leisure sports drawn from other evidence. First, the equipment types implicated only a narrow range of provincial and early national practices. The inventories contained no goods that would have advantaged or had meaning in animal baiting, fistfighting, or even cudgeling. In part perhaps this was a matter of economy. To the extent that the market responded to demands of consumers, manufacturers and craftspeople made and sold goods to people who could afford them, and few lower-rank colonists could do so. The kinds of goods available on the market were also likely a function of the state of the practices, however. Card and billiard tables, specialized fowling pieces, and distinctively crafted fishing hooks and sleighs were sold and acquired only for certain kinds of practices. These were formalized, even ritualized sports and dis-

Table 4. Percentages of Total Selected Maryland
Sporting Goods, by County

County	1770	1790	1810
Anne Arundel	8	9	10
Baltimore	8	37	49
Frederick	0	3	4
Worcester	23	6	12

Sources: Prerogative Court and Probate Records of Baltimore, Anne
Arundel, Worcester, and Frederick counties, Maryland State Archives, Annapolis.

plays composed of stylized, repetitious movements arranged in distinctive
sequences of action and maintained as such by conventions and rules—and
now by equipment—that enhanced performances and made cultural statements. They were, in short, gentry sports, "leisure" sports, that the emerging middle rank adopted.

This proliferation of sporting goods, although on something less than
a revolutionary scale, probably sharpened the connection between the sports
for which they were sold and leisure as a distinctive sphere of life. One who
owned a relatively expensive card table, let alone a pair of them, was not
likely to use it as an ordinary table for ordinary tasks. The same was true
for fowling pieces and sulkies. The former required a distinctive kind of
shot that was ineffective against bigger prey, whereas the latter was too small
and not particularly comfortable for use as either a wagon or a carriage.
Moreover, anyone who wished to display this fashionable equipment and
to enjoy him- or herself with peers would do so in a time and place convenient for partners or opponents—in leisure.

Finally, the inventory data confirm the demographic and geographic
boundaries of leisure and leisure sports. The simple fact of the matter is
that not all colonists or early national Americans experienced or acknowledged leisure as a distinctive time for certain endeavors. In the eighteenth
century leisure and leisure sports began and remained a European-American male construction, and to the extent that ownership of goods did more
than make the use and contouring of performances possible, it also suggests that upper- and middle-rank men made many of the decisions about

the content and structure of leisure sports and other recreations. This was especially true if they lived in urbanizing areas, where the segmenting impact of capitalism on time, place, and tasks was pronounced.

⊷⊜⊶

The construction of leisure as time for "new schemes of utility" was an important event in the history of early American sports. By locating particular practices in leisure, gentlemen and eventually middle-rank men eroded the ties that particular games and matches had to ordinary tasks, ties that linked the contests and performances, as well as the movements therein, with physical labor practices and traditional, even residual rituals. Sports in leisure incorporated and concocted emergent forms of action, as subscription races, bowling on greens, and fox hunting suggest. These practices in turn anticipated the sports of subsequent generations of upper- and middle-rank Americans, sports whose movements and skills did not draw from ordinary work tasks, sports like baseball.

Sports and other physical recreations removed from the realm of labor and ordinary life more generally also called for their own behavioral guidelines. Thus, some early national gentlemen reframed and clarified the "right actions" of the early eighteenth-century Chesapeake gentry as a specific code, the code of the "sportsman." Rather than state what one did not do, as men like William Byrd and Robert "King" Carter had, the code of the sportsman specified what one did do. A sportsman displayed refinement and genteel manners; he acted courteously, bravely, and generously. He killed only "one brace of woodcocks and two of partridges," and he did so with great skill, "missing only two shots." He also dismissed an "unqualified sportsman" as a "most ignorant and conceited pupp[y] or a coward."[59] The amateur code, which was important to later "modern" sports and which was also a male code, was already in the making.

In their own time, however, the construction and exploitation of leisure as time for "new schemes of utility" and the association of some sports and other recreations with it provided their makers with significant cultural power. In part this power derived from the economic dimensions of leisure itself. Leisure was an expensive but potentially profitable commodity, for the practices of leisure, including sports and other physical recreations, resulted in dollars and cents for their makers and work for laborers. Leisure and leisure sports also afforded their makers and consumers with ideological and social leverage. In controlling both the means for making and

188

the content of the messages conveyed by leisure sports, late colonial and early national upper-rank men and some of their middle-rank emulators reaffirmed leisure as a male domain, just as they affirmed virtue to be a female attribute. They consigned women to a separate sphere, an unequal sphere, a sphere of "amusements" and "entertainments" but not active sports. They also marginalized the lower rank, both as workers in genteel leisure enterprises and as people whose sports were not leisure practices. Eventually matches and games of poor and laboring Americans would not even be considered to be sports, for in the emergent style of late eighteenth-century upper- and middle-rank Anglo-American men lay a base for "modern" athletic team sports, especially the holy trinity of the dominant culture in the United States in the nineteenth and twentieth centuries: baseball, football, and basketball.

Epilogue: People of Prowess

William Dunlap was not unlike other men of his race and class in northern cities after the Revolution. He had been born in 1766, when the states
were still colonies, and he died in 1839, as segments of the booming population were beginning to trek westward beyond the Mississippi River and
just before controversies over states' rights and slavery heated up. As a young
adult Dunlap married into a Connecticut family whose business consisted
of importing china and running a hardware store, and his wife's family's
money underlay his rise into the upper middle class and financed some of
his many business ventures. Before he turned forty Dunlap had painted
portraits and watercolor scenes, managed a theater and written some plays,
and fancied himself as something of a historian and a naturalist. Much of
this work took place in New York City, where Dunlap belonged to the
Manumission Society and a professional men's organization known as the
Friendly Club, but he also owned a farm in nearby Perth Amboy, New
Jersey. By 1806, however, Dunlap's talents had apparently betrayed his interests, and he declared bankruptcy. His life was never the same.[1]

Before his economic condition deteriorated, Dunlap's life involved more
than work, as the diary he kept for nearly a decade and a half after 1797
reveals. These were his own middle years, his thirties and early forties, and
they were full, enjoyable years. The Dunlaps lived in the city for much of
the year, and William spent evenings and weekends, his nonworking time,
playing backgammon at his club or hunting on nearby Staten Island. In

the summers the family moved to the farm at Perth Amboy, where the air was fresh and the pace of life slower. For weeks at a time Dunlap's regimen was the same. He rose early, completed a few chores, and then went either by himself or with one of his sons to hunt the small animals and birds that inhabited the woods and meadows. In some stretches rarely a weekday passed when Dunlap did not hunt. Saturdays, on the other hand, were for family outings. Sometimes Dunlap took his children and their friends, all laden with "Fishing tackling & my fowling equipage," on a "sporting expedition." At other times the entire family, including his wife and daughters, went along to "shoot and fish"; to walk, usually for several miles; or even to ride in the carriage, which made for a "pleasant, rambling excursion."[2] Sundays also saw the Dunlaps walking, over the river and through the woods as it were, hiking in solidarity and for the exercise. Churchgoing was apparently not something that kept the family from its recreations.

In these activities, as well as in his efforts to paint and manage theaters, William Dunlap was the beneficiary of the late colonial gentry's cultural inventiveness, their construction of leisure as a separable sphere of life. Dunlap and others like him had, of course, dispensed with some of the constraints that the earlier upper rank had imposed on the term. Leisure no longer meant unengaged time committed to "schemes of utility" to middle-class urbanites. Now visible agents of leisure in their own right, the Dunlaps of the early national years had reconstructed it as nonworking time, which they continued to fill with "acceptable" sports like hunting, hiking, swimming, boating, and games. On occasion as well, they watched other people perform on the race track, in the circus, or in an exhibition of physical strength, agility, or speed, and they never seemed to acknowledge that such displays, for which they had leisure, made work for others. They were simply participating in what they had turned into a custom in the new republic—enjoying one's leisure—and they probably took for granted their clearly bounded realms of labor and leisure, of work and recreations.

In early national cities like New York, William Dunlap's leisure patterns and practices were relatively common, at least among middle- and upper-class men. They were not the only experiences, however, as even Dunlap's diary makes clear. One of these episodes began when the Dunlap couple and some friends left the city for "a jaunt to the Falls of Pesaick [Passaic]" on a Tuesday in early June 1797. The men and women alike intended to have a pleasant day of healthful exercise by walking "to the falls, climbing the rock near the Canal." On the way, however, they passed through Dutch settlements, where an affair that few of them had ever seen was in progress.

The locals were celebrating the "Pinkster" holiday, and doing so, to Dunlap's astonishment, in a public, democratic fashion. Everyone seemed to be involved. There were women and children who "look'd particularly neat"; beyond them "blacks as well as their masters were frolicking." The traffic was heavy, and "waggon's full of rustic beaux & belles" clogged the road. Many of the revelers apparently had a single destination in mind: "every public house is crowded with merry makers."[3] Like Benjamin Berry had years earlier, the ordinary keepers were doing a booming business as the community celebrated joyously and probably a bit raucously.

Dunlap was clearly surprised by what he saw, but he need not have been. The Pinkster holiday stretched far back in time. It had originated as a Pentecostal celebration among the Dutch; the term *Pinkster* itself derived from "Pfingsten," the Dutch word for Pentecost. Early in the eighteenth century, however, Africans in New York appropriated the event. Already legitimated as festive days in the North Atlantic world, the days surrounding Pentecost made for a break in their work. Agricultural and urban workers alike gathered in a central location, traded goods and foodstuffs they had gathered for other items of value, and danced. Not the ritualized affairs common among European Americans, the dances were demonstrative performances, displays of prowess often concocted on the spot by men and women who had few opportunities to move freely and express their feelings. Such physical performances were at once competitive and cooperative practices, and they involved commercial exchanges. The dancers put on a good show for those who watched, translating their emotions and even telling stories with their physical actions. But they were also contesting for place in the gathered community, as well as for money or items of material worth.[4]

Precisely how much of this dancing persisted in the "frolicking" Dunlap observed is unclear. In any event the Pinkster holiday, now partially secularized and reappropriated by people of Dutch descent, remained meaningful to people in northeast New Jersey and southern New York in ways that Dunlap had not understood. Moreover, although it was distinctive, the Pinkster holiday was not unique, at least in the sense of being the only such affair. Dunlap's cultural myopia notwithstanding, the newly constructed United States remained a land of multiple styles, both of living and of sports and other physical recreations. Indeed, for every Dunlap, there were thousands of Americans living in the young republic who neither shared nor understood his separable worlds of labor and leisure and his sports.

Some of these people had more in common with the Pinkster celebrants, especially those of African descent, than they did with northern, urban, middle-class men like Dunlap. Many African Americans remained slaves on plantations and farms in the South, although their lives had changed, subtly if not dramatically, by the end of the colonial period. They raised wheat, cotton, and livestock rather than the colonial staple, tobacco, for example; they practiced specialized work skills; and they took great solace in extended families. Nevertheless, they still gauged time in terms of crops and climate rather than hours. They also depended on religious and community events to secure breaks from labor, to gather kin and friends, and to express their feelings and display their prowess in dances, matches, and other recreative contests that required little equipment and certainly no fashionable middle- or upper-class sporting goods. In all, the boundaries that Dunlap knew were neither relevant nor meaningful to many enslaved African Americans.[5]

Nor were these boundaries particularly meaningful to other laborers in the urbanizing North. Dockworkers, teamsters, and people who worked in the textile and shoe industries or on the fishing and whaling ships, among others, had little appreciation for and insufficient means of obtaining the sporting experiences of a Dunlap or his divided realms of labor and leisure. Some of these people did have access to the still-expanding realm of commercial entertainments, however. Some members of the urban laboring class, including poor women, whose opportunities for other forms of employment were diminishing in the face of immigration and industrialization, even found work as faro and card dealers or prostitutes. Many of the commercializing events—cockfights, sleight-of-hand displays, and tight-rope exhibitions, for example—also remained tied to taverns and to the seasons and the times of day when the customers, mostly laboring men, could attend. Their opportunities in turn depended not on distinctive, regularized nonworking "leisure" time but on economic and climatic conditions and the demands of employers. Intermittent festivals and festive days also remained important. Some of these were long-standing craft and trade celebrations, whereas others were emergent local and national holidays such as Independence Day (4 July).[6]

Another segment of the early national population was neither enslaved nor urban dwelling, and many of their experiences were distinctive from one another, as all were from Dunlap's. Some people were small plantation owners in the South who continued to eke out marginal profits from rice, cotton, and livestock operations; who hunted and fished at will; and who boxed and gouged to defend their honor, much as had their mid-eighteenth-century forebears. Others had migrated to the fertile river valleys and plains west of the Appalachian Mountains, where they had restarted the processes of farm and community building and to which they brought and then adapted some sports they had known in the East. Fire hunting, for example, occurred in Ohio, but the prey was occasionally bats rather than deer. Finally, and increasingly to the west of the Mississippi River, lay the strongholds of Native Americans, many of whom continued to live off and in harmony with the land, who hunted buffalo and elk as a part of the course of ordinary life, who gambled extensively for goods of material worth, and for whom religious and other tribal festivals still included games and other contests.[7]

Another dramatic counterpoint to Dunlap's experiences comes from the life of a woman whose story Laurel Thatcher Ulrich has so richly retold: Martha Ballard. Ballard lived far from the lights of Broadway, first in Worcester County, Massachusetts, where she was born three decades before Dunlap, and then in Hallowell, Maine, just north of the point where the Kennebec River flows into the Atlantic Ocean, where she died in 1812. Like William Dunlap, however, Martha Ballard had many talents and responsibilities. She was a mother, a midwife, an agricultural producer, and a trader, as well as a farmer's spouse and social arbiter. Her life was full and rich, but during the years after 1785, when she maintained a diary, it was never one of leisure. As was the case with many women in the late eighteenth and early nineteenth centuries—and well beyond—Martha Ballard did not have, nor did she see herself as having, either "unengaged time" or nonworking time.[8]

She did know sports and other physical recreations, some of which resembled long-standing practices—in forms, sites, and relationships—more than they did Dunlap's leisure ones. Ballard's husbands and sons hunted and fished in ways known to several generations of men in New England villages, and Martha's labors in part freed the men to pursue wild game and river trout. Within the largely agricultural and fishing communities surrounding Hallowell, neighbors and kin also gathered to celebrate a special occasion, to raise a house or barn, or to complete some other task. In June and July 1788, for example, locals rebuilt a sawmill that had burned, and on at least one occasion she noted a "vast concorse [*sic*] of men and children." Fortunately, in Martha's judgment, "not many" of the former were "disguised with Licquor [*sic*]," and the evening ended pleasantly as "the young folks had a dance" until midnight.[9]

Martha herself quilted, and quilting parties, followed by dances, were relatively common, if irregular, in Hallowell. She may also have enjoyed the sleighing parties or "frolics" that enlivened the long Maine winters.[10] Beyond these practices, however, Ballard had few opportunities for active physical participation in sports. Both her age—she was already in her mid-forties when her diary began—and the prevailing expectations of her gender apparently combined to ensure that she would operate as a producer of recreations and as a moral overseer, as a "republican mother."

Had she the interest in, the means of, or the Jacobean "liberty" to do so, however, Martha Ballard might have enjoyed more sports and physical recreations. She certainly had a good deal of strength and stamina. To deliver the babies of women who lived far apart, Martha had to travel by horseback or canoe, and on more than one occasion she had to make her way across a flooding river. She could also climb steep, rocky hills and make her way through the woods. She was, in short, a woman of considerable physical prowess. But then, they were all people of prowess.

⋅⇾⩥◉⩤⇽⋅

They had always been so, which is the point. Sports and other physical recreations had long been important to early Anglo-Americans, as well as to other Americans, both native-born and migrants. When this story began in England, games, matches, and other contests were an important part of the fabric of ordinary life. In their extraordinary contexts as well—the festivals that announced or concluded the seasons, the celebrations of villagers, the coronations of monarchs—sporting practices were significant affairs. They resulted from and expressed the interests, values, and relations of people. They enabled English people to resist authority or exhibit solidarity. They produced enjoyment and perhaps renown or things of material value. And no one, not even radical English reformers, thought of eliminating sports and other recreations entirely. They wished only to find a "right" place for them.

This matter of locating, or relocating, sports and other physical recreations was a central theme in the experiences of early Anglo-Americans. It appeared early, when emerging capitalists and reformist Protestants in England moved to impose their version of social order, which included regularized work, and to make recreational performances dependent on and beneficial to labor and laborers. This was not a movement completed quickly or without resistance, in part because it ran counter to popular, long-standing patterns and practices, especially the leisure preference. Some people on both sides of the Atlantic did view sports as laborlike, especially insofar as they expected economically desirable and advantageous ends. At no point in the seventeenth century, however, were traditional practices and relationships transformed. Nor, for that matter, were they by the end of the next century. The experiences of Dunlap's Pinkster celebrants testify to that fact.

Nonetheless, in this ongoing quest to relocate sporting practices, colonists on the mainland of North American did alter the forms, sites, and understandings of some matches and displays of prowess. Practices like quarter-mile horse racing and football formalized and acquired conventions, which made repetitive performances possible. These performances in turn encouraged, and quite early on, the geographic spread of some sports and the assignment of emergent meanings to them, both among and across groups of people. Particular sports—thoroughbred racing in the Chesapeake, bull baits in Philadelphia, and abelarding in the southern piedmont, for instance—even emerged as autonomous, central events in the lives of some colonists. They did so in part, however, because they continued to incorporate in dramatic scenes of contest or display the physical actions and movements that remained meaningful in everyday life.

The process of formalizing, at least as undertaken by Anglo-American men with substantial wealth and leverage over laborers, also changed the face and place of colonial sports in a more dramatic way. Defining particular times and places for such practices, demarcating the physical actions by rules, assigning distinctive expectations and behavioral codes, using specialized equipment—these were some of experiences through which gentlemen removed games and contests from ordinary life and work. Simultaneously changes in labor relations and the kinds of necessary tasks these men performed, improved clock technology, and different notions about the organization and use of time combined to encourage the construction of leisure, the emergent social site for genteel sports and recreations. Even before the middle of the eighteenth century, leisure—and leisure sports—constituted a separable category of experience. Then the gentry and others quickly exploited, commercialized, and emulated leisure. In so doing the late colonial and early national upper rank augmented its social leverage. Leisure and leisure sports were fashionable; they were desirable; they were both instruments and symbols of gentry hegemony.

In time—perhaps by the turn of the nineteenth century, but certainly by the 1820s—the genteel sporting style to which leisure sports and recreations were central became the dominant style. An emergent urban middle class was already appropriating and adapting it, and even urban laborers were drawn into it as both performers and spectators. The latter group made up a portion of the large crowds—as large as 70,000—that flocked to race courses on Saturdays to watch the "great" North-South thoroughbred matches in the 1820s. Sporting magazines that emerged in cities like Baltimore and New York made leisure sports their subjects. The growing number of equipment manufacturers and retailers, who now operated even in the Midwest, made leisure sportsmen their objects. The medical profession prescribed the health-rendering exercises of leisure sports. And it was training in and for leisure sports that educators incorporated in school curricula by the 1830s.[11]

The rest of the story, one might say, is history. Leisure and leisure sports, constructed by the colonial upper rank and borrowed and reframed in subtle ways by the early national urban middle class, persisted into the mid-nineteenth century, when they became the base for "modern" sports, the practices of white, male, urban middle-class men. In their time they too became the dominant and dominating type. The cultural myopia of historians of modern sport notwithstanding, however, they were never the only type. But that is another story.

Notes

⤙═◦═⤚

Introduction

1. Jane Carson, *Colonial Virginians at Play* (Charlottesville, Va., 1965); Edmund S. Morgan, *American Slavery–American Freedom: The Ordeal of Colonial Virginia* (New York, 1975), 71–91; idem, *The Puritan Dilemma: The Story of John Winthrop* (Boston, 1958), 8–10; Rhys Isaac, *The Transformation of Virginia 1740–1790* (Chapel Hill, N.C., 1982), esp. 88–114; Timothy H. Breen, "Horses and Gentlemen: The Cultural Significance of Gambling among the Gentry of Virginia," *William and Mary Quarterly*, 3d ser., 34 (Apr. 1977): 239–57; David H. Fischer, *Albion's Seed: Four British Folkways in America* (New York, 1989), 146–51, 360–64, 552–55, 735–40; J. Thomas Jable, "Pennsylvania's Early Blue Laws: A Quaker Experiment in the Suppression of Sport and Amusements, 1682–1740," *Journal of Sport History* 1 (Spring 1974): 107–22; Hans-Peter Wagner, *Puritan Attitudes toward Recreation in Early Seventeenth-Century New England* (Frankfurt am Main, 1982); Elliott Gorn, "'Gouge and Bite, Pull Hair and Scratch': The Social Significance of Fighting in the Southern Backcountry," *American Historical Review* 90 (Feb. 1985): 18–43. See also Bruce C. Daniel's new book in which he revisits the Puritans' approach to what remains modern leisure and relies primarily on literary evidence: *Puritans at Play: Leisure and Recreation in Colonial New England* (New York, 1995).

2. *Oxford English Dictionary*, 2d ed., 20 vols. (Oxford, 1989), s.v. "sport." Dennis Brailsford and, for a later time period, Hugh Cunningham noted similar problems in assigning modern meanings to these words. See Dennis Brailsford, *Sport, Time, and Society: The British at Play* (London, 1991), xi–xii and ch. 1; Hugh Cunningham, *Leisure in the Industrial Revolution c.1780–c.1880* (New York, 1980), 13. See also Peter Bailey, *Leisure and Class in Victorian England: Rational Recreation and the Contest for Control, 1830–1885* (London, 1987), 8–20.

3. John Loy Jr., "The Nature of Sport: A Definitional Effort," *Quest* 10 (May 1968): 1–15. As have others, Loy drew on anthropological and philosophical discussions of these phenomena. See, for example, Roger Caillois, *Man, Play and Games,* trans. Meyer Barash (New York, 1961); John M. Roberts and Brian Sutton-Smith, "Child Training and Game Involvement," *Ethnology* 1 (1962): 166–85; and Gregory P. Stone, "American Sports: Play and Display," *Chicago Review* 9 (Fall 1955): 83–100.

4. Allen Guttmann, *From Ritual to Record: The Nature of Modern Sports* (New York, 1978), esp. 15–55. In his first chapter Guttmann opens with a typology that is similar to Loy's, except that he injects "contest" between games and sports, based on the work of Roger Caillois.

5. Johan Huizinga, *Homo Ludens—A Study of the Play-Element in Culture* (Boston, 1955 [1938]), 28, 196.

6. See, for example, Foster R. Dulles, *A History of Recreation: America Learns to Play,* 2d ed. (New York, 1965); Daniel T. Rodgers, *The Work Ethic in Industrial America, 1850–1920* (Chicago, 1978); Rosemary Deem and Graeme Salaman, eds., *Work, Culture, and Society* (Philadelphia, 1985): Kathryn Grover, ed., *Hard at Play: Leisure in America, 1840–1940* (Amherst, Mass., 1992); John R. Kelly and Geoffrey Godbey, *The Sociology of Leisure* (State College, Pa., 1992); Gary S. Cross, *Time and Money: The Making of Consumer Culture* (London, 1993).

Throughout this book I use *work* as Stephen Innes does, as meaning "productive labor." Innes argues that Marx's distinction between work and labor is inappropriate for early America, and I suggest that it is so for early modern Britain as well. See Innes, ed., *Work and Labor in Early America* (Chapel Hill, N.C., 1988), 20.

7. Thorstein Veblen, *The Theory of the Leisure Class,* rev. ed. (New York, 1934 [1899]).

8. The literature on the locus and "development" of modern American sports in mid-nineteenth-century cities is extensive, but three works adequately present the assumptions, central arguments, and limits of what is a style, or urban, male, middle-class sport, as well as the modernization model on which this type depends. See Melvin Adelman, *A Sporting Time: New York City and the Rise of Modern Athletics, 1820–1870* (Urbana, Ill., 1986); George Kirsch, *The Creation of American Team Sports: Baseball and Cricket, 1838–72* (Urbana, Ill., 1989); and Steven A. Riess, *City Games: The Evolution of American Urban Society and the Rise of Sports* (Urbana, Ill., 1989).

9. I have struggled with the adequacy of terms such as *customary, traditional,* and *residual.* The first two do not really imply the subtle changes that people imposed on long-standing practices. Nevertheless, the alternative posed by Raymond Williams—*residual*—is also not satisfactory, in part because few practices were really the residue of past forms and formations through the seventeenth century. Consequently I have settled on the lesser of evils, *customary* and *traditional,* and employ *residual* only later, once a group did construct an alternative form or forma-

tion. As chapter 1 will indicate, I do employ Williams's term *emergent.* See Raymond Williams, *Marxism and Literature* (New York, 1977), 121–22; idem, *Problems in Materialism and Culture: Selected Essays* (London, 1980), 40–42.

10. Peter Mathias, *The Transformation of England: Essays in the Economic and Social History of England in the Eighteenth Century* (New York, 1979), 155–56.

Chapter 1: Sport in the Old World

1. This is the famous Book, or Declaration, of Sports incident, which culminated in the national edict "The Kings Majesties Declaration to his Subjects Concerning Lawful Sports to be Used" in 1618. For historians' treatments of the episode, see Kenneth L. Parker, *The English Sabbath: A Study of Doctrine and Discipline from the Reformation to the Civil War* (Cambridge, 1988), 149–60; Nancy L. Struna, "The Declaration of Sports Reconsidered," *Canadian Journal of History of Sport* 14 (Dec. 1983): 44–68; Roger C. Richardson, "Puritanism and the Ecclesiastical Authorities: The Case of the Diocese of Chester," in Brian Manning, ed., *Politics, Religion, and the English Civil War* (London, 1973), 3–33; Dennis Brailsford, *Sport and Society: Elizabeth to Anne* (London, 1969), 99–108; James Tait, "The Declaration of Sports for Lancashire," *English Historical Review* 32 (Oct. 1917): 561–68; Lionel A. Govett, *The King's Book of Sports* (London, 1890).

2. Quoted in Parker, *English Sabbath*, 148.

3. William Kethe, *A Sermon Made at Blanford Forum, in the Countie of Dorset* (London, 1571), 8; Christopher Hill, *Society and Puritanism in Pre-Revolutionary England* (London, 1964), 191.

4. Govett, *Book of Sports*, 25.

5. David Underdown, *Revel, Riot and Rebellion: Popular Politics and Culture in England 1603–1660* (Oxford, 1985), 69, 47; Roger B. Manning, *Village Revolts: Social Protest and Popular Disturbances in England 1509–1640* (Oxford, 1988), 211–14; Keith V. Thomas, *Man and the Natural World: A History of the Modern Sensibility* (New York, 1983), 64–67; Peter Burke, *Popular Culture in Early Modern Europe* (New York, 1978), esp. 207–23; F. G. Emmison, *Elizabethan Life: Disorder* (Chelmsford, 1970), 229–30.

6. Govett, *Book of Sports*, 31

7. Quoted in Underdown, *Revel, Riot and Rebellion*, 65.

8. Carl Bridenbaugh, *Vexed and Troubled Englishmen, 1590–1642* (New York, 1968).

9. For a broader theoretical discussion of the political significance of sports, see Richard Gruneau, "Freedom and Constraint: The Paradoxes of Play, Games, and Sport," *Journal of Sport History* 7 (Winter 1980): 68–86.

10. Joseph Strutt, *The Sports and Pastimes of the People of England* (Detroit, 1968 [1801]), 208–9; John Stowe, *A Survey of London*, ed. Charles L. Kingsford, 2 vols. (Oxford, 1971 [1603]), 1:91–95; Richard Carew, *Survey of Cornwall* (New York, 1969 [1602]), 76–77; Richard Holt, *Sport and the British: A Modern History* (Oxford, 1989), 16–17; Thomas, *Man and the Natural World*, 144.

11. Quoted in Underdown, *Revel, Riot and Rebellion*, 46.

12. Francis Burns, *Heigh for Cotswold! A History of Robert Dover's Olimpick Games* (Chipping Camden, 1981).

13. Carew, *Survey of Cornwall*, 76.

14. Ibid., 74–75.

15. Ibid., 74. On football more generally, see Norbert Elias and Eric Dunning, "Folk Football in Medieval and Early Modern Britain," in Eric Dunning, ed., *The Sociology of Sport: A Selection of Readings* (London, 1971), esp. 126–29; Francis P. Magoun, "Football in Medieval England and in Middle English Literature," *American Historical Review* 35 (Oct. 1929): 33–45.

16. Dorothy G. Spicer, *Yearbook of English Festivals* (New York, 1954), 191; Thomas, *Man and the Natural World*, 144–45.

17. Thomas, *Man and the Natural World*, 145.

18. E. O. James, *Seasonal Feasts and Festivals* (New York, 1961), 298–99; T. F. Thistleton-Dyer, *British Popular Customs: Past and Present* (London, 1876), 31–32; Brailsford, *Sport and Society*, 55–56.

19. Carew, *Survey of Cornwall*, 77; Strutt, *Sports and Pastimes*, 70; James Rice, *History of the British Turf: From Earliest Times to the Present Day*, 2 vols. (London, 1879), 1:3–13; Roger Longrigg, *The English Squire and His Sport* (New York, 1977), 81–82; idem, *The History of Horse Racing* (New York, 1972), 39–41; Thomas, *Man and the Natural World*, 59–60.

20. Winton U. Solberg, *Redeem the Time: The Puritan Sabbath in Early America* (Cambridge, Mass., 1977), 23; Strutt, *Sports and Pastimes*, 274–93; James, *Seasonal Feasts*, 298–99, 309–11; A. R. Wright, *British Calendar Customs: England*, ed. T. E. Lones, 3 vols. (London, 1936–38), 1:22–28, 2:85–90; Ann Kussmaul, *Servants in Husbandry in Early Modern England* (Cambridge, 1981), 50. A fine, recent discussion of the location of sports in festivals and rituals is Dennis Brailsford, *Sport, Time, and Society: The British at Play* (London, 1991), 2–12.

21. Norman Ault, ed., *Seventeenth Century Lyrics from the Original Texts* (London, 1928), 191; Robert W. Malcolmson, *Popular Recreations in English Society 1700–1850* (Cambridge, 1973), 28–29, 48; Carew, *Survey of Cornwall*, 69–70; Strutt, *Sports and Pastimes*, 273–93; Lu Emily Pearson, *Elizabethans at Home* (Stanford, Calif., 1957), 529; Holt, *Sport and the British*, 14–15; Burke, *Popular Culture*, 182–204.

22. Strutt, *Sports and Pastimes*, 62, 174, 178. On work and leisure rhythms, see Lindsey Charles and Lorna Duffin, eds., *Women and Work in Pre-industrial England* (London, 1985); Kussmaul, *Servants in Husbandry*; Keith Thomas, "Work and Leisure in Pre-Industrial Society," *Past & Present* 29 (1964): 50–66.

23. The best work on English alehouses is Peter Clark, *The English Alehouse: A Social History 1200–1830* (London, 1983). See also Keith Wrightson, "Alehouses, Order and Reformation in Rural England, 1590–1660," in Stephen Yeo and Eileen Yeo, eds., *Popular Culture and Class Conflict 1590–1914: Explorations in the History of Labour and Leisure* (Atlantic Highlands, N.J., 1981), 1–27; Malcolmson, *Popular Recreations*, 72–73.

24. Quoted in Underdown, *Revel, Riot and Rebellion*, 63. See also Carew, *Survey of Cornwall*, 69.

25. Burns, *Heigh for Cotswold;* Christopher Whitfield, ed., *Robert Dover and the Cotswold Games: Annalia Dubrensia* (London, 1962).

26. Strutt, *Sports and Pastimes*, 105–26; Alan Young, *Tudor and Jacobean Tournaments* (London, 1987). For a fuller discussion of upper-rank sports, see Thomas S. Henricks, *Disputed Pleasures: Sport and Society in Preindustrial England* (Westport, Conn., 1991). On fencing as commercial display and entertainment, see Mary McElroy and Kent Cartwright, "Public Fencing Contests on the Elizabethan Stage," *Journal of Sport History* 13 (Winter 1986): 193–211.

27. Brailsford, *Sport and Society*, 26–27; Pearson, *Elizabethans at Home*, 531.

28. Sir Thomas Elyot, *The Boke Named the Governour*, ed. Henry H. S. Croft, 2 vols. (London, 1883 [1531]).

29. Roger Ascham, *The Schoolmaster*, ed. Lawrence V. Ryan (Ithaca, N.Y., 1967 [1570]); Sir Humphrey Gilbert, *Queene Elizabethe's Academy: A Booke of Precedence*, ed. Frederick J. Furnivall (London, 1869 [1564]).

30. James Stuart, *Basilikon Doron*, in Charles H. McIlwain, ed., *The Political Works of James I* (Cambridge, Mass., 1928), 48–50.

31. Manning, *Village Revolts*, 287–89.

32. Chester Kirby, "The English Game Law System," *American Historical Review* 38 (Jan. 1933): 240–62; Gervase Markham, "Country Contentments," in J. Dover Wilson, ed., *Life in Shakespeare's England* (Cambridge, 1949), 16; P. B. Munsche, *Gentlemen and Poachers: The English Game Laws, 1671–1831* (New York, 1981), 9–10; Thomas, *Man and the Natural World*, 145–46; Charles Young, *The Royal Forests of Medieval England* (Philadelphia, 1979); Matt Cartmill, *A View to Death in the Morning: Hunting and Nature through History* (Cambridge, Mass., 1993), 60–65.

33. Frederick J. Furnivall, ed., *Captain Cox, His Ballads and Books: or, Robert Laneham's Letter 1575* (Hertford, 1890), 123–24. See also John Nichols, ed., *Progresses and Public Progressions of Queen Elizabeth*, 3 vols. (London, 1823), 1:308, 2:277.

34. Munsche, *Gentlemen and Poachers*, 11; Kirby, "English Game Law System," 240–41.

35. Manning, *Village Revolts*, 284–92.

36. Quoted in ibid., 285.

37. Ibid.

38. H. S. Bennett, *Life on the English Manor: A Study of Peasant Conditions 1150–1400* (New York, 1937), 265; G. B. Harrison, *An Elizabethan Journal Being a Record of Those Things Most Talked of during the Years 1591–1594* (London, 1928), 44; William S. Davis, *Life in Elizabethan Days* (New York, 1930), 238; Munsche, *Gentlemen and Poachers*, 11; Govett, *Book of Sports*, 23.

39. Strutt, *Sports and Pastimes*, 43–46; Brailsford, *Sport and Society*, 30.

40. Peter Mathias, *The Transformation of England: Essays in the Economic and Social History of England in the Eighteenth Century* (New York, 1979), 137–56; Hill, *Society and Puritanism*, 124–25.

41. David Levine and Keith Wrightson, *The Making of an Industrial Society: Whickham, 1560–1765* (Oxford, 1991); Ian W. Archer, *The Pursuit of Stability: Social Relations in Elizabethan London* (Cambridge, 1991); Paul Slack, *Poverty and Policy in Tudor and Stuart England* (London, 1988); Richard Lachmann, *From Manor to Market: Structural Change in England, 1536–1640* (Madison, Wis., 1987); A. L. Beier, *Masterless Men: The Vagrancy Problem in England 1560–1640* (London, 1985); John E. Martin, *Feudalism to Capitalism: Peasant and Landlord in English Agrarian Development* (Atlantic Highlands, N.J., 1983); Joan Thirsk, *The Rural Economy of England: Collected Essays* (London, 1984); E. A. Wrigley and R. S. Schofield, *The Population History of England, 1541–1871: A Reconstruction* (Cambridge, Mass., 1981); J. A. Yelling, *Common Field and Enclosure in England 1450–1850* (Hamden, Conn., 1977); Peter Clark and Paul Slack, *English Towns in Transition 1500–1700* (London, 1976); Peter Laslett, *The World We Have Lost: England before the Industrial Age* (New York, 1965); Lawrence Stone, *Crisis of the Aristocracy, 1580–1640* (Oxford, 1965); idem, "Social Mobility in England, 1500–1700," *Past & Present* 20 (Apr. 1966): 16–55; Ephraim Lipson, *The Economic History of England*, 3 vols. (London, 1956–59), 3:248–49.

42. G. W. Prothero, ed., *Select Statutes and Other Constitutional Documents Illustrative of the Reigns of Elizabeth and James I*, 4th ed. (Oxford, 1913), 47–48. On the emergent interests in regulating labor as a factor in production, see Richard H. Tawney and Eileen Power, eds., *Tudor Economic Documents*, 2 vols. (London, 1924), 1:360, 384.

43. Prothero, ed., *Select Statutes*, 72–73, 96–104. See also Buchanan Sharp, *In Contempt of All Authority: Rural Artisans and Riot in the West of England, 1586–1660* (Berkeley, Calif., 1980), 31–34.

44. James, "His Majesties Declaration."

45. Underdown, *Revel, Riot and Rebellion*, 50–51; Hill, *Society and Puritanism*, 189–90; Emmison, *Elizabethan Life*, 229–30; Harrison, *Elizabethan Journal*, 105–6, 242–43. For the broader European reformation of popular culture, see Burke, *Popular Culture*, 207–34.

46. Quoted in Underdown, *Revel, Riot and Rebellion*, 51.

47. John Northbrooke, *Distractions of the Sabbath* (London, 1579), 175–76.

48. Underdown, *Revel, Riot and Rebellion*, 54–55. On the emerging Puritan movement, see Patrick Collinson, *English Puritanism* (London, 1983); William Hunt, *The Puritan Movement: The Coming of Revolution in an English County* (Cambridge, Mass., 1983); Nicholas Tyacke, "Puritanism, Arminianism and Counter Revolution," in Conrad Russell, ed., *The Origins of the English Civil War* (New York, 1973), 119–43; Felicity Heal and Rosemary O'Day, eds., *Church and Society in England: Henry VIII to James I* (Hamden, Conn., 1977); Hill, *Society and Puritanism*; idem, *Intellectual Origins of the English Revolution* (Oxford, 1965);

49. Richard Hakluyt, *Discourse of Western Planting*, in E. G. R. Taylor, ed., *The Original Writings & Correspondence of the Two Richard Hakluyts*, 2 vols. (London, 1935). My interpretation draws from multiple sources, including Levine and Wright-

son, *The Making of an Industrial Society;* Archer, *The Pursuit of Stability;* Slack, *Poverty and Policy;* Lachmann, *From Manor to Market.*

50. On the argument about labor as social duty, see William Perkins, *Works,* 3 vols. (London, 1616–18), 3:774–79; Richard Baxter, *The Autobiography of Richard Baxter,* ed. N. H. Keeble (London, 1974), 241; Hill, *Society and Puritanism,* 129. See also Kemper Fullerton, "Calvinism and Capitalism," *Harvard Theological Review* 21 (July 1928): 163–95; Charles George and Katherine George, "Protestantism and Capitalism in Pre-Revolutionary England," *Church History* 27 (Dec. 1858): 351–71; Solberg *Redeem the Time,* 44.

51. J. E. Neale, *Elizabeth I and Her Parliaments,* 2 vols. (New York, 1958), 1:58–59, 395; Hill, *Society and Puritanism,* 152–61; Parker, *English Sabbath;* J. W. Allen *English Political Thought, 1603–1660,* 2 vols. (London, 1938), 2:269; Solberg, *Redeem the Time,* 46, 70. See also Brailsford, *Sport, Time, and Society,* 16–23.

52. Henrich Bullinger, *The Decades of Henry Bullinger,* ed. Thomas Harding, 4 vols. (Cambridge, 1849–52); Richard Greenham, *Works* (London, 1599); Nicholas Bownde, *The Doctrine of the Sabbath* (London, 1595); Perkins, *Works,* 1:774–75; Phillip Stubbes, *The Anatomie of Abuses,* ed. Frederick J. Furnivall (London, 1879), 174, 157; John Downame, *The Christian Warfare* (London, 1634), 969–90; John Addy, *Sin and Society in the Seventeenth Century* (London, 1989), 106–7; Solberg, *Redeem the Time,* 49–51; Hans-Peter Wagner, *Puritan Attitudes toward Recreation in Early Seventeenth-Century New England* (Frankfurt am Main, 1982); J. Thomas Jable, "The English Puritans: Suppressors of Sport and Amusement?" *Canadian Journal of History of Sport* 7 (May 1976): 33–40; Dennis Brailsford, "Puritanism and Sport in Seventeenth Century England," *Stadion* 1 (1975): 316–30.

53. Francis White, *A Treatise of the Sabbath-Day* (London, 1635), 234.

54. Hill, *Society and Puritanism,* 197; Solberg, *Redeem the Time,* 158.

55. Munsche, *Gentlemen and Poachers,* 8–19.

56. Underdown, *Revel, Riot and Rebellion,* 84, 56, 61–62.

57. William Laud, *Works,* 7 vols. (Oxford, 1847–60), 6:318–19; Charles I, "Declaration to His Subjects Concerning Lawful Sports to Be Used on Sundays, 1633," in Samuel R. Gardiner, ed., *The Constitutional Documents of the Puritan Revolution 1628–1660* (Oxford, 1889), 31–35. In the same year William Prynne restated the Puritans' opposition to unlawful sports and gaming and more or less went on the offensive by saying that the people had access to many other sports—indeed, a sufficient number of "honest recreations . . . with which to refresh themselves" (*Histrio-Mastrix: The Players Scourge, or Actors Tragaedie, Divides into Two Parts* [London, 1633], 966).

58. John Harland, ed., *The Lancashire Lieutenancy under the Tudors and Stuarts* (Manchester, 1859), 218.

59. Hugh R. Trevor-Roper, *Archbishop Laud 1573–1645* (London, 1940), 158, 250–52; Brailsford, *Sport and Society,* 105; Solberg, *Redeem the Time,* 77–78; Parker, *English Sabbath,* 182–96.

Chapter 2: A Grand Scheme

1. David B. Quinn, *England and the Discovery of America, 1481–1620* (New York, 1974); David B. Quinn and A. N. Ryan, *England's Sea Empire* (Boston, 1983).

2. William Strachey, *The Historie of Travell into Virginia Britannia,* eds. Louis B. Wright and Virginia Freund (London, 1953 [1612]), 13; "Nova Brittania: Offering Most Excellent Fruites by Planting in Virginia" (1609), in Peter Force, ed., *Tracts and Other Papers Relating Principally to the Origin, Settlement, and Progress of the Colonies in North America,* 4 vols. (Cloucester, Mass., 1963), 1: chap. 6, pp. 5–8.

3. Strachey, *Historie,* 14.

4. Richard Hakluyt, *A Discourse of Western Planting,* in E. G. R. Taylor, ed., *The Original Writings & Correspondence of the Two Richard Hakluyts,* 2 vols. (London, 1935): 2:211–326. Another significant work by Hakluyt the younger was *The Principal Navigations, Voiages and Discoveries of the English Nation,* 2 vols. (London, 1965 [1589]). See also David B. Quinn, *Set Fair for Roanoke: Voyages and Colonies, 1584–1606* (Chapel Hill, N.C., 1985), esp. 1–19.

5. Hakluyt, *Discourse,* 2:214.

6. Ibid., 2:215–20, 313–18.

7. Ibid., 2:222.

8. Ibid., 2:222–33; quotation on 233.

9. Ibid., 2:234.

10. Ibid., 2:235. As were most of the Hakluyts' arguments, this point was reinforced in later writings; see, for example, Richard Hakluyt the elder, "Pamphlet for the Virginia Enterprise" (1585), in Taylor, ed., *Writings & Correspondence,* 2:327.

11. Hakluyt, *Discourse,* 2:234.

12. Ibid., 2:319, 234–36. Throughout this and later chapters I use *work* as Stephen Innes does, as meaning "productive labor." Innes argues that Marx's distinction between work and labor is inappropriate for early America, and I suggest that it is inappropriate for early modern Britain as well. See Innes, ed., *Work and Labor in Early America* (Chapel Hill, N.C., 1988), 20.

13. Hakluyt, *Discourse,* 2:235. The occupations are listed on 320–24.

14. Ibid., 2:282. For a broader discussion of the propagandists' vision of New World colonization as a development scheme, see David Cressy, *Coming Over: Migration and Communication between England and New England in the Seventeeth Century* (Cambridge, 1987), esp. 37.

15. Hakluyt, *Principall Navigations,* 2:711.

16. Letter from Ralph Lane to Richard Hakluyt, lawyer, 3 September 1585, in Taylor, ed., *Writings & Correspondence,* 2:347. See also Karen O. Kupperman, *Roanoke: The Abandoned Colony* (Lanham, Md., 1984); David B. Quinn, *The Roanoke Voyages,* 2 vols. (Cambridge, 1955); and David B. Quinn and Alison M. Quinn, eds., *Virginia Voyages from Hakluyt* (London, 1973).

17. Thomas Harriot, "A Briefe and True Report of the New Found Land of Virginia" (1588), in Hakluyt, *Principall Navigations,* 2:763.

18. "Nova Brittania," in Force, *Tracts,* 1: chap. 6, pp. 12–19.

19. See, for example, ibid., 10–11; "Instructions for the Virginia Company" (1606), probably written by Hakluyt the younger, in Taylor, ed., *Writings & Correspondence,* 2:495; "Christopher Levett's Plans of 1628," in James P. Baxter, *Christopher Levett of York, the Pioneer Colonist in Casco Bay* (Portland, Me., 1893), 128–39. See also note 41 to this chapter.

20. "A True Declaration of the Estate of the Colonie in Virginia "(1610), in Force, ed., *Tracts,* 3: chap. 1, p. 22.

21. Strachey, *Historie,* 117.

22. "The Relation of Thomas Yong, 1634," in Albert C. Myers, ed., *Narratives of Early Pennsylvania, West New Jersey, and Delaware 1630–1707* (New York, 1912), 48. John Smith may hold the record for what are probably tall tales about kill ratios. He claimed that Jamestown planters downed 148 birds with three shots; see Smith, *The Complete Works of Captain John Smith,* ed. Philip L. Barbour, 3 vols. (Chapel Hill, N.C., 1986), 1:245 (hereinafter cited as *Works*).

23. Hakluyt, *Discourse,* 2:318. On Native American cultures, see William Cronon, *Changes in the Land: Indians, Colonists, and the Ecology of New England* (New York, 1983); James H. Merrell, *The Indians' New World* (Chapel Hill, N.C., 1989); Peter H. Wood, Gregory A. Waselkov, and M. Thomas Hatley, eds., *Powhatan's Mantle: Indians in the Colonial Southeast* (Lincoln, Nebr., 1989); Daniel K. Richter, *The Ordeal of the Longhouse: The Peoples of the Iroquois League in the Era of European Colonization* (Chapel Hill, N.C., 1992).

24. Strachey, *Historie,* 114. See also Smith, *Works,* 1:162.

25. "Winslow's Relation," in Alexander Young, ed., *Chronicles of the Pilgrim Fathers of the Colony of Plymouth, from 1602 to 1625* (Boston, 1841), 363. William Cronon has a lengthy discussion of Native American work patterns and makes the point that the English migrants (literate ones who left records) were critical of American Indian males who, in their judgment, worked little. But the English not only misread what was happening among Native Americans but also apparently either forgot or failed to recognize the little value placed on work among many of their contemporaries; see Cronon, *Changes in the Land,* esp. 34–53.

26. Smith, *Works,* 2:118, 1:164.

27. Strachey, *Historie,* 83.

28. "Winslow's Relation," in Young, ed., *Chronicles of the Pilgrim Fathers,* 307.

29. Smith, *Travels and Works of Captain John Smith,* ed. Edward Arber, 2 vols. (Edinburgh, 1910), 1:cxiv (hereinafter cited as *Travels and Works).*

30. Strachey, *Historie,* 84.

31. Ibid., 75.

32. Smith, *Works,* 1:160–75. For an extensive discussion of Smith's relations with and treatment of the native Virginians, see Karen O. Kupperman, ed., *Captain John Smith: A Select Edition of His Writings* (Chapel Hill, N.C., 1988), 135–203.

33. Smith, *Works,* 1:350.

34. Ibid., 1:347.

35. Ibid.

36. Ibid., 1:346–47.

37. Francis Higginson, "New England's Plantation" (1630), in Alexander Young, ed., *Chronicles of the First Planters of the Colony of Massachusetts Bay, from 1623 to 1636* (Boston, 1846), 253 (hereinafter cited as *Chronicles of Massachusetts*).

38. "Relation of Yong," in Clayton C. Hall, ed., *Narratives of Early Maryland, 1633–1684* (New York, 1910), 297, 299.

39. Perry Miller, *Errand into the Wilderness* (New York, 1964), 1; William Bradford, *Of Plymouth Plantation 1620–1647*, ed. Samuel E. Morison (New York, 1952), 62. As they arrived in Cape Cod in winter, Bradford recalled that what they saw was "but a hideous and desolate wilderness, full of wild beasts and wild men." See also Peter N. Carroll, *Puritanism and the Wilderness: The Intellectual Significance of the New England Frontier 1629–1700* (New York, 1969).

40. Cressy, *Coming Over*, 14.

41. "Nova Brittania," 21; John Winthrop, *Journal*, ed. James K. Hosmer, 2 vols. (New York, 1908), 1:9–11; William Morrell, "New-England, or a Briefe Enarration" (1625), *Massachusetts Historical Society Collections*, 4th ser., 1 (1852): 218; Young, ed., *Chronicles of Massachusetts*, 95–96, 183; Edmund S. Morgan, *American Slavery–American Freedom: The Ordeal of Colonial Virginia* (New York, 1975), 45; Everett Emerson, ed., *Letters from New England: The Massachusetts Bay Colony, 1629–1638* (Amherst, Mass., 1976), 1–2; Richard P. Gildrie, *Salem, Massachusetts, 1629–1683: A Covenant Community* (Charlottesville, Va., 1975), 5–6; Christine L. Heyrman, *Commerce and Culture: The Maritime Communities of Colonial Massachusetts 1690–1750* (New York, 1984), 31–34.

42. The mortality figures for Virginia are based on Smith, *Travels and Works*, 1:cxxix; Gary M. Walton and James F. Shepherd, *The Economic Rise of Early America* (Cambridge, 1979), 37; see also James R. Perry, *The Formation of a Society on Virginia's Eastern Shore, 1615–1655* (Chapel Hill, N.C., 1990), 11. The Plymouth figures draw from "Bradford's and Winslow's Journal" (better known as "Mourt's Relation"), in Young, ed., *Chronicles of the Pilgrim Fathers*, 197–98.

43. See, for example, "Governor Bradford's History of Plymouth Colony," in Young, ed., *Chronicles of the Pilgrim Fathers*, 97–105.

44. Ibid., 104.

45. Ibid., 161–63; "Bradford's and Winslow's Journal," in Young, ed., *Chronicles of the Pilgrim Fathers*, 198; Bradford, *Of Plymouth Plantation*, 94.

46. Smith, *Works*, 1:210–35; idem, *Travels and Works*, 1:lxxii; Carl Bridenbaugh, *Jamestown 1544–1699* (New York, 1980), 28–31; Charles E. Hatch Jr., *The First Seventeen Years in Virginia 1607–1624* (Charlottesville, Va., 1957), 1–29.

47. Thomas Morton, "New English Canaan" (1632), in Force, *Tracts*, 2: chap. 5, pp. 89–92; Bradford, *Of Plymouth Plantation*, 204–6; Richard Drinnon, "The Maypole of Merry Mount," *Massachusetts Review* 21 (Summer 1980): 382–410; Michael Zuckerman, "Pilgrims in the Wilderness: Community, Modernity, and the Maypole at Merry Mount," *New England Quarterly* 50 (June 1977): 255–77.

48. "Bradford's and Winslow's Journal," in Young, ed., *Chronicles of the Pilgrim Fathers,* 231; see also Syndey V. James, ed., *Three Visitors to Early Plymouth* (Plymouth, Mass., 1963), 29.

49. "Bradford's and Winslow's Journal," in Young, ed., *Chronicles of the Pilgrim Fathers,* 210–11.

50. "A True Declaration of the Estate of the Colonie in Virginia," in Force, ed., *Tracts,* 3: chap. 1, p. 20; Morgan, *American Slavery–American Freedom,* 73–74; Bridenbaugh, *Jamestown,* 34; Wesley F. Craven, *The Southern Colonies in the Seventeenth Century, 1607–1689* (Baton Rouge, 1970).

51. Morgan, *American Slavery–American Freedom,* 70.

52. Smith, *Works,* 1:258–59. Twelve years later, in his *General Historie,* he revised the estimate to six hours (ibid., 2:208).

53. Smith, *Works,* 2:225.

54. Samuel M. Bemiss, ed., *The Three Charters of the Virginia Company of London with Seven Related Documents, 1606–1621* (Williamsburg, Va., 1957), 52; "The New Life of Virginea . . . Being the Second Part of Nova Brittania" (1612), in Force, ed., *Tracts,* 1: chap. 7, p. 13.

55. *For the Colony in Virginea Britannia: Lawes Divine, Morall, and Martiall, etc.,* comp. William Strachey, ed. David H. Flaherty (Charlottesville, Va., 1969 [1612]), 9–14.

56. Ibid., 20, 19.

57. Ibid., 29, 32, 36.

58. Ibid., 79.

59. Smith, *Works,* 2:239

60. Ibid., 1:262.

61. "Bradford's and Winslow's Journal," in Young, ed., *Chronicles of the Pilgrim Fathers,* 170.

62. Bradford, *Of Plymouth Plantation,* 120–21.

63. Ibid., 97.

64. "Cushman's Discourse," in Young, ed., *Chronicles of the Pilgrim Fathers,* 264.

65. Bradford, *Of Plymouth Plantation,* 105; "Bradford's and Winslow's Journal," in Young, ed., *Chronicles of the Pilgrim Fathers,* 199–201.

66. "Bradford's and Winslow's Journal," in Young, ed., *Chronicles of the Pilgrim Fathers,* 234.

67. John White, *The Planters Plea* (1630), in Force, ed., *Tracts,* 3: chap. 3, p. 41.

68. Young, ed., *Chronicles of Massachusetts,* 189.

69. Ibid., 188, 190.

70. Morton, "New English Canaan," 49.

71. Ibid., 89–90; Bradford, *Of Plymouth Plantation,* 204–5.

72. Bradford, *Of Plymouth Plantation,* 207–10; Drinnon, "Maypole of Merry Mount," 391; Zuckerman, "Pilgrims in the Wilderness," 257–58.

73. Bridenbaugh, *Jamestown,* 59; Perry, *Formation of a Society,* 17–19, 245; Morgan, *American Slavery–American Freedom,* 82–83, 92–95; Walton and Shepherd,

Economic Rise, 39. Bernard Bailyn has claimed that land speculation by Anglo-American colonists was "a universal occupation" from the beginning; see Bailyn, *The Peopling of British North America: An Introduction* (New York, 1986), 66. On the populations see Morgan, *American Slavery–American Freedom,* 98; Hatch, *First Seventeen Years,* 144–46; Craven, *Southern Colonies,* 183; Cressy, *Coming Over,* 63, 68; Emerson, ed., *Letters from New England (1629–38),* 93. The Virginia population would have been significantly higher had the mortality rate not remained so high; as of 1624 three out of every four colonists had died. See Kupperman, *Captain John Smith,* 253; Bridenbaugh, *Jamestown,* 20, 44–45.

74. Smith, *Works,* 1:346.

Chapter 3: Change and Persistence in Colonial Sporting Life, 1620s–1670s

1. Bernard Bailyn, *Voyagers to the West* (New York, 1986), 243; Stephen Innes, ed., *Work and Labor in Early America* (Chapel Hill, N.C., 1988), 6–7.

2. James R. Perry, *The Formation of a Society on Virginia's Eastern Shore, 1615–1655* (Chapel Hill, N.C., 1990), 11–27; David H. Fischer, *Albion's Seed: Four British Folkways in America* (Oxford, 1989), 207–11; Russell R. Menard, "The Tobacco Industry in the Chesapeake Colonies, 1617–1730: An Interpretation," *Research in Economic History* 5 (1980): 109–77; Gloria L. Main, *Tobacco Colony: Life in Early Maryland, 1650–1720* (Princeton, N.J., 1982), 9–47; Paul G. E. Clemens, *The Atlantic Economy and Colonial Maryland's Eastern Shore: From Tobacco to Grain* (Ithaca, N.Y., 1980), 41–79; Wesley F. Craven, *The Southern Colonies in the Seventeenth Century, 1607–1689* (Baton Rouge, 1970), 183. The most recent and adequate discussion of the seventeenth-century Chesapeake is Lois Green Carr, Russell R. Menard, and Lorena Walsh, *Robert Cole's World: Agriculture and Society in Early Maryland* (Chapel Hill, N.C., 1991); see 12–13 for these early years. On the broad interests in landholding, see Bernard Bailyn, *The Peopling of British North America: An Introduction* (New York, 1986), 66; William Cronon, *Changes in the Land: Indians, Colonists, and the Ecology of New England* (New York, 1983), 77–78, 168. See also David Quinn, "Why They Came," in David Quinn, ed., *Early Maryland in a Wider World* (Detroit, 1982), 122–36.

3. Much of the evidence about recreations is in the negative form, especially in laws and court cases. In some sources, however, evidence about recreations is notable only for its absence. See, for example, Andrew White (Father), "A Relation of the Colony of Lord Baron Baltimore, in Maryland, Near Virginia," in Peter Force, ed., *Tracts and Other Papers Relating Principally to the Origin, Settlement, and Progress of the Colonies in North America,* 4 vols. (Cloucester, Mass., 1963), 4: chap. 12, p. 34.

4. Edmund S. Morgan, *American Slavery–American Freedom: The Ordeal of Colonial Virginia* (New York, 1975), 98–107; Carl Bridenbaugh, *Jamestown 1544–1699* (New York, 1980), 44–45; James Horn, "Adapting to a New World: A Comparative Study of Local Society in England and Maryland, 1650–1700," in Lois Green Carr, Philip D. Morgan, and Jean B. Russo, eds., *Colonial Chesapeake Society* (Chapel

Hill, N.C., 1988), 134–39; J. Frederick Fausz, "Merging and Emerging Worlds: Anglo-Indian Interest Groups and the Development of the Seventeenth-Century Chesapeake," in ibid., 50–51.

5. John Smith, *Travels and Works of Captain John Smith*, ed. Edward Arber, 2 vols. (Edinburgh, 1910), 2:564. See also *The Records of the Virginia Company in London*, ed. Susan M. Kingsbury, 4 vols. (Washington, D.C., 1906–35), 3:706.

6. Bridenbaugh, *Jamestown*, 54–55; Perry, *Formation of Virginia Society*, 202–3. Historians of the seventeenth-century Chesapeake generally maintain that few upper-rank English people migrated to the region; see, for example, Russell R. Menard, "Economy and Society in Early Colonial Maryland" (Ph.D. diss., University of Iowa, 1975), 263.

7. *Records of the Virginia Company*, 4:235. See also *The Statutes-at-Large, Being a Collection of All the Laws of Virginia (1619–1792)*, ed. William W. Hening, 13 vols. (Richmond, 1819–1823), 2:417–18 (hereinafter cited as *Virginia Statutes*).

8. "Proceedings of the Virginia Assembly, 1619," in Lyon Tyler, ed., *Narratives of Early Virginia 1606–1625* (New York, 1907), 263. Laws often stressed the goal of "industriousness"; see, for example, *Virginia Statutes*, 1:114.

9. "Proceedings of the Virginia Assembly," 263.

10. *Records of the Virginia Company*, 3:208.

11. Ibid., 3:208; "Proceedings of the Virginia Assembly," 273; *Virginia Statutes*, 1:123, 126, 144. Long ago Perry Miller maintained that religion was the "really energizing propulsion" in the colonization of Virginia (*Errand into the Wilderness* [New York, 1964], 101). Later and a bit more broadly Darrett Rutman argued that religion was a critical component of the mental worlds of seventeenth-century people (*American Puritanism* [Philadelphia, 1970], 4–5).

12. Perry, *Formation of Virginia Society*, 17; Morgan, *American Slavery–American Freedom*, 141–42; Menard, "Economy and Society," 320; Carr, Menard, and Walsh, *Robert Cole's World*, 13; Bridenbaugh, *Jamestown*, 41. These estimated figures do vary in the literature, but the range and increased production per laborer appear firm. Morgan claimed that a Virginia laborer could produce 1,500 pounds per year by the 1640s, or double the production of the 1620s, whereas Menard's estimates for Maryland, used here, are not as high. I determined the initial per capita figure by dividing Bridenbaugh's figures for Virginia exports in 1618 (50,000 pounds) by the total population. Perry presented a slightly lower figure (41,000 pounds), but using this number would have made the subsequent increase even more striking. I have tried to err on the conservative side in all the figures.

13. Bridenbaugh, *Jamestown*, 20; Menard, "Economy and Society," 319–21; Gary M. Walton and James F. Shepherd, *The Economic Rise of Early America* (Cambridge, 1979), 134–36. For Maryland during and after the late 1630s, Carr, Menard, and Walsh estimated production at 100,000 pounds of tobacco, or an annual average of 600 pounds per laboring male. Individual production limits may have been as high as 700–750 pounds. They also argued that labor productivity increased even more after midcentury (*Robert Cole's World*, 42–43).

14. Both free and unfree laborers lived and worked in the Chesapeake, under different kinds of agreements with owners and employers. See Morgan, *American Slavery–American Freedom,* 220–23; Lorena S. Walsh, "Land, Landlord, and Lease-holder: Estate Management and Tenant Fortunes in Southern Maryland, 1642–1820," *Agricultural History* 59 (July 1985): 373–96; Lois Green Carr and Russell R. Menard, "Servants and Freedmen in Early Colonial Maryland," in Thad W. Tate and David L. Ammerman, eds., *The Chesapeake in the Seventeenth-Century: Essays on Anglo-American Society* (Chapel Hill, N.C., 1979), 209–12; Perry, *Formation of Virginia Society,* 138–39; Darrett Rutman and Anita Rutman, *A Place in Time: Middlesex County, Virginia 1650–1750* (New York, 1984), 71–75. On proportions of migrants who were servants and on conditions of servitude, see David Galenson, *White Servitude in Colonial America: An Economic Analysis* (Cambridge, 1981), 49–50; James Horn, "Servant Emigration to the Chesapeake," in Tate and Ammerman, eds., *Chesapeake in the Seventeenth-Century,* 94–95. About conditions all colonists faced, see Horn, "Adapting to a New World," 160–61. Mortality rates remained high through much of the century. Russell Menard has estimated that 17 percent of all immigrant males died before age thirty and 70 percent before age fifty ("Immigrants and Their Increase: The Process of Population Growth in Early Colonial Maryland," in Aubrey C. Land, Lois Green Carr, and Edward Papenfuse, eds., *Law, Society, and Politics in Early Maryland* [Baltimore, 1977], 93; "Economy and Society," 254).

15. "The Trappan'd Maiden: Or, The Distressed Damsel," cited in Nancy F. Cott, ed., *Root of Bitterness: Documents of the Social History of American Women* (New York, 1972), 31–33.

16. *Archives of Maryland,* ed. William Hand Browne et al., 72 vols. (Baltimore, 1883–1972), 4:74, 75–79, 82–84, 86–88. See also Raphael Semmes, *Captains and Mariners of Early Maryland* (Baltimore, 1937), 11–12, 23, 731; Perry, *Formation of Virginia Society,* 42; John Hervey, *Racing in America,* 2 vols. (New York, 1944), 1:15; Roger Longrigg, *The History of Horse Racing* (New York, 1972), 105–6.

17. *Archives of Maryland,* 1:45–46, 52–54, 159, 286; *Virginia Statutes,* 1:261, 300–301; *County Court Records of Accomack-Northampton, Virginia, 1632–1640,* ed. Susie M. Ames (Washington, D.C., 1954), 128–29, xlii–xliii. See also Perry, *Formation of Virginia Society,* 141–42, 177, 202–3, 208–10, 230.

18. *Accomack-Northampton Records,* 60–61.

19. Menard, "Economy and Society," 268.

20. Letter, Robert Ryece to John Winthrop, Suffolk, 9 September 1636, in Winthrop Papers, *Massachusetts Historical Society Collections,* 4th ser., 6 (1863): 408; Ryece to Winthrop, 1 March 1636, 411.

21. Stephen Foster, *The Long Argument: English Puritanism and the Shaping of New England Culture, 1570–1700* (Chapel Hill, N.C., 1991); William Hunt, *The Puritan Moment: The Coming of Revolution in an English County* (Cambridge, Mass., 1983); Derek Hirst, *Authority and Conflict: England, 1603–1658* (Cambridge, Mass., 1986); Buchanan Sharp, *In Contempt of All Authority: Rural Artisans and Riot in the*

West of England, 1586–1660 (Berkeley, 1980); Nancy L. Struna, "The 'Declaration of Sports' Reconsidered," *Canadian Journal of History of Sport* 14 (Dec. 1983): 44–68.

22. Cited in Edmund S. Morgan, *The Puritan Dilemma: The Story of John Winthrop* (Boston, 1958), 39.

23. John White, "Brief Relation," in Alexander Young, ed., *Chronicles of the First Planters of The Colony of Massachusetts Bay, from 1623 to 1636* (Boston, 1846), 13–14; Edward Johnson, *The Wonder Working Providence of Sions Saviour,* ed. J. Franklin Jameson (New York, 1959), 55, 248; David Cressy, *Coming Over: Migration and Communication between England and New England in the Seventeenth Century* (Cambridge, 1987), 52, 67–68, 129; Virginia D. Anderson, *New England's Generation: The Great Migration and the Formation of Society and Culture in the Seventeenth Century* (Cambridge, 1991).

24. Daniel Vickers, "Competency and Competition: Economic Culture in Early America," *William and Mary Quarterly,* 3d ser., 48 (July 1991): 3–39.

25. Ibid. For discussion of the interests of the migrants, both economic and religious, see Timothy H. Breen and Stephen Foster, "The Puritans' Greatest Achievement: A Study of Social Cohesion in Seventeenth-Century Massachusetts," *Journal of American History* 60 (June 1973): 5–22; Cressy, *Coming Over,* 74–81, 178. See also John F. Martin, *Profits in the Wilderness: Entrepreneurship and the Founding of New England Towns in the Seventeenth Century* (Chapel Hill, N.C., 1991).

26. *The Records of the First Church in Boston,* ed. Richard D. Pierce, 2 vols. (Boston, 1961), 1:27 (26 January 1640); *The Records of the Governor and the Company of Massachusetts Bay,* ed. Nathaniel B. Shurtleff, 5 vols. (New York, 1968), 1:82, 140, 2:179–80 (hereinafter cited as *Massachusetts Records*); "Salem Town Records, 1634–1659," *Essex Institute Historical Collections* 9 (1868): 13; Sidney Perley, *The History of Salem,* 3 vols. (Salem, 1924–28), 1:331; Edmund S. Morgan, *The Founding of Massachusetts* (New York, 1964), 403; Winton U. Solberg, *Redeem the Time: The Puritan Sabbath in Early America* (Cambridge, Mass., 1977), 77, 131; David D. Hall, *Worlds of Wonders, Days of Judgment: Popular Religious Belief in Early New England* (New York, 1989), 5–10.

27. This antisport and play interpretation had appeared fairly consistently in the writings of historians since the late nineteenth century. An early version that used only laws and sermons as evidence was that of William Weeden, *Economic and Social History of New England,* 2 vols. (Cambridge, Mass., 1890). See also John A. Krout, *Annals of American Sport* (New Haven, Conn., 1929); Jesse F. Steiner, *Americans at Play* (New York, 1933); Foster Rhea Dulles, *A History of Recreation: America Learns to Play* (New York, 1940); John R. Betts, "Mind and Body in Early American Thought," *Journal of American History* 54 (Mar. 1968): 796–805.

The only monograph to attempt to reexamine the Puritans' position (the antiposition) originated as a doctoral dissertation and was largely unrevised. See Hans-Peter Wagner, *Puritan Attitudes toward Recreation in Early Seventeenth-Century New*

England (Frankfurt am Main, 1982). Wagner concluded that the Puritans were not as dour as early historians had portrayed them and that they both encouraged and practiced some sports and exercises. Allen Guttmann discussed Wagner's argument within a synthetic work on modern American sport but then reframed the older antisport interpretation as one in which the Puritans "retarded the emergence of modern sports" (*A Whole New Ball Game: An Interpretation of American Sports* [Chapel Hill, N.C., 1988], 23–34; quotation on 34). See also Bruce C. Daniels, "Sober Mirth and Pleasant Poisons: Puritan Ambivalence toward Leisure and Recreation in Colonial New England," *American Studies* 34 (Spring 1993): 121–37; and idem, *Puritans at Play: Leisure and Recreation in Colonial New England* (New York, 1995).

28. John Robinson, *Observations of Knowledge & Virtue* (London, 1625), 143.

29. John Winthrop, *Winthrop Papers*, 6 vols. (Boston, 1929–47), 1:201–2.

30. John Winthrop, *Journal*, ed. James K. Hosmer, 2 vols. (New York, 1908), 1:32.

31. Richard Mather, "Journal" (1635), in Young, ed., *Chronicle of Massachusetts*, 460.

32. William Hammon to Sir Simonds D'Ewes, 26 September 1633, in Everett Emerson, ed., *Letters from New England: The Massachusetts Bay Colony, 1629–1638* (Amherst, Mass., 1976), 110–11.

33. William Wood, "New-Englands Prospect" (1634), in Young, ed., *Chronicles of Massachusetts*, 407–8.

34. *Massachusetts Records*, 1:236; Perley, *History of Salem*, 2:25–27.

35. Francis Higginson, "New-Englands Plantation" (1630), in Young, ed., *Chronicles of Massachusetts*, 261, noted six to seven horses. In 1633 Hammon complained that the colonists did not "have but four mares" and five "team of bullock and horse in the country" (in Emerson, ed., *Letters from New England*, 112). See also Longrigg, *History of Horse Racing*, 106.

36. Wood, "New-Englands Prospect," 404; Perley, *History of Salem*, 2:25–27; Cressy, *Coming Over*, 150. John Winthrop Jr. apparently employed a Native American as a "huntsman" in 1634, but there is no evidence that other men did. See Charles Brooks, *History of the Town of Medford, Middlesex County, Massachusetts*, rev. ed. (Boston, 1886 [1855]), 37.

37. Christopher Hill has claimed that New Englanders realized the "full theoretical consequences" of the Puritan position on the necessity and dignity of labor, as their English contemporaries did not (*Society and Puritanism in Pre-Revolutionary England* [New York, 1964], 141). On covenants, the calling doctrine, and the Puritans' social ethic, see Perry Miller, *The New England Mind: The Seventeenth Century* (Boston, 1939); Edmund S. Morgan, *The Puritan Family: Religion and Domestic Relations in Seventeenth-Century New England*, rev. ed. (New York, 1966), esp. 66–78; Stephen Foster, *Their Solitary Way: The Puritan Social Ethic in the First Century of Settlement in New England* (New Haven, Conn., 1971), 99–106.

38. John Winthrop cited in Morgan, *Puritan Dilemma*, 8–9.

39. This phrase was also common in the writings of English Puritans. See, for example, John Downame, *Guide to Godlynesse* (London, 1622), 164. See also

Fischer, *Albion's Seed,* 147. Civil authorities in Massachusetts particularly encouraged physical exercises that benefited the "publicke weale & safety," such as were central to military training. They not only allowed the Military Company of Massachusetts Bay to assemble anytime but also ordered youths between the ages of ten and sixteen to receive training in the use of arms (*Massachusetts Records,* 1:250, 327, 2:99).

40. *Massachusetts Records,* 4, pt. 1:366–67. Any pastime, according to Boston minister John Cotton, was unlawful when it served no "higher end than our own pleasure" ("A Practical Commentary, or an Exposition with Observations, Reasons and Uses upon the First Epistle Generall of John" [London, 1656], 299–300). Authorities in nearby Plymouth also condemned idleness and idlers (William Bradford, *Of Plymouth Plantation 1620–1647,* ed. Samuel E. Morison [New York, 1952], 299–300). John F. Martin has argued that Puritan cosmology linked idleness and industry to two powerful, and oppositional, images. Puritans believed that the former was a condition, and perhaps a cause, of the wilderness, the wasteland. Industry, or labor, in turn, underlay improvements in the "garden" (*Profits in the Wilderness,* 115–16).

41. *Massachusetts Records,* 2:179–80.

42. Young, ed., *Chronicle of Massachusetts,* 168. See also David T. Konig, *Law and Society in Puritan Massachusetts: Essex County, 1629–1692* (Chapel Hill, N.C., 1979), 3.

43. Winthrop, *Journal,* 1:112.

44. For drunkenness, see *Massachusetts Records,* 1:271–72, 280; for poor and unsettled persons, 1:264; for tobacco, 1:126, 241–42; for taverns, 1:213. See also "Captain Roger Clap's Memoirs," in Young, ed., *Chronicles of Massachusetts,* 361–63; Winthrop, *Journal,* 1:108, 325; Winthrop Family, "Letters," *Massachusetts Historical Society Collections,* 4th ser., 7 (1865): 24–25; Richard P. Gildrie, *Salem, Massachusetts 1629–1683: A Covenant Community* (Charlottesville, Va., 1975), 47.

45. Lyle Koehler, *A Search for Power: The "Weaker Sex" in Seventeenth-Century New England* (Urbana, Ill., 1980), 352; *Massachusetts Records,* 1:90, 203, 267, 313.

46. Winthrop, *Papers,* 2:147; Young, ed., *Chronicles of Massachusetts,* 183. Letters from early immigrants, such as Francis Higginson (in Salem) and Winthrop, advised future migrants about the type and quantities of goods and food to brings (Emerson, ed., *Letters from New England,* 26–27, 46–47, 88). See also Cressy, *Coming Over,* 43–46.

47. Winthrop, *Journal,* 2:42; Emerson, ed., *Letters from New England,* 11.

48. Letter, Thomas Weld to his former parish in Terling, Essex, from Roxbury, June/July 1633, in Emerson, ed., *Letters from New England,* 96.

49. Letter, Edmund Browne to Sir Simonds D'Ewes, Sudbury, 7 September 1638, in ibid., 227.

50. William Wood, "Description of Massachusetts" (1634), in Young, ed., *Chronicles of Massachusetts,* 413.

51. Winthrop, *Papers,* 3:126; Cressy, *Coming Over,* 47–49.

52. In 1642 the General Court even ordered towns to choose men to ensure that parents fulfilled their duties to train "up their children in learning & labor" (*Massachusetts Records*, 2:6, 179–80). See also Cressy, *Coming Over*, 266.

53. Winthrop, *Journal*, 1:112, 2:24; Emerson, ed., *Letters from New England*, 65, 92; Darrett Rutman, *Winthrop's Boston* (New York, 1965), 184; Joseph G. Holland, *History of Western Massachusetts*, 2 vols. (Springfield, Mass, 1855), 1:63. In his *Journal* Winthrop included, with supporting commentary, John Cotton's statement of "false principles," which the minister delivered in response to Robert Keayne (1:317–18). Cotton condemned contemporaries for selling goods at high prices, even though they often bought them cheaply, and for taking advantage of their skills (by demanding high wages). For a fine discussion of the family organization of labor, the persisting demand for it, and the differences between New England and Chesapeake labor, see Daniel Vickers, "Working the Fields in a Developing Economy: Essex County, Massachusetts, 1630–1675," in Innes, ed., *Work and Labor*, 49–69, esp. 57–60.

54. Letter, John Eliot to Sir Simonds D'Ewes, Roxbury, 18 September 1633, in Emerson, ed., *Letters from New England*, 107.

55. Mechel Sobel, *The World They Made Together: Black and White Values in Eighteenth-Century Virginia* (Princeton, N.J., 1987), 21–22. Sobel maintains that the notion of time held by ordinary British people enabled them to order activities "concurrently rather than sequentially." E. P. Thompson made this point earlier ("Time, Work-Discipline, and Industrial Capitalism," *Past and Present* 38 [1967]: 56–97).

56. Henry Glassie, *Pattern in the Material Folk Culture of the Eastern United States* (Philadelphia, 1968); E. P. Thompson, "Eighteenth-Century English Society: Class Struggle without Class?" *Social History* 3 (1978), 152–53; Richard Bushman, "American High-Style and Vernacular Cultures," in Jack Greene and J. R. Pole, eds., *Colonial British America: Essays in the New History of the Early Modern Era* (Baltimore, 1984), 370–72. My argument draws much from Bushman's synthesis, in its entirety, 345–82.

57. David Hall has framed the long-running cultural change in different terms, calling it the "steady dissolution of traditional culture" (*Worlds of Wonder*, 10). A series of fits and starts and an unevenness over time may more adequately characterize the process.

58. John Josselyn, "An Account of Two Voyages to New-England" (1675), *Massachusetts Historical Society Collections*, 3d ser. (1883): 349; *Archives of Maryland*, 53:633; George Alsop, "A Character of the Province of Maryland" (1666), in Clayton C. Hall, ed., *Narratives of Early Maryland, 1633–1684* (New York, 1910), 357; John Hammond, "Leah and Rachel, Or, the Two Fruitful Sisters Virginia and Maryland" (1656), in Force, *Tracts*, 3: chap. 14, p. 2. On the Chesapeake, see Menard, "Economy and Society," 444–45; Carr, Menard, and Walsh, *Robert Cole's World*, 55–69; Lois Green Carr and Lorena S. Walsh, "Economic Diversification and Labor Organization in the Chesapeake, 1650–1820," in Innes, ed., *Work and Labor*, 154–55.

59. See, for example, Samuel Maverick, "A Briefe Description of New England and the Severall Townes Therein," *Massachusetts Historical Society Proceedings*, 2d ser., 1 (1885): 238; Samuel Danforth, "Journal, March 1649–July 1674," *New England Historical and Genealogical Register* 34 (1880): 362; *Virginia Statutes*, 2:12; Annie L. Jester, *Domestic Life in Virginia in the Seventeenth Century* (Charlottesville, Va., 1957), 70; Lorena S. Walsh, "Community Networks in the Early Chesapeake," in Carr, Morgan, and Russo, eds., *Colonial Chesapeake Society*, 200–241; Michael Graham, "Meetinghouse and Chapel: Religion and Community in Seventeenth-Century Maryland," in ibid., 242–47; Perry, *Formation of Virginia Society*, 68, 90–93, 114, 193; Horn, "Adapting to a New World," 169–72.

60. *Archives of Maryland*, 52:207–10.

61. Letter, John Endecott to John Winthrop, Salem, 28 July 1640, *Massachusetts Historical Society Collections*, 4th ser., 6 (1863): 141–42; *Massachusetts Records*, 4, pt. 1:200. See also Roger Thompson, *Sex in Middlesex: Popular Mores in a Massachusetts County, 1649–1699* (Amherst, Mass., 1986), 84, 90–93; Winthrop, *Journal*, 2:42; Samuel E. Morison, *Harvard College in the Seventeenth Century*, 2 vols. (Cambridge, Mass., 1936), 2:465–71; Fischer, *Albion's Seed*, 164–65; Rutman, *Winthrop's Boston*, 180–81; Thomas F. Waters, *Ipswich in the Massachusetts Bay Colony* (Ipswich, 1905), 123–24.

62. Josselyn, "An Account of Two Voyages," 267–68.

63. In all the colonies the legislatures periodically renewed these laws and in some cases made them more inclusive. See, for example, *Massachusetts Records*, 4, pt. 1: 150–51, 347, and 4, pt. 2: 395; *Town and Selectmen's Records of Newtowne and Cambridge 1630–1703* (Cambridge, Mass., 1901), 164, 178, 231; *Archives of Maryland*, 1:343, 2:414–15; *Virginia Statutes*, 2:48. For general discussions of the Sabbath laws and their similarities across the colonies, see Solberg, *Redeem the Time*, esp. 94–99 for this period. He claimed that the Sabbath served to check the "dehumanizing" effect that the frontier had on colonists.

64. *Virginia Statutes*, 1:401–2, 2:126; Essex Quarterly Court, 5:39, 7:364; Justin Windsor, ed., *The Memorial History of Boston 1630–1880*, 3 vols. (Boston, 1880), 1:229. See also *Archives of Maryland*, 2:346.

65. *Massachusetts Records*, 3:242, 359, 399, 449, 4, pt. 1: 150–51, 222, 366–67, 324–25, and 4, pt. 2: 453; *Massachusetts Court of Assistants Records 1630–1692*, 3 vols. (Boston 1901), 3:201; Joseph H. Smith, ed., *Colonial Justice in Western Massachusetts* (Cambridge, Mass., 1961), 257. Town leaders in the colony were also concerned with "strangers," whom they accused of creating "ill conveniencyes" (*The Early Records of the Town of Dedham*, ed. Don G. Hall [Dedham, 1894], 123; *Records of the Town of Braintree, 1640–1793*, ed. Samuel A. Bates [Randolph, Mass., 1886], 5–6). See also *Archives of Maryland*, 1:286, 375; Ralph T. Whitelaw, *Virginia's Eastern Shore: A History of Northhampton and Accomack Counties*, 2 vols. (Gloucester, Mass., 1968), 1:35.

66. *Massachusetts Records*, 2:172–73, 3:173, 4, pt. 1: 287; *Virginia Statutes*, 2:18–19, 112–13, 268–69; *Archives of Maryland*, 41:47–48. See also Kym S. Rice, *Early Amer-*

ican Taverns: For the Entertainment of Friends and Strangers (Chicago, 1983), 23; Edward Field, *The Colonial Tavern: A Glimpse of New England Town Life in the Seventeenth and Eighteenth Centuries* (Providence, R.I., 1897), 29; Perry, *Formation of Virginia Society*, 141–42, 177.

67. *Archives of Maryland*, 3:493–94; *Massachusetts Records*, 3:195, 201, 224. The surge in acts and laws in Massachusetts in the 1650s and 1660s lends some credence to historians' arguments that civil and clerical leaders believed that colonists were straying from the goals of the initial generations, even if it does not support an actual declension. See, for example, Robert G. Pope, *The Half-Way Covenant: Church Membership in Puritan Neighborhoods* (Princeton, N.J., 1969). For the counter view, that religious commitment and experience persisted even though formal membership may have dropped, see Hall, *Worlds of Wonders*.

68. On Sabbath violations see, for example, *Archives of Maryland*, 1:404, 53:250–51, 429, 54:27, 41, 78, 193; Henry Nourse, ed., *The Early Records of Lancaster, Massachusetts, 1643–1725* (Lancaster, Mass., 1884), 91–92; Holland, *History of Western Massachusetts*, 1:51. David Hall has maintained that the laws regulating some behaviors, such as the prohibition of dancing at weddings in ordinaries, were neither enforced nor enforceable since weddings were rites of passage (*Worlds of Wonders*, 210). Kenneth Lockridge suggested that civil authorities turned to law as one solution to disorder in the seventeenth century (*Settlement and Unsettlement in America* [New York, 1981], 70–71). Historians have challenged his contention that disorder was pervasive and increasing as the century lengthened but not this point about official culture's perception and use of law.

69. Increase Mather, "Autobiography," ed. M. G. Hall, *American Antiquarian Society Proceedings* 71 (1961), 291; Cotton Mather, *The Diary of Cotton Mather*, ed. Worthington C. Ford, 2 vols. (New York, 1911), 1:69; Carl Bridenbaugh, "Baths and Watering Places of Colonial America," *William and Mary Quarterly*, 3d. ser., 3 (Apr. 1946): 152; *Harvard College Records*, 3 vols. (Boston, 1955), 3:330.

70. *Archives of Maryland*, 10:1982–93, 54:313, 57:296; *Virginia Statutes*, 1:248, 437, 2:96–97, 535; *Calendar of Virginia State Papers*, ed. William P. Palmer, 11 vols. (Richmond, 1875–93), 1:1; "Body of Liberties of 1641," in Edwin Powers, *Crime and Punishment in Early Massachusetts, 1620–1692* (Boston, 1966); Sarah F. McMahon, "'A Comfortable Subsistence': A History of Diet in New England, 1630–1850" (Ph.D. diss., Brandeis University, 1982); Henry M. Miller, "An Archeological Perspective on the Evolution of Diet in the Colonial Chesapeake, 1620–1745," in Carr, Morgan, and Russo, eds., *Colonial Chesapeake Society*, 183–85; Carr et al., *Robert Cole's World*, 95; Vickers, "Competency and Competition," 18; Semmes, *Captains and Mariners*, 12–13; *Dedham Records*, 44, 93; *Massachusetts Records*, 2:192–93.

71. This discussion reflects my unease with employing Raymond Williams's three-part historical culture scheme—residual, dominant, and emergent—in the colonies during much of the seventeenth century. Traditional English practices do not appear to have become residual forms, "mere" residue of once vital practices, during the third quarter of the century. For his framing, see his *Marxism and Lit-*

erature (New York, 1977), 121–22, and *Problems in Materialism and Culture: Selected Essays* (London, 1980), 40–42.

72. David W. Conroy noted a similar process affecting public drinking in Massachusetts in the second half of the seventeenth century, and he attributed the "divorcing [of] drink from religious observance" to the ministers. See his *Public Houses: Drink and the Revolution of Authority in Colonial Massachusetts* (Chapel Hill, N.C., 1995), 81.

Chapter 4: Sports and Colonial Popular Culture, 1680s–1730s

1. Quoted in Albert B. Hart, *Commonwealth History of Massachusetts*, 5 vols. (New York, 1927–30), 2:280; Thomas F. Waters, *Ipswich in the Massachusetts Bay Colony* (Ipswich, Mass., 1905), 357; Amos E. Jewett and Emily M. Jewett, *Rowley, Massachusetts: Mr. Ezechi Rogers' Plantation, 1639–1850* (Rowley, Mass., 1946), 51.

2. Isaac N. P. Stokes, *The Iconography of Manhattan Island, 1498–1909*, 6 vols. (New York, 1967), 4:451–52, 497; *Boston Gazette*, 23–30 May 1726; William Byrd, *The Secret Diary of William Byrd of Westover, 1709–1712*, ed. Louis B. Wright and Marion Tinling (Richmond, Va., 1941), 144, 151, 153, 155, 158; idem, *The London Diary (1717–1721) and Other Writings*, ed. Louis B. Wright and Marion Tinling (New York, 1958), 25, 411; J. Thomas Jable, "Pennsylvania's Early Blue Laws: A Quaker Experiment in the Suppression of Sport and Amusements, 1682–1740," *Journal of Sport History* 1 (Spring 1974): 107–22; *Documents Relative to the Colonial History of the State of New York*, ed. Edmund B. O'Callaghan, 15 vols. (Albany, N.Y., 1856–87), 14:620; John Hervey, *Racing in America*, 2 vols. (New York, 1944), 1:6–8; W. G. Stanard, "Racing in Colonial Virginia," *Virginia Magazine of History and Biography* 2 (Jan. 1895): 293–305; Samuel Sewall, *The Diary of Samuel Sewall*, 3 vols. (New York, 1972), 3:193; "Salem Town Records, 1659–1691," *Essex Institute Historical Collections* 43 (Jan. 1907): 47; Joseph G. Holland, *History of Western Massachusetts: The Counties of Hampden, Hampshire, Franklin, and Berkshire*, 2 vols. (Springfield, Mass., 1855), 2:219. This timing of horse racing seems to have depended primarily on the presence of sufficient stock in the colonies. Racing on commons and village streets was illegal in Massachusetts because the matches endangered pedestrians, but occasionally people raced there anyway.

Another practice that supposedly emerged in a colony (Maryland) at this point is jousting. It remains Maryland's state sport, but I have found no evidence that any Marylanders competed in jousts this early. For a romantic account, see Hanson Hiss, "The Knights of the Lance in the South," *Outing* 31 (Jan. 1898): 338–44. For an account that is probably more accurate, locating jousting in the antebellum years, see G. Harrison Orians, "The Origin of the Ring Tournament in the United States," *Maryland Historical Magazine* 36 (Sept. 1941): 263–77.

3. See, for example, Joshua Hempstead, "Diary of Joshua Hempstead, 1711–1758," *New London Colony Historical Society Collections* 1 (1901): 5, 29; Samuel Dexter, "Extracts from the Diary of Rev. Samuel Dexter, of Dedham," *New England Histor-*

ical and Genealogical Register 13 (Oct. 1859): 308; Joseph Green, "Diary of Rev. Joseph Green of Salem Village," *Essex Institute Historical Collections* 10 (Mar. 1869): 94; Ebenezer Parkman, "The Diary of Ebenezer Parkman, 1719–1728 and 1729–1738," ed. Francis B. Walett, *Proceedings of the American Antiquarian Society* 71 (Apr. 1961): 99, 105, 118; and note 36 to this chapter.

4. "An Account of the Province of Carolina, by Samuel Wilson, 1682," in Alexander S. Salley Jr., ed., *Narratives of Early Carolina 1650–1708* (New York, 1911), 170.

5. John Lawson, *A New Voyage to Carolina*, ed. Hugh T. Lefler (Chapel Hill, N.C., 1967 [1709]), 158.

6. *Archives of Maryland*, ed. William Hand Browne et al., 72 vols. (Baltimore, 1883–1972), 38:21, 29:197–98; Anon., "Narrative of a Voyage to Maryland, 1705–06," *American Historical Review* 12 (Jan. 1907): 337. See also Gabriel Thomas, "An Historical and Geographical Account of Pennsilvania and of West-New-Jersey," in Albert C. Myers, ed., *Narratives of Early Pennsylvania, West New Jersey, and Delaware 1630–1707* (New York, 1912), 321.

7. Robert Beverley, *The History and Present State of Virginia*, ed. Louis B. Wright (Chapel Hill, N.C., 1947 [1705]), 308–10. See also Jasper Danckaerts, *Journal of Jasper Danckaerts, 1679–1680*, ed. J. Franklin Jameson and Bartlett B. James (New York, 1913), 123.

8. Beverley, *History*, 312, 154–55; William Byrd, *The Prose Works of William Byrd of Westover*, ed. Louis B. Wright (Cambridge, Mass., 1966), 139, 299–300; John Fontaine, *The Journal of John Fontaine, an Irish Huguenot Son in Spain and Virginia, 1710–1719*, ed. Edward P. Alexander (Williamsburg, Va., 1972), 113; James H. Merrell, *The Indians' New World* (Chapel Hill, N.C., 1989), 34–35. There was also a public roundup of horses running wild on Long Island; see Stokes, *Iconography*, 4:312.

9. David Vickers, "Work and Life on the Fishing Periphery of Essex County, Massachusetts, 1620–1675," in David D. Hall and Philip C. F. Smith, eds., *Seventeenth-Century Massachusetts* (Boston, 1984), 83–119; Alice Morse Earle, *Customs and Fashions in Old New England* (New York, 1893), 239; Charles A. Hanna, *The Wilderness Trail: Or, The Ventures and Adventures of the Pennsylvania Traders on the Allegheny Path* (New York, 1972); Joseph J. Kelley, *Pennsylvania: The Colonial Years, 1681–1776* (Garden City, N.Y., 1980); Wayland F. Dunaway, *The Scotch-Irish of Colonial Pennsylvania* (Baltimore, 1981); Graham R. Hodges, *New York City Cartmen, 1667–1850* (New York, 1986), 46. See also Marcus Rediker, *Between the Devil and the Deep Blue Sea: Merchant Seamen, Pirates, and the Anglo-American Maritime World 1700–1750* (Cambridge, 1987), esp. 59–60, 77–111.

10. Parkman, "Diary," 68, 100, 129; *The Colonial Laws of New York from the Year 1664 to the Revolution*, 5 vols. (Albany, N.Y., 1894–96), 1:296; Stokes, *Iconography*, 4:307, 377; Mary R. M. Goodwin, "Eighteenth Century Fairs," Colonial Williamsburg Foundation research report (Williamsburg, 1955), 17; Francis Louis Michel, "The Journey of Francis Louis Michel, 1701–02," *Virginia Magazine of History and*

Biography 24 (Apr. 1916): 129; Anon., "Narrative of a Voyage to Maryland, 1705–06," *American Historical Review* 12 (Jan. 1907): 334–35; Aubrey C. Land, *The Dulanys of Maryland: A Biographical Study of Daniel Dulany, the Elder (1685–1753), and Daniel Dulany, the Younger (1722–1797)* (Baltimore, 1955), 49–50; Edmund S. Morgan, *Virginians at Home: Family Life in the Eighteenth Century* (Williamsburg, Va., 1952), 86.

11. John J. Waters, "The Traditional World of the New England Peasants: A View from Seventeenth-Century Barnstable," *New England Historical and Genealogical Register* 130 (Jan. 1976): 4; John Marshall, Diary 1689–1711, 28 June 1697, Massachusetts Historical Society, Boston; Elroy S. Thompson, *History of Plymouth, Norfolk and Barnstable Counties* (New York, 1928), 790; Henry B. Parkes, "New England in the Seventeen Thirties," *New England Quarterly* 3 (July 1930): 410–11; Morgan, *Virginians at Home*, 88–89; Stokes, *Iconography*, 4:443, 500; Benjamin Walker, "Diary of Benjamin Walker, Jr.," *Publications of the Colonial Society of Massachusetts* 28 (1930–33): 243–44; Sewall, *Diary*, 1:122, 3:217; William Stephens, *The Journal of William Stephens 1741–1745*, ed. E. Merton Coulter, 2 vols. (Athens, Ga., 1958), 2:86–7, 145, 183, 216.

12. Danckaerts, *Journal*, 271; Parkman, "Diary," 395, 400, 442; Walker, "Diary," 243; Sewall, *Diary*, 2:42, 235; *The Early Records of Lancaster, Massachusetts 1643–1725* (Lancaster, Mass., 1884), 186; Michel, "Journey," 129; Byrd, *Secret Diary*, 413, 415, 417; Philip A. Bruce, *Social Life of Virginia in the Seventeenth Century* (New York, 1907), 242.

13. Sarah Kemble Knight, *The Journal of Madam Knight* (New York, 1935), 51.

14. See chapter 7 and Francis LeJau, *The Carolina Chronicle of Dr. Francis LeJau, 1706–1717*, ed. Frank J. Klingberg (Berkeley, Calif., 1956), 69; Stokes, *Iconography*, 4:427, 432; Myers, ed., *Narratives of Early Pennsylvania*, 229, 253, 262; Jable, "Pennsylvania's Early Blue Laws," 112; Mary N. Stanard, *Colonial Virginia, Its People and Customs* (Philadelphia, 1917), 148; Kym S. Rice, *Early American Taverns: For the Entertainment of Friends and Strangers* (Chicago, 1983), 36; Charles E. Clark, *The Eastern Frontier: The Settlement of Northern New England, 1610–1763* (New York, 1970), 28, 322; Lyle Koehler, *A Search for Power: The "Weaker Sex" in Seventeenth-Century New England* (Urbana, Ill., 1980), 340; *New England Courant*, 30 April 1722; *Boston News-Letter*, 26 April–3 May 1714. The most helpful discussion of taverns are Peter Thompson, "A Social History of Philadelphia's Taverns, 1683–1800" (Ph.D. diss., University of Pennsylvania, 1989); David W. Conroy, *In Public Houses: Drink and the Revolution of Authority in Colonial Massachusetts* (Chapel Hill, N.C., 1995).

15. Sewall, *Diary*, 1:196; see also *Massachusetts Court of Assistants Records 1630–1692*, 3 vols. (Boston 1901), 1:197, 3:194.

16. Bernard Bailyn, "The Challenge of Modern Historiography," *American Historical Review* 87 (Feb. 1982): 10–12.

17. Jim Potter, "Demographic Development and Family Structure," in Jack P. Greene and J. R. Pole, eds., *Colonial British America: Essays in the New History of the Early Modern Era* (Baltimore, 1984), 123–56; Gary B. Nash, "Social Develop-

ment," in ibid., 245; David Cressy, *Coming Over: Migration and Communication between England and New England in the Seventeenth Century* (Cambridge, 1987), 70; John J. Waters, *The Otis Family in Provincial and Revolutionary Massachusetts* (Chapel Hill, N.C., 1968), 48–49; Paul G. E. Clemens, *The Atlantic Economy and Colonial Maryland's Eastern Shore: From Tobacco to Grain* (Ithaca, N.Y., 1980), 63–69; Russell R. Menard, "Economy and Society in Early Colonial Maryland" (Ph.D. diss., University of Iowa, 1975), 424–25; Gregory A. Stiverson, *Poverty in a Land of Plenty: Tenancy in Eighteenth-Century Maryland* (Baltimore, 1977); Ian K. Steele, *The English Atlantic, 1675–1740: An Exploration of Communication and Community* (New York, 1986), 272.

18. The restrictions on life in New Amsterdam resembled those in the British North American mainland colonies and, in some instances, may have been harsher. *The Records of New Amsterdam from 1653 to 1674*, 7 vols. (New York, 1897), 6:405; *Laws and Ordinances of New Netherland, 1638–1674*, comp. Edmund B. O'Callaghan (Albany, N.Y., 1868), 20, 205–6, 258–63, 320, 366, 448–49, 461; J. Franklin Jameson, ed., *Narratives of New Netherland 1609–1664* (New York, 1909), 88; Stokes, *Iconography*, 4:114, 148–49, 189, 328, 391; Oliver A. Rink, *Holland on the Hudson: An Economic and Social History of Dutch New York* (Ithaca, N.Y, 1986).

19. Gary B. Nash, *The Urban Crucible: Social Change, Political Consciousness, and the Origins of the American Revolution* (Cambridge, Mass., 1979), 19.

20. *Records of New Amsterdam*, 6:401–4.

21. Danckaerts, *Journal*, 47; Stokes, *Iconography*, 4:451–52.

22. *Minutes of the Common Council of the City of New York, 1675–1776*, 8 vols. (New York, 1905), 1:92–93; Stokes, *Iconography*, 4:316, 320–21.

23. See notes 7 and 8 to this chapter and Salley, ed., *Narratives of Early Carolina*, 170; LeJau, *Carolina Chronicle of Dr. Francis LeJau*, 68, 169; Lawson, *A New Voyage*, 33; Merrell, *Indians' New World*, 36–39. William Byrd II also recorded shooting contests using bows and arrows, and although archery practice had a long history in Britain, Byrd's comments suggest a Native American rather than a British influence on the contests in which he engaged. He and his mates were practicing for hunting, not defense (*Secret Diary*, 114, 129, 156, 348). It is also probable that the barbecues that southern colonists eventually enjoyed drew from the Indians' practice of eating roasted meats, what Lawson called "barbakues" (*A New Voyage*, 42). Furthermore, by no means does this focus on the South suggest that hunting practices in the North were not varied or did not incorporate Native American customs.

24. Louis Green Carr and Lorena S. Walsh, "The Planter's Wife: The Experience of White Women in Seventeenth-Century Maryland," *William and Mary Quarterly*, 3d ser., 34 (Oct. 1977): 542–71; Russell Menard, "British Migration to the Chesapeake Colonies in the Seventeenth Century," in Lois Green Carr, Philip D. Morgan, and Jean B. Russo, eds., *Colonial Chesapeake Society* (Chapel Hill, N.C., 1988), 128–30.

25. Quoted in Morgan, *Virginians at Home*, 88–89.

26. Hempstead, "Diary," 24; James Jeffrey, "James Jeffrey's Journal for the Year 1724," *Essex Institute Historical Collections* 36 (Oct. 1900): 331–38.

27. Koehler, *Search for Power*, 119–20, 339–40, 357, 433.

28. Ibid., 110–14, 121; Julia Spruill, *Women's Life and Work in the Southern Colonies* (Chapel Hill, N.C., 1938), 293–94; Francis M. Manges, "Women Shopkeepers, Tavernkeepers, and Artisans in Colonial Philadelphia" (Ph.D. diss., University of Pennsylvania, 1958).

29. David Galenson, *Traders, Planters, and Slaves: Market Behavior in Early English America* (Cambridge, 1986); John J. McCusker and Russell R. Menard, *The Economy of British America 1607–1789* (Chapel Hill, N.C., 1985), 56–68; E. A. Wrigley and R. S. Schofield, *The Population History of England, 1541–1871: A Reconsideration* (London, 1981), 179–87, 219–21; Russell R. Menard, "From Servants to Slaves: The Transformation of the Chesapeake Labor System," *Southern Studies* 16 (Winter 1977): 355–90. Other factors certainly affected both the demographic and economic developments in particular locales in these decades. See, for example, Christine L. Heyrman, *Commerce and Culture: The Maritime Communities of Colonial Massachusetts 1690–1750* (New York, 1984), 54–56, 224–27.

30. See, for example, Joshua Gee Jr., College Memorandum Book, 1714–1715, in Davis Papers II, 1681–1747, Massachusetts Historical Society, Boston; *Records of the Suffolk County Court, 1671–1680*, 2 vols. (Boston, 1964), 1:91, 230; Catharine P. Hargrave, *A History of Playing Cards and a Bibliography of Cards and Gaming* (Boston, 1933), 58; Abbott L. Cummings, ed., *Rural Household Inventories, 1675–1775* (Boston, 1964), 282.

31. *Minutes of the Common Council of New York*, 2:134, 138; Stokes, *Iconography*, 4:429; *Journal of House of Representatives of Massachusetts*, ed. Worthington C. Ford et al., 45 vols. (Boston, 1919–76), 2:174, 178; John S. Ezell, "When Massachusetts Played the Lottery," *New England Quarterly* 22 (Sept. 1949): 316–35; John F. Watson, *Annals of Philadelphia* (Philadelphia, 1830), 710–12; *Boston Evening-Newsletter*, 22–29 August 1715, 11–18 November 1717; *Boston Gazette*, 22–29 May 1721, 6–13 August 1722, 19–26 April 1725.

32. Quoted in Watson, *Annals of Philadelphia*, 239. Entrepreneurs also organized and advertised the initial dancing schools; see "Proceedings of the Visitors of William and Mary College, 1716," *Virginia Magazine of History and Biography* 4 (1896–97): 169; Sewall, *Diary*, 1:103–4; *Boston News-Letter*, 1 March 1713.

33. "Letter from William Penn to the Committee of the Free Society of Traders, 1683," in Myers, ed., *Narratives of Early Pennsylvania*, 228–29. On the later development and significance of the fur trade in the Susquehanna River region, see Peter C. Mancall, *Valley of Opportunity: Economic Culture along the Upper Susquehanna, 1700–1800* (Ithaca, N.Y., 1991), 47–70.

34. This scenario is impressionistic but not unrealistic. It draws from evidence about the practices of many early Americans who had small freeholds in backcountry regions, engaged in a range of economic activities, and generally followed the residual task discipline.

35. See, for example, Sewall, *Diary*, 1:393, 3:111, 158, 193; Cotton Mather, *The Diary of Cotton Mather*, ed. Worthington C. Ford, 2 vols. (New York, 1911), 2:144, 367; Benjamin Lynde, *The Diaries of Benjamin Lynde and of Benjamin Lynde, Jr.* (Boston, 1880), 132–33. The emergent "high style" of government officials, including civil servants, and merchants was one dimension of the starker unequal distribution of wealth that was emerging in eastern towns such as Boston and Salem. See note 50 to this chapter.

36. See note 3 to this chapter and Lawrence Hammond, "Diary of Lawrence Hammond," *Massachusetts Historical Society Proceedings*, 2d ser., 7 (Jan. 1892): 147; Joseph Gerrish, Diary 1717–19, 23 April 1718, Massachusetts Historical Society, Boston; Zaccheus Collins, Diary, 1726–50, 18 August 1722, 27 June 1727, 21 August 1728, Essex Institute, Salem, Mass.; Green, "Diary," 76, 92, 100, 102; Peter Thacher, "Private Dairy, April 1679–February 1699," in A. K. Teek, *The History of Milton, Massachusetts* (Boston, 1887), 641.

37. See note 1 to this chapter.

38. Robert E. Moody, ed., *The Saltonstall Papers 1607–1815* (Boston, 1972), 270–72.

39. The Body of Liberties of 1641 prohibited cruelty to animals and hence baits.

40. Gambling in the Chesapeake in this period is addressed in chapter 5 and by Timothy H. Breen, "Horses and Gentlemen: The Cultural Significance of Gambling among the Gentry of Virginia," *William and Mary Quarterly*, 3d ser., 34 (Apr. 1977): 239–57. Large landowners in the Carolinas gambled, as did New Yorkers of all ranks and races. The legislatures in Virginia, Maryland, and New York also moved to limit ordinaries and to contain, if not to suppress, tavern gambling. There were also gambling cases in the court records of Massachusetts, but their numbers were small in comparison to incidences of other crimes. See, for example, *Records of the Suffolk County Court*, 2 vols. (Boston, 1933), 2:162; *Court of Assistants Records*, 1:235; *Plymouth Court Records 1689–1859*, ed. David T. Konig, 16 vols. (Wilmington, Del., 1978), 1:196, 235, 2:21; Edwin Powers, *Crime and Punishment in Early Massachusetts, 1620–1699* (Boston, 1966), 404–8.

41. Sabbatarian policy prevailed in all the colonies, but with the possible exception of Pennsylvania, the strictures against work, travel, and sports were irregularly enforced, even as the laws were regularly continued. See, for instance, *The Statutes-at-Large, Being a Collection of All the Laws of Virginia (1619–1792)*, ed. William W. Hening, 13 vols. (Richmond, 1819–1823), 2:361–62, 395–401; *Archives of Maryland*, 17:419, 38:44–48; *Acts and Laws of His Majesty's Province of the Bay in New England*, 8 June 1692; *Journal of the House of Representatives of Massachusetts*, 1:137, 154; Stokes, *Iconography*, 4:391, 497; Jable, "Pennsylvania's Early Blue Laws," 115–17.

42. See, for example, David S. Lovejoy, *The Glorious Revolution in America* (Middleton, Conn., 1987); Patricia Bonomi, *Under the Cope of Heaven: Religion, Society and Politics in Colonial America* (New York, 1986), 30–38; Richard R. Johnson, *Adjustment to Empire: The New England Colonies, 1675–1715* (New Brunswick, N.J., 1981); Sung Bok Kim, *Landlord and Tenant in Colonial New York: Manorial Society,*

1664–1775 (Chapel Hill, N.C., 1978), 44–56; Edmund S. Morgan, *American Slavery–American Freedom: The Ordeal of Colonial Virginia* (New York, 1975), 250–70; Lois Green Carr and David W. Jordan, *Maryland's Revolution of Government, 1689–1692* (Ithaca, N.Y., 1974). My argument also draws on Antonio Gramsci's concept of hegemony and historical blocs; see his *Selections from the Prison Notebooks*, ed. and trans. Quentin Hoare and G. N. Smith (New York, 1971).

43. Peter Burke, *Popular Culture in Early Modern Europe* (New York, 1978), 1.

44. This argument draws from Richard Bushman, "American High-Style and Vernacular Cultures," in Greene and Pole, eds., *Colonial British America,* 370–73.

45. Darret B. Rutman, "Assessing the Little Communities of Early America," *William and Mary Quarterly,* 3d. ser., 43 (Apr. 1968): 163–78; quotation on 174.

46. The power of this construction was diminishing, but Edward Taylor, a Connecticut minister and poet, restated it clearly. He called the body a "mud well tent where Matters are Dead elements" (*The Poems of Edward Taylor,* ed. Donald E. Stanford [New Haven, Conn., 1960], 209).

47. Sewall, *Diary,* 2:303.

48. Ibid., 1:122, 167, 312–13.

49. Sewall also noted cards strewn on his lawn, to "mock me," he believed (ibid., 1:498). In nearby Charlestown revelers reerected a maypole that authorities had cut down, and ninepins players, although harassed by authorities, kept returning to play their games at "Mt. Whoredom," probably the slope of Beacon Hill (ibid., 1:178, 3:51–52). My suggestions about laborers' opposition and resistance to the dominant culture are influenced by E. P. Thompson, *The Making of the English Working Class* (New York, 1966); James C. Scott, *The Moral Economy of the Peasant: Rebellion and Subsistence in Southeast Asia* (New Haven, Conn., 1976); Craig Calhoun, *The Question of Class Struggle: Social Foundations of Popular Radicalism during the Industrial Revolution* (Chicago, 1982).

50. James Henretta, "Economic Development and Social Structure in Colonial Boston," in Gary B. Nash, ed., *Class and Society in Early America* (Englewood Cliffs, N.J., 1970), esp. 133–38; Nash, *Urban Crucible,* 16, 63; Waters, *The Otis Family,* 48–49.

Chapter 5: Sport and Rank Making in the Chesapeake

1. The full covenants are reprinted in W. G. Stanard, "Racing in Colonial Virginia," *Virginia Magazine of History and Biography* 2 (Jan. 1895): 296–98. This chapter is a revised version of an article published as "The Formalizing of Sport and the Formation of an Elite: The Chesapeake Gentry, 1650–1720s," *Journal of Sport History* 13 (Winter 1986): 212–34, used with permission.

2. Stanard, "Racing in Colonial Virginia," 297.

3. Ibid.

4. The literature on the gentry is extensive, but representative works include Louis B. Wright, *The First Gentlemen of Virginia: Intellectual Qualities of the Early Colonial Ruling Class* (San Marino, Calif., 1940); Aubrey C. Land, *The Dulanys of*

Maryland: A Biographical Study of Daniel Dulany, the Elder (1685–1753), and Daniel Dulany, the Younger (1722–1797) (Baltimore, 1955); Bernard Bailyn, "Politics and Social Structure in Virginia," in James M. Smith, ed., *Seventeenth Century America: Essays in Colonial History* (Chapel Hill, N.C., 1959), 90–115; Jack P. Greene, "Foundations of Political Power in the Virginia House of Burgesses, 1720–1776," *William and Mary Quarterly* 16 (Oct. 1959): 485–506; idem, *The Quest for Power* (Chapel Hill, N.C., 1963); Clifford Dowdey, *The Virginia Dynasties* (Boston, 1969); Carole Shammas, "English-Born and Creole Elites in Turn-of-the-Century Virginia," in Thad W. Tate and David L. Ammerman, eds., *The Chesapeake in the Seventeenth Century: Essays on Anglo-American Society* (Chapel Hill, N.C., 1979), 274–96; David L. Jordan, "Political Stability and the Emergence of a Native Elite in Maryland, 1600–1715," in ibid., 143–73; Martin H. Quitt, *The Virginia House of Burgesses: The Social and Economic Basis of Political Power* (New York, 1989).

5. Timothy H. Breen, "Horses and Gentlemen: The Cultural Significance of Gambling among the Gentry of Virginia," *William and Mary Quarterly*, 3d ser., 34 (Apr. 1977): 239–57; quotation on 257.

6. John Hervey, *Racing in America*, 2 vols. (New York, 1944), 1:14–17; Roger Longrigg, *The History of Horse Racing* (New York, 1972), 105–6. No comprehensive history of seventeenth-century taverns exists, but estate inventories and legislative and court records provide fragmentary information about what tavernkeepers owned. For descriptions, see Philip A. Bruce, *Social Life of Virginia in the Seventeenth Century* (New York, 1907); Mary N. Stanard, *Colonial Virginia, Its People and Customs* (Philadelphia, 1917); Jane Carson, *Colonial Virginians at Play* (Williamsburg, Va., 1965).

7. George Alsop, "A Character of the Province of Maryland" (1666), in Clayton C. Hall, ed., *Narratives of Early Maryland, 1633–1685* (New York, 1910), 357.

8. Russell R. Menard, "Economy and Society in Early Colonial Maryland" (Ph.D. diss., University of Iowa, 1975), 268.

9. Ibid., 79, 84–85, 243–48, 263–67, 444–45; Paul G. E. Clemens, *The Atlantic Economy and Colonial Maryland's Eastern Shore: From Tobacco to Grain* (Ithaca, N.Y., 1980), 48–49: Lorena S. Walsh, "Servitude and Opportunity in Charles County, 1658–1705," in Aubrey C. Land, Lois Green Carr, and Edward C. Papenfuse, eds., *Law, Society and Politics in Early Maryland* (Baltimore, 1977), 123; Gloria L. Main, *Tobacco Colony: Life in Early Maryland, 1650–1720* (Princeton, N.J., 1982); Darrett B. Rutman and Anita H. Rutman, *A Place in Time: Middlesex County, Virginia 1650–1750* (New York, 1984), 67–69, 188–91; Edmund S. Morgan, *American Slavery–American Freedom: The Ordeal of Colonial Virginia* (New York, 1975); Henry Glassie, *Folk Housing in Middle Virginia* (Knoxville, Tenn., 1975), 75.

10. Menard, "Economy and Society," 324, 414–17, 429–35, 445–47; idem, "Population, Economy, and Society in Seventeenth-Century Maryland," *Maryland Historical Magazine* 79 (Spring 1984): 86; Clemens, *Atlantic Economy*, 48–52; Wesley Frank Craven, *White, Red and Black: The Seventeenth-Century Virginian* (Charlottesville, Va., 1971), 5; Walsh, "Servitude and Opportunity," 127.

11. *For the Colony in Virginea Britannia: Lawes Divine, Morall, and Martiall, etc.* (1612), comp. William Strachey, ed. David H. Flaherty (Charlottesville, Va., 1969), 32, 34, 79, 84; *County Court Records of Accomack-Northampton, Virginia, 1632–1640,* ed. Susie M. Ames (Washington, D. C., 1954), 60–61; *The Statutes-at-Large, Being a Collection of All the Laws of Virginia (1619–1792),* ed. William W. Hening, 13 vols. (Richmond, 1819–1823), 1:114, 123, 126–27, 144, 173, 261, 2:44–46, 268–69 (hereafter cited as *Virginia Statutes*). See also John M. Findlay, *People of Chance: Frontiers of Gambling and Society in America from Jamestown to Las Vegas* (New York, 1986), 11–43.

12. *Archives of Maryland,* eds. William Hand Browne, et al., 72 vols. (Baltimore, 1883–1972), 1:500–501.

13. *Virginia Statutes,* 2:268–69, 3:44–46, 361–62.

14. *Archives of Maryland,* 2:434–35, 7:65–68.

15. Joyce Oldham Appleby, *Economic Thought and Ideology in Seventeenth-Century England* (Princeton, N.J., 1978); Peter Mathias, *The Transformation of England: Essays in the Economic and Social History of England in the Eighteenth Century* (New York, 1979), 137–45; Lawrence W. Stone, "Social Mobility in England, 1500–1700," *Past & Present* 20 (Apr. 1966): 16–55; E. E. Rich, "The Population of Elizabethan England," *Economic History Review* 2 (1949–50): 249; Peter Clark and Paul Slack, *English Towns in Transition 1500–1700* (London, 1976); Buchanan Sharp, *In Contempt of All Authority: Rural Artisans and Riot in the West of England, 1586–1660* (Berkeley, Calif., 1980).

16. *Archives of Maryland,* 54:499.

17. Ibid., 54:550–51.

18. Ibid., 54:594, 599. Another case from the same period appeared in the Accomack County, Virginia, records. This involved "a very poore Man," Thomas Davis, who had lost 500 pounds of tobacco or stock as the result of a race loss. The play debt distinction did not appear in the course of the court's discussion, but the court did request a decision about the legality of the wager from the governor. This suggests that the justices may have considered the English precedent (16 January 1666, Accomack County, Orders, 1666–70, 9).

19. 22 August 1695, Northumberland County Order Book, 1678–1698, pt. 2, 707–8; January 1694, 643; 7 April 1693, Westmoreland County Order Book, 1690–98, 92; Stanard, "Racing in Virginia," 296–98.

20. *Archives of Maryland,* 4:74, 75–79, 82–84, 86–88; Henry M. Miller, "An Archaeological Perspective on the Evolution of Diet in the Colonial Chesapeake, 1620–1745," in Lois Green Carr, Philip D. Morgan, and Jean B. Russo, eds., *Colonial Chesapeake Society* (Chapel Hill, N.C., 1988), 176–99.

21. 10 September 1674, York County Deeds, Orders, Wills, 1672–94, 85. See also Standard, "Racing in Virginia," 294; Hervey, *Racing in America,* 1:17.

22. These figures are taken from Testamentary Proceedings, Inventories and Accounts, 1, pt. 1, 1674–1704, Maryland Hall of Records, Annapolis.

23. *Virginia Statutes,* 1:128, 271, 2:35–37; *Archives of Maryland,* 7:275, 277, 292, 296, 302–3, 338, 480–81, 13:13, 549–50.

24. Francis Nicholson, "Proclamation about the College and Orders for Prize Games for Bachelors," in "Extracts from Records of Surry County," *William and Mary Quarterly*, 1st ser., 11 (Oct. 1902): 86–87. See also Robert Beverley's criticism of Nicholson's arrangement in *The History and Present State of Virginia*, ed. Louis B. Wright (Chapel Hill, N.C., 1947 [1705]), 97–98.

25. Beverley, *History and Present State of Virginia*, 308–10; Stephen Bordley, Letterbooks 1727–35, 22 January and 15 February 1728, Maryland History Society, Baltimore; William Byrd, *The Secret Diary of William Byrd of Westover, 1709–1712*, ed. Louis B. Wright and Marion Tinling (Richmond, Va., 1941), 25, 114, 120, 123, 144, 151–58; Durand of Dauphiné, *A Huguenot Exile in Virginia; or, Voyages of a Frenchman Exiled for His Religion, with a Description of Virginia and Maryland*, ed. and trans. Gilbert Chinard (New York, 1934), 148; Richard B. Davis, ed., *William Fitzhugh and His World, 1676–1701: Letters and Other Documents* (Chapel Hill, N.C., 1963), 384; John Fontaine, *The Journal of John Fontaine, an Irish Huguenot Son in Spain and Virginia, 1710–1719*, ed. Edward P. Alexander (Williamsburg, Va., 1972), 87, 121; Hugh Jones, *The Present State of Virginia* (1724), ed. Richard L. Morton (Chapel Hill, N.C., 1956), 70, 87; William Woodford, *Woodford Letter Book, 1723–1737*, ed. Catesby W. Stewart (Verona, Va., 1977), 229.

26. Byrd, *Secret Diary*, 75.

27. Breen, "Horses and Gentlemen," 239–57.

28. Alexander Hamilton, Letterbook of Dr. Alexander, 1739–43, letter 5 (20 October 1743), Dulany Papers, Box 2, Maryland Historical Society, Baltimore; William H. Kenney, *Laughter in the Wilderness* (Kent, Ohio, 1976), 208–9; Carson, *Colonial Virginians at Play*, 164–65.

29. William Byrd, *The Prose Works of William Byrd of Westover*, ed. Louis B. Wright (Cambridge, Mass., 1966), 139, 299–300.

30. Ibid. See also Fontaine, *Journal*, 113.

31. *Virginia Gazette*, 19 November 1736; William Byrd once refused to allow his "man" to attend a horse race "because there was nothing but swearing and drinking there" (*Secret Diary*, 75).

32. Byrd, *Prose Works*, 278–79.

33. Ibid., 373–74.

34. *Virginia Gazette*, 30 September 1737. For a discussion of a more narrowly constructed code of honor evoked in duelling among eighteenth-century British gentry and nobility, see Donna T. Andrews, "The Code of Honour and Its Critics: The Opposition to Duelling in England, 1700–1800," *Social History* 5 (Oct. 1980): 409–34. Dickson D. Bruce Jr. and Bertram Wyatt-Brown have established the significance of honor in duelling among nineteenth-century Americans (Bruce, *Violence and Culture in the Antebellum South* [Austin, Tex., 1979], 73; Wyatt-Brown, *Southern Honor: Ethics and Behavior in the Old South* [Oxford, 1982], 350–61).

35. Beverley, *History of Virginia*, 153–54. This sense of moderation may have extended as well to the care of their horses, which gentlemen expected. Writing in 1721 James Hollyday threatened to prosecute his neighbor if "my horses come to

any Damage." Working on land owned by Richard Bennett (a wealthy Maryland-er), Thomas Rowland had seized Hollyday's stock because it had roamed into his cornfield (letter, James Hollyday to Thomas Rowland, 21 November 1721, Lloyd Collection, Maryland Historical Society, Baltimore).

36. Breen, "Horses and Gentlemen," 257.

37. The losses of latter-day gentry appear to have ranged from £500 to £2,000, but William Byrd III's largest single gambling loss was £10,000. These practices are discussed in chapter 7. In contrast, Byrd's father noted in 1712 that he played cards and won forty shillings, but then he lost ten pounds at dice and resolved not to play again (Byrd, *Secret Diary*, 516). The tobacco-to-specie translation draws from Clemens, *Atlantic Economy*, 226. He identified the price of Talbot County, Maryland, tobacco in 1720 as one pence per pound. Prices fluctuated by county and by year; consequently, a range rather than a firm amount may best approximate gambling wagers. On British upper-rank gambling during and after the Restoration, see Roger Longrigg, *The English Squire and His Sport* (New York, 1977), 139–40; James Rice, *History of the British Turf: From Earliest Times to the Present Day*, 2 vols. (London, 1879), 1:312.

38. Cited in Longrigg, *History of Horse Racing*, 56.

39. 16 Charles II, ch. 17; 9 Anne, ch. 14.

40. William Byrd II to Charles Boyle, Earl of Orrey, 5 July 1726, in "Virginia Council Journals, 1726–1753," *Virginia Magazine of History and Biography* 32 (Jan. 1924): 27; Marion Tinling, ed., *The Correspondence of the Three William Byrds of Westover, Virginia, 1684–1776*, 2 vols. (Charlottesville, Va., 1977), 1:355.

41. Louis B. Wright, ed., *Letters of Robert Carter 1720–1727: The Commercial Interests of a Virginia Gentleman* (San Marino, Calif., 1940), 79–80. See also Main, *Tobacco Colony*, 167–239.

42. Cited in Dowdey, *Virginia Dynasties*, 153.

43. Fairfax Harrison, "The Will of Charles Carter of Cleve," *Virginia Magazine of History and Biography* 31 (Jan. 1923): 39.

44. This conclusion draws on Breen, "Horses and Gentlemen," 243, 256; Rhys Isaac, *The Transformation of Virginia 1740–1790* (Chapel Hill, N.C., 1982), 119; Wyatt-Brown, *Southern Honor*, 344.

45. Byrd, *Prose Works*, 249.

46. Letter, William Gooch to Thomas Gooch, Bishop of Norwich, 18 September 1727, letters of Governor William Gooch, 1727–51, typescript, Colonial Williamsburg Foundation, Williamsburg.

47. Cited in Dowdey, *Virginia Dynasties*, 355.

48. Wright, ed., *Letters of Robert Carter*, 99, 258–59.

49. See, for example, *Virginia Statutes*, 2:35–37; Longrigg, *History of Horse Racing*, 48, 57–62; idem, *The English Squire*, 81–82, 138–39; Allen E. Begnaud, "Hoofbeats in Colonial Maryland," *Maryland Historical Magazine* 65 (Fall 1970): 207–38.

50. Russell R. Menard, "From Servants to Slaves: The Transformation of the Chesapeake Labor System," *Southern Studies* 16 (Winter 1977): 355–90; idem, "Econ-

omy and Society," 86–88; Morgan, *American Slavery–American Freedom*, esp. 295–15; David Galenson, *White Servitude in Colonial America: An Economic Analysis* (Cambridge, 1981).

51. Menard, "Economy and Society," 346–47; Allan Kulikoff, *Tobacco and Slaves: The Development of Southern Cultures in the Chesapeake, 1680–1800* (Chapel Hill, N.C., 1986), 37–44; Lois Green Carr and Lorena S. Walsh, "Economic Diversification and Labor Organization in the Chesapeake, 1650–1820," in Stephen Innes, ed., *Work and Labor in Early America* (Chapel Hill, N.C., 1988), 144–88.

52. Byrd, *Prose Works*, 100.

53. Philip Ludwell, "Boundary Line Proceedings, 1710," *Virginia Magazine of History and Biography* 5 (July 1897): 10.

54. Jones, *Present State of Virginia*, 48.

55. Prowess, in this context, intended "manly" valor, courage, physical skill, and strength and had been extolled for nearly two centuries in European courtesy literature and subsequent civility manuals. See Dennis Brailsford, *Sport and Society: Elizabeth to Anne* (London, 1969), 185–97, 223–30; and note 59 to this chapter.

56. Byrd, *Prose Works*, 291, 397.

57. Fontaine, *Journal*, 104.

58. Woodford, *Letter Book*, 229.

59. See, for example, Sir Thomas Elyot, *The Boke Named the Governour*, ed. Henry H. S. Croft (London, 1883 [1531]); Roger Ascham, *The Schoolmaster*, ed. Lawrence V. Ryan (Ithaca, N.Y., 1967 [1570]); Humphrey Gilbert, *Queene Elizabethe's Academy: A Booke of Precedence*, ed. Frederick J. Furnivall (London, 1869 [1564]); Henry Peacham, *Compleat Gentleman*, ed. Virgil B. Heltzel (Ithaca, N.Y., 1962 [1622]); Wright, *First Gentlemen*, 149–53, 206, 210, 335; Roberta J. Park, "Strong Bodies, Healthful Regimens, and Playful Recreations as Viewed by Utopian Authors of the 16th and 17th Centuries," *Research Quarterly* 49 (Dec. 1978): 498–511.

60. This argument draws on Raymond Williams's suggestions about the often dramatic social exchanges among groups of people in fluid, dynamic periods. The late seventeenth and early eighteenth centuries were just such a time in the Chesapeake. See *The Sociology of Culture*, esp. 57–86.

61. Darrett B. Rutman, "Assessing the Little Communities in Early America," *William and Mary Quarterly*, 3d ser., 43 (Apr. 1986): 174.

62. Jack P. Greene has contended that the Chesapeake squires wanted to become as nearly like their peers in Britain as possible. For a discussion of the idealizing of metropolitan culture by colonials, see "Search for Identity: An Interpretation of the Meaning of Selected Patterns of Social Response in Eighteenth-Century America," *Journal of Social History* 3 (Spring 1970): 189–220. As Breen has noted as well, however, the evidence about their sporting practices does not suggest that they consciously copied British forms and customs; Breen, "Horses and Gentlemen," 242, n. 9.

63. Jones, *Present State of Virginia*, 32, 43.

64. G. E. Mingay, *English Landed Society in the Eighteenth Century* (London,

1963); Robert W. Malcolmson, *Popular Recreations in English Society 1700–1850* (Cambridge, 1973), 56–67. Malcolmson maintained that patronage declined among the English gentry as the eighteenth century proceeded, largely for economic reasons. This withdrawal was not particularly evident in the Chesapeake until after midcentury, and then it was not complete. For genteel support of gatherings and sports of ordinary people, see Anon., "Narrative of a Voyage to Maryland, 1705–06," *American Historical Review* 12 (Jan. 1907): 334–35; Francis Louis Michel, "The Journey of Francis Louis Michel, 1701–02," *Virginia Magazine of History and Biography* 24 (Apr. 1916): 129; Byrd, *Secret Diary*, 414–15; *Virginia Gazette*, 19 November 1736; Stanard, *Colonial Virginia*, 257–58; Bruce, *Social Life*, 242.

65. Menard, "Economy and Society," 258–59; Edmund Morgan, "Slavery and Freedom," *Journal of American History* 54 (June 1972): 20–21; Kenneth Lockridge, *Settlement and Unsettlement in Early America* (Cambridge, 1981), 66–68; Gary B. Nash, "Social Development," in Jack P. Greene and J. R. Pole, eds., *Colonial British America Essays in the New History of the Early Modern Era* (Baltimore, 1984), 244–45; Stephen S. Webb, "The Strange Career of Francis Nicholson," *William and Mary Quarterly*, 3d ser., 23 (Oct. 1966): 527; Russell R. Menard, "Immigrants and Their Increase: The Process of Population Growth in Early Colonial Maryland," in Land, Carr, and Papenfuse, eds., *Law, Society, and Politics,* 98; Clemens, *Atlantic Economy,* 63–69; Louis Green Carr and Lorena S. Walsh, "The Planter's Wife: The Experience of White Women in Seventeenth-Century Maryland," *William and Mary Quarterly*, 3d ser., 34 (Oct. 1977): 542–71; Mary Beth Norton, "The Evolution of White Women's Experience in Early American," *American Historical Review* 89 (June 1984): 593–619.

66. These races were probably small and local affairs. No precise crowd figures exist, but given the extensive land surrounding a focal plantation and the country organization of Maryland and Virginia, perhaps several hundred people constituted a good-sized crowd. Moreover, a gentleman dealt directly and intimately with his neighbors and his county, rather than with all the people in a region.

67. Beverley, *History of Virginia,* 312–13.

68. See, for example, Anon., "Voyage to Maryland, 1705–06," 337; Michel, "Journey, 1701–02," 21–22; Fontaine, *Journal,* 87, 104; John Clayton, "Virginia Game and Field Sports: Descriptions of Them by the Botanist Clayton in 1739," *Virginia Magazine of History and Biography* 7 (Oct. 1899): 174. Estate inventories from Maryland, sampled in ten-year intervals from 1680 to 1730, revealed virtually no equipment specifically appropriate for sports (Inventories and Accounts, 1680, Liber 7, 1690, Liber 11 HB no. C, 1700, Liber 57, Liber WT, 1710, Liber WB, nos. 3–8; Inventories, 1720, Liber TB, nos. 4, 76–78, 1730, Liber EHC no. 10, Liber CC no. 11, Maryland Hall of Records, Annapolis). In 1712–13 (old style) the Virginia Assembly noted and deplored the increase in horses (*Virginia Statutes,* 4:46–49). In 1728 the Assembly passed an antigambling act that encompassed virtually all previous acts and most activities and copied almost verbatim an act of Parliament (*Virginia Statutes,* 4:214–18). In 1733 the Maryland Assembly considered but did not pass

a similar act (*Archives of Maryland,* 39:10). No evidence exists to suggest that the British law restricting horse racing had any currency in the Chesapeake after the turn of the century.

69. *Archives of Maryland,* 24:244, 275.

70. Breen apparently had another sense of this word in mind than do I. Although he called gentry races exclusive events, he did not suggest that others did not race.

71. A helpful discussion on deference is in J. G. A. Pocock, "The Classical Theory of Deference," *American Historical Review* 81 (June 1976): 516–23. Darrett and Anita Rutman discussed the quality of individuals' performances and skills in the context of public work and status; see *A Place in Time,* esp. ch. 5. This discussion also draws from Clifford Geertz, *The Interpretation of Cultures* (New York, 1973), 3–30, 412–53; and Victor Turner, *The Ritual Process* (Chicago, 1969) and *Dramas, Fields, and Metaphors* (Ithaca, N.Y., 1974).

72. Morgan, *American Slavery–American Freedom,* esp. 338–87.

Chapter 6: Mid-Eighteenth-Century Sporting Styles

1. Eric Hobsbawm, "Introduction: Inventing Traditions," in Eric Hobsbawm and Terence Ranger, eds., *The Invention of Tradition* (Cambridge, 1983), 1–15 (quotations on 1). Some of the material in this chapter, especially about the gentry, appeared in my "Sport and the Awareness of Leisure," in Cary Carson, Ronald Hoffman, and Peter J. Albert, eds., *Of Consuming Interests: The Style of Life in the Eighteenth Century* (Charlottesville, Va., 1994), 406–43.

2. Charles Dickens, *A Tale of Two Cities* (New York, 1938 [1859]), 13.

3. John Adams, *Diary and Autobiography of John Adams,* ed. Lyman H. Butterfield, 4 vols. (Cambridge, 1961–62), 1:13–14, 73, 27.

4. Ibid., 1:140–41.

5. Lyman H. Butterfield, ed., *Adams Family Correspondence,* 2 vols. (Cambridge, Mass., 1963), 1:44–45.

6. Ibid., 1:285–86.

7. Probably the best discussions of British upper-rank sporting practices and interests in the seventeenth and eighteenth centuries remain J. H. Plumb, "The Commercialization of Leisure in Eighteenth-Century England," in Neil McKendrick, John Brewer, and J. H. Plumb, *The Birth of a Consumer Society: The Commercialization of Eighteenth-Century England* (Bloomington, Ind., 1982), 265–85; Robert W. Malcolmson, *Popular Recreations in English Society 1700–1850* (Cambridge, 1973); Dennis Brailsford, *Sport and Society: Elizabeth to Anne* (London, 1969).

8. My understanding of gentility, refinement, and cultivation owes much to Richard Bushman, *The Refinement of America: Persons, Houses, Cities* (New York, 1992). See also Stow Persons, *The Decline of American Gentility* (New York, 1973); Howard Mumford Jones, *O Strange New World: American Culture, The Formative Years* (New York, 1967); Edwin H. Cady, *The Gentleman in America: A Literary Study*

in American Culture (Syracuse, N.Y., 1949); John E. Mason, *Gentlefolk in the Making: Studies in the History of English Courtesy Literature and Related Topics from 1531 to 1774* (Philadelphia, 1935); Virgil B. Heltzel, *Chesterfield and the Tradition of the Ideal Gentleman* (Chicago, 1925).

9. See, for example, John Rowe, *Letters and Diary of John Rowe, Boston Merchant, 1759–1762, 1764–1779,* ed. Anne R. Cunningham (Boston, 1903), 71–120; William Tudor, ed., *Deacon Tudor's Diary* (Boston, 1896), 2, 6, 38; Anna Green Winslow, *Diary of Anna Green Winslow,* ed. Alice M. Earle (Boston, 1894), 28; Ellen W. Spofford, "Personal Sketches of Early Inhabitants of Georgetown, Massachusetts," *Essex Institute Historical Collections* 41 (Apr. 1905): 169–70; *Maryland Gazette,* 3 March 1774; Philip Vickers Fithian, *Journal and Letters of Philip Vickers Fithian, 1773–1774: A Plantation Tutor of the Old Dominion,* ed. Hunter Dickinson Farish (Williamsburg, Va., 1943), 201–3; George F. Dow, ed., *The Holyoke Diaries* (Salem, Mass., 1911), 63, 74; James D. Phillips, *Salem in the Eighteenth Century* (Boston, 1937), 179–80. Marylanders also sailed yachts; see note 53 to this chapter and *Maryland Gazette,* 3 March 1774.

10. See, for example, William Bartram, *Travels of William Bartram,* ed. Mark Van Doren (New York, 1955), 11–12; Anon., "Journal of a French Traveller in the Colonies, 1765," *American Historical Review* 27 (Oct. 1921): 72, 76; James Gordon, "Diary of Colonel James Gordon, of Lancaster County, Virginia," *William and Mary Quarterly,* 1st ser., 11 (Oct. 1902): 108, 196; Dow, ed., *Holyoke Diaries,* 47, 49, 51, 54, 59, 62, 64, 71, 79; John Harrower, *The Journal of John Harrower, an Indentured Servant in the Colony of Virginia, 1773–1776,* ed. Edward M. Riley (Williamsburg, Va., 1963), 46; John Clayton, "Virginia Game, and Field Sports: Descriptions of Them by the Botanist Clayton in 1739," *Virginia Magazine of History and Biography* 7 (Oct. 1899): 173–74; John F. Watson, *Annals of Philadelphia* (Philadelphia, 1830), 238; Charles Carroll, "Extracts from the Carroll Papers," *Maryland Historical Magazine* 12 (Dec. 1917): 356; Francis Goelet, "Extracts from Capt. Francis Goelet's Journal, Relative to Boston, Salem and Marblehead &c., 1746–50," *New England Historical and Genealogical Review* 24 (Jan. 1870): 54–55, 57; William Stephens, *The Journal of William Stephens 1741–1745,* ed. E. Merton Coulter, 2 vols. (Athens, Ga., 1958), 2:6, 108.

11. See notes 9 and 10 to this chapter and Isaac N. P. Stokes, *The Iconography of Manhattan Island, 1498–1909,* 6 vols. (New York, 1967), 4:722; Eliza Pinckney, *The Letterbook of Eliza Lucas Pinckney 1739–1762,* ed. Elise Pinckney (Chapel Hill, N.C., 1972), 57; *Maryland Gazette,* 25 July, 8 August 1754, 14 November 1754, 5 February 1765, 7 February 1765; Robert K. Brock, *Archibald Cary of Ampthill, Wheelhorse of the Revolution* (Richmond, Va., 1937), 5; Jane Carson, *Colonial Virginians at Play* (Williamsburg, Va., 1965), 185–86.

12. See, for example, *South Carolina Gazette,* 31 October 1741, 7 November 1741; Stephens, *Journal,* 2:155, 164, 192–94, 248; Peter Gordon, *The Journal of Peter Gordon, 1732–1735,* ed. E. Merton Coulter (Athens, Ga., 1963), 30; *New York Post-Boy,* 12 November 1759.

13. This argument draws especially from Lorena S. Walsh, "Plantation Management in the Chesapeake, 1620–1820," *Journal of Economic History* 49 (June 1989): 393–406; Lois Green Carr and Lorena S. Walsh, "Economic Diversification and Labor Organization in the Chesapeake, 1650–1820," in Stephen Innes, ed., *Work and Labor in Early America* (Chapel Hill, N.C., 1988), 144–88; Philip D. Morgan, "Task and Gang Systems: The Organization of Labor on New World Plantations," in ibid., 189–220; Thomas M. Doerflinger, *A Vigorous Spirit of Enterprise: Merchants and Economic Development in Revolutionary Philadelphia* (Chapel Hill, N.C., 1986); Cynthia A. Kierner, *Traders and Gentlefolk: The Livingstons of New York, 1675–1790* (Ithaca, N.Y., 1992); Joyce E. Chaplin, *An Anxious Pursuit: Agricultural Innovation and Modernity in the Lower South, 1730–1815* (Chapel Hill, N.C., 1993). My interpretation of the gentry's approach to work differs from that recently offered by Gordon S. Wood. He maintained that gentlemen (no women cited) consistently and persistently disliked and disavowed labor, which they saw as "servile," and they preferred leisure and idleness, which he linked together. Some of them, perhaps most commonly in the Carolinas, undoubtedly did hold and act on these positions, as I acknowledge later, but I believe that Wood's position states the case too starkly. He frames work as manual labor, offers little evidence about what upper-rank men actually did, and does not consider possible changes in either their constructions of or their performances in leisure. See *The Radicalism of the American Revolution: How a Revolution Transformed a Monarchical Society into a Democratic One Unlike Any That Had Ever Existed* (New York, 1992), esp. 33–39, 107, 170–72.

14. Pinckney, *Letterbook*, 51.

15. Ibid., 7, 35, 39–40, 147–48, 153.

16. In 1768 alone Washington went fox hunting fifty times, each time for three to four hours. He hunted foxes most frequently in the winter months, and seven and eight outings per month were not uncommon through the early 1770s (*The Diaries of George Washington*, ed. Donald Jackson, 2 vols. [Charlottesville, Va., 1976], e.g., 1:30–118, 2:119–206). On the importance of slaves to the economy and the ideology of southern planters, see Allan Kulikoff, *Tobacco and Slaves: The Development of Southern Cultures in the Chesapeake, 1680–1800* (Chapel Hill, N.C., 1986); Russell R. Menard, "Slavery, Economic Growth, and Revolutionary Ideology in the South Carolina Low Country," in Ronald Hoffman, John J. McCusker, Russell R. Menard, and Peter J. Albert, eds., *The Economy of Early America: The Revolutionary Period, 1763–1790* (Charlottesville, Va., 1988), 244–74; Peter A. Coclanis, *The Shadow of a Dream: Economic Life and Death in the South Carolina Low Country, 1670–1920* (New York, 1988); Rachel N. Klein, *Unification of a Slave State: The Rise of a Planter Class in the South Carolina Backcountry, 1760–1808* (Chapel Hill, N.C., 1990). Gentlemen eschewing labor and relishing leisure are central points in Gordon S. Wood's arguments in *The Radicalism of the American Revolution* (New York, 1991), esp. 36–39 and 271–86. He conflates leisure and idleness, however.

17. Landon Carter, *The Diary of Colonel London Carter of Sabine Hall, 1752–1778*, ed. Jack P. Greene, 2 vols. (Charlottesville, Va., 1965), 1:352, 379, 522, 550; 2:630, 638,

640–41, 755, 870 996, 1012; Robert Wormeley Carter, Almanac Diary 1765, 16 December 1765, microfilm, Colonial Williamsburg Foundation, Williamsburg, Va.; Louis Morton, "Robert Wormeley Carter of Sabine Hall," *Journal of Southern History* 3 (Aug. 1946): 356–57.

18. William Milnor Jr., *An Authentic Historical Memoir of the Schuylkill Fishing Company of the State in Schuylkill* (Philadelphia, 1830); The Schuylkill Fishing Company, *A History of the Schuylkill Fishing Company of the State in Schuylkill, 1732–1888* (Philadelphia, 1889); Carl Bridenbaugh, *Cities in the Wilderness: The First Generation of Urban Life in America 1625–1742* (New York, 1955), 440; William Douglass, *A Summary, Historical and Political, of the First Planting, Progressive Improvements, and Present State of the British Settlements in North America*, 2 vols. (London, 1755), 2:216; Alexander Hamilton, *Gentleman's Progress: The Itinerarium of Dr. Alexander Hamilton, 1744*, ed. Carl Bridenbaugh (Chapel Hill, N.C., 1948), 115–16. Another club, the South River Club, may have existed near Annapolis, Maryland, but I have found no contemporary evidence to confirm its existence. See South River Club Collection, Maryland Historical Society, Baltimore; Swepson Earle, *The Chesapeake Bay Country* (Baltimore, 1924), 180. The club did play cricket against men from other counties by 1754 (*Maryland Gazette*, 14 November 1754). For Carolina jockey clubs, see *South Carolina Gazette*, 17 March 1757, 20 June 1761; Fairfax Harrison, *John's Island Stud* (Richmond, Va., 1931), 101–31; John B. Irving, *History of the Turf in South Carolina* (Charleston, 1857), 33–36. The jockey club in Charleston had formed in 1734, but apparently it did not survive and reorganized in the 1750s (*South Carolina Gazette*, 1 June, 16 August 1734). A Maryland jockey club may also have organized in the 1730s, but it too met regularly only after midcentury.

19. Milnor, *Schuylkill Fishing Company*, 2.

20. Hamilton, *Gentleman's Progress*, 116; *Benjamin Franklin's Proposals for the Education of Youth in Pennsylvania, 1749* (Ann Arbor, Mich., 1927), 10.

21. See, for example, *Virginia Gazette*, 2 June 1738, 12 September 1745, 28 November 1745, 12 May 1768; *Boston Gazette*, 15 October 1751, 17 May 1762; *Georgia Gazette*, 16 May 1765, 11 May 1774, 14 September 1774; *Maryland Gazette*, 6 December 1745, 19 June 1755, 24 December 1761, 27 March 1766; *Pennsylvania Gazette*, 16 April 1752; letter, John Gibson to Mrs. John Ross, 14 July 1741, Gibson-Maynadier Papers, Maryland Historical Society, Baltimore; John Norton, *John Norton & Sons: Merchants of London and Virginia*, ed. Francis N. Mason (Richmond, 1937), 24, 42–43, 101, 125, 329; Isaac Osgood, Account Book 1768–1770, 14 March 1768, 28 June 1768, 5 January 1769, Haverhill Public Library, Haverhill, Mass.; Francis Jerdone, Cargo Waste Book, 1748–1749, 18, 20–24, 27, 37–38, 41, 53–38, 66, 70, 73, 82, 88, 93–97, 101, 125, Colonial Williamsburg Foundation, Williamsburg; Stokes, *Iconography*, 4:674.

22. *Maryland Gazette*, 9 December 1747; *Boston Gazette and Country Journal*, 20 January 1766, 6 April 1766; Stokes, *Iconography*, 4:674–75, 531, 5:1065, 1071; Phillips, *Salem in the Eighteenth Century*, 185–86; *Harvard College Records*, 3 vols. (Boston, 1955), 1:40; Robert Carter, Letterbook, 1764–68, 22 December 1767, microfilm,

Colonial Williamsburg Foundation, Williamsburg; Thomas Anburey, *Travels through the Interior Parts of America*, 2 vols. (Boston, 1923 [1789]), 2:208–9; Carter, *Diary of London Carter*, 1:71. For a discussion of the Georgian emphasis on symmetry, see James F. Deetz, *In Small Things Forgotten: The Archaeology of Early American Life* (Garden City, N.Y., 1977).

23. Stokes, *Iconography*, 4:533, 549, 575, 605, 620–22, 632, 638, 647–48, 667, 743; John Hervey, *Racing in America 1665–1865*, 2 vols. (New York, 1944), 1:31–32, 57; Roger Longrigg, *The History of Horse Racing* (New York, 1972), 108; Fairfax Harrison, "The Equine FFVs: A Study of the Evidence of the English Horses Imported into Virginia before the Revolution," *Virginia Magazine of History and Biography* 35 (Oct. 1927): 329–70; Francis Culver, *Blooded Horses of Colonial Days* (Baltimore, 1922); W. G. Stanard, "Racing in Colonial Virginia," *Virginia Magazine of History and Biography* 2 (Jan. 1895): 301–2; John Austin Stevens, "Early New York Racing History," *Wallace's Monthly Magazine* 3 (Oct. 1877): 782–88; David Ridgely, ed., *Annals of Annapolis* (Baltimore, 1841), 115–16, 126–27; Watson, *Annals of Philadelphia*, 238–39; Davis, *Fledgling Province*, 174–75; J. Thomas Scharf, *History of Maryland*, 3 vols. (Baltimore, 1897), 2:731; Frederick G. Usilton, *History of Kent County 1630–1916* (n.p., n.d.), 182–83. See also almost any number of the major provincial newspapers in spring and fall months.

24. Josiah Quincy, "Journal of Josiah Quincy, Junior, 1773," ed. Mark A. DeWolf Howe, *Massachusetts Historical Society Proceedings* 49 (June 1916): 467. For racing in eastern Massachusetts, see *Early Records of the Town of Worcester*, 4 vols. (Worcester, Mass., 1878–82), 2:65; Samuel Gardner, "Diary for the Year 1759 Kept by Samuel Gardner of Salem," *Essex Institute Historical Collections* 49 (Jan. 1913): 7; Peter Kimball, Journal 1760–67, 22 April 1760, Essex Institute, Salem, Mass.; *Boston Gazette*, 20 October 1760; *Essex Journal*, 18 May 1774; Howard Russell, *The Long Deep Furrow: Three Centuries of Farming in New England* (Hanover, N.H., 1976), 162–65.

25. See, for example, Breeding Book of John Tayloe, Tayloe Papers, Virginia State Library, Richmond; Robert Carter, Letterbook, 1764–1768, 16; *Maryland Gazette*, 5 July 1764, 11 February 1768, 28 October 1773, 29 September 1774; *South Carolina Gazette*, 24 March 1764; *Virginia Gazette*, 3 March, 21 April 1774; Culver, *Blooded Horses*, 55–71.

26. See, for example, Stokes, *Iconography*, 5:1128–29; *Maryland Gazette*, 8 August 1765, 11 February 1768; *Maryland Journal and Baltimore Advertiser*, 30 April 1782; *Virginia Gazette and Alexandria Advertiser*, 7 October 1790.

27. Benjamin Franklin, *Benjamin Franklin's Memoirs*, ed. Max Farrand (Berkeley, Calif., 1949), 4, 122–24. See also Michael Zuckerman, "Identity in British America: Unease in Eden," in Nicholas Canny and Anthony Pagden, eds., *Colonial Identity in the Atlantic World 1500–1800* (Princeton, N.J., 1987), 115–57.

28. William Eddis, *Letters from America*, ed. Aubrey Land (Cambridge, Mass., 1969), 112.

29. Thomas Cushman, Diary 1761, 1766, 1775, 26 June 1766, Massachusetts Historical Society, Boston.

30. See, for example, William Homes, "Diary of Rev. William Homes of Chilmark, Martha's Vineyard, 1689–1746," *New England Historical and Genealogical Register* 50 (Apr. 1896): 163; Peter Kimball, Journal 1760–1767, 16 May 1760, 7, Essex Institute, Salem, Mass.; James Parker, "Extracts from the Diary of James Parker of Shirley, Mass.," *New England Historical and Genealogical Register* 69–70 (1915–16): 15, 120; *Town Records of Manchester*, 2 vols. (Salem, Mass., 1889), 2:69; *Proceedings at the Centennial Celebration of the Incorporation of the Town of Longmeadow* (Longmeadow, Mass., 1884), 221; *Boston Weekly News-Letter*, 20 September 1759, 20 October 1759; Anne Grant, *Memoirs of an American Lady: With Sketches of Manners and Scenery in America, as They Existed Previous to the Revolution* (New York, 1809), 36–37; Gottlieb Mittleberger, *Journey to Pennsylvania*, eds. and trans. Oscar Handlin and John Clive (Cambridge, Mass., 1960), 60; Clayton, "Virginia Game," 173–74; William J. Hinke and Charles E. Kemper, eds., "Moravian Diaries of Travel through Virginia," *Virginia Magazine of History and Biography* 11 (Oct. 1903): 123; Samuel Kercheval, *A History of the Valley of Virginia*, 3d ed. (Woodstock, Va., 1902 [1833]), 263–65, 283–84, 388–89; Lewis P. Summer, *History of Southwest Virginia, 1746–1786, Washington County, 1777–1870* (Baltimore, 1966), 127–29; Anon., "Journal of a French Traveler, 1765," 72; Janet Schaw, *Journal of a Lady of Quality; Being the Narrative of a Journey from Scotland to the West Indies, North Carolina, and Portugal, in the Years 1774 to 1776*, ed. Evangeline W. Andrews and Charles M. Andrews (New Haven, Conn., 1931), 149. The timing of hunting and fishing seems to have depended not just on work patterns and what had become customary but also on the migratory rhythms of animals, fish, and fowl.

31. Aubrey C. Land, *The Dulanys of Maryland: A Biographical Study of Daniel Dulany, the Elder (1685–1753) and Daniel Dulany, the Younger (1722–1797)* (Baltimore, 1955), 182–83; Watson, *Annals of Philadelphia*, 239–43, 309, 379–85, 432–23; Edmund S. Morgan, *Virginians at Home: Family Life in the Eighteenth Century* (Williamsburg, Va., 1952), 87–88; *Maryland Gazette*, 13 September 1745, 24 March 1747, 8 September 1747, 14 June 1753; John Brickell, *The Natural History of North-Carolina* (Dublin, 1911 [1737]), 40; Grant, *Memoirs*, 51–53; Joseph Merrill, *History of Amesbury and Merrimac* (Haverhill, Mass., 1880), 206; Samuel Phillips Savage, Diaries 1770–1795, 14 January 1770, Massachusetts Historical Society, Boston; Stokes, *Iconography*, 4:565; Nicholas Cresswell, *The Journal of Nicholas Cresswell 1774–1777* (New York, 1924), 26; Mittleberger, *Journey to Pennsylvania*, 85; Harold E. Davis, *The Fledgling Province: Social and Cultural Life in Colonial Georgia 1733–1776* (Chapel Hill, N.C., 1976), 174; Shane White, "'It Was a Proud Day': African Americans, Festivals, and Parades in the North, 1741–1834," *Journal of American History* 18 (June 1994): 13–50.

32. See, for example, Brickell, *Natural History*, 33, 40; Watson, *Annals of Philadelphia*, 351; Cresswell, *Journal*, 30; Philip Vickers Fithian, *Journal, 1775–1776*, ed. Robert G. Albion and Leonidas Dodson (Princeton, N.J., 1934), 180; John Entick, *Present State of the British Empire*, 4 vols. (London, 1774), 4:438; Anon., "Observations in Several Voyages and Travels in America: From the London Magazine, July,

1746," *William and Mary Quarterly,* 1st ser., 15 (Jan. 1907): 158; Jonathan Green, Diary 1738–1752, 27 February 1740, 1 March 1741, in Linscott Papers 1653–1922, Massachusetts Historical Society, Boston.

33. Probably the clearest recent argument about the transfer and persistence of Old World ways is David H. Fischer, *Albion's Seed: Four British Folkways in America* (New York, 1989). For the persistence of some dimensions of Old World experiences, see David Brody, "Time and Work during Early American Industrialism," *Labor History* 30 (1985): 18–35; Alfred F. Young, "English Plebeian Culture and Eighteenth-Century American Radicalism," in Margaret Jacob and James Jacob, eds., *The Origins of Anglo-American Radicalism* (London, 1984), 185–212; David S. Cohen, "How Dutch Were the Dutch of New Netherland?" *New York History* 38 (1981): 43–60; R. J. Dickson, *Ulster Emigration to Colonial America, 1718–1775* (London, 1966).

34. Kercheval, *History of the Valley,* 57–58. See also Albert B. Faust, *The German Element in the United States,* 2 vols. (Boston, 1909), 1:178.

35. Joseph Doddridge, *Notes on the Settlement and Indian Wars of the Western Parts of Virginia and Pennsylvania, from 1763 to 1783,* ed. Alfred Williams (New York, reprint ed., 1973 [1876]), 102–6; Kercheval, *History of the Valley,* 266–69.

36. Stephens, *Journal,* 1:24, 27, 67, 2:86–7, 145, 183, 216. In 1739 Edwin Belke also informed the Society for Promoting Christian Knowledge that the "Common People take the Liberty of playing at Foot ball every Lordsday" in Charleston, South Carolina. Belke was distressed about this practice and about the fact that parish officials did little or nothing about it (Minutes of the S.P.C.K., 10 April 1739, 18:70–71, Marylebone, England; Alison Olson kindly provided this reference).

37. David Fischer maintained that ball playing had some following in New England before the Revolution (*Albion's Seed,* 148–51), but I have found little evidence of games like town ball, except among youths. Fischer did not identify the contemporary sources that might substantiate his claim (except for a Quaker woman's criticism). Colonel James Gordon did note that he and three visitors played ball in March 1759 in Virginia, so amorphous games were probably played irregularly. I suspect that most ball games among adults, cricket being a major exception, organized primarily after the Revolution. By 1802 the *Norfolk Herald* offered a defense of the "national manly game of Bandy" (13 November 1802). Isaiah Thomas's oft-cited *A Little Pretty Pocket Book* (Worcester, Mass., 1787) describes the games of children and youths.

38. See notes 31 and 32 to this chapter and John Boyle, "Boyle's Journal of Occurrences in Boston, 1759–1778," *New England Historical and Genealogical Register* 84 (July 1930): 364; Brickell, *Natural History,* 32; Grant, *Memoirs,* 54–56; Mittleberger, *Journey to Pennsylvania,* 89. Women raced horses elsewhere as well; see Fithian, *Journal 1773–74,* 266; Herman Mann, *The Female Review: Life of Deborah Sampson* (New York, 1972), 167.

39. See note 13 to this chapter.

40. Richard Bushman has explored the limits of persistence in "American High-

Style and Vernacular Cultures," in Jack Greene and J. R. Pole, eds., *Colonial British America: Essays in the New History of the Early Modern Era* (Baltimore, 1984), 370–73.

41. Samuel Checkley, "Diary of Rev. Samuel Checkley, 1735," ed. Samuel Green, *Colonial Society of Massachusetts Publications* 12 (1908–9): 295, 305; Samuel Greenleaf, Diary 1756, 5 November 1756, Massachusetts Historical Society, Boston; James Ferguson, Notebook 1745–65, 5 November 1745, 5 November 1764, Massachusetts Historical Society, Boston; Goelet, "Journal," 61; Rowe, *Diary*, 67; *Boston Gazette and Country Journal*, 30 October 1769; *Essex Gazette*, 2–9 November 1773; Joshua Coffin, *History of Newbury* (Boston, 1845), 249–51; Ashley Bowen, *The Journals of Ashley Bowen (1728–1813) of Marblehead*, ed. Philip C. F. Smith, 2 vols. (Boston, 1973), 2:367, 416; Stokes, *Iconography*, 4:426, 446, 554, 612, 673.

42. Paul A. Gilje, *The Road to Mobocracy: Popular Disorder in New York City, 1763–1834* (Chapel Hill, N.C., 1987), esp. 25–30.

43. James Freeman, Notebook 1745–65, 5 November 1745, Massachusetts Historical Society, Boston; Checkley, "Diary," 290.

44. The extensive literature about the street politics of ordinary colonists, their expressions of common interests including notions of moral economy, and their resistance to the dominant culture includes, besides Gilje, Ronald Schultz, *The Republic of Labor: Philadelphia Artisans and the Politics of Class, 1720–1830* (New York, 1993); Barbara Clark Smith, "Food Rioters and the American Revolution," *William and Mary Quarterly*, 3d ser., 51 (Jan. 1994): 3–38; Alfred F. Young, ed., *Beyond the American Revolution: Explorations in the History of American Radicalism* (DeKalb, Ill., 1993); idem, *The American Revolution: Explorations in the History of American Radicalism* (DeKalb, Ill., 1976); Dirk Hoerder, *Crowd Action in Revolutionary Massachusetts, 1765–1780* (New York, 1977); John P. Reid, "In a Defensive Rage: The Uses of the Mob, the Justification in Law, and the Coming of the American Revolution," *New York University Law Review* 49 (1974): 1043–91.

45. Brickell, *Natural History*, 39; Anburey, *Travels*, 2:227–28; John F. D. Smyth, *A Tour in the United States of America (1784)*, 2 vols. (New York, 1968), 1:22.

46. Stokes, *Iconography*, 4:646; Parker, "Diary," 15, 122; J. E. Norris, ed., *History of the Lower Shenandoah Valley* (Chicago, 1890), 326; Doddridge, *Notes on the Settlement*, 122–25; Anburey, *Travels*, 2:240; Kercheval, *History of the Valley*, 285; Gordon, *Journal*, 43.

47. Elliott J. Gorn, "'Gouge and Bite, Pull Hair and Scratch': The Social Significance of Fighting in the Southern Backcountry," *American Historical Review* 90 (Feb. 1985): 18–43. See also Fithian, *Journal 1773–74*, 183, 240–41; Kenneth P. Bailey, *Thomas Cresap, Maryland Frontiersman* (Boston, 1944), 25; Thomas Lewis, *The Fairfax Line: A Journal of 1746*, ed. John W. Wayland (New Market, Va., 1925), 65. The North Carolina legislature declared gouging a felony in 1749 and then restated and expanded the "crime" as one of "malicious maiming and wounding" in 1754 (*The State Records of North Carolina*, ed. Walter Clark, 15 vols. [Winston, Goldsboro, and Raleigh, N.C., 1895–1914], 6:320, 340). Post-Revolutionary journals and

accounts of travelers to the backcountry often contain vivid descriptions of fighting, which apparently changed little. See, for example, Moreau de St.-Mery, *Moreau de St.-Mery's American Journey (1793–1798)*, trans. and ed. Kenneth Roberts and Anna M. Roberts (Garden City, N.Y., 1947), 328–29; Charles Janson, *The Stranger in America 1793–1806* (New York, 1935), 308–9; Thomas Ashe, *Travels in America* (London, 1809), 82–85.

48. Watson, *Annals of Philadelphia*, 239–40. Bullbaiting also persisted in New York and New Jersey; see *New York Gazette*, 26 September 1763; Stokes, *Iconography*, 5:1131, 1135; Harry B. Weiss and Grace M. Weiss, *Early Sports and Pastimes in New Jersey* (Trenton, N.J, 1960), 59–60. Gander pulling, in which one literally tried to separate the body from the head of a goose by pulling on the feet while the goose's head was tied by a rope (and which may have been Dutch in origin), was also relatively common and persistent in New York and the deep South; see Stokes, *Iconography*, 4:146; Esther Singleton, *Dutch New York* (New York, 1968); *South Carolina Gazette*, various numbers in 1744 and 1745; and A. B. Longstreet, *Georgia Scenes in the First Half Century of the Republic* (New York, 1852), 117.

49. *Essex Gazette*, 2 August 1768; *Boston Gazette and Country Journal*, 16 October 1769; Parker, "Diary," 14, 121; Joseph E. A. Smith, *The History of Pittsfield, Massachusetts, from the Year 1734 to the Year 1800* (Boston, 1869), 205–6; Julia Spruill noted a similar contest among women of "poorer classes" in the South (*Women's Life and Work in the Southern Colonies* [Chapel Hill, N.C., 1938]). See also Nancy L. Struna, "'Good Wives' and 'Gardeners,' 'Spinners and Fearless Riders': Middle- and Upper-rank Women in the Early American Sporting Culture," in J. A. Mangan and Roberta J. Park, eds., *From "Fair Sex" to Feminism: Sport and the Socialization of Women in the Industrial and Post-Industrial Eras* (London, 1987), 235–55.

50. Benjamin Rader, *American Sports: From the Age of Folk Games to the Age of Televised Sports*, 2d ed. (Englewood Cliffs, N.J., 1990).

51. For midcentury comments on the dislike for labor by small and marginal planters and farmers, which were usually criticisms as well, see, for example, Brickell, *Natural History*, 30; Marion Tinling, ed., *The Correspondence of the Three William Byrds of Westover, Virginia, 1684–1776*, 2 vols. (Charlottesville, Va., 1977), 2:487–88. Unlike Brickell, however, William Byrd II blamed whites' dislike of physical labor on the slaves. At the time of the Revolution, Elkanah Watson concluded that "the poor white man would rather starve than work, because the negro works." He probably overstated the case without entirely misstating it (*Men and Times of the Revolution; or the Memoirs of Elkanah Watson*, ed. Winslow C. Watson [New York, 1856], 61). Apprentices, servants, and laborers in a northern colony like Pennsylvania, on the other hand, probably worked diligently, at least when they could get work, and this pattern may help to account for the evidence of recreations primarily in the evenings (see n. 48). See, for example, Sharon V. Salinger, *"To Serve Well and Faithfully": Labor and Indentured Servants in Pennsylvania, 1682–1800* (Cambridge, 1987), esp. 82–114; Billy G. Smith, *The "Lower Sort": Philadelphia's Laboring People, 1750–1800* (Ithaca, N.Y., 1990).

52. For a fine discussion of mutual obligations observed in rituals in Virginia, see A. G. Roeber, "Authority, Law, and Custom: The Rituals of Court Day in Tidewater Virginia, 1720 to 1750," *William and Mary Quarterly*, 3d ser., 37 (Jan. 1980): 29–52. Richard Bushman has also argued that "exchange and assimilation" between the ranks "went on constantly" ("American High-Style and Vernacular Cultures," 374).

53. See, for example, Goelet, "Journal," 53; Robert F. Kelley, *American Rowing: Its Background and Traditions* (New York, 1932), 14–17; Jennie Holliman, *American Sports, 1785–1835* (Durham, N.C., 1931), 155. Lord Baltimore brought a "yacht" to the Chesapeake Bay as early as 1676 as well, but it was used for defense. Vessels for pleasure also appeared in larger New England harbors before the end of the seventeenth century, and the sailing of clippers and packets does not appear to have been restricted to New York.

54. See note 21 to this chapter and chapter 8.

55. See, for example, George Washington, *The Diaries of George Washington*, ed. John C. Fitzpatrick, 4 vols. (Boston, 1925), 3:124; Fithian, *Journal 1773–73*, 177; *Maryland Gazette*, 25 April 1754; Thomas E. Campbell, *Colonial Caroline: A History of Caroline County, Virginia* (Richmond, Va., 1954), 419.

56. The round and oval tracks, usually a mile in circumference, probably dated from the 1730s and 1740s. John Hervey initially identified the distinctiveness of American tracks from British straight "courses" (*Racing in America*, 1:31–32). See also *Maryland Gazette*, 25 April 1754; *Virginia Gazette*, 28 April 1774; Harrower, *Journal*, 40–65; Smyth, *Tour in the United States*, 20.

57. This argument draws from Timothy H. Breen, *Tobacco Culture: The Mentality of the Great Tidewater Planters on the Eve of the Revolution* (Princeton, N.J., 1985); Bernard Bailyn and Philip D. Morgan, eds., *Strangers within the Realm: Cultural Margins of the First British Empire* (Chapel Hill, N.C., 1991); Alison G. Olson, *Making the Empire Work: London and American Interest Groups 1690–1790* (Cambridge, Mass., 1992).

58. Devereux Jarratt, "The Autobiography of the Reverend Devereux Jarratt 1732–1793," *William and Mary Quarterly*, 3d ser., 9 (1952): 361.

59. Gary Kulik, "Dams, Fish, and Farmers: Defense of Public Rights in Eighteenth-Century Rhode Island," in Stephen Hahn and Jonathan Prude, eds., *The Countryside in the Age of Capitalist Transformation* (Chapel Hill, N.C., 1985), 25–50. My understanding of how ordinary people used ordinary activities like sports to resist domination owes much to E. P. Thompson, "The Moral Economy of the English Crowd in the Eighteenth Century," *Past and Present* 50 (Feb. 1971): 76–135; idem, *Whigs and Hunters: The Origin of the Black Act* (London, 1975).

60. Thirty Years of Records of Taunton, 1760–1793, cases of two justices of the peace (John Godfrey, 1744–54, and George Godfrey, 1765–77), comp. George Godfrey, 1 August 1749, Old Colony Historical Society, Taunton, Mass.; Alexander Hamilton, Letterbook of Dr. Alexander Hamilton, 1739–43, letter 5, 20 October 1743, Dulany Papers, Box 2, Maryland Historical Society, Baltimore.

61. Anburey, *Travels*, 2:201–3.

Chapter 7: Taverns and Sports

1. Alvin Dohme, *The Shenandoah: The Valley Story* (Washington, D. C., 1972), 27–28; J. E. Norris, ed., *History of the Lower Shenandoah Valley* (Chicago, 1890), 459. When Elbridge Gerry rode through the town in 1813, it was still called Battletown (*The Diary of Elbridge Gerry, Jr.* [New York, 1927], 134).

2. Johann David Schoepf, *Travels in the Confederation [1783–1784]*, trans. and ed. Alfred J. Morrison, 2 vols. (New York, 1968), 2:46.

3. On English alehouses, see Peter Clark, *The English Alehouse: A Social History 1200–1830* (London, 1983); Keith Wrightson, "Alehouses, Order and Reformation in Rural England, 1590–1660," in Steven Yeo and Eileen Yeo, eds., *Popular Culture and Class Conflict 1590–1914: Explorations in the History of Labour and Leisure* (Atlantic Highlands, N.J., 1981), 1–27; Mass Observation, *The Pub and the People* (London, 1986). On taverns in the colonies, see David W. Conroy, *In Public Houses: Drink and the Revolution of Authority in Colonial Massachusetts* (Chapel Hill, N.C., 1995); Peter Thompson, "A Social History of Philadelphia's Taverns, 1683–1800" (Ph.D. diss., University of Pennsylvania, 1989); Kym S. Rice, *Early American Taverns: For the Entertainment of Friends and Strangers* (Chicago, 1983); Patricia A. Gibbs, "Taverns in Tidewater Virginia, 1700–1774" (master's thesis, William and Mary College, 1968); Francis Manges, "Women Shopkeepers, Tavernkeepers and Artisans in Colonial Philadelphia" (Ph.D. diss., University of Pennsylvania, 1958); Marian D. Terry, *Old Inns of Connecticut* (Hartford, 1937); Elise D. Lathrop, *Early American Inns and Taverns* (New York, 1936); Edwin Field, *The Colonial Tavern* (Providence, R.I., 1897); Alice Morse Earle, *Stage-Coach and Tavern Days* (New York, 1900). Helpful for a later, comparative perspective is Perry Duis, *The Saloon: Public Drinking in Chicago and Boston 1880–1920* (Urbana, Ill., 1983).

4. Rural taverns, according to travelers who had some basis for comparison, were less well equipped and furnished and operated at standards barer than those of urban ones. For a comparison after the Revolution, see Schoepf, *Travels in the Confederation*, 1:237. On the proliferation of taverns in rural areas, see Harold E. Davis, *The Fledgling Province: Social and Cultural Life in Colonial Georgia 1733–1776* (Chapel Hill, N.C., 1976), 118; Robert D. Mitchell, *Commercialism and Frontier: Perspectives on the Early Shenandoah Valley* (Charlottesville, Va., 1977), 208.

5. "A Further Account of the Province of Pennsylvania, by William Penn, 1685," in Albert C. Myers, ed., *Narratives of Early Pennsylvania, West New Jersey and Delaware 1630–1707* (New York, 1967), 260.

6. *Minutes of the Provincial Council of Pennsylvania, from the Organization to the Termination of the Proprietary Government*, 10 vols. (Philadelphia, 1851–52), 1:527–28.

7. Richard Bushman, *The Refinement of America: Persons, Houses, Cities* (New York, 1992), 161; Rice, *Early American Taverns*, 125; John F. Watson, *Annals of Philadelphia* (Philadelphia, 1830), 463; Billy G. Smith and Gary B. Nash, "The Population of Eighteenth-Century Philadelphia," *Pennsylvania Magazine of History and Biography* 99 (1975): 362–72.

8. Thomas Brennan, *Public Drinking and Popular Culture in Eighteenth-Century Paris* (Princeton, N.J., 1988).

9. See, for example, *The Statutes-at-Large, Being a Collection of All the Laws of Virginia (1619–1792)*, ed. William W. Hening, 13 vols. (Richmond, 1819–1823), 6:71–76 (hereinafter cited as *Virginia Statutes*); *The Laws of Maryland*, ed. William Kilty, 2 vols. (Annapolis, Md., 1799–1800), 1 (1780): chap. 24; *Acts and Laws of His Majesty's Province of the Bay in New England*, 1726–30: 13, 101–4, 1742: act 6, 13–14 (hereinafter cited as *Massachusetts Province Code of Laws*).

10. Descriptions of taverns and tavern activities are common in the accounts of eighteenth-century travelers and in subsequently written local histories. See, for example, Schoepf, *Travels in the Confederation*, 1:361; Moreau de St.-Mery, *Moreau de St.-Mery's American Journey (1793–1798)*, trans. and ed. Kenneth Roberts and Anna M. Roberts (Garden City, N.Y., 1947), 102; Charles Brooks, *History of the Town of Medford, Middlesex County, Massachusetts*, rev. ed. (Boston, 1886), 389. When he was traveling through western South Carolina recruiting supporters of independence in 1775, William Tennant stayed at a different tavern every night (Journal 1775, South Caroliniana Library, Columbia).

11. The licensees are listed by year in Baltimore County Court Minutes, 1755–80, Maryland Hall of Records, Annapolis.

12. Rice, *Early American Taverns*, 125–33.

13. Nancy L. Struna, "Gender and Sporting Practice in Early America," *Journal of Sport History* 18 (Spring 1991): 15–22.

14. In Maryland applicants for licenses often listed an occupation, which suggests that they may have seen tavernkeeping as an additional trade rather than an alternative one. See also Thompson, "A Social History of Philadelphia's Taverns"; Donald R. Lemmon and Ida Brooks Kellam, eds., *The Wilmington Town Book, 1743–1778* (Raleigh, N.C., 1973), 200; Daniel Fisher, "Narrative of Daniel Fisher," in Louise P. du Bellet, *Some Prominent Virginia Families* (Baltimore, 1976), 767; Schoepf, *Travels in the Confederation*, 1:30; *Minutes of the County Court, Union County, South Carolina, 1785–1789*, ed. Brent Holcomb (Easley, S.C., 1979), 323, 325, 337, 359; Davis, *Fledgling Province*, 120; Ann Cross, Accounts, 1774–84, in Paul Cross Papers, 1768–1803, South Caroliniana Library, Columbia.

15. William Black, "Journal of William Black," ed. R. Alonzo Brock, *Pennsylvania Magazine of History and Biography* 2 (1878): 41; Watson, *Annals of Philadelphia*, 39; Davis, *Fledgling Province*, 117–18; A. D. Watson, "Ordinaries in Colonial Eastern North Carolina," *North Carolina Historical Review* 45 (Jan. 1968): 67–88. Examples of arrests and indictments are in *Plymouth Court Records 1686–1859*, ed. David T. Konig, 16 vols. (Wilmington, Del., 1978), 3:244, 248, 258; Thirty Years of Records of Taunton, 1760–93, cases of two justices of the peace (John Godfrey, 1744–54, and George Godfrey, 1765–77, comp. George Godfrey, Old Colony Historical Society, Taunton, Massachusetts; Lyman Chalkley, *Chronicles of the Scotch-Irish Settlement in Virginia (Augusta County Records, 1745–1800)*, 3 vols. (Baltimore, 1965), 1:334; Thomas E. Campbell, *Colonial Caroline: A History of Caroline County,*

Virginia (Richmond, Va., 1954), 415; Norris, *History of the Lower Shenandoah Valley,* 120. For taxes, see Isaac N. P. Stokes, *The Iconography of Manhattan Island, 1498–1909,* 6 vols. (New York, 1967) 4:615; *Archives of Maryland,* ed. William Hand Browne et al., 72 vols. (Baltimore, 1883–1972), 52:147, 506, 54:496; *Records of the City of Baltimore (Special Commissioners) 1782–1797* (Baltimore, 1909), 129, 157, 191, 225–26; Catharine P. Hargrave, *A History of Playing Cards and a Bibliography of Cards and Gaming* (Boston, 1930), 286–87. For concerns about retailing without a license, see Baltimore Court Minutes, Criminal Fines, 1762–75, Maryland Hall of Records, Annapolis.

16. Stokes, *Iconography,* 5:1059; Schoepf, *Travels in the Confederation,* 2:4; Rice, *Early American Taverns,* 20–21, 33; Bushman, *Refinement of America,* 161–64.

17. Francis Goelet, "Extracts from Capt. Francis Goelet's Journal, Relative to Boston, Salem and Marblehead &c., 1746–50," *New England Historical and Genealogical Review* 24 (Jan. 1870): 53; *New-York Post Boy,* 22 March 1748, 22 March 1748; *New-York Weekly Journal,* 26 January 1736; Anne Grant, *Memoirs of an American Lady: With Sketches of Manners and Scenery in America, as They Existed Previous to the Revolution* (New York, 1809), 56; Philip Padelford, ed., *Colonial Panorama, 1775* (San Marino, Calif., 1939), 49; William Stephens, *The Journal of William Stephens 1741–1745,* ed. E. Merton Coulter, 2 vols. (Athens, Ga., 1958), 1:81–82; Robert W. Carter, Almanac Diary of Robert Wormeley Carter, 1765, 16 December, microfilm M-5, Colonial Williamsburg Foundation, Williamsburg. See also Ruth Painter, "Tavern Amusements in Eighteenth-Century America," *Americana* 11 (Jan. 1916): 92–115.

18. See, for example, Mary Newton Stanard, *Colonial Virginia, Its People and Customs* (Philadelphia, 1917), 148–49; *New-York Post Boy,* 6 November 1749; *New-York Mercury,* 13 August 1753; Field, *The Colonial Tavern,* 154; Isaac Bangs, *Journal of Lieutenant Isaac Bangs, April 1 to July 29, 1776,* ed. Edward Bangs (Cambridge, Mass., 1890), 56.

19. Stokes, *Iconography,* 5:1068, 1092, 1094; *Boston Evening Post,* 11 January 1773; *New-York Gazette,* 10 May 1762, 26 September 1763; Mary DeWitt Freeland, *The Records of Oxford, Massachusetts* (Albany, N.Y., 1894), 261; *New-York Journal,* 3 March 1735.

20. Hugh Jones, *The Present State of Virginia,* ed. Richard L. Morton (Chapel Hill, N.C., 1956 [1724]), 84; *South Carolina Gazette,* 24 February 1732, 13 May 1732; John Brickell, *The Natural History of North-Carolina* (Dublin, 1911 [1737]), 40; James Jeffrey, "James Jeffrey's Journal for the Year 1724," *Essex Institute Historical Collections* 2 (Apr. 1860): 66; Philip Vickers Fithian, *Journal and Letters of Philip Vickers Fithian, 1773–1774: A Plantation Tutor of the Old Dominion,* ed. Hunter Dickinson Farish (Williamsburg, Va., 1943), 19, 96, 121–22; Henry B. Weiss and Grace M. Weiss, *Early Sports and Pastimes in New Jersey* (Trenton, N.J., 1960), 64–65.

21. Carl Bridenbaugh, *Cities in the Wilderness: The First Generation of Urban Life in America 1625–1742* (New York, 1955), 275, 435; Francis Jerdone, "Letter Book, 1746–1759," *William and Mary Quarterly,* 1st ser., 11 (Jan. 1903): 153, 155; Watson, *Annals*

of Philadelphia, 239; Stokes, *Iconography,* 5:1160; Andrew Burnaby, *Travels through the Middle Settlements in North-America in the Years 1759 and 1760: With Observations upon the State of the Colonies,* 2 vols. (Ithaca, N.Y., 1968), 2:128–29; J. Thomas Scharf, *History of Maryland,* 3 vols. (Baltimore, 1897), 2:75; Jane Carson, *Colonial Virginians at Play* (Williamsburg, Va., 1965), 159–62; Jennie Holliman, *American Sports 1785–1835* (Durham, N.C., 1931), 124–29. See also Richard E. Powell Jr., "Sport, Social Relations and Animal Husbandry: Early Cock-fighting in North America," *International Journal of the History of Sport* 10 (Dec. 1993): 295–312; Clifton D. Bryant, *Some Sociological Observations on a Socially Disvalued Sport* (Blacksburg, Va., 1982).

22. Clifford Geertz, "Deep Play: Notes on the Balinese Cockfight," *Daedalus* 101 (Winter 1972): 1–37.

23. Jeremy Bentham, *The Theory of Legislation,* ed. C. K. Ogden, trans. Richard Hildreth (New York, 1931), 106n.

24. Rhys Isaac, *The Transformation of Virginia 1740–1790* (Chapel Hill, N.C., 1982), esp. 101–20.

25. Ibid.

26. See, for example, Robert W. Carter, Almanac Diary 1768, 2–7 May, William and Mary College Library, Williamsburg, Va.; "Letters from and to George Hume," *Virginia Magazine of History and Biography* 20 (Oct. 1912): 413: "Cock Fight, 1767," *Virginia Magazine of History and Biography* 10 (1902–3): 325; Elkanah Watson, *Men and Times of the Revolution, or the Memoirs of Elkanah Watson,* ed. Winslow C. Watson (New York, 1856), 261–62.

27. See, for example, *Virginia Gazette,* 27 February 1752, 22 February 1770, 27 May 1773.

28. See, for example, Field, *The Colonial Tavern;* Paton Yoder, "The American Inn, 1775–1850: Melting Pot or Stewing Kettle?" *Indiana Magazine of History* 59 (June 1963): 135–51; Patricia Click, *The Spirit of the Times: Amusements in Nineteenth-Century Baltimore, Norfolk, and Richmond* (Charlottesville, Va., 1989), 87. Recently David Conroy has also argued that taverns and public drinking contributed to the emergence of a more open, less paternalistic and authoritarian public political culture in eighteenth-century Massachusetts. Of the two sets of claims, Conroy's measured conclusion seems the more reasonable; see *In Public Houses,* especially chaps. 4–5. A more complete regional analysis of the social consequences of sporting events, at least by rank, might support this argument.

29. See notes 17 and 19 to this chapter and *South Carolina Gazette,* 27 March–3 April 1742; *New-York Mercury,* 13 May 1765; John Adams, *Diary and Autobiography of John Adams,* ed. Lyman H. Butterfield, 4 vols. (Cambridge, 1961–62), 1:172–73; Alexander Graydon, *Alexander Graydon's Memoirs of His Own Time* (Philadelphia, 1846), 82, 92–93.

30. Campbell, *Caroline County, Virginia,* 410–12; Alonzo May, "Mays Dramatic History of Baltimore," part 6, 1747–1819, Maryland Historical Society, Baltimore; John Boyle, "Boyle's Journal of Occurrences in Boston, 1759–1778," *New England*

Historical and Genealogical Register 84 (July 1930): 253; Stokes, *Iconography*, 4:632, 641, 724, 787, 797; Watson, *Annals of Philadelphia*, 239.

31. See, for example, *Maryland Gazette*, 7 February 1754; Letterbook of Dr. Alexander Hamilton, 1739–43, letter 5, 20 October 1743, Box 2, Dulany Papers, Maryland Historical Society, Baltimore; Thirty Years Records of Taunton, 1 August 1749; Charles Woodmason, *The Carolina Backcountry on the Eve of the Revolution: The Journal and Other Writings of Charles Woodmason, Anglican Itinerant,* ed. Richard J. Hooker (Chapel Hill, N.C., 1953), 129; *Boston Evening Post,* 14 January 1740; Robert C. Twombly, "Black Resistance to Slavery in Massachusetts," in William L. O'Neill, ed., *Insights and Parallels: Problems and Issues of American Social History* (Minneapolis, Minn., 1973), 35–54.

32. See, for example, Thomas Anburey, *Travels through the Interior Parts of America,* 2 vols. (Boston, 1923 [1789]), 2:201–3; Norris, *History of the Lower Shenandoah Valley,* 459.

33. Anne Arundel County Court, Judgment Records, 1734–75, 1B6, November 1747, 605, Maryland Hall of Records, Annapolis.

34. This subject requires much more study, but see Christine Stansell, *City of Women: Sex and Class in New York 1789–1860* (Urbana, Ill., 1986), 3–18, 105–29, 171–216; N. E. H. Hull, *Female Felons: Women and Serious Crime in Colonial Massachusetts* (Urbana, Ill., 1987); Nancy L. Struna, "The Recreational Experiences of Early American Women," in D. Margaret Costa and Sharon R. Guthrie, eds., *Women and Sport: Interdisciplinary Perspectives* (Champaign, Ill., 1994), 54.

35. Black, "Journal," 130–31.

36. *Records of the Town of Braintree, 1640–1793,* ed. Samuel A. Bates (Randolph, Mass., 1886), 418.

37. *Minutes of the Common Council of the City of New York, 1675–1776,* 8 vols. (New York, 1905): 4:311–12.

38. *Archives of Maryland,* 44:411; *The Colonial Records of the State of Georgia,* comp. Allen D. Candler and Lucian L. Knight, 25 vols. (Atlanta, Ga., 1904–16), 18:218.

39. *Archives of Maryland,* 44:402.

40. Ibid., 42:133–34; *Massachusetts Province Code of Laws,* 1742, 52–53; *Boston Weekly News-Letter,* 5 July 1750.

41. *Minutes of the Common Council of New York,* 4:311–12.

42. Stephens, *Journal,* 1:69. For other criticisms, see *Virginia Gazette,* 2 January 1751; *Boston Evening Post,* 25 March 1751.

43. John Gerard William DeBrahm, *DeBrahm's Report of the General Survey in the Southern District of North America,* ed. Louis DeVorsey (Columbia, S.C., 1971), 82. Drinking beverages with some alcoholic content, including beer, cider, wine, and harder liquor, was common throughout the colonies, even among children.

44. See, for example, *Boston Weekly News Letter,* 5 July 1750; *Georgia Gazette,* 20 July 1774; James Gordon, "Diary of Colonel James Gordon, of Lancaster County, Virginia," *William and Mary Quarterly,* 1st ser., 11 (Oct. 1902): 112; Thomas Lewis, *The Fairfax Line: A Journal of 1746,* ed. John W. Wayland (New Market, Va., 1925),

6; *Minutes of the Common Council of New York,* 6:44–45; *Massachusetts Province Code of Laws,* 1742, act 5, 9–13; *Archives of Maryland,* 42:133–34; *Virginia Statutes,* 4:428. General histories of drink and drinking include William J. Rorabaugh, *The Alcoholic Republic: An American Tradition* (New York, 1979); Mark E. Lender and James K. Martin, *Drinking in America: A History* (New York, 1982); Geraldine Youcha, *Women and Alcohol: A Dangerous Pleasure* (New York, 1986); Susanna Barrow and Robin Room, *Drinking: Behavior and Belief in Modern History* (Berkeley, Calif., 1991).

45. See, for example, *Boston Weekly News Letter,* 5 July 1750. This argument, which was fairly common, may help to account for provincial assemblies' orders to tavernkeepers to limit the credit they extended; see, for example, *The Colonial Laws of New York,* 5 vols. (Albany, N.Y., 1894–96), 2:952, 3:756–59. Also, local communities, especially in New England, occasionally reacted to the poverty of those whom they saw as idlers and in some places even established workhouses; see *Records of the Town of Plymouth,* ed. W. T. Davis, 3 vols. (Plymouth, Mass., 1889–1903), 3:257. Orphanages may also have been partly a response to poverty and the prospects for idle lives among children.

46. See, for example, Francis Asbury, *The Journal and Letters of Francis Asbury,* ed. Elmer T. Clark, J. Manning Potts, and Jacob S. Payton, 3 vols. (Nashville, Tenn., 1958), 1:50, 68; Woodmason, *Carolina Backcounty,* 47; Johann Martin Bolzius, "Johann Martin Bolzius Answers a Questionnaire on Carolina and Georgia," ed. and trans. Klaus G. Leowald, Beverly Starika, and Paul S. Taylor, *William and Mary Quarterly,* 3d ser., 14–15 (1957–58): 239–40; George Washington, *The Writings of George Washington, 1745–1756,* ed. John C. Fitzpatrick, 39 vols. (1931–1944), 1:317; letter, Samuel Chase to his children, 8 July 1784, in Samuel Chase Letters, Maryland Historical Society, Baltimore.

47. See, for example, *New-York Gazette,* 11–18 February 1734; *Boston Evening Post,* 25 March 1751; Bolzius, "Bolzius Answers a Questionnaire," 240; *Colonial Records of Georgia,* 20:82; Anon., "Observations in Several Voyages and Travels in America: From the London Magazine, July, 1746," *William and Mary Quarterly,* 1st ser., 15 (Apr. 1907): 222; Adams, *Diary and Autobiography,* 1:77, 128–29; Thomas Jefferson, Account Books, 1767–82, 1769, 21, 25, Library of Congress, Washington, D.C.

48. George Webb, *The Office and Authority of a Justice of Peace* (Williamsburg, Va., 1736), 165–66.

49. *Massachusetts Province Code of Laws,* 1759, 33–35; *Virginia Statutes,* 10:205.

50. There was also a double standard: even as institutional and individual critics complained about gamblers and gaming, some of them gambled themselves, and they organized and participated in lotteries. See, for example, *Virginia Statutes,* 6:453–61; *Boston Gazette,* 23 January 1758; Alice Morse Earle, *Customs and Fashions in Old New England* (New York, 1893), 254; John S. Ezell, *Fortune's Merry Wheel: The Lottery in America* (Cambridge, 1960); Robert C. Johnson, "The Lotteries of the Virginia Company 1612–1621," *Virginia Magazine of History and Biography* 74 (July 1966): 259–92; G. Robert Blakey, "State Conducted Lotteries: History, Prob-

lems, and Promises," *Journal of Social Issues* 35 (Summer 1979): 62–85; John M. Findlay, *People of Chance: Gambling in American Society from Jamestown to Las Vegas* (New York, 1986), esp. 11–43.

51. See, for example, Brickell, *Natural History*, 39, 335–66; Fithian, *Journal 1773–74*, 1:140; Washington, *Writings*, 1:289–99; Edmund S. Morgan, *Virginians at Home: Family Life in the Eighteenth Century* (Williamsburg, Va., 1952), 77.

52. Timothy H. Breen, "Horses and Gentlemen: The Cultural Significance of Gambling among the Gentry of Virginia," *William and Mary Quarterly*, 3d ser., 34 (Apr. 1977): 243–56.

53. Isaac, *Transformation of Virginia*, 119.

54. Bertram Wyatt-Brown, *Southern Honor: Ethics and Behavior in the Old South* (Oxford, 1982), 344.

55. Virtually every law passed to regulate taverns or gambling (often the same) contained a clause about not operating "to the prejudice of the neighboring inhabitants" (*Virginia Statutes*, 6:71). Work agreements, especially those signed by apprentices, also prohibited gambling and in some cases tavern visits; see Roland D. Sayer, "The Ilsley-Chase Account Books," *Essex Institute Historical Collections* 86 (Apr. 1950): 179.

56. *Virginia Statutes*, 5:102–3, 229, 6:76–81. By 1762 Virginia law did allow tavern-keepers to recover some debts, especially from liquor sales (*Virginia Statutes*, 7:595–96). This change may have been a result of specie shortages, which had existed during the Seven Years War; see Joseph A. Ernst, *Money and Politics in America, 1755–1775: A Study in the Currency Act of 1764 and the Political Economy of Revolution* (Chapel Hill, N.C., 1973), 46. Georgians could recover no more than forty shillings (£2). For limits on amounts recoverable in other colonies and concerns about losses, see Brickell, *Natural History*, 257–58; Robert H. Moody, ed., *The Saltonstall Papers 1607–1815*, Massachusetts Historical Society Collections 80 (1972): 368–69.

57. *Massachusetts Province Code of Laws, 1759–60*, 33–35.

58. *The State Records of North Carolina*, ed. Walter Clark, 15 vols. (Winston, Goldsboro, and Raleigh, N.C., 1895–1914), 5:78–80, 250–53, 6:611–13, 677, 838. The Anglican minister Charles Woodmason offered a similar critique in the late 1760s (*Carolina Backcountry*, 47, 96).

59. *Pennsylvania Gazette*, 16 April 1752.

60. Ibid.

61. William Stith, "The Sinfulness and Pernicious Nature of Gaming: A Sermon Preached before the General Assembly of Virginia, at Williamsburg, March 1st, 1752" (Williamsburg, 1752), 6–10. Stith and other William and Mary College officers also prohibited gambling among students; see William Stith, "Journal of the Meetings of the President and Masters of William and Mary College," *William and Mary Quarterly*, 1st ser., 2 (July 1893): 54–55.

62. Adams, *Diary and Autobiography*, 1:14, 190–91.

63. Letter, William Nelson to Samuel Athawes, 16 May 1771, Nelson Letterbook, microfilm, Colonial Williamsburg Foundation, Williamsburg, Va.

64. Landon Carter, *The Diary of Colonel London Carter of Sabine Hall, 1752–1778,* ed. Jack P. Greene, 2 vols. (Charlottesville, Va., 1965), 2:870.

65. Cited in Elizabeth Evans, *Weathering the Storm: Women of the American Revolution* (New York, 1989), 345.

66. Anon., "Journal of a French Traveller in the Colonies, 1765," *American Historical Review* 26 (July 1921): 742–42; David Mead, "Recollections of William Byrd III," *Virginia Magazine of History and Biography* 37 (Oct. 1929): 310; Robert Wormeley Carter, Almanac Diary 1768, 7 May, William and Mary College Library, Williamsburg, Va.; Louis Morton, "Robert Wormley Carter of Sabine Hall," *Journal of Southern History* 12 (Aug. 1946): 345–65; Louis B. Wright, *The First Gentlemen of Virginia: Intellectual Qualities of the Early Colonial Ruling Class* (San Marino, Calif., 1940), 312, 327.

67. James Maury, "A Dissertation on Education in the Form of a Letter from James Maury to Robert Jackson, July 17, 1762," ed. Helen D. Bullock, *Papers of the Albemarle County Historical Society,* 2 vols. (1941–42), 2:42, 46.

68. This argument borrows from Timothy H. Breen, "Narrative of Commercial Life: Consumption, Ideology, and Community on the Eve of the American Revolution," *William and Mary Quarterly,* 3d ser., 50 (July 1993): 471–501.

69. Jeanne Boydston provides a fine, concise discussion of the economic-uneconomic constructions in the late colonial years; see *Home and Work: Housework, Wages, and the Ideology of Labor in the Early Republic* (New York, 1990), esp. 27–29.

70. *Journals of the Continental Congress 1774–1789,* ed. Worthington C. Ford et al., 34 vols. (Washington, D. C., 1904–37), 1:78. See also "Marblehead Regulations Restraining Amusements in 1775," *Essex Institute Historical Collections* 62 (Jan. 1906): 88; Joseph E. A. Smith, *History of Pittsfield, Massachusetts, from the Year 1734 to the Year 1800* (Boston, 1869), 374–81; Janet Schaw, *Journal of a Lady of Quality; Being the Narrative of a Journey from Scotland to the West Indies, North Carolina, and Portugal, in the Years 1774 to 1776,* ed. Evangeline W. Andrews and Charles M. Andrews (New Haven, Conn., 1931), 149; Stokes, *Iconography,* 4:868, 870.

Chapter 8: Upper- and Middle-Rank Leisure and Sports

1. *Virginia Gazette,* 4 November 1775, 3. Some of the material in the second half of this chapter appeared in my "Sport and the Awareness of Leisure," in Cary Carson, Ronald Hoffman, and Peter J. Albert, eds., *Of Consuming Interests: The Style of Life in the Eighteenth Century* (Charlottesville, Va., 1994), 406–43.

2. Ibid.

3. Many historians, sociologists, and American studies scholars have treated leisure as unchanging, although they differ about whether it should be framed as a portion of time or as a category of experience. See, for example, Fritz Redlich, "Leisure-time Activities: A Historical, Sociological, and Economic Analysis," *Explorations in Entrepreneurial History,* 2d ser., 3 (Fall 1965): 3–41; Michael R. Marrus, *The Rise of Leisure in Industrial Society* (St. Louis, 1974); Max Kaplan, *Lei-*

sure in America: A Social Inquiry (New York, 1960); Joffre Dumazedier, *Toward a Society of Leisure*, trans. Stewart E. McClure (New York, 1967); Patricia Click, *The Spirit of the Times: Amusements in Nineteenth-Century Baltimore, Norfolk, and Richmond* (Charlottesville, Va., 1989). Important exceptions include Lewis Mumford, *Technics and Civilization* (London, 1934); Sebastian De Grazia, *Of Time, Work, and Leisure* (London, 1967); Hugh Cunningham, *Leisure in the Industrial Revolution c. 1780–c.1880* (New York, 1980); Stephen Yeo and Eileen Yeo, eds., *Popular Culture and Class Conflict 1590–1914: Explorations in the History of Labour and Leisure* (Atlantic Highlands, N.J., 1981); Roy Rosenzweig, *Eight Hours for What We Will: Workers and Leisure in an Industrial City, 1870–1920* (Cambridge, 1983); Stephen J. Ross, *Workers on the Edge: Work, Leisure, and Politics in Industrializing Cincinnati, 1788–1890* (New York, 1985); John Clarke and Chas Critcher, *The Devil Makes Work: Leisure in Capitalist Britain* (Urbana, Ill., 1985); Peter Bailey, *Leisure and Class in Victorian England: Rational Recreation and the Contest for Control, 1830–1885* (London, 1987).

4. Keith Thomas, *Religion and the Decline of Magic* (New York, 1971), 623; E. P. Thompson, "Time, Work-Discipline and Industrial Capitalism," *Past & Present* 38 (1967): 56–97, esp. 57–65.

5. Thompson, "Time, Work-Discipline and Industrial Capitalism."

6. This argument draws on the literature about changes in late seventeenth- and eighteenth-century economic structures and relations and social organization, only some of which speaks directly about leisure. See, for example, David Cannadine, "The Theory and Practice of the English Leisure Classes," *Historical Journal* 21 (1978): 461–62; Joyce Oldham Appleby, *Economic Thought and Ideology in Seventeenth-Century England* (Princeton, N.J., 1978); Peter Clark, ed., *The Transformation of English Provincial Towns* (London, 1984); J. M. Golby and A. W. Purdue, *The Civilisation of the Crowd: Popular Culture in England 1750–1900* (London, 1984). See also note 50 to this chapter. By no means, however, did the actions and intentions of owners and managers radically or unilaterally alter residual labor-leisure patterns among many kinds of English laborers; see, for example, E. P. Thompson, *The Making of the English Working Class* (New York, 1966); John Rule, *The Labouring Classes in Early Industrial England, 1750–1850* (London, 1986); idem, *The Experience of Labour in Eighteenth-Century Industry* (London, 1981); Manfred A. Bienefeld, *Working Hours in British Industry: An Economic History* (London, 1972); Mark Harrison, *Crowds and History: Mass Phenomena in English Towns, 1790–1835* (Cambridge, 1988).

7. J. H. Plumb, "The Commercialization of Leisure in Eighteenth-Century England," in Neil McKendrick, John Brewer, and J. H. Plumb, *The Birth of a Consumer Society: The Commercialization of Eighteenth-Century England* (Blooomington, Ind., 1982), 265–85; Angus McInnes, "The Emergence of a Leisure Town: Shrewsbury 1660–1760," *Past & Present* 120 (Aug. 1988): 53–87; Peter Clark, *Country Towns in Pre-Industrial England* (Leicester, 1986). For a more extensive summary of the sports popular among eighteenth-century Britons than Plumb's, see Richard Holt, *Sport and the British: A Modern History* (Oxford, 1989), 12–73.

8. Roger Longrigg, *The History of Horse Racing* (New York, 1972), 63 (see also 57–62).

9. Francis LeJau, *The Carolina Chronicle of Dr. Francis LeJau, 1706–1717*, ed. Frank J. Klingberg (Berkeley, 1956), 97. That leisure was time for necessary, nonphysical tasks, and as such was quite different from idleness, is one of the points that I think Gordon Wood does not consider. See note 13 to chapter 6 and *The Radicalism of the American Revolution: How a Revolution Transformed a Monarchical Society into a Democratic One Unlike Any That Had Ever Existed* (New York, 1992), esp. 33–39, 107, 170–72.

10. William Stephens, *The Journal of William Stephens 1741–1745*, ed. E. Merton Coulter, 2 vols. (Athens, Ga., 1958), 2:1, 250–51.

11. Leisure used in this sense appears often in diaries, letters, and pamphlets written by provincial upper-rank men. See, for example, Joseph Seccombe, "Business and Diversion Inoffensive to God, and Necessary for the Comfort and Support of Human Society: A Discouse Utter'd in Part at Ammanskeeg-Falls, in the Fishing Season" (Boston, 1743 [1739]); Ralph K. Hagedorn, *Benjamin Franklin and Chess in Early America* (Philadelphia, 1958), 15–16. Examples from later gentry appear in George Washington, *The Writings of George Washington, 1745–1789*, ed. John C. Fitzpatrick, 39 vols. (Washington, 1931), 1:458; Richard Henry Lee, *The Letters of Richard Henry Lee*, ed. James C. Ballagh, 2 vols. (New York, 1911), 1:82, 108–9, 205. Women rarely employed the term, however, nor did they suggest that they saw themselves as having leisure. They did express concerns about being idle or idling their time away, however. See, for example, "Some Family Letters of the Eighteenth Century" (Maria Carter of Sabine Hall to her cousin Maria Carter of Cleve, 1756), *Virginia Magazine of History and Biography* 15 (Apr. 1908): 432–33; Elizabeth Evans, *Weathering the Storm: Women of the American Revolution* (New York, 1989), 43.

12. *Virginia Gazette*, 27 December 1752, 1; 8 December 1752, 1; 24 January 1752, 1; *Pennsylvania Gazette*, 23 April 1752, 1.

13. The equipment prices derive from estate inventory registrations in Maryland. The journals and account books of many Revolutionary and post-Revolutionary era provincial gentlemen contain some evidence about fees, wagers, and other expenses associated with sports and recreations. Few of these, however, appear to have been as systematically maintained as were the accounts of John Marshall, the future chief justice of the Supreme Court; see *The Papers of John Marshall*, ed. Herbert A. Johnson, 3 vols. (Chapel Hill, N.C., 1974), 1:299, 302–7, 315–19, 2:354–67, 382, 387.

14. Few gentlemen appear to have earned significant and regular incomes from gambling, stud fees, or any other practice associated with sports and recreations. From the 1760s–1780s stud fees ranged between five and eight pounds sterling "for the season" and between twenty and forty shillings "for the leap," and in either case an owner would have to have numerous clients to pay even the initial cost of the stallion. See also William Russell Account Book, accounts for horse racing, 1774–

83, Maryland Historical Society, Baltimore; Rebecca Ridgely Account Book, 1790–1805, 23, 25, 34, Box 1, Maryland Historical Society; Moreau de St.-Mery, *Moreau de St.-Mery's American Journey (1793–1798)*, trans. and ed. Kenneth Roberts and Anna M. Roberts (Garden City, N.Y., 1947), 77. The expenses associated with racing and other recreations also added to the rising living costs for gentlemen and gentlewomen, which for some people became real burdens. In the case of South Carolina planters, Bolzius claimed that one could spend a minimum of £100 just to keep "a genteel family" in Charleston for a part of the years; this sum did not include even a "carriage and horses" and probably not gambling or racing costs (Johann Martin Bolzius, "Johann Martin Bolzius Answers a Questionnaire on Carolina and Georgia," ed. and trans. Klaus G. Leowald, Beverly Starika, and Paul S. Taylor, *William and Mary Quarterly*, 3d ser., 14–15 [1957–58]: i:243).

15. Isaac N. P. Stokes, *The Iconography of Manhattan Island, 1498–1909*, 6 vols. (New York, 1967), 4:1214, 1289, 1309, 1311, 1495; *Maryland Gazette and Baltimore Advertiser*, 8 October 1782, 3; Francisco de Miranda, *The New Democracy in America: Travels of Francisco de Miranda in the United States, 1783–84*, trans. Judson P. Wood, ed. John S. Ezell (Norman, Okla., 1963), 54; John Enys, *The American Journals of John Enys*, ed. Elizabeth Cometti (Syracuse, 1976), 194, 204; Francis Baily, *Journal of a Tour in the Unsettled Parts of North America in 1796 and 1797* (London, 1856), 101; Elbridge Gerry, *The Diary of Elbridge Gerry, Jr.* (New York, 1927), 190, 196.

16. The fullest discussion of British fashions and leisure entrepreneurs remains McKendrick, Brewer, and Plumb, *The Birth of a Consumer Society*. For theater, see Jean-Christophé Agnew, *Worlds Apart: The Market and the Theater in Anglo-American Thought, 1550–1750* (Cambridge, 1986). Similarly, the most erudite and comprehensive treatment of the interests of and borrowing by the provincial upper rank on the matter of British fashions and gentility is Richard Bushman, *The Refinement of America: Persons, Houses, Cities* (New York, 1992).

17. Stokes, *Iconography*, 4:544, 616–17, 641–42, 724, 5:1195, 1207; John F. Watson, *Annals of Philadelphia* (Philadelphia, 1830), 408; *Georgia Gazette*, 25 September 1765, 21 May 1766, 22 June 1768; Alonzo May, "Mays Dramatic History of Baltimore," part 1, Maryland Historical Society, Baltimore; J. Thomas Scharf, *The Chronicles of Baltimore* (Baltimore, 1874), 112–13, 229; *Virginia Gazette and Alexandria Advertiser*, 22 April 1790; Johann David Schoepf, *Travels in the Confederation [1783–1784]*, trans. and ed. Alfred J. Morrison, 2 vols. (New York, 1968), 1:90. Putting on plays in the colonies, to be sure, preceded the appearance of London acting companies.

18. May, "Mays Dramatic History of Baltimore," part 6, 1747–1819, "Shows in Taverns and Coffee Houses in Baltimore Town."

19. See, for example, Stokes, *Iconography*, 4:787, 797, 1314; *Records of the City of Baltimore (Special Commissioners) 1782–1797* (Baltimore, 1909), 179, 338.

20. Carl Bridenbaugh, "Baths and Watering Places of Colonial America," *William and Mary Quarterly*, 3d ser., 3 (1946): 153–81; Henry Wansey, *Henry Wansey and His American Journal, 1794*, ed. David John Jeremy (Philadelphia, 1970), 95, 218–19; Enys, *American Journal*, 221–11; Schoepf, *Travels in the Confederation*, 1:534, 2:310–

11; Ferdinand Bayard, *Travels of a Frenchman in Maryland and Virginia with a Description of Philadelphia and Baltimore in 1791*, ed. Ben C. McCary (Williamsburg, Va., 1950), 51–52. This is the period when Coney Island (Gravesend) and Governor's Island emerged as resorts for New York City; see Stokes, *Iconography*, 4:1281–82, 5:1310; Wansey, *American Journal*, 134. See also Carl Bridenbaugh, *Cities in the Wilderness: The First Generation of Urban Life in America 1625–1742* (New York, 1955), 442.

21. Watson, *Annals of Philadelphia*, 430–31; Stokes, *Iconography*, 1:384, 4:748, 5:1298, 1305, 1319, 1341.

22. *New York Independent Journal*, 13 August 1788; *New York Daily Advertiser*, 28 April 1803.

23. On the increasing passivity of upper- and middle-rank women, especially urban ones, in recreational scenes, see, for example, Miranda, *The New Democracy*, 29, 162; Robert Hunter, *Quebec to Carolina in 1785–1786: Being the Travel Diary and Observations of Robert Hunter, Jr., a Young Merchant of London*, ed. Louis B. Wright and Marion Tinling (San Marino, Calif., 1943), 243. Many of the men's comments are less direct but perhaps no less telling about the marginalizing of women. Charles Janson, for example, saw an "abundance of Ladies, decorated as if for a ball," seated at the race course in Georgetown, west of Washington, D.C. (Janson, *The Stranger in America 1793–1806* [New York, 1935], 216). Claude Blanchard also observed women in Providence, Rhode Island, at a turtle frolic, which started with a picnic and ended with dancing. He noted that the women sat either opposite the men or in a different room, and he did not think that they danced well (*The Journal of Claude Blanchard [1780–83]*, ed. Thomas Balch and William Duane [Albany, N.Y., 1876], 65). I suspect that although many of the describers were male, they were not misrepresenting women's physical activity levels. Women themselves provided few indications that they understood or experienced leisure as men did. See also note 11 to this chapter and Nancy L. Struna, "Gender and Sporting Practice in Early America, 1750–1810," *Journal of Sport History* 18 (Spring 1991): 10–31.

24. Linda K. Kerber, "'History Can Do It No Justice': Women and the Reinterpretation of the American Revolution," in Ronald Hoffman and Peter J. Albert, eds., *Women in the Age of the Revolution* (Charlottesville, Va., 1989), 3–42; idem, "The Republican Ideology of the Revolutionary Generation," *American Quarterly* 37 (1985): 474–95; Mary Beth Norton, *Liberty's Daughters: The Revolutionary Experiences of American Women, 1750–1800* (Boston, 1980); Carroll Smith-Rosenberg, "Domesticating 'Virtue': Coquettes and Revolutionaries in Young America," in Elaine Scarry, ed., *Literature and the Body: Essays on Populations and Persons* (Baltimore, 1988), 160–84.

25. *New York Daily Advertiser*, 4 July 1801.

26. Stokes, *Iconography*, 4:632.

27. *New-York Mercury*, 13 August 1753, 17 September 1753.

28. John Boyle, "Boyle's Journal of Occurrences in Boston, 1759–1778," *New England Historical and Genealogical Register* 84 (July 1930): 253.

29. Wansey, *American Journal*, 76; May, "Mays Dramatic History," part 6, 30 October 1787; St.-Mery, *American Journal*, 54, 58.

30. *Columbian Mirror and Alexandria Advertiser*, 22 October 1795, 2; May, "Mays Dramatic History," part 6, 1787.

31. Gilbert Streeter, "Salem before the Revolution," *Essex Institute Historical Collections* 32 (Jan. 1896): 51–52.

32. Stokes, *Iconography*, 4:621; John Rowe, *Letters and Diary of John Rowe, Boston Merchant, 1759–1762, 1764–1779*, ed. Anne R. Cunningham (Boston, 1903), 249; *Virginia Gazette*, 22 October 1772, 2; Watson, *Annals of Philadelphia*, 239.

33. *New York Daily Advertiser*, 27 September 1786; Stokes, *Iconography*, 5:1205.

34. Ibid., 5:1205, 1231; May, "Mays Dramatic History," part 6, 21 June 1785.

35. John Hervey, *Racing in America 1665–1865*, 2 vols. (New York, 1944), 1:247–48, 2:4–25; William H. Robertson, *The History of Thoroughbred Racing in America* (Englewood Cliffs, N.J., 1964), 31–33.

36. *New York Daily Advertiser*, 10 August 1793.

37. *Minutes of the Common Council of the City of New York, 1675–1776*, 8 vols. (New York, 1905), 2:140, 142; *Records of the City of Baltimore*, 238.

38. Stokes, *Iconography*, 5:1334; St.-Mery, *American Journal*, 345; J. Thomas Scharf and Thompson Westcott, *History of Philadelphia, 1609–1884*, 2 vols. (Philadelphia, 1884), 2:952–53. He also appeared in small towns from Virginia to New York.

39. Stokes, *Iconography*, 5:1314, 1316.

40. Precisely when pits, especially for cockfighting, emerged in Britain is unclear. They probably existed by the reign of Edward III and perhaps earlier. Joseph Strutt claimed that Henry VIII had one built at the palace at Whitehall (*The Sports and Pastimes of the People of England* [Detroit, 1968 (1801)], 224). Pits apparently were not a part of the physical environment of the earliest Elizabethan theaters; see William Ingram, *The Business of Playing: The Beginnings of Adult Professional Theater in Elizabethan London* (Ithaca, N.Y., 1992).

41. Stokes, *Iconography*, 1:385, 5:1338–39; Isaac J. Greenwood, *The Circus: Its Origin and Growth Prior to 1835* (New York, 1970 [1898]).

42. Charles G. Steffins, *The Mechanics of Baltimore: Workers and Politics in the Age of Revolution, 1763–1812* (Urbana, Ill., 1984), 265; Billy G. Smith, *The "Lower Sort": Philadelphia's Laboring People, 1750–1800* (Ithaca, N.Y., 1990), 92–125, 230–38; Sean Wilentz, *New York City and the Rise of the American Working Class 1788–1850* (New York, 1984), 50–51; Cynthia J. Shelton, *The Mills of Manayunk: Industrialization and Social Conflict in the Philadelphia Region, 1787–1837* (Baltimore, 1986), 43, 52.

43. These differences were manifested in various ways even in the nineteenth century. Actors struggled to get the courts to recognize their contracts as legally binding on employers shortly after the Civil War. Then professional baseball players found themselves defined as members of the league rather than distinctive employees after 1876, at least until contracts of sorts came with the reserve clause in 1879. Even in the twentieth century, however, ideological, if not experiential, dif-

ferences persist, as even the formation of guilds by actors and associations by professional athletes—rather than unions—suggests. This matter has not received the attention from historians that it deserves.

44. *Maryland Journal and Baltimore Advertiser,* 9 May 1790.

45. May, "Mays Dramatic History," part 6, 1782.

46. See, for example, *Records of the City of Baltimore,* 157–58, 228, 288, 330. At least two black men received the approval of the city to display their physical prowess, so work opportunities were not limited to whites and African Americans were not limited to the roles of prize fighters or jockeys.

47. Hunter, *Quebec to Canada,* 145; Miranda, *New Democracy,* 148; Stokes, *Iconography,* 5:1253, 1314, 1330; Edmund Berkeley Jr., "Quoits, the Sport of Gentlemen," *Virginia Cavalcade* 15 (Summer 1965): 11–21; Click, *Spirit of the Times,* 74; *Maryland Gazette,* 20 February 1783, 2; *Maryland Journal and Baltimore Advertiser,* 30 April 1782, 4; *Minutes of the Common Council of New York,* 6:133–36. For a broad-ranging interpretation of the emergence of the weekend, especially in bourgeois Western cultures, see Witold Rybczynski, *Waiting for the Weekend* (New York, 1991).

48. This argument draws on works that have explored changes in eighteenth-century cultural forms and social patterns. See especially Bushman, *Refinement of America;* Stephanie Grauman Wolf, *As Various as Their Land: The Everyday Lives of Eighteenth-Century Americans* (New York, 1993); Jack P. Greene, *Pursuits of Happiness: The Social Development of Early Modern British Colonies and the Formation of American Culture* (Chapel Hill, N.C., 1988); Tamara P. Thornton, *Cultivating Gentlemen: The Meaning of Country Life among the Boston Elite 1785–1860* (New Haven, Conn., 1989); Jan Lewis, *The Pursuit of Happiness: Family Values in Jefferson's Virginia* (Cambridge, 1983).

49. Stuart M. Blumin, *The Emergence of the Middle Class: Social Experience in the American City, 1760–1900* (Cambridge, 1989); Gary B. Nash, *The Urban Crucible: Social Change, Political Consciousness, and the Origins of the American Revolution* (Cambridge, Mass., 1979); Jackson Turner Main, *The Social Structure of Revolutionary America* (Princeton, N.J., 1965). See also James A. Henretta, *The Origins of American Capitalism: Collected Essays* (Boston, 1991), 256–94.

50. McKendrick, Brewer, and Plumb, *The Birth of a Consumer Society;* Lorna Weatherill, *Consumer Behaviour and Material Culture in Britain, 1660–1760* (London, 1988); Carol Shammas, *The Pre-Industrial Consumer in England and America* (Oxford, 1990); Joan Thirsk, *Economic Policies and Projects: The Development of a Consumer Society in Early Modern England* (Oxford, 1978).

51. Lois Green Carr and Lorena S. Walsh, "Consumer Behavior in the Colonial Chesapeake," in Carson, Hoffman, and Albert, eds., *Of Consuming Interest,* 59–66; Lorena S. Walsh, Gloria L. Main, Lois Green Carr, Jackson Turner Main, and Billy G. Smith, "Toward a History of the Standard of Living in British North America," *William and Mary Quarterly,* 3d ser., 45 (Jan. 1988): 116–70; Gloria L. Main and Jackson Turner Main, "Standards and Styles of Living in Southern New England, 1640–1774," *Journal of Economic History* 48 (1988): 27–46; Timothy H. Breen, "'Baubles of

Britain': The American and Consumer Revolutions of the Eighteenth Century," *Past & Present* 119 (May 1988): 73–104; idem, "An Empire of Goods: The Anglicization of Colonial America, 1690–1776," *Journal of British Studies* 25 (1986): 467–99; Robert Blair St. George, ed., *Material Life in America 1600–1860* (Boston, 1988).

52. *Virginia Gazette*, 24 September 1772.

53. *Virginia Gazette and Alexandria Advertiser*, 7 October 1790, 4.

54. Weatherill, *Consumer Behaviour*, 165.

55. On analyses and the limits of estate inventory data, see Lois Green Carr and Lorena S. Walsh, "Inventories and the Analysis of Wealth and Consumption Patterns in St. Mary's County, Maryland, 1658–1777," *Historical Methods* 8 (1980): 81–104; Gloria L. Main, "The Correction of Biases in Colonial American Probate Records," *Historical Methods Newsletter* 8 (1974): 10–28; Alice Hanson Jones, *American Colonial Wealth: Documents and Methods*, 3 vols. (New York, 1977), esp. vol. 3.

56. Marylynn Salmon, *Women and the Law of Property in Early America* (Chapel Hill, N.C., 1986); Toby L. Ditz, "Ownership and Obligation: Inheritance and Patriarchal Households in Connecticut, 1750–1821," *William and Mary Quarterly*, 3d ser., 47 (Apr. 1990): 235–65; idem, *Property and Kinship: Inheritance in Early Connecticut 1750–1820* (Princeton, N.J., 1986); Carole Shammas, Marylynn Salmon, and Michel Dahlin, *Inheritance in America: Colonial Times to the Present* (New Brunswick, N.J., 1987); Daniel Scott Smith, "Inheritance and the Social History of Early American Women," in Hoffman and Albert, eds., *Women in the Age of the Revolution*, 45–66.

57. Data from inventories in the parish containing Charleston, South Carolina, reinforce these suggestions (inventories, 1770, 1790, 1810, State Archives, Columbia, S.C.).

58. Richard S. Walsh and William L. Fox, eds., *Maryland: A History* (Annapolis, Md., 1983); Steffins, *Mechanics of Baltimore*, 3–4.

59. John Randolph, *Letters of John Randolph to a Young Relative* (Philadelphia, 1834), 15, 26, 109, 128–29. See also Thomas P. Cope, *Philadelphia Merchant: The Diary of Thomas P. Cope, 1800–1851* (South Bend, Ind., 1978), 159. For a recent discussion of upper-rank merchants constructing manly identity, see Toby L. Ditz, "Shipwrecked; or, Masculinity Imperiled: Mercantile Representations of Failure and the Gendered Self in Eighteenth-Century Philadelphia," *American Historical Review* 18 (June 1994): 51–80.

Epilogue

1. See William Dunlap, *Diary of William Dunlap (1766–1839): The Memoirs of a Dramatist, Theatrical Manager, Painter, Critic, Novelist, and Historian* (New York, 1969), xii–xix, for a brief synopsis of his life.

2. Ibid., 321, 338.

3. Ibid., 64.

4. E. A. A., "Sassafras and Swinglingtow; or, Pinskter Was a Holiday," *American Notes and Queries: A Journal for the Curious* 6 (1964): 35–40; A. J. Williams-

Myers, "Pinkster Carnival: Africanisms in the Hudson River Valley," *Afro-Americans in New York Life and History* 9 (1985): 7–17; Shane White, "Pinkster: Afro-Dutch Syncretization in New York City and the Hudson Valley," *Journal of American Folklore* 101 (1989): 68–75; idem, "'It Was a Proud Day': African Americans, Festivals, and Parades in the North, 1741–1834," *Journal of American History* 18 (June 1994), esp. 18–25; Joyce D. Goodfriend, *Before the Melting Pot: Society and Culture in Colonial New York City, 1664–1730* (Princeton, N.J., 1992), 122–24; Paul A. Gilje, *The Road to Mobocracy: Popular Disorder in New York City, 1763–1834* (Chapel Hill, N.C., 1987), 19; Alice Morse Earle, *Colonial Days in Old New York* (New York, 1896), 195–201.

5. David Wiggins, "Good Times on the Old Plantation: Popular Recreations of the Black Slave in the Antebellum South, 1810–1860," *Journal of Sport History* 4 (1977): 260–84; Eugene D. Genovese, *Roll, Jordan, Roll: The World the Slaves Made* (New York, 1974); Barbara Jeanne Fields, *Slavery and Freedom on the Middle Ground: Maryland During the Nineteenth Century* (New Haven, Conn., 1985); Ira Berlin and Philip D. Morgan, eds., *The Slaves' Economy: Independent Production by Slaves in the Americas* (London, 1991); Allan Kullikoff, *The Agrarian Origins of American Capitalism* (Charlottesville, Va., 1992); Ira Berlin and Philip D. Morgan, eds., *Cultivation and Culture: Labor and the Shaping of Slave Life in the Americas* (Charlottesville, Va., 1993).

6. Elliot J. Gorn, *The Manly Art: Bare-Knuckle Prize Fighting in America* (Ithaca, N.Y., 1986); Sean Wilentz, "Artisan Republican Festivals and the Rise of Class Conflict in New York City, 1788–1837," in Michael E. Frisch and Daniel J. Walkowitz, eds., *Working-Class America* (Urbana, Ill., 1983), 37–77; idem, *New York City and the Rise of the American Working Class 1788–1850* (New York, 1984); David R. Roediger and Philip S. Foner, *Our Own Time: A History of American Labor and the Working Day* (Westport, Conn., 1989); David Brody, "Time and Work during Early American Industrialism," *Labor History* 30 (1989): 5–46. There is little evidence to suggest that working women participated in the festivals and contests of men, even in their residual roles as producers (except prostitutes), which may be another indicator of the declining conditions for women, especially poor women. See Mary H. Blewett, *Men, Women, and Work: Class, Gender and Protest in the New England Shoe Industry* (Urbana, Ill., 1988), Christine Stansell, *City of Women: Sex and Class in New York 1789–1860* (Urbana, Ill., 1986).

7. See, for example, Thomas Ashe, *Travels in America* (London, 1809), 82–85; Thomas Chalkley, *Journal of Thomas Chalkley* (New York, 1808), 93; Moreau de St.-Mery, *Moreau de St.-Mery's American Journey (1793–1798),* trans. and ed. Kenneth Roberts and Anna M. Roberts (Garden City, N.Y., 1947), 328–29; Charles Janson, *The Stranger in America 1793–1806* (New York, 1935), 308–10, 337; Jennie Holliman, *American Sports 1785–1835* (Durham, N.C., 1931); Elliott J. Gorn, "'Gouge and Bite, Pull Hair and Scratch': The Social Significance of Fighting in the Southern Backcountry," *American Historical Review* 90 (Feb. 1985): 18–43; Stewart Culin, *Games of the North American Indians* (New York, 1975).

8. Laurel T. Ulrich, *A Midwife's Tale: The Life of Martha Ballard, Based on Her Diary, 1785–1812* (New York, 1990).

9. Ibid., 71, 146.

10. Ibid., e.g., 136, 147.

11. See, for example, Melvin Adelman, *A Sporting Time: New York City and The Rise of Modern Athletics, 1820–1870* (Urbana, Ill., 1986), 31–54; Nancy L. Struna, "The North-South Races: The Transformation of American Thoroughbred Racing, 1823–1850," *Journal of Sport History* 8 (Summer 1981): 28–57; John R. Betts, "Sporting Journalism in Nineteenth-Century America, *American Quarterly* 5 (1953): 39–56; idem, "Mind and Body in Early American Thought," *Journal of American History* 54 (Mar. 1968): 787–805; Roberta J. Park, "Athletes and Their Training in Britain and America, 1800–1914," in Jack W. Berryman and Roberta J. Park, eds., *Sport and Exercise Science* (Urbana, Ill., 1992), 57–108; idem, "Physiology and Anatomy Are Destiny!? Brains, Bodies, and Exercise in Nineteenth Century American Thought," *Journal of Sport History* 18 (Spring 1991): 31–63.

Index

✦⇒◉⇐✦

Nancy L. Struna is a faculty member in the Department of Kinesiology and has an affiliate appointment in the Department of History at the University of Maryland, College Park. She has published extensively on early American sport and popular culture and is currently the president of the North American Society for Sport History.

Books in the Series Sport and Society

Muhammad Ali, the People's Champ   *Edited by Elliott J. Gorn*

People of Prowess: Sport, Leisure, and Labor in Early Anglo-America
Nancy L. Struna

Reprint Editions

The Nazi Olympics   *Richard D. Mandell*

Sports in the Western World (Second Edition)   *William J. Baker*